MAKING A LIVING

MAKING A LIVING

Technology and Change

R. Alan Hedley

The University of Victoria

HarperCollins*Publishers*

Sponsoring Editor: Alan McClare
Project Editor: Thomas R. Farrell
Cover Design: Stacy Agin
Production Assistant: Linda Murray
Photo Research: Mira Schachne
Compositor: Publishing Synthesis, Ltd.
Printer and Binder: R.R. Donnelley & Sons Company
Cover Printer: New England Book Components

MAKING A LIVING: Technology and Change

Library of Congress Cataloging-in-Publication Data

Hedley, R. Alan
    Making a living : technology and change / R. Alan Hedley.
      p. cm.
    Includes index.
    ISBN 0-06-042751-5
    1. Work. 2. Industrialization. 3. Technological innovations-
-Economic aspects. 4. Social change. I. Title.
HD6955.H36 1992
   306.3'6—dc20   91-30478
                     CIP

92 93 94 9 8 7 6 5 4 3 2

In memory of

WALLY EURCHUK

An ordinary human being who made a difference

Contents

List of Tables, Figures, and Boxes

Chapter 3   The Industrial Revolution

Chapter 4 Major Transformational Theories

FIGURES

BOXES

Chapter 5 Industrialization in the World Today

TABLES

FIGURES

BOXES

Chapter 6 Occupational and Labor Force Structure

TABLES

Chapter 7   Formal Organizations

Chapter 8   Transnational Corporations

Chapter 9   Workers and Work

Chapter 10   Worker-Management Relations

Chapter 11.   Work, Worker, and Society

Chapter 12   *Work in the Twenty-first Century: Prospects and Problems*

Preface

The human species has existed on this planet for thousands of years, but only during the last two and a half centuries have we been able to overcome in any significant way our inherent physical and mental limitations. This book deals with some of the revolutionary changes that have occurred in that recent span of history. It takes as its starting point the industrial revolution, which began in Great Britian during the latter part of the eighteenth century.

The industrial revolution harnessed inanimate energy and changed the nature of the work we perform, the skills we employ, and the kinds of organization we establish. It also changed the very structure of the society in which it occurred, with the result that industrialized countries are qualitatively different from nonindustrial countries. Be it urbanization, level of national output, population growth, development of an infrastructure, rate of innovation, or quality of social life, industrialization "explains" more of the differences between nations than any other complex set of forces.

The harnessing of inanimate energy unwittingly opened Pandora's box. In the thousands of years prior to the industrial revolution, the cumulative impact of human populations upon the earth and its ecosystem was negligible. We are now realizing, however, that many of the "marvels of technology" carry with them heavy tangible costs, costs that can affect the earth's capacity for sustained growth, including the capacity to support successive generations. Consequently, we are beginning to recognize the need to balance short-term gains against long-term losses. While we have reaped untold benefits as a result of industrialization, there is the debit side of the ledger to consider.

By any measure, we are now involved in a period of rapid social change. Many experts argue that we are currently experiencing a revolution every bit as intense and consequential as the industrial revolution was in its time. The information revolution, based on technological breakthroughs in computers, microelectronics, and telecommunications, is expanding our mental capabilities much as the industrial revolution augmented our physical capacities. To put it crudely, one was a revolution primarily of "brawn" the other is more related to "brain."

To understand both revolutions, this book uses three analytic strategies. First, it traces the history of industrialization from its origins in the industrial revolution to the present—in Chapters 1 to 4—and draws inferences about the various effects of industrialization over time. A second, complementary strategy makes cross-national comparisons of all nations in the world for which adequate data exist, in Chapter 5. The purpose of this analysis is to establish a rank ordering of countries with respect of their level of industrialization, and then to note other significant differences that vary with industrialization.

The third analytical strategy involves an intensive comparison of three highly industrialized countries—-Great Britian, the United States, and Japan—in Chapters 6 to 11. Britian was the first industrial nation and maintained its productive pre-eminence until the middle of the nineteenth century. It was superseded by the United States, which dominated world industrial production through much of the twentieth century. Finally, as Japan is now challenging the United States for world industrial supremacy, it too is an appropriate choice for comparison. Each of these countries is an industrial superpower, and each has at some point reached the pinnacle of industrial might. Consequently, an examination of their similarities can reveal common, possibly universal, features and effects of industrialization. Particularly given the different (non-European) cultural origins of Japan, such an analysis will help to lay bare the essential characteristics and consequences of this complex process.

Through an examination of the history of industrialization, as well as two separate comparative analyses searching for both differences and similarities, the book arrives at an approximation of the industrialization process and the effects it has caused, in Chapter 12, and explores the future based on limited projections as to what developments are most likely.

ACKNOWLEDGMENT

Although an author's name appears on the cover of a book, this is not the full story of authorship. As I state in Chapter 3 regarding invention which is a type of authorship, it is "a combination, albeit ingenious, of already known elements."

> What is really involved is a process of a cumulative accretion of useful knowledge, to which many people make essential contributions, even though the prize and reognition are usually accorded to the one actor who happens to be on the stage at a critical moment. (Rosenberg, 1982: 48—49)

Accordingly, I should like to acknowledge some of these many people and their essential contributions.

In the first ring of authorship of this book are the following: the late Kaspar D. Naegele, who turned me on to sociology and imbued me with a sociological imagination; the late Joan Woodward, from whom I learned the excitement of industrial and organizational research and who gave me the confidence to grow as a sociologist; Robert Dubin, my advisor and mentor, from who I stole probably more than I realize; W. S. Robinson, who introduced me to Hume's dilemma and other problems of social research; Thomas C. Taveggia, my fellow graduate student, friend, and colleague, who read and heavily criticized every single word of the original manuscript; Robert Hagedorn, my friend, reality contact, and willing sounding board for the past twenty years; and Darby Carswell, my wife and best friend, who contributed to the manuscript with her usual perceptive and empathetic criticism.

In the second ring of authorship are the sociologists, historians, economists, social commentators, practitioners, and others whose names appear in the bibliography. As this book is a summary, evaluation, and attempt to project the course of industrialization, quite obviously these writers are indispensable to the process. I hope that I have interpreted them well.

I should also like to thank Jack P. Gibbs for reviewing a portion of the manuscript and providing criticism that only he can. During his Lansdowne appointment at the University of Victoria, he was most stimulating at the Friday afternoon seminars. I also want to thank the following reviewers for their helpful comments:

Kevin T. Leicht, Penn State University
Aloo Driver, American International College
Mark Lazerson, SUNY Stony Brook
Sandra L. Albrect, University of Kansas
Heidi Gottfried, Purdue University

During my research and my life I have met many hundreds of workers from a diversity of occupations at all hierarchical levels. They have provided me with the substance to form my abstractions, which were then challenged by my students. These two groups also share in the authorship this book.

Finally, my appreciation and thanks go to Mollie Lister who typed the entire manuscript at least twice, some parts considerably more. Somehow through it all she managed to retain her sense of humor.

R. ALAN HEDLEY

Chapter

1

Making It in Postindustrial Society

The industrial transformation has multiplied the means, not the goals, of human existence.

Davis, 1985, p. 19

The major goal in any society is survival: of the society and of the individuals within it. In order to survive, both as a social system and as individuals, we must work to produce the goods and services that sustain us. Through work we make a living, and the type of work we do determines in large part the quality of that living.

This book examines the institution of work, how it has evolved and changed since the industrial revolution, which began in England just 200 years ago. It examines the process of industrialization and how its differential rate of introduction has produced enormous disparity among the nations of the world. It also examines the structural features of contemporary industrialized societies—the occupational and labor force structure, the organizational base, and the stratification system that is based largely on the work we do. And finally, it examines the motivations, reactions, and behavior of individual workers and how they fit into this complex whole. By way of introduction, this chapter will discuss the major elements that characterize industrial society, the revolutionary technological changes that have occurred, and the consequences these changes have had for individuals in society.

Before we begin, let me offer some advice to the reader. You will gain more from the analysis that follows if you can symbolically remove yourself from your present context and all that it involves. Attempt to suspend your present reality—

the many social positions you occupy, your interaction patterns, the complex social systems within which you operate—and adopt the eyes of "the stranger" or "the visitor" who makes infrequent trips to our planet in order to observe what is happening and the new developments that are taking place. This is the perspective of the social analyst who attempts to view the world abstractly to learn what in general is occurring and how it came about. When the analysis is concluded, you should have a better appreciation of how you and your activities fit into the overall scheme of things, because the changes I am going to describe are having and have had a profound impact upon all of us—the ways we think and the ways we behave, in short, the ways in which we live.

ELEMENTS OF THE INDUSTRIAL TRANSFORMATION

From the eyes of our perennial visitor, 200 years is not a long time. Given current standards, it is less than three lifetimes, or less than one-tenth of one percent of the total time that *Homo sapiens* has inhabited the face of this earth. Yet in this brief interval since the industrial revolution, we have achieved more change in the ways in which we live and in how we relate to our environment than in all the many thousands of years previous. In terms of impact upon human existence, only the agricultural revolution some 9000 years earlier is comparable. This revolution saw the discovery and domestication of various grains and the consequent establishment throughout many parts of the world of sedentary human settlements (see Lenski and Lenski, 1982, p. 134ff). Largely replacing the hunting, gathering, and herding societies of earlier times, these new agricultural communities were the precursors of life as we know it today. Although subsequent developments were notable and many, they pale in significance with those that occurred during late eighteenth century Europe.

The industrial revolution and all that it engendered was as far reaching in the transformation of human society as the agricultural revolution was in the basic establishment of that society. Important elements in this transformation include: (1) the separation of work from nonwork activities and the creation of a labor market; (2) increasing bureaucratization of all social activities; (3) the development of a societal infrastructure; (4) the systematic application of various forms of inanimate energy to all kinds of human endeavor; and (5) the widespread proliferation of technological innovations. In order to appreciate the magnitude of this societal transformation, we will examine each element in detail.

Work and the Labor Market

We take for granted the complex institutional arrangement whereby diverse individual talents and aptitudes are channeled into suitable employment opportunities and job vacancies are filled by appropriately qualified candidates. This arrangement is all the more remarkable when it is considered that many new labor force recruits are now filling jobs that did not even exist when these jobholders first entered school. For example, during the past 16 years (i.e., 12 years of school and

4 years of college), the services-producing, tertiary sector of the economy has expanded substantially in all industrialized nations (see Bednarzik and Shiells, 1989). In many cases, the new jobs created in this sector are the result of technological breakthroughs that have opened up new employment opportunities in areas such as health, medicine, and radiology; computers and electronic data processing; and electrical and electronic engineering (see Bureau of Labor Statistics, 1988). According to Rajan and Pearson (1986), new technologies, changing work methods, and the redistribution of jobs between and within sectors all contribute to changes in the occupational structure, and thus maintain the labor market in a dynamic state of perpetual flux. Under these fluid conditions, employees manage to find jobs that interest them, and employers hire applicants who are suitably qualified.

The labor market was first formally established during the industrial revolution as a consequence of the factory system of production. Paul Mantoux (1961, pp. 25–26), in a detailed chronicle of the beginnings of the factory system in England, describes its essential features:

> The factory system concentrates and multiplies the means of production so that the output is both accelerated and increased. Machinery is employed, which accomplishes with infallible precision and prodigious rapidity the heaviest and most complicated tasks. Its motive power is not the limited and irregular effort of human muscles, but either natural forces such as wind and running water, or artificial forces such as steam or electricity; these are tractable, regular and indefatigable, and can be increased indefinitely and at will. A vast number of persons, men, women and children, are brought together to tend the machines, all with specialized tasks—mere wheels within wheels. Implements more and more complicated, workmen more and more numerous and highly organized, these make up great undertakings, which are indeed industrial commonwealths. And, as the mainspring of this terrific activity, as a cause and as an end, behind this use of human labour and of mechanical force, capital is at work, swept forward by its own law—the law of profit—which urges it ceaselessly to produce, in order ceaselessly to grow.

From this description, we can discern the following points: (1) Factories were located close to available energy sources that were not always near existing population centers; (2) they were large in order to justify the huge capital costs of machinery and to achieve economies of scale; (3) they employed large numbers of workers, "all with specialized tasks"; and (4) they were organized to accommodate rigid and continuous production schedules in order that they might fully utilize the expensive machinery. Consequently, employers in sometimes remote locations could not leave to chance the availability of workers in sufficient number and with appropriate training who would be on hand to work around the clock. More formal mechanisms were required. Thus was created an explicit labor market in which both employers and workers could advertise their respective needs. Through this now institutionalized arrangement, a better fit between job demand and worker supply has resulted.

Today, this arrangement has been perfected to the point where it is now possible to make limited projections of labor force growth and to predict which occupations are likely to grow most rapidly (see Chapter 6). Every other year, the U.S. Bureau of Labor Statistics "identifies the principal factors that affect job prospects and indicates how these are expected to affect the occupation in the future" (BLS,

1988, p. 8). Other industrialized countries also publish projections that are designed to ensure that future occupational demand will be met by an adequate supply of appropriately trained personnel (see, for example, Rajan and Pearson, 1986). Armed with these projections, other institutionalized agencies within society (e.g., government bureaus, vocational training institutes, and educational organizations) can plan their respective programs accordingly. However, it is possible to make these projections only to the extent that there is an explicitly defined labor force and movements into it, within it, and out of it are charted meticulously. This requires that organizations be established with the express purpose of obtaining these statistics and maintaining the resulting records (e.g., Bureau of Labor Statistics). Consequently, as indicated previously, not only is modern industrial society characterized by a formally defined labor force, it is also highly organized.

Organizational Base

The twentieth century has been called "the age of organization" because in a very real sense large-scale organizations encompass most aspects of everyday life and so affect how we think and behave.The most effective solution to resolving the problems of coordination has been the formal complex organization. The evolution of formal organization and its envelopment of contemporary industrialized society was aptly described by Drucker (1964) in his monumental study of General Motors:

> Only a lifetime ago, at the turn of the century, the social world of Western man might have been represented as a prairie on which man himself was the highest eminence. A small hill—government—rose on the horizon, but while it was larger than anything else there, it was still quite low. Today by contrast, man's social world whether West or East, resembles the Himalayas. Man seems to be dwarfed by the giant mountains of large-scale organization all around him. Here is the Mount Everest of modern government. Next to it there are the armed forces, which in every country devour the lion's share of national production. Then come the towering cliffs of large business corporations and, scarcely less high and forbidding, the peaks of the large, powerful labor unions; then, the huge universities, the big hospitals—all of them creatures of this century. (Drucker, 1964, p. vii)

While it may be acknowledged that formal organizations are not a twentieth century creation in that they were functioning in ancient Egypt and classical Greece and Rome, nevertheless it is also true that never before have they occupied such a central and all-encompassing role as they do today. Whether it be the job that we have, the food we buy, the television we watch, or the newspaper we read, almost all our daily activities, even within the family, take place in an organizational context.

Organizations are extensions of ourselves. They permit the achievement of goals and resolution of problems otherwise unattainable on an individual basis. Complex tasks and functions such as the administration of government bureaus, the provision of hospital treatment and care, the manufacture of automobiles, and the building and launching of space satellites are all broken down into their constituent elements such that people knowledgeable in various aspects of the task, and perhaps located in different geographical regions, may apply their differential

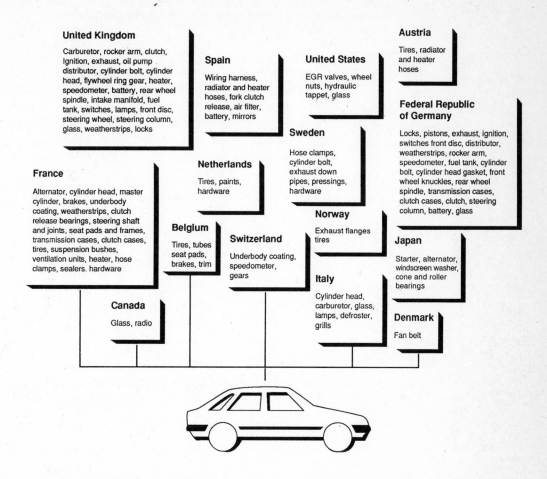

United Kingdom

Carburetor, rocker arm, clutch, Ignition, exhaust, oil pump distributor, cylinder bolt, cylinder head, flywheel ring gear, heater, speedometer, battery, rear wheel spindle, intake manifold, fuel tank, switches, lamps, front disc, steering wheel, steering column, glass, weatherstrips, locks

Spain

Wiring harness, radiator and heater hoses, fork clutch release, air filter, battery, mirrors

United States

EGR valves, wheel nuts, hydraulic tappet, glass

Austria

Tires, radiator and heater hoses

Federal Republic of Germany

Locks, pistons, exhaust, ignition, switches front disc, distributor, weatherstrips, rocker arm, speedometer, fuel tank, cylinder bolt, cylinder head gasket, front wheel knuckles, rear wheel spindle, transmission cases, clutch cases, clutch, steering column, battery, glass

Sweden

Hose clamps, cylinder bolt, exhaust down pipes, pressings, hardware

France

Alternator, cylinder head, master cylinder, brakes, underbody coating, weatherstrips, clutch release bearings, steering shaft and joints, seat pads and frames, transmission cases, clutch cases, tires, suspension bushes, ventilation units, heater, hose clamps, sealers. hardware

Netherlands

Tires, paints, hardware

Norway

Exhaust flanges tires

Belgium

Tires, tubes seat pads, brakes, trim

Switzerland

Underbody coating, speedometer, gears

Japan

Starter, alternator, windscreen washer, cone and roller bearings

Italy

Cylinder head, carburetor, glass, lamps, defroster, grills

Canada

Glass, radio

Denmark

Fan belt

Figure 1.1 The International Car (Component Network of the European Ford Escort) Source: World Bank, 1987, p. 39.

expertise to the ultimate objective of the organization. This is called a division of labor (horizontal differentiation), and it is coordinated through vertical differentiation or the creation of a hierarchy in which successive levels of managers guide the process through to completion.

So successful have these complex organizations become in the realization of their objectives that there is now an *international* division of labor in which large (transnational) corporations, utilizing all the world's resources (e.g., labor, energy, raw materials, professional expertise, markets, and so on), conduct their operations to the utmost advantage. Many of the goods we use today are produced by transnational corporations employing an international division of labor. Figure 1.1 illustrates how extensive this division of labor can be.

Table 1.1 **A COMPARISON OF ANNUAL SALES OF LEADING INDUSTRIAL CORPORATIONS AND THE GROSS DOMESTIC PRODUCTS OF SELECTED NATIONS** In Millions of Dollars (1988–1990)

Nation or corporation	GDP or sales[1]	Nation or corporation	GDP or sales
United States	$4,847,310	Unilever	$39,972
Japan	2,843,710	Pakistan	34,050
United Kingdom	702,370	Chrysler	30,868
General Motors	125,126	Toshiba	30,182
Royal Dutch/Shell	107,204	Nigeria	29,370
Exxon	105,885	Honda	27,070
Ford Motor	98,275	Singapore	23,880
Norway	91,050	Imperial Chemical	23,348
Saudi Arabia	72,620	Chile	22,080
IBM	69,018	Morocco	21,990
Toyota	64,516	Eastman Kodak	19,075
Venezuela	63,750	Xerox	18,382
British Petroleum	59,541	Mazda	16,913
General Electric	58,414	Hewlett-Packard	13,233
Hitachi	50,686	Sudan	11,240
Matsushita	43,516	Anheuser-Busch	10,751
Greece	40,900	Coca-Cola	10,406
Nissan	40,217	Ecuador	10,320

[1]Gross domestic product (GDP) measures the total final output of goods and services produced by residents and nonresidents of an economy.

Sources: For annual sales of corporations, *Fortune* 1991, pp. 245–247; for GDP, World Bank, 1990, pp. 182–183.

The rise of the modern industrial corporation and the power it holds are reflected in Table 1.1, which compares the annual sales of some of the world's largest companies with the gross domestic products (i.e., total output of goods and services) of selected countries. When it is considered that General Motors, the leading corporation in sales in 1990, had revenues approaching one-fifth of the GDP of the United Kingdom and surpassed by far the combined national output of Nigeria, Singapore, Chile, Morocco, Ecuador, and the Sudan, some appreciation is gained of the awesome might of these giant enterprises. In this context, the statement by Wilson (1952)—"what's good for General Motors is good for the country"—contains more than a kernel of truth.

Societal Infrastructure

Industrialized nations are comprised of interdependent, constantly interacting networks of public and private organizations. Whether it be international banks running credit checks for their transnational corporate clients, or government

Table 1.2   INSTITUTION OF FIVE SOCIAL SECURITY PROGRAMS IN TWENTY
INDUSTRIALIZED COUNTRIES,* 1900–1967

	Number of countries with program				
Type of program	1900	1915	1930	1945	1967
Work injury compensation	9	18	20	20	20
Old age pension	3	11	13	18	20
Sickness benefit	5	12	14	16	17
Unemployment benefit	0	4	13	18	19
Family allowance	0	0	2	10	18

*The countries include fourteen European nations plus the United States, Canada, Japan, Australia, New Zealand, and Israel.

Source: Mishra, 1973, p. 546.

regulatory agencies ensuring that occupational health and safety standards are being met, or a nationally federated union body mounting a lobbying campaign, there is increased interaction and interdependence among organized units of industrial society such that action in any one sector can have multiple effects throughout. Consequently, another feature of contemporary developed societies is the necessary coordination of activities, processes, and people into an organized whole. This is called the infrastructure, or underlying foundation, of a society.

Never before have there been so many competing, disparate, and yet legitimate demands made on social systems with limited abilities to satisfy all. Because the resolution of one set of problems requires valuable (and scarce) resources and has repercussions for other problems and other segments of society, complex interrelated organizations have evolved whereby problems are identified, priorities established, plans devised, and programs implemented in an attempt to provide the greatest good for society as a whole.

A complex and pervasive infrastructure capable of responding to the many needs of all the citizenry is a distinctive feature of modern industrialized societies. While obviously there are imperfections, and the fit between individual and society is often less than ideal, nevertheless at no other time has the state been set up to ensure the provision of essential goods and services to the entire populace. One study demonstrating just this point was carried out by Mishra (1973) in which he noted when various social security programs and free compulsory education were instituted in twenty industrialized countries from 1900 to 1970.[1] Over time, each country has established a relatively standard and uniform framework of social security benefits which has now been extended to cover the vast majority of the population in these countries (see Table 1.2). In addition, all countries require at least seven years of schooling for the young, and two-thirds demand a mininimum of nine years.

Mishra's thesis is that the industrialization process itself is largely responsible for the type of services that are provided. With regard to education, he argues that industrial technology demands an educated populace in order that it may perform an increasingly complex set of tasks, while the provision of social security programs is in direct response to various contingencies surrounding work. Thus, work injury compensation, a direct consequence of work, had been legislated in all twenty countries in 1945, and benefits relating to old age, sickness, and unemployment were similarly present in most. However, family allowance benefits, which are unrelated to the performance of work, were available in only half of these countries during the same period.

The infrastructure of a society is the institutionalized response of its people to the central problems faced by the society. Thus, in industrialized nations the infrastructure is not only responsible for educational and social security needs, but it also regulates and deals with a whole host of other problems relating to health, housing, welfare, economic development, transportation and communication, the administration of justice, the arts, and the protection of national sovereignty. Normally, anywhere from one-quarter to one-half of an industrial country's Gross National Product (the total value of goods and services produced annually within the country) is used to support this infrastructure (World Bank, 1987, p. 247).[2]

As problems surface due to society change, so also must the infrastructure respond to these new changes. For example, because of wide-ranging breakthroughs in prolonging life, there are increasingly larger cohorts of old people in industrial society. Problems arise in the ability of the system to support an ever-growing retired population; and also there are severe personal problems for older people who are systematically stripped of one of their principal sources of individual identity—their role as workers and producers in society. Other problems such as the fit between the services that a society supplies and the demands that its citizenry make also abound. As the age distribution of a society changes, various public and private agencies must respond in order to accommodate these changes. For example, nowadays there is demand for an increasing volume and variety of services for the elderly at the same time that there is a diminishing need for primary-school facilities. In short, our ability to prolong life produces new problems with which we as a society, as members of organized groups, and as individuals must learn to cope.

Inanimate Energy

As the history of industrialization involves increasing organization, so too is it characterized by increasing mechanization, that is, the replacement of human beings in the work process by complex tools, machinery, and equipment. While a factory at the time of the industrial revolution was notable for its "vast number of persons, men women, and children, . . . brought together to tend the machines" (Mantoux, 1961, p. 26), contemporary modern factories are remarkable for the relative absence of workers employed directly in the production process. Self-regulating, integrated systems of equipment and machinery have been designed to transform raw material into finished goods, completely without human intervention. The box item on flexible manufacturing systems (Box 1-1) describes one such automated production process.

With increasing mechanization comes a commensurate reliance on inanimate energy to drive the machinery. Coal was the fuel of choice in industrializing Great Britain during the eighteenth and nineteenth centuries, and mines were hard pressed to keep up with the ever-growing demand:

> In 1800 the total annual coal production of Britain was about 10 million tonnes. By 1850 this had climbed to 60 million tonnes and by 1900 it had reached 225 million tonnes a year. More coal was consumed in the two years 1899 and 1900 than in the whole century between 1700 and 1800 (Foley, 1981, p. 56).

While the production of coal in Britain between 1800 and 1900 increased by a factor of 22.5, its population grew only three and a half times. It was industrial mechanization that was largely responsible for the tremendous increase in per capita consumption; and as the industrial revolution spread to other countries, so too was there a corresponding increase in their per capita energy consumption. By 1925 the industrialized countries of North America, Western Europe, Oceania, and Japan were responsible for nearly 90 percent of the total energy consumed in the world; the United States itself used almost half (Darmstadter, 1971, p. 10).

Today, the industrially developed market economies account for just over half the world's energy consumption. By contrast, the less developed countries, which constitute slightly more than three-quarters of the world's population, use only 17 percent of total energy consumed (International Energy Agency, 1989, p. 31). Consequently, as energy consumption is related to mechanization, so also is it related to economic development. In a cross-national study of 34 countries, Darmstadter and his colleagues (1977, p. 3) report a strong correlation ($r = .85$) between per capita energy consumption and per capita gross national product. Thus, while industrialization contributes toward an improved standard of living, it is also costly in terms of taxing available energy sources.

It is anticipated that primary energy requirements will increase by more than half between 1987 and 2005 (International Energy Agency, 1989, p. 31). Aside from industrial activities, energy also is required for the transport and residential-commercial sectors of society. Indeed, recent growth in energy consumption in the developed economies, particularly in North America, has been taken up largely by the transport sector. With almost half a billion motor vehicles now on the roads throughout the world and an average annual growth rate of nearly five percent, the transportation sector is rapidly becoming the largest total energy consumer (Bleviss, 1990).

Recently, much concern has been expressed about energy use and its effects on the environment. At no time in the history of humankind have we had the ability to alter (and to destroy) our natural habitat as we have today. For example, greenhouse gases (i.e., carbon dioxide, nitrous oxide, chlorofluorocarbons, and methane), by-products of fossil fuel combustion, aerosol propellants, refrigerants, and other industrial agents are producing global warming, which if left unchecked could result in massive flooding of the world's lowlands and in droughts on the plains (see Spash and d'Arge, 1989). In the view of the United Nations-sponsored

Box 1-1   Flexible Manufacturing Systems

In the following account, Jaikumar (1989) describes flexible automation. The core of this strategy is the flexible manufacturing system (FMS), which is "a computer-control-led configuration of semi-independent work stations connected by automated handling systems" (Jaikumar, 1989, p. 124). FMS almost completely displaces the need for human intervention in the operation phase of manufacture.

"In most FMS installations, incoming raw workpieces arrive at a workstation where they are positioned into fixtures on pallets. When information on a fixtured workpiece (typically an identifying number) is entered informing the FMS controller that the workpiece is ready, the FMS supervisor (computer) takes charge, performing all the necessary operations to completion in any of a number of machines, moving workpieces between machines, responding to contingencies, and assigning priorities to the jobs in the system.

"The supervisor first sends a transporter to the load/unload station to retrieve a pallet. The loaded pallet then keeps moving in a loop until a machine becomes available to perform the first operation. When a shuttle (a position in the queue) becomes available, the transporter stops and a transfer mechanism removes the pallet, freeing the transporter to respond to the next move request.

"Parts received by a machine must be accurately located relative to the machine tool spindle. The inspection to accomplish this can be done manually, using standard instruments, or by coordinate measuring machines. The appropriate machining offsets are calculated from the measurements and communicated to the supervisor.

"Meanwhile, the supervisor has determined whether all the tools required for the machining operations are present in the tool pocket and requested needed tools from either off-line tool storage or a tool crib/tool chain within the system. When all the required tools are loaded, the supervisor downloads the NC (numeric control) part program to the machine controller from the FMS control computer.

"The process of making sure that the part is, in fact, what the computer thinks it is is termed 'qualifying' the part. Qualifying includes making sure that all previous operations have been completed, that the part is dimensionally within tolerance limits, and that it is accurately located. Tools, too, must be qualified. Tool geometry, length, diameter, and wear are all examined, either manually or under computer control. When both the workpiece and the tool have been qualified, the tool, part, or program offsets necessary to correct for systematic error have to be established.

"When the set-up activities are completed, machining begins. The FMS monitors the tool during machining. If it breaks, a contingent procedure is invoked. Some advanced FMSs have in-process inspection and adaptive control, whereby a continuous measurement of metal removal is made and compared to defined process parameters. Compensating corrections for any deviations are made during machining. Adaptive control in FMS is still very rudimentry and technically quite difficult with present-day technology.

"The finished, or machined, part is moved to the shuttle to await a transporter. After being loaded onto the transporter, the pallet moves to the next operation, or else circulates in the system, or is unloaded at some intermediate storage location until the machine required for the next operation becomes available.

"The computer controls the cycles just described for all parts and machines in the system, performing scheduling, dispatching, and traffic coordination functions. It also collects statistical and other manufacturing information from each station for reporting systems. As all the activities are under precise computer control, effects of part program changes, decision rules for priority assignment, contingent control, and part-portfolio mix can be captured."

Source: Jaikumar, 1989, pp. 122–123.

World Commission on Environment and Development, "it is impossible to separate economic development issues from environment issues; many forms of development erode the environment resources upon which they must be based, and environmental degradation can undermine economic development" (World Commission, 1987, p. 3). As Box 1.2 illustrates, the price of economic development can be very high, affecting current inhabitants of the earth and also generations yet to come. With anticipated energy use being half again as much by the beginning of the next century, clearly we cannot delay further the search for solutions to the economic development–environmental degradation dilemma.

Technological Innovation

The personal and structural changes that we are now experiencing in industrial society are so widespread, profound, and rapid that some social commentators have suggested that change itself and our ability to deal with it is the most serious of contemporary social problems. Alvin Toffler (1970) and other futurists (Naisbitt, 1982) have conveyed in most dramatic terms the types of change we are experiencing and the rapidity with which these changes are occurring. First Toffler:

> . . . if the last 50,000 years of man's existence were divided into lifetimes of approximately sixty-two years each, there have been about 800 such lifetimes. Of these 800, fully 650 were spent in caves.
>
> Only during the last seventy lifetimes has it been possible to communicate effectively from one lifetime to another—as writing made it possible to do. Only during the last six lifetimes did masses of men ever see a printed word. Only during the last four has it been possible to measure time with any precision. Only in the last two has anyone anywhere used an electric motor. And the overwhelming majority of all the material goods we use in daily life today have been developed within the present, the 800th, lifetime. (Toffler, 1970, p. 14)

Box 1-2   A World at Risk

The World Commission on Environment and Development first met in October 1984 and published its report 900 days later, in April 1987. Over those few days,

- The drought-triggered, environment–development crisis in Africa peaked, putting 35 million people at risk, killing perhaps a million.
- A leak from a pesticides factory in Bhopal, India, killed more than 2,000 people and blinded and injured 200,000 more.
- Liquid-gas tanks exploded in Mexico City, killing 1,000 and leaving thousands more homeless.
- The Chernobyl nuclear reactor explosion sent nuclear fallout across Europe, increasing the risks of future human cancers.
- Agricultural chemicals, solvents, and mercury flowed into the Rhine River during a warehouse fire in Switzerland, killing millions of fish and threatening drinking water in the Federal Republic of Germany and the Netherlands.
- An estimated 60 million people died of diarrheal diseases related to unsafe drinking water and malnutrition; most of the victims were children.

Source: World Commission on Environment and Development, 1987, p. 3.

And now Naisbitt:

> Between 6,000 and 7,000 scientific articles are written each day.
> Scientific and technical information now increases 13 percent per year, which means it doubles every 5.5 years.
> But the rate will soon jump to perhaps 40 percent per year because of new, more powerful information systems and an increasing population of scientists. That means that data will double every twenty months. (Naisbitt, 1982, p. 24)

According to Toffler (1970, p. 25), the "growling engine of change" is technology. One technological innovation spurs additional discovery and invention in an ever-widening sphere of related applications and at an ever-increasing rate. Furthermore, some of these subsequent discoveries and inventions lead to independent applications, which in turn spawn their own trajectories of development. The result is an interrelated complex of self-perpetuating and self-propelling innovations such that the material basis of society changes, thus provoking sometimes radical changes in how we lead our lives and how we relate to one another.

Take as an example technological developments in telecommunications, microelectronics, and information transfer. Three previously independent and major inventions—the telephone, television, and the computer—have now been integrated such that they are revolutionizing the design and functioning of the modern farm, factory, and office. In the office, the traditional typewriter, desk calculator, copier, filing cabinet, telephone, and telex have been or are being replaced by the integrated electronic workstation, which in turn is connected to similar workstations in a "real-time" (i.e., instantaneous) network throughout the organization, and indeed throughout the world.

These workstations have the capability to access public and private data banks, to maintain huge electronic files that can be retrieved and reproduced in a matter of seconds, and to send electronic mail or form the basis for a video teleconference at the same time that they are performing the more mundane office chores, such as writing and editing memos and writing and copying standard personalized letters to clients or colleagues whose addresses are drawn automatically from "memory" (see Rochell, 1988). Ongoing developments in these and other fields such as artificial intelligence, satellite technology, and superconductors promise even more. For example, should current work in developing "high-temperature" superconducting material yield the results anticipated, such a resistance-free communication line could

> transmit the text equivalent of one thousand Encyclopedia Britannicas per second, more than 15 million two-way voice conversations or more than 10,000 full-color television channels. Such a transmission line could transmit the entire 25 million books of the Library of Congress, the world's largest library, in two minutes . . . . (Meredith, 1987, p. 25)

The fact that we are undergoing such rapid change in every facet of our experience and that this is such a recent phenomenon means that our coping mechanisms, both individual and organizational, and our ability to adapt are not (yet) fully developed. Among our (mal)adaptive mechanisms is the tendency to deny or reject the changes that are actually occurring. We carve out our own niches and attempt to repel unwelcome intrusions. However, the changes that we are now witnessing have profound long-term implications for all our social institutions and the pattern of our daily living. As Gerard Piel, publisher of the *Scientific American*, has stated, "we are living in a revolution . . . yet we manage to fit the changes in the way we live and make our livings into the picture of the society we grew up with, suppressing any recognition of the impact of change on those values and institutions" (cited in Royal Commission . . . , Vol. 1, 1985, p. 125).

The labor movement is one such institution that is presently experiencing great difficulty as a result of the impact of change. Responding not only to technological upheavals in the world of work, but also to a radical restructuring of the labor force, the international division of labor, greater female labor force participation, changing contexts of work, and greater intervention of state employers, unions are discovering that their ideological heritage, traditional demands, and organizational tactics leave them ill equipped to represent the interests of the modern contemporary worker. Particularly in the United States, where union membership has declined steadily since 1945 (Cornfield, 1986, p. 1113), unions are struggling to adopt strategies that will permit them to reoccupy their hard-won position of power vis-à-vis the employer (see Kochan et al., 1986).

TECHNOLOGICAL REVOLUTIONS

The magnitude of the changes that are occurring has prompted some writers to suggest that we are currently undergoing a revolution every bit as intense as the industrial revolution some two hundred years earlier. Labeled the information revolution because it is based on the radical and comprehensive reorganization, processing, manipulation, and transfer of information, it has produced changes that go far beyond this technical base. Its consequences involve quite simply the restructuring of society. For example, given the fact that we can achieve instantaneous electronic access virtually anywhere in the world, this means it is now no longer necessary to perform much of the work we do within explicitly defined space and time limits. While we are still contractually responsible for achieving organizational goals, much more flexibility is built into the system.

Because most work today involves the manipulation of information rather than materials, former space/time constraints become redundant. Instead, workers can be linked to each other in a free-floating electronic network. Where and, within certain limits, when they perform their duties is largely irrelevant. According to Cordell (1985, p. 33), "by the mid-1990s, an estimated 15 percent of the workforce may be telecommuting, that is, working away from a central office."

Consider briefly the implications of telecommuting for some of our established institutional arrangements. What consequences does it have for the family? Certainly it could ease some of the current problems surrounding day care, at the same time that it could radically alter existing marital relations and the household division of labor. It is also possible that there would be a slowing of urbanization as it would no longer be necessary for many workers to locate close to the business core. This in turn would have consequences for arterial and transportation systems as well as communities that surround the major urban centers.

The relationship between the employee and the organization will also undergo substantial change. For example, what will become of employee identification, commitment, and loyalty to the company when the major linkage is electronic instead of physical? Will informal social interaction, which now occurs at the workplace, reappear between formally communicated information transfers; and what consequences will this have for interpersonal relationships in general? Also, the whole area of labor relations will experience yet another upheaval as professional and clerical unions attempt to institute computer-driven solidarity.

Herbert Simon (1987), a Nobel prize winner in economics and a leader in research on artificial intelligence, has addressed the issue of the relationship between technical and social change, and, to use his words, "what makes technology revolutionary." He maintains that "when technology reshapes society, it is not the result of a single invention but of a host of additional, completely unanticipated inventions, many of them of the same order of magnitude as the first one in the chain" (Simon, 1987, p. 7). Consequently, similar to the steam engine in the original industrial revolution, the computer by itself was not revolutionary. Its origins can be traced to the Electronic Numerical Integrator and Computer (ENIAC), which was developed during World War II, and earlier to the inventions of Charles Babbage and Herman Hollerith in the latter part of the nineteenth century (see Rochell, 1988). However, it was not until hitherto unrelated inventions were combined that the seeds of revolutionary change were sown.

Simon notes three features that accompany revolutionary technology. First, many of the changes that occur as a result of a fundamental technological innovation are completely unpredictable and therefore unanticipated. Consider the reactions of the inventors of the automobile or the airplane were they to return now to witness all the changes their inventions have produced. They could not possibly have even imagined, let alone predicted, the complete and total restructuring of society that was to follow. (See Box 1-3.)

A second feature of revolutionary technology is that it is introduced and accepted into society through what Simon calls "education by immersion." The first widespread adoption and use of the computer occurred with the introduction of the hand-held calculator less than two decades ago. These instruments, many of which are more powerful than the garage-size, first-generation computers, are now found in virtually every home and office. Then came electronic cash registers, basically electronic bookkeepers, which also were widely dispersed throughout society, including the local corner store. And finally, we are now ensconced in the middle of the personal or microcomputer revolution such that a very large and ever-growing proportion of the population has had hands-on experience. Simon's point is that with a fundamental technological invention we learn by doing rather than waiting until an appropriate instructional apparatus is established. In short, the technology revolutionizes our behavior.

Simon's third feature is the generality of the technological innovation, that is, an invention must have general applicability for it to be truly revolutionary. This was evident in the case of the steam engine, electricity, and the internal combustion engine, as it is with the computer. Each of these inventions permits the user to apply it in innumerable ways and in a variety of tasks.

Returning to the relationship between technological and social change, Simon sounds both optimistic and cautionary:

> Technological revolutions are not something that "happen" to us. We make them, and we make them for better or for worse. Our task is not to peer into the future to see what computers will bring us, but to shape the future that we want to have—a future that will create new possibilities for human learning, including, perhaps most important of all, new possibilities for learning to understand ourselves. (Simon, 1987, p. 11)

The fact that technological innovations have social consequences and that revolutionary technology produces revolutionary social change is an extremely important point that we will deal with throughout this book. Increasingly, it is necessary to adopt a longer-range, more comprehensive perspective in order to give direction to and maintain control of our collective existence.

If we apply Simon's criteria for establishing what is technologically revolutionary (see also Piatier, 1983, pp. 226–27), it is possible to identify four such revolutions. These are presented in Table 1.3 together with some of their important characteristic features. Obviously, such a representation can only include those

Box 1-3   Computer Error

Two features of computers, their internal consistency and their speed, can have disastrous consequences if programming errors are made. Because many thousands of "similar" cases can be wrongly classified instantaneously, inappropriate or even harmful action may be taken before the error is identified. The following newspaper article is amusing, but the results of other computer errors could be far more fateful.

> **"PARIS**—About 41,000 shocked Parisians have been branded pimps, murderers, and extortionists in an act of random 'blackmail' apparently caused by a computer error, a city official said Tuesday.
>
> "The slurs were dropped through Paris mailboxes last Friday morning, shattering domestic calm and causing panic.
>
> "A spokesman for the city office responsible for collecting fines said many of the officially signed letters mistakenly attributed routine traffic fines to crimes such as racketeering and running prostitution rings.
>
> "He said 41,000 letters of apology were on their way."

Source: Victoria *Times-Colonist*, 6 September 1989, p. A1.

items considered to be most salient, and hence many features are omitted. However, you should be able to appreciate the distinctiveness and uniqueness of each period.

Agricultural Revolution

These four technological (and social) revolutions may be categorized according to the major activities engaged in by the societies involved. The agricultural revolution, occurring approximately 9000 years ago, was marked by the establishment for the first time of societies in which the main activity was subsistence-level cultivation, with herding, hunting, and gathering being assigned secondary importance. These developments in turn resulted in the formation of semipermanent settlements and the accumulation of goods consisting of increasingly sophisticated tools, weapons, and other artifacts. It is important to note that the agricultural revolution, although revolutionary in its impact upon the evolution of human society, did not occur rapidly. Rather it evolved over a period of several thousand years in which increasing refinements were instituted in the pattern of sedentary human existence (see Lenski and Lenski, 1982, pp. 134–148).

Two Industrial Revolutions

The industrial revolution, beginning in the mid-eighteenth century, sparked a series of changes that reconstituted the entire basis of agricultural England. Some

Table 1.3   TECHNOLOGICAL REVOLUTIONS

Important characteristics	Technological revolutions			
	Agricultural	**Industrial**	**Transportation & communication**	**Information**
Date (approx.)	7000 B.C.	1750	1900	1950
Key inventions/ innovations	Plant cultivation	Steam engine	Electricity; internal combustion engine	Computer; nuclear fission
Power	Muscle; wind; water; fire	Coal-fired steam	Electricity; oil	Nuclear energy; solar power
Tools	Hand tools; plow; kiln	Factory system; machine tools	Assembly line; power tools	Integrated automated systems; computer; robotics; lasers
Skills	Physical strength; farming; basic craft skills	Skilled trades and semiskilled machine operatives	Skilled trades and semiskilled machine operatives	System monitors; professional services; human relations skills
Materials	Stone; bone; wood; hides; clay; metals	Textiles; iron; steel	Sheet metal; copper; rubber; glass; chemicals	Plastics; aluminum; super-alloys; synthetics; petrochemicals; aquaculture; genetic engineering
Transportation	Animal power; wheel; sailboat	Steam locomotive; steamship	Automobile; diesel locomotive; aircraft	Jet aircraft; helicopter; rocket; space ship; atomic-powered trains and vessels
Communication	Word of mouth; signs; sounds (later, written messages)	Newspaper printed on steam press; postal service	Telephone; telegraph; radio; movies	Television; telex; fax transmission; computer networks; satellites; microwaves; video cassettes
Medium of exchange	Barter	Money	Money	Electronic

Sources: Lenski and Lenski, 1982, pp. 134–142 and 242–255; Miller and Form, 1980, pp. 38–56; Piatier, 1983.

early manifestations included the interplay between technological innovations in the spinning and weaving functions of the textile industry, and the commercial application of the steam engine by James Watt (see Chapter 3). The earlier established factory system of production became entrenched as it was necessary to build large plants in order to utilize the power of steam efficiently. Factories were built to manufacture not only textiles but also iron, steel, agricultural equipment, and machine tools. By the end of the eighteenth century, industrial production had replaced agriculture as the major economic activity in England (see Hedley, 1986c, pp. 490–491).

Mechanical power and the factory system were responsible for the widespread change from subsistence to market production. No longer were goods produced only for one's needs but for a larger amorphous market of consumers. To take advantage of the increased capacity of mechanized production, industrial entrepreneurs had to create a demand for the great volume of goods. In this way, industrialization produced what we have come to call the marketplace. Various goods are produced according to the demand that exists for them.

In order to get the goods to market and to obtain raw materials for manufacture, there was also a great expansion and improvement in transportation. In fact, this was the second stage of the industrial revolution as the steam engine was applied directly to rail and ship. Increased production required ever-increasing access to surrounding areas, and it was this concern that at least in part initiated the subsequent revolution in transportation and communication.

By the beginning of the twentieth century, the industrial revolution had spread to Germany, France, and the United States, with the latter supplanting Great Britain as the world industrial leader. Together these four nations accounted for nearly three-quarters of all manufacturing output (Lenski and Lenski, 1982, p. 249). With the textile, iron, and steel industries already well established, attention turned to the development and application of electricity and the internal combustion engine, both actually invented in the previous century. Particularly in the United States with its vast territory, improved transportation and communication were crucial factors in the integration and consolidation of the new republic.

It was during this third technological revolution that industrial production assumed preeminence as the major economic activity in these then developing countries. Contributing to this were innovations in the organization of industrial work, first with the introduction of scientific management and industrial engineering principles by Frederick W. Taylor (1911), and later with the establishment of the assembly line by Henry Ford (1922). Both these industrial practitioners were responsible for implementing a minute division of labor such that many workers, all with minimal skill and training, could complete their individual and specialized tasks according to precise time specifications, which resulted in the manufacture of complex products such as automobiles, tractors, electric motors, and household appliances. These more efficient methods of mass production most certainly contributed to the United States maintaining its supremacy in world industrial production during this period.

Information Revolution

The years during World War II were a time of intense technological development in which government-sponsored research centers produced myriad inventions and discoveries that were applied to the war effort. Some of these, most notably the work in nuclear fission and rocketry, contributed directly to the arsenal of the warring nations, whereas others such as materials development (plastics, superalloys, aluminum, and synthetics) made more indirect contributions. A third area of con-

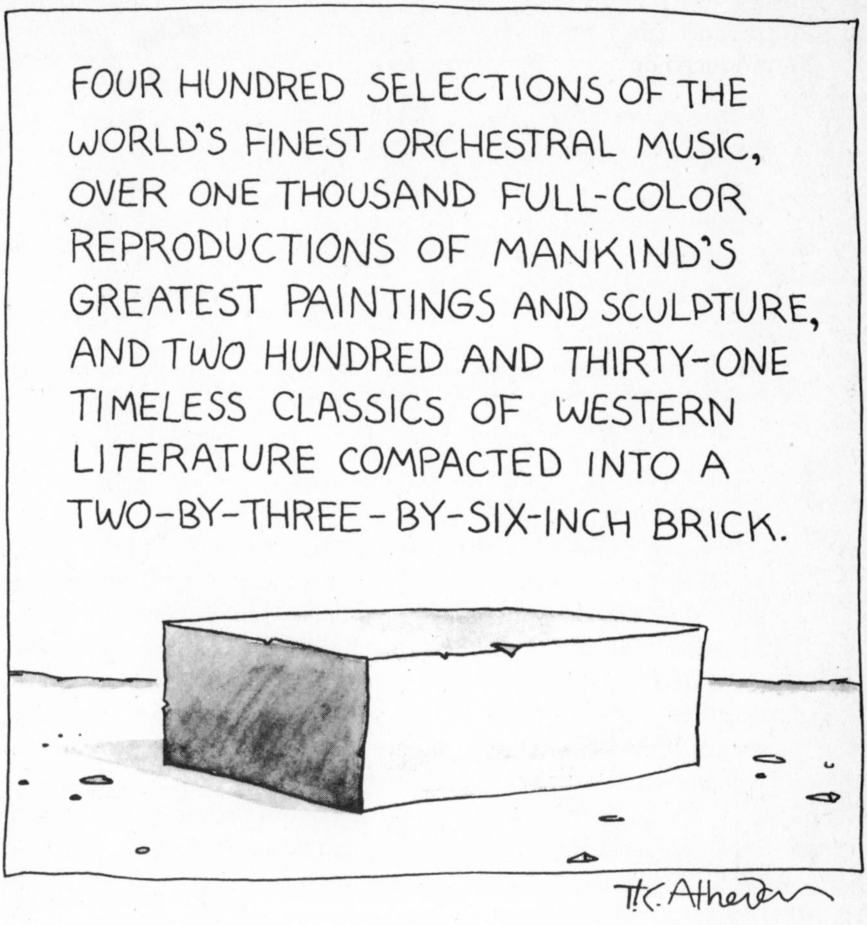

FOUR HUNDRED SELECTIONS OF THE
WORLD'S FINEST ORCHESTRAL MUSIC,
OVER ONE THOUSAND FULL-COLOR
REPRODUCTIONS OF MANKIND'S
GREATEST PAINTINGS AND SCULPTURE,
AND TWO HUNDRED AND THIRTY-ONE
TIMELESS CLASSICS OF WESTERN
LITERATURE COMPACTED INTO A
TWO-BY-THREE-BY-SIX-INCH BRICK.

Figure 1.2 Drawing by T. K. Atherton. © 1983 The New Yorker Magazine, Inc.

centration involved the development of reliable and high-speed support systems;
and it was in this context that the computer and the telecommunications industry
were created and set the stage for the information revolution that was to follow.[3]

In the postwar period, advances in computer technology catapulted development as engineers and managers alike became aware of the enormous potential for
systematic information processing in all fields of endeavor. Most significant among
these advances were "real-time" processing, miniaturization, increased memory
storage, greater capability and versatility, and reduced cost. Today, according to
Robert Borchers, associate director of the Lawrence Livermore National Laboratory, the most powerful computer, containing 240,000 computer chips, can do in
one second what it took a year to do in 1952 (Rochell, 1988, p. 14).

The computer chip, the core of the microelectronics and telecommunications
industries, has transformed industrial society. Jobs in the information sector, that

Table 1.4   WORLD INDUSTRIAL OUTPUT BY SELECTED COUNTRIES, 1888, 1948, 1986

Country	1888	1948	1986
United States	32%	43%	28%
United Kingdom	18	8	4
Germany	13	5	8
France	11	4	3
Russia	8	13	24
Japan	no data	1	5
All others	17	26	28
Total	99	100	100

Sources: Calculated from W. S. Woytinsky and E. S. Woytinsky, *World Population and Production: Trends and Outlooks* (New York: Twentieth Century Fund, 1953); United Nations *Statistical Yearbook 1948*; United Nations *Monthly Bulletin of Statistics*.

is, the part of the economy that produces, processes, and distributes information goods and services, are now more numerous and produce more of the wealth than the industrial and agricultural sectors combined (Naisbitt, 1982, pp. 20–22). Furthermore, this same computer chip has radically altered the nature of work in the more traditional sectors (see the special issue on "The Mechanization of Work" in *Scientific American*, 1982). From a simple thermostat to a "smart" robot to an automatic factory, the computer chip can be used in any machine or network of machines that manipulates information.

An important consequence of computerization is that virtually all of the repetitive mechanical jobs in society can be accomplished more efficiently and more productively using computers instead of people. Indeed, almost daily, current developments are expanding the range of computer applications possible such that the skills required in an information society are quite different from those in an industrial society. Also, with information in all its many aspects becoming an increasingly important commodity, the occupational structure itself is undergoing substantial change. This has resulted in a growing demand for administrative and professional services as well as other occupations that require nonroutine, face-to-face interaction.

Table 1.4 lists the percentage distribution of total industrial output by the leading manufacturing nations at roughly 50-year intervals over the past 100 years. These figures reflect in part the impact of the three technological revolutions occurring earlier in these countries. The most recent figures reveal that the earlier concentration in industrial production is now being diffused as other countries are experiencing their own industrial revolutions. The data also indicate the changing focus of the developed countries toward the production and distribution of information rather than manufactured goods. For example, whereas these six nations account for 72% of world industrial output in 1986, together they represent 83% of all registered patents in force (Kurian, 1984, pp. 217–218). Patents may be used as an indicator of the thrust toward information production.

In 1967, Daniel Bell coined the term *postindustrial society* to draw attention to the fact that the developed nations were in the throes of revolutionary change and that their economies were no longer geared primarily to industrial production. Piatier (1983) has summarized the major activities in a postindustrial society that involve the production of information:

1. activities concerned with the augmentation of intellectual human capital (education and training);
2. activities dealing with the augmentation of knowledge and exploitable ideas (research, R & D);
3. activities involving the collection, expression, and modification of information in the strict sense of the word;
4. nonmaterial transport (e.g., telecommunications);
5. activities of organization, arbitrage, decision, division, and so on;
6. activities linked to the allocation of rights to goods and services (money, finance, control of property, etc.). (Piater, 1983, p. 232)

Together these activities indicate the structural shift occurring in the world's most developed economies. This trend, along with the other elements of the industrial transformation discussed above, has important consequences for the individual living in a contemporary postindustrial, information-generating society. Let us now briefly examine the effects of this transformation from the individual's perspective.

THE INDIVIDUAL IN POSTINDUSTRIAL SOCIETY

In the preceding sections, we established that postindustrial societies have formally defined labor forces; are highly organized; have developed infrastructures capable of responding to the needs of the populace; are extremely energy intensive; are technologically innovative; and are increasingly geared to the provision of services rather than the production of goods. In this section, we establish the meaning of these structural changes for ordinary citizens living in these societies. While it may be asserted that the quality of their lives has improved both in relation to previous generations and compared to people in less-developed societies, there are also costs. In general, because of the high rate of change that also characterizes postindustrial societies, people are under more stress now than ever before. Thus, there are both benefits and costs arising from the great transformation we have experienced.

Quality of Life

Consider first human life itself. At no time in the history of humankind have we been able to delay death for so long as we can now. Children born today in any of the industrially developed countries can expect to live an average of 15 years longer than their grandparents, and 15 to 20 years longer than similar children born elsewhere in the world (*1988 World Population Data Sheet*, Gee, 1983). Not only will these children live longer, but also the quality of their lives will be vastly superior.

They may expect a level of medical treatment, nutrition, housing, education, and other social services without precedent. Furthermore, the benefits of both increased life expectancy and increased quality of living are extended more uniformly throughout contemporary developed societies than they were previously or than they are in less developed societies (Murdoch, 1980).

By any reasonable measure, the bulk of the world's population who live in nonindustrialized countries have not satisfied their basic human needs for food, water, and shelter. "Estimates of the extent of hunger in the world range widely, but there is general agreement that more than 1 billion people are chronically undernourished. Deaths related to hunger and starvation average 50,000 a day" (Sivard, 1985, p. 27). In 47 countries, mainly in Africa and Asia, which together represent 30 percent of the world's population, per capita caloric intake is below the minimum level required to sustain life (Sivard, 1985, p. 27).

The Population Crisis Committee in Washington, D.C., has constructed an international human suffering index comprised of ten measures of human welfare, each scored on a scale from 0 (no suffering) to 10 (extreme). Table 1.5 presents the 10 worst and the 10 best countries in terms of human suffering. Note that all the countries in which suffering is most acute are in industrially underdeveloped Africa or southern Asia, and that the countries in which there is least suffering are all, without exception, highly industrialized. Over two-thirds of the world's population live in conditions that the Population Crisis Committee characterizes as "extreme" or "high" human suffering, that is, between 50 and 100 points on the index. None of these countries is classified as industrial. Of the 27 countries with "minimal human suffering" (i.e., below 25 on the scale), all are industrialized with the exception of oil-rich Trinidad and Tobago.

In 1965, social psychologist Hadley Cantril published the results of his ambitious cross-national interview survey of nearly 20,000 citizens representatively sampled from 13 different countries,[4] entitled *The Pattern of Human Concerns*, Cantril sought to uncover the strivings, satisfactions, and situations of ordinary people as perceived by them. He found that the stage of development of a country gives particular shape to these aspirations and worries:

> . . . the vast majority of people's hopes and fears were found to revolve around the complex of well-being rather simply defined in terms of a decent standard of living, a more secure family life with opportunities for children. In underdeveloped countries, an appreciable number of people hoped for technological advances, which would speed improvements in their standards of living. Modern technology with all its faults obviously tends to alleviate the burdens people have borne for so many centuries and opens up more opportunities for more satisfactions in terms of greater security, better health, and self-development in a variety of ways. It is not until a people have achieved the high standard of living technology has made possible that they can begin to sense the huge new problems, which emerge because of it and which so vex the more sophisticated observers of the modern scene (Cantril, 1965, pp. 313–314).

Box 1-4, **India and the United States,** involves two of the countries that Cantril surveyed, the former at the lowest level of economic development and the latter

Table 1.5   INTERNATIONAL HUMAN SUFFERING INDEX

HUMAN SUFFERING INDEX

	Human suffering index total	Gross national product per capita	Average annual rate of inflation	Average annual growth of labor force	Average annual growth of urban population	Infant mortality	Daily per capita calorie supply % of requirement	Access to clean drinking water	Energy consumption per capita	Adult literacy	Personal freedom/governance	0 20 40 60 80 100
10 Worst												
Mozambique	95	10	10	6	10	10	10	9	10	10	10	
Angola	91	9	10	6	10	10	8	8	10	10	10	
Afghanistan	88	10	7	4	10	10	7	10	10	10	10	
Chad	88	10	6	5	10	9	10	8	10	10	10	
Mali	88	10	6	6	7	10	10	9	10	10	10	
Chana	87	9	10	8	9	6	10	6	10	9	10	
Somalia	87	9	8	6	9	10	8	7	10	10	10	
Niger	85	10	6	7	10	9	6	7	10	10	10	
Burkina Faso	84	10	6	4	8	10	9	7	10	10	10	
Central African Rep.	84	9	6	6	8	9	7	9	10	10	10	
10 Best												
Switzerland	4	0	0	0	0	0	0	0	4	0	0	
West Germany	5	2	1	0	0	1	0	0	1	0	0	
Luxembourg	6	1	4	0	1	0	0	0	0	0	0	
Netherlands	7	3	2	1	0	0	0	0	1	0	0	
United States	8	0	4	2	1	1	0	0	0	0	0	
Belgium	9	3	3	0	1	0	0	0	2	0	0	
Canada	9	1	5	2	1	0	0	0	0	0	0	
Austria	9	3	2	0	0	1	0	0	3	0	0	
Denmark	9	2	5	0	0	0	0	0	2	0	0	
Japan	11	2	1	1	1	0	3	0	3	0	0	

Source: Population Crisis Committee, 1987.

at the highest. This presentation reveals dramatically the structural differences involved in these two stages of development as well as how contextual features shape and bound people's perceptions and aspirations. A decade later, George Gallup (1976) launched a 70-nation opinion poll in which he emerged with essentially similar findings, that is, a direct relationship between national economic development and individual feelings of happiness and well-being.

Box 1-4   India and the United States: Making It in an LDC and an MDC (an Objective and Subjective Assessment)

Statistics are used to summarize information and to highlight certain essential characteristics of it. In the comparison that follows, India, a less-developed country (LDC), and the United States, a more-developed country (MDC), are contrasted on certain dimensions that have considerable impact on the quality of life for individuals in these countries.* These data indicate the differences in the relationship between person and environment.

In the subjective assessment that follows, in which Indians and Americans were asked to provide their own definitions of a "decent standard of living," the reader will appreciate what the objective data mean in terms of how people live their lives.

A. Objective Assessment

Characteristics	India	United States
Population (millions) 1988	816.8	246.1
Area (millions of sq. km)	3.29	9.36
Population density (persons per sq. km)	248	26
Crude birth rate (per 1000 pop.)	33	16
Crude death rate (per 1000 pop.)	13	9
Natural increase (% annual increase)	2.0%	0.7%
No. of years to double population (at current rate)	35	99
Infant mortality rate (per 1000 births)	104	10
Total fertility rate (avg. no. of children per woman)	4.3	1.8
Life expectancy at birth (years)	54	75
Daily calorie supply per capita (1985)	2189	3663
Population per physician (1981)	3700	500
Population per nursing person (1981)	4670	180
Number enrolled in school as % of age group (1984)		
Primary: Male	105%	102%
Female	73	100
Secondary: Male	44	95
Female	23	95
Higher education: Total	9	57

* According to classification developed by the United Nations, more-developed countries (MDCs) include all those in Europe and North America (excluding Mexico) plus the USSR, Japan, Australia, and New Zealand. These are generally what we refer to as postindustrial societies. All other countries are classified as less developed (LDCs). See the *1988 World Population Data Sheet.*

Gross National Product per capita (US$) 1986	$270	$17,500
% distribution of household income (c. 1980)		
Highest 20% of population earn	49.4%	39.9%
Fourth quintile	20.5	25.0
Third quintile	13.9	17.9
Second quintile	9.2	11.9
Lowest 20% of population earn	7.0	5.3
Total central govt. expenditure as % of GNP (1985)	16.7%	24.5%
% distribution of government expenditures (1985)		
Defense	18.8%	24.9%
Education	1.9	1.8
Health	2.4	11.3
Housing, community amenities, social security	4.4	31.6
Economic services (development and regulation)	27.0	8.3
Other (general administration, etc.)	45.5	22.1

B. Subjective Assessment

"A decent standard of living"

India

I hope in the future I will not get any disease. Now I am coughing. I also hope I can purchase a bicycle. I hope my children will study well and that I can provide them with an education. I also would sometime like to own a fan and maybe a radio.
(40-year-old skilled worker earning $30 a month)

My main wish is that my land produce enough so that I may be able to repay my debts as I have to pay a great deal of money to money-lenders now. I should some day like enough money to educate my children.
(60-year-old Hindu of moderate education)

I should like above all to know that I could live a life without the possibility of starvation. I should also like to get some education and then get a job as soon as possible.
(20-year-old man who is a Harijan earning 60 rupees, about $12 a month)

United States

These days one has to work so hard, there is always someone pushing you. I would like a slower pace in living, more time for the simplicities of life. I'd like to put my four sons through college so they don't have to work as hard as I have. I would be a fool if I didn't want more money and a nice house to live in, a new car, and a chance to travel.
(46-year-old skilled worker)

Materially speaking, I would like to provide my family with an income to allow them to live well—to have the proper recreation, to go camping, to have music and dancing lessons for the children, and to have family trips. I wish we could belong to a country club and do more entertaining. We just bought a new home and expect to be perfectly satisfied with it for a number of years.
(28-year-old lawyer)

(continued on next page)

India

I would like to construct a well and set up an electric pump on my land. I also need enough manure to get the maximum yield from the land.
(38-year-old owner-cultivator now earning about $35 a month)

The main thing I wish for is to have some money at my disposal so I could marry off my daughter. I also need to have better produce from my land so I can repay the money-lender. If I get these wishes then my life will be very comfortable.
(50-year-old illiterate, owner-cultivator, earning about $20 a month)

I wish for an increase in my wages, because with my meager salary I cannot afford to buy decent food for my famiy. If the food and clothing problems were solved, then I would feel at home and be satisfied. Also if my wife were able to work the two of us could then feed the family and I am sure would have a happy life and our worries would be over.
(30-year-old sweeper, monthly income around $13)

I wish that I had some money so that I could repair my house so that we could at least have a roof over us. As it is now, I am not safe from strong winds and rains.
(60-year-old midwife, monthly income around $15)

I wish my son could be employed in a factory on a regular basis. Then my old age would be saved from rotting and he could support the family in my absence. I hope the government will start some cottage industry in our village so that we can earn a living. (60-year-old laborer earning about $18 a month)

United States

I would like a reasonable enough income to maintain a house, have a new car, have a boat, and send my four children to private schools.
(34-year-old laboratory technician)

I would like financial security and enough to be able to quit work and stay home with the children.)
(34-year-old bus driver)

I would like a new car. I wish all my bills were paid and I had more money for myself. I would like to play more golf and to hunt more than I do. I would like to have more time to do the things I want to and to entertain my friends.
(Black bus driver, 24-years-old)

If I had more money I could build a home, get married, move out of the city, and take a long vacation. I would like to be able to take my bride to Europe.
(26-year-old clerk)

I want to see that my children are happily married and financially secure. I want enough money to travel and go back to school and study and learn to be a psychologist.
(49-year-old mechanic)

I hope that when I retire I will have enough money to travel, not necessarily in top style. We have had a nice comfortable home life raising our children and have enjoyed it. Now I'd like to do a few different things, like traveling.
(52-year-old insurance agent)

Sources: Objective data from World Bank (1987); *1988 World Population Data Sheet*. Subjective data from Cantril (1965, pp. 205–207, 221–223).

Individual–Environment Stress

Changes in the environment place pressure upon individuals to adapt to them, and the greater and more varied the changes, the greater the consequent pressure. This was the hypothesis that prompted the research of Holmes and Rahe (1967), which led to their pioneering development of the social readjustment rating scale of life events. They argued that pressure (stress) is a function of the amount of change, whether positively or negatively perceived, and the consequent readjustment that this change involves for the individual. Holmes and Rahe constructed 43 life events rank ordered according to their perceived degree of necessary readjustment, and then correlated these with the incidence of stress as manifested through various behavioral disorders. According to Dohrenwend and Dohrenwend (1984, p. 3), "Holmes and his colleagues have reported statistically significant relations between a quantitative index of the amount of change entailed in recent life events and disorders or disabilities ranging from myocardial infarction and childhood leukemia to poor teacher performance and low college grade point average." (See Box 1-5, **Burnout: Vocabulary of the Eighties**.)

Although the study of stress caused by increased environmental change is relatively recent, stress more generally is defined as the result of an inadequate person–environment fit (Kasl, 1978), and in this sense, it is not a new phenomenon. According to this definition, stress arising out of change is the result of a relatively indeterminate environment in which individuals are uncertain of their parameters. For example, it is impossible to predict at this moment all jobs and occupations that will be in existence even 10 years from now. Obviously, this indeterminacy most affects the young, all of whom must ultimately make some type of vocational choice based on incomplete knowledge. Examination of the *Dictionary of Occupational Titles* (DOT) over regular intervals since its inception in 1939 indicates that the overlap or degree of fit between successive editions is continuously deteriorating; in other words, it is becoming increasingly difficult to plan a career. Furthermore, it is likely that young people entering the labor force now will experience more radical career change throughout their working lives than has occurred with previous generations.

The DOT also reveals a greater *number* of occupations from one edition to the next. Although editions are not exactly comparable due to changing definitions and classification systems used, nevertheless the sheer volume of increase in the number of jobs listed over time indicates the increased variety and therefore choice available. In this case, stress can arise from virtually unlimited choice and the fact that there are few established guidelines by which to decide. As well as occupational listings, this applies to educational/training choices and indeed to optional lifestyles.

As an example of the choices with which we are inundated, compare the departments and course listings of a university today with one only 20 years ago. The contemporary university not only has the traditional disciplines represented like its earlier counterpart, but it also has brand-new departments as well as various interdisciplinary configurations. In my own university, there are departments of chemistry, economics, and philosophy, as there were 20 years earlier.

Box 1-5   Burnout: Vocabulary of the Eighties

A sociological definition of "culture" is a "shared set of symbols and their definitions or meanings prevailing in a society" (Curtis and Lambert, 1986, p. 61). Language is thus an intrinsic aspect of culture and reflects the behavior and values occurring within it. Particularly in times of rapid social change, new terms as well as old terms with new meanings are coined to denote novel things, processes, experiences, and our reactions to these.

As late as 1974, "burnout," according to the authoritative *Webster's New World Dictionary*, did not include the psychoemotional meaning which we now attribute to this term. It was defined only physically as "the point at which missile fuel is completely burned up and the missile enters its free-flight phase," or alternatively as "damage caused by overheating." However, ten years later in the 1984 edition of *Webster's*, these definitions were expanded to reflect popular usage of the term: "a state of emotional exhaustion caused by the stresses of one's work or responsibilities."

Using language as our guide, it would appear that prior to the 1980s our culture had no particular need for this special meaning of burnout, but had to coin it subsequently to indicate a new reality.

However, it now also offers programs in child care, computer science, health information science, leisure studies, and robotics as well as interdisciplinary offerings in biochemistry and microbiology, environmental studies, Pacific and Asian studies, and women's studies. Consequently, today's student has both the advantage and the dilemma of choice. Actually, if one considers the total range and variety of educational and training institutions available today compared with the previous era, together with the fact that all vocational applications are not known, the decision-making process can be truly bewildering.

Greater choice in this case arises directly out of the phenomenal expansion of knowledge we are experiencing and the consequent specialization that this entails. In order to master increasingly detailed and complex fields of study, it is necessary to carve them up into ever smaller domains of inquiry. Thus, as well as there being an overall expansion of subjects and disciplines, there is also increased specialization and the creation of subareas *within* disciplines.

Forty years ago, David Riesman (1961, originally published 1950) wrote an insightful treatise titled *The Lonely Crowd* in which he attempted to explain the changes he was witnessing around him. He argued that particular character types evolve or are produced from the structural changes that occur in society. He offered evidence that suggested that a new major character type was becoming prominent in the American urban–industrial core. Labeled the "other-directed" type, its features are consonant with the fact that individuals in contemporary postindustrial society have few unquestioned, stable norms upon which they may base their actions.

> What is common to all the other-directed people is that their contemporaries are the source of direction for the individual—either those known to him or those with whom he is indirectly acquainted, through friends and through the mass media. This source is of course "internalized" in the sense that dependence on it for guidance in life is implanted early. The goals toward which the other-directed person strives shift with that guidance: it is only the process of striving itself and the process of paying close attention to the signals from others that remains unaltered throughout life. (Riesman, 1961, p. 21)

The picture that emerges of the individual in postindustrial society is one who is buffeted by myriad changes that interfere in some part with the rational pursuit of personal life goals. Although offered more choices, the outcomes of these choices are not always certain, thus frustrating action. Not able to rely extensively on past standards or practices, this individual consequently looks to others for direction and guidance.

Consequently, while individuals in contemporary postindustrial society may very likely be under a great deal of stress due to the rapid structural changes they are experiencing, nevertheless they are also happier with the quality of their lives and their ability to make choices than their fellow beings in less-developed parts of the world who are more concerned with problems of immediate survival. To paraphrase Herbert Simon, part of the choice that we exercise as individuals and as members of various organized groups is the determination of appropriate goals and objectives. To the extent that we do this, and *then* set into motion the technological and organizational means necessary to achieve them, we can shape our own destiny instead of becoming technologically enslaved.

As a final indication of the vastly changed world in which we live and with which we must cope, examine the list in Box 1-6, **When I Was Your Age . . . .** In this chapter alone, I have mentioned 60 innovations which were not present in your grandparents' day, many of which have altered radically today's society. I have tried to present the most important developments in order to give you a flavor of the uniqueness of the period we are living in, but this list is by no means exhaustive. It is, however, indicative of the excitement, the challenge, and the problems that we face.

In a very real sense, this chapter is an overture to what is to come in the remaining chapters. I have provided examples and illustrations of the global impact of industrialization from its beginnings slightly more than 200 years ago. I have discussed how industrialization improves the quality of life at the same time that it introduces new problems in our relationships to the environment, to society, and to each other. I have noted the features of the technological revolutions we have experienced, how the pace of technical innovation is quickening, and the consequences for both individuals and society. In the chapters to come, each of these themes will be expanded beginning first with the very important notion of social change.

Box 1-6   # When I Was Your Age . . .

How many times did you hear this while growing up? Think of your grandparents at the age you are now, and attempt to reconstruct their society, noting how different it was from your society today. To demonstrate this difference, search through this chapter for words, inventions, and concepts that are familiar to you but which were unknown in your grandparents' day (approx. 1940).

The list below reveals some of the startling developments we have experienced in just two generations.

aerosol propellants	integrated electronic workstation
aquaculture	international division of labor
artificial intelligence	jet aircraft
atomic-powered train	lasers
automation	microcomputer
burnout	microelectronics
computer	microwaves
computer chip	nuclear energy
computer error	nuclear fallout
computer memory	nuclear fission
computer science	nuclear reactor
copying machine	numeric control
data bank	plastics
day care	postindustrial society
electronic calculator	real-time network
electronic cash register	robotics
electronic data processing	rocket
electronic files	satellite technology
electronic mail	space satellite
electronic network	space ship
fax transmission	superalloys
flexible manufacturing systems	superconductors
genetic engineering	telecommunications
global manufacturing	telecommuting
global warming	television
greenhouse gases	telex
health information science	transnational corporation
helicopter	video cassette
information revolution	video teleconference
information transfer	women's liberation movement

SUMMARY

1.1 The beginnings of contemporary modern society were formed 200 years ago with the onset of the industrial revolution in England.

1.2 As a consequence of the factory system of production, labor markets were established to coordinate more effectively occupational demand with the supply of appropriately trained workers.

1.3 An inherent feature of industrialization is organization. The twentieth century has been called the age of organization in that virtually every facet of contemporary society has an organizational base. Large-scale industrial organizations can span several countries in their operations and are as powerful as many nation states (see Table 1.1).

1.4 Contemporary industrial societies have infrastructures or underlying coordinating foundations that are established to deal with the central problems faced by the populace. The industrialization process itself is largely responsible for the problems created and the services rendered.

1.5 Another defining characteristic of industrialization is mechanization, that is, the steady replacement of human beings by machines in the production process. Mechanization relies upon inanimate energy for its driving force. The industrially developed market economies that account for less than one-fifth of the world's population use over one-half of all energy consumed. By-products of energy consumption are causing severe damage to the environment.

1.6 The industrial transformation is also remarkable for the many major technological innovations it has spawned. At no other time in the history of the world has the rate of technological change been so rapid. In turn, these innovations have been largely responsible for the restructuring of society that has occurred.

1.7 When several major technological innovations are combined, the result is a techno-logical revolution. Three important features of a technological revolution are: (1) many of the changes produced are unpredictable; (2) innovations are adopted en masse through "education by immersion"; and (3) major innovations are generally applicable.

1.8 In the history of humankind, there have been four technological revolutions: (1) agricultural; (2) industrial; (3) transportation and communication; and (4) information (see Table 1.3).

1.9 The quality of life of ordinary citizens in modern postindustrial societies has improved both in relation to previous generations and compared to people in less developed societies. There is a direct relationship between national economic development and individual feelings of happiness and well-being.

1.10 The increased rate of change in contemporary society is a source of stress between individual and environment. Stress arises from the indeterminacy of the environment as well as the fact that it involves almost limitless choice. The chapter concluded by listing 60 major recent innovations whose cumulative effect is a relatively high level of stress.

NOTES

1. The countries he examined were fourteen European nations plus the United States, Canada, Japan, Australia, New Zealand, and Israel.

2. Gross national product (GNP) and gross domestic product (GDP) are two slightly different measures of national output. GNP "measures the total domestic and foreign output claimed by residents," whereas GDP "measures the total final output of goods and services produced by an economy—that is, by residents and nonresidents" (World Bank, 1987, pp. 268, 271).

3. A fourth area of militarily supported research was in the application of the social sciences to the war effort. See, for example, the four-volume work *Studies in Social Psychology in World War II* (Stouffer et al., 1950), which was based on data collected by social scientists in the Research Branch of the Information and Education Division of the U.S. War Department. The individual volumes are:
   I. *The American Soldier: Adjustment During Army Life*
   II. *The American Soldier: Combat and Its Aftermath*
   III. *Experiments on Mass Communication*
   IV. *Measurement and Prediction*

4. Ranked from lowest to highest on a national socioeconomic index developed by Cantril, the countries he surveyed included: India, Nigeria, Egypt, Dominican Republic, Brazil, Philippines, Yugoslavia, Panama, Cuba, Poland, Israel, West Germany, and the United States.

Chapter
2

Social Change

Without time, . . . there is no change. Without change, however, there is no sense of time.

Moore, 1963, p. 23

*A*s mentioned, industrialization began slightly more than 200 years ago, and because of the tremendous changes it produced, it was called a "revolution." Chapter 2 will examine industrialization from the perspective of social change. In the first section, we will look at changes brought about by the industrial revolution as perceived by early social theorists. This retrospective view presents the important distinction between dichotomies and continua or changes in kind versus changes in degree. It also examines the several dimensions that comprise the complex concept of industrialization and how these are measured over time. Next, we will note that whether or not change occurs is partially dependent upon the level of analysis we employ. For example, what may be interpreted as change at the "individual" level of analysis may be construed as stability if "society" becomes the focus of concern. There is also a discussion of the actual ways in which change is measured in this section. The chapter will conclude with a brief examination of major theories of social change, most of these in fact having been devised to explain how this complex process of industrialization has produced so many of the changes that we are currently experiencing.

DICHOTOMIES AND CONTINUA

In most theories of social change, industrialization or some aspect of it is employed as the independent or causal variable to explain some other change that has occurred or is occurring. Industrialization as an independent variable has been used to explain diverse phenomena such as the change from extended to nuclear families, declining death and birth rates, urbanization, secularization, and increases in deviant behavior. That is, the changes that were introduced as a result of the industrialization process have caused or produced other substantial changes within society.

The Great Dichotomy

Early theorists saw these changes brought about by the industrial revolution as changes in kind rather than of degree. Because these changes were so extensive and occurred over a relatively short period of time (nothing like this had ever happened before), they were interpreted as producing a qualitative "revolutionary" change in society. According to these theorists, the values, norms, mode of social organization, and interaction patterns of the earlier agriculturally based society were literally transformed by the events of the industrial revolution into a completely different (industrial) social system. Employing what is termed an *ideal type* analysis, these theorists attempted to distill all those features that they thought characterized or typified an agricultural society, and then contrasted these with how they presumed these same features operated within industrial society.[1] Thus, they ended up with two sets of almost diametrically opposed attributes. Later labeled "the great dichotomy" by subsequent sociologists, many of these features are presented in Table 2.1.

While it may be argued, for example, that prior to the industrial revolution English society was primarily agriculturally based, and that subsequent to this development its economy was predominantly supported by manufactured goods, the point is that in *no* society, either before or after the industrial revolution, does one set of activities (e.g., agriculture) totally exclude the other (manufacturing). Similarly, whereas informal social relations are more characteristic of agricultural than of industrial societies, formal relations nevertheless do still take place. Likewise, formal relations are not the exclusive interactional pattern in industrial societies.

Ideal types are just that; they are analytical constructs or abstracted forms that do not find their counterparts in the real world. Their utility lies more in the features they uncover rather than in their ability to provide an accurate and valid portrayal of empirical reality. As Wilbert Moore (1963) has noted,

> Although such modes of classification are "primitive" in the sense that they attempt analysis in terms of attributes rather than variables, they are not useless. It is the beginning of wisdom to identify the dichotomies as polar extremes on a range of variation, and the pursuit of wisdom to observe that pure types do not concretely exist. A very considerable gain in wisdom results, however, from recognizing the paired alternatives as conflicting principles of social organization and regulation, both of which are persistent in groups and societies. Emphasis on one alternative in the values and norms of any society does not dispel or dismiss its counterpart. (Moore, 1963, p. 66)

Table 2.1 THE GREAT DICHOTOMY

From the time of Marx, Durkheim, and Weber to the present, sociologists have attempted to spell out the variety and types of social change that occurred as a result of the technological changes brought about by the industrial revolution. Table 2.1 is a simplified presentation; it is based on positing agricultural and industrial societies as dichotomies. In fact, each type of society possesses characteristics of the other.

Social dimension	Agricultural society	Industrial society
Economy	Agricultural Subsistence production Simple division of labor Barter exchange	Industrial Market production Complex division of labor Money exchange
Culture	Homogeneous standards Based on consensus	Heterogeneous standards Differentiation
Values	Traditional Sacred Ceremony and ritual	Innovative Secular Functional instrumental orientation
Social organization	Traditional Based on kinship	Rational-legal (bureaucratic) Based on merit
Social control	Informal moral pressure	Impersonal bureaucratic control mechanisms
Social relations	Informal Mechanical solidarity	Formal Organic solidarity
Mode of behavior	Based on custom and tradition	Based on contract

Source: Adapted from Hedley, 1986c, p. 492.

It is important to realize that whereas significant changes have taken place as a result of industrialization, and various analysts have identified the most prominent of these, this does not mean that there is no continuity and that elements of one form of society are not also common to the other type of society. This very point was made by Gusfield (1967) in his examination of what he termed "misplaced polarities in the study of social change."

Based on his research in India, Gusfield identified seven common fallacies in the assumptions underlying the agricultural–industrial, or as he called it, the traditional–modern polarity:

Fallacy 1. Developing societies have been static societies There is a tendency to think that all less-developed countries have always existed in their present form simply waiting for their own chances at development. Gusfield points to the rich dynamic history of India as a counterexample, but other cases abound (e.g., China, Egypt, Iran [Persia], Mexico, and Peru). Although industrialization does produce significant societal change, this does not preclude other substantial changes from occurring independently.

Fallacy 2. Traditional culture is a consistent body of norms and values   According to Durkheim's notion of mechanical solidarity (see Durkheim, 1964, originally published in 1893) in which similarities in values and norms are emphasized, one might be led to believe that all values and norms are consistently held and practiced in traditional society. However, one has only to look at how religious or spiritual leaders are often in direct opposition to political leaders to see that a diversity of values and norms is not only possible, but also very likely.

Fallacy 3. Traditional society is a homogeneous social structure   Following from the previous point, Gusfield notes that even within a so-called traditional society distinct subgroups and subcultures do exist, to which the Indian caste system bears testimony. Homogeneity cannot be assumed simply because traditional societies have a more simple division of labor than do industrial societies.

Fallacy 4. Old traditions are displaced by new changes   While it is true that changes are constantly occurring within any society, this does not mean that the new must necessarily *replace* the old. There are many instances in which both old and new coexist and are used interchangeably by many members of society. Magic and medicine is one example, as is Box 2-1, **Make a Dream Come True**.

Fallacy 5. Traditional and modern forms are always in conflict   In 1973, Ronald Dore published his study, *British Factory–Japanese Factory*, in which he noted that although Great Britain and Japan, both island countries dependent upon the import of raw materials for manufacture, are now postindustrial nations, they are nevertheless each very different and took different paths to achieve modernization. These differences in large part stem from their unique cultures, which far from impeding their respective development actually enhanced it. Kerr and his colleagues (1964) suggest that national development (i.e., modernization) occurs along lines most amenable to the ruling indigenous elite classes most of whom assumed their exalted positions in earlier traditional times.

Fallacy 6. Tradition and modernity are mutually exclusive systems   As may be witnessed previously, tradition and modernity are frequently mutually reinforcing rather than systems in conflict. Although status in modern contemporary organizations is ideally based on achieved rather than ascribed criteria, empirically both are often present. For example, Porter (1965) in his study of elites in Canada found "a thin but none the less perceptible thread of kinship" present among the elite network, while Haq in his study of Pakistan noted "the growing concentration of industrial income and wealth in the hands of only 22 family groups . . . (who) controlled . . . about two-thirds of the industrial assets, 80% of banking, and 70% of insurance in Pakistan" (cited in Murdoch, 1980, p. 243).

Fallacy 7. Modernizing processes weaken tradition   While it is true that the processes of modern communication and transportation increase the possibility of a world culture, at the same time they permit the diffusion of traditional cultures.

Box 2-1   Make a Dream Come True

One explanation for social change is to increase control and thus mastery over our individual and collective existence, and to this end we have put science and technology to work in all manner of forms. However, notwithstanding all of our expertise and ingenuity, we can never predict with absolute certainty what will happen tomorrow. Because of this, both traditional and innovative modes of dealing with the future coexist as alternative and sometimes complementary coping mechanisms.

On the same day you read about new scientific discoveries and technological breakthroughs in your newspaper, you will also be able to read facsimiles of the following:

Give a final push to make a dream come true. Just because others have given up is no reason for you to follow suit! Loved ones give you greater freedom. Money pressures diminish.

Someone could try to give you a hard time today. Shore up your defenses and disregard meaningless ultimatums. Put love at the top of your priority list.

Revenge is sweet, but if you carry it too far, you could have the tables turned on you. Unconventional hours are difficult for your loved ones, but reduce your commuting time.

Pay closer attention to your money and how it is being spent by others. A surprising revelation could lead you to make swift changes.

People of the same traditional culture but living in different regions can more easily maintain contact with one another and reinforce old values.

Each fallacy reveals a problem that is raised if we do not calibrate our measuring instruments according to the complexity of the task at hand. Very probably, the intent of the original authors of "the great dichotomy" was to highlight in as forceful a fashion as possible the changes brought about by the industrial revolution. Thus, they categorized all societies into just two types in a kind of crude "before and after" research design. While it may be said that they succeeded in emphasizing the changes that had occurred, at the same time their theoretical models severely distorted the empirical social systems they were characterizing. Later sociologists, partly in reaction against these distortions, provided more empirically valid descriptions of the changes that actually had taken place (see, for example, Gans, 1962; Hauser, 1965; Young and Willmot, 1957).

While it may seem ludicrous in retrospect that anyone would conceive of such a simple two-category classification scheme, in fact it is a very common strategy employed to focus on one constellation of factors (often very loosely defined) as opposed to another. Consider for example Type A and Type B personalities, introverts and extroverts, developed and underdeveloped countries, democratic and totalitarian regimes, or even stability and change. In ordinary conversation too, we often resort to presenting concepts and things in "either–or" terms (e.g., good–bad, cheap–expensive, ugly–beautiful).

The construction of dichotomies, that is, the division of phenomena into two mutually exclusive, contrasting categories, is at best a shorthand, heuristic technique employed to simplify and to emphasize one or more features that the presenter thinks are important. However, in the case of complex phenomena such as human personalities or social systems, the resulting dichotomies are grossly inadequate descriptions of what they are purporting to portray. In some instances, the cases within one category of the dichotomy may be more different from each other than they are from the so-called opposite examples. This is precisely the point that Gusfield (1967) was making in his analysis of "misplaced polarities" (see also Hagedorn, 1969).

Dimensions of Industrialization

Dichotomies as theoretical abstractions are crude representations of reality compared to continua, which reflect gradients or degrees along specified dimensions or variables. To state that agricultural societies are based on kinship and that industrial societies are based on merit (see Table 2.1) does not tell us very much, and may actually conceal more than is revealed. How, for instance, do we determine whether or not this is an accurate statement?

In Chapter 1, during my discussion of the four technological revolutions, I classified societies according to the major (economic) activities engaged in by them. Thus, it is possible, for example, to rank order all countries by the percent of the labor force that is employed in agriculture, or the percent that agriculture contributes to the gross domestic product (GDP) of each country. Alternatively, one could engage in similar rankings with respect to industry (percent of labor force employed in industry and percent contribution of industry to GDP). Although the agricultural rankings would approximate the inverse of the industrial rank orders, they would not be exact opposites in that employment and earnings in agriculture and industry do not exhaust all the sectors of economic activity (i.e., the services or tertiary sector remains). The point here is that we are really dealing with *two* dimensions—an agricultural continuum or variable *and* an industrial one. As long as there are more than two types of economic activity, one is not and cannot be the opposite of the other.

In a significant way, the early theorists were confused in their analyses of societal changes incurred by the industrial revolution. In the first place, they treated two cross-cutting dimensions (the agricultural and the industrial) as only one. Instead of examining agricultural and postagricultural *or* preindustrial and industrial societies, they dealt exclusively with agricultural and industrial societies, thereby concentrating on different aspects before and after the industrial revolution. In the second place and following from their original strategy, further confusion resulted from the conclusions flowing from these analyses, as once again

Table 2.2   THE EFFECT OF INDUSTRIALIZATION ON THE DETERMINATION OF ECONOMIC STATUS

Level of industrialization	Criteria for Economic Status Determination			
	Kinship	Merit	Other	Total (%)
High	_____	_____	_____	100
Medium	_____	_____	_____	100
Low	_____	_____	_____	100
Total	_____	_____	_____	100

different dimensions or variables were identified as the result. For example, most of the contrasting characteristics listed under agricultural society and industrial society in Table 2.1 are not opposite ends of the same dimensions. They are features of quite different variables, and herein lies the basis for and explanation of the "misplaced polarities."

In the analysis of change, it is absolutely crucial to deal with the same (independent and dependent) variables before *and* after. If, for example, industrialization is thought to produce various social changes, then the job of the analyst is to identify a number of societies at various stages in the industrialization process. It is then possible to measure other aspects of these same societies to determine whether or not the degree of industrialization has an effect.

In Table 2.2, I have provided a revised example from an entry contained in Table 2.1, that is, the effect of industrialization on the determination of one's economic status. In this retreatment, you will note that both kinship *and* merit are considered as possibilities for economic status determination under *each* condition of industrialization. (Note also that there is a residual "other" category for cases in which the determination of economic status is not a function of either kinship connections or merit considerations, e.g., a lucky accident or winning the lottery.)

The strategy implied by Table 2.2 involves three steps: (1) Assign countries to categories on the basis of their level of industrialization; (2) for each of these categories, calculate the proportions in which economic status is assigned according to kinship, merit, and other criteria; and (3) evaluate whether the differences in status determination *between* levels of industrialization are significant. Contrast this strategy with that implied in Table 2.1 in which kinship (or merit) is examined in one type of society but omitted from consideration in the uniquely labeled other society. Unfortunately, this method of "comparison" is still all too prevalent, and thus you should ensure that like things are being compared and contrasted on the same dimensions before drawing possibly erroneous conclusions. Incidentally, the analytical strategy employed in Table 2.2 is the *only* way in which an answer may be provided to the question posed at the beginning of this section.

Table 2.2 raises another interesting issue, and that is the conceptualization and measurement of industrialization. We have already ascertained that it is a com-

Table 2.3   DIMENSIONS AND MEASURES OF INDUSTRIALIZATION

1. *Economic activity/labor*
   (a) Percent of labor force in industry
   (b) Percent of labor force in manufacturing

2. *Economic output/productivity*
   (a) Percent contribution of industry to GDP
   (b) Percent share of value added in manufacturing to GDP
   (c) Gross output per employee in manufacturing
   (d) Earnings per employee in manufacturing

3. *Factory system/machine production/mechanization*
   (a) Number of manufacturing establishments employing fifty or more workers per capita
   (b) Number of manufacturing establishments employing fifty or more workers as a percent of all manufacturing establishments

4. *Energy source/use*
   (a) Energy consumption per capita (kilograms of oil equivalent)
   (b) Total cost of fuels and purchased electric energy per employee in manufacturing

5. *Technology/skills/techniques*
   (a) Percent of professional and technical workers in labor force
   (b) Registered patents in force per capita
   (c) Registered industrial designs in force per capita

References for measures: Hagedorn et al., 1971; Kurian, 1984; World Bank, 1987.

plex process involving industrial manufacture, but unless we can measure it we cannot determine with any degree of precision how extensive it is within various societies nor what effects it causes.

One of the original and most basic definitions of industrialization is provided by Kerr and his colleagues (1964, p. 14): "the actual course of transition from the preceding agricultural or commercial society toward the industrial society." The actual processes involved in this transition are "economic growth or increasing income per capita, mechanization of production, and increasing size of production organizations" (Faunce and Form, 1969, p. 3). To these processes, Smucker (1980, p. 1) in his definition of industrialization adds "the replacement of human skills in the production of goods and services with machines and the replacement of human or animal energy with inanimate sources of power."

Industrialization is a complex process comprised of a number of interrelated dimensions or variables. Table 2.3 specifies these dimensions and lists available measures that have been used to indicate them. The first two of these dimensions reflect the changes in activity that occur in a shift from an agricultural-based economy to one based on industry; that is, there is a change in what people do for a living (labor force activity), and what they do contributes to the overall wealth of the nation (economic output). The third dimension (factory system/machine production/mechanization) takes into account the organization of this economic activity, while the fourth reflects its energy or power source. Finally, the fifth dimension (technology/skills/techniques) exemplifies the systematic methods and innovative practices by which this economic activity is pursued.

Ideally, all these dimensions and their measures should covary such that progress or development along one dimension is mirrored by similar progress along the others. Unfortunately, this is not often the case (see Hagedorn et al., 1971). As an illustration of this point, Canada, as measured by energy consumption per capita (item 4a in Table 2.3), is the most industrialized country in the world; but when measured by percent share of value added in manufacturing to GDP (item 2b), its industrial preeminence drops to 36th place, being outperformed by nations such as Mexico, Egypt, Zimbabwe, Uruguay, Turkey, Philippines, Peru, Bolivia, Zambia, Thailand, Pakistan, and Senegal (see World Bank, 1987, pp. 51, 218–19).[2]

Feldman and Moore (1969, p. 59) have noted that "the industrialization process . . . comprises a complex of social changes that are neither precisely determinate in sequence nor finite in duration." This statement becomes more understandable to the extent that one realizes that for industrialization to occur, it must take place in some physical (e.g., resources, climate, territorial size), social (e.g., population, culture, history, political structure), and temporal (e.g., time and rate of introduction) context. Therefore, it is not really surprising that this process will be manifested in more or less different forms in countries such as Canada, Switzerland, the United States, Japan, Great Britain, Brazil, and Singapore. Because industrialization is such a complex multidimensional process, it may be a wiser strategy in many instances to break it down and study the changes occurring along its various dimensions and the effects these produce rather than to attempt to understand and explain its global impact (see Dubin, 1969, pp. 60–63).

LEVELS AND UNITS OF ANALYSIS

During the course of our lives, each of us experiences many changes as we pass through the various stages of the life cycle. The physiological changes in our bodies are accompanied by different social roles and responsibilities, or, as Shakespeare put it, "one man in his time plays many parts, his acts being seven ages." As we pass from infancy through childhood and finally reach adult status, we are bombarded with novel experiences and ideas; we are in a process of constant change. Yet, even as we marvel at the changes we are experiencing as individuals, we become increasingly aware that "in *every* society, *every* individual has an age role and a sex role" (Lenski and Lenski, 1982, p. 49 [italics added]). In other words, what is novel for us is commonplace within society. "Social relationships in all mammalian societies . . . are organized to take account of age and sex differences" (Lenski and Lenski, 1982, p. 47).

Is the above example an illustration of change or stability? The answer depends upon whether the focus of study is on individuals (e.g., explaining individuals' reactions to life cycle changes) or society (e.g., the mechanisms by which orderly continuity is maintained in society). Basically, researchers are interested in dependent variables—in how and why these vary in terms of independent or causal variables. Depending on which dependent variables they select, they may be involved in different levels of analysis.

Levels of Analysis

Traditionally, sociology is comprised of two orientations: macro-sociology and micro-sociology. "A macro perspective studies the large scale structures and processes of society. A micro perspective studies the small scale structures and process of society" (Hagedorn, 1986, p. 12). Actually, as Wallace (1969, p. 45) points out, this is yet another case where a continuum is presented as a dichotomy.[3] Although some sociologists extend the dichotomy and speak of macro, mezzo (middle), and micro levels (see, for example, Berg, 1979, and Ford, 1988), in fact, sociological variables range over many levels of analysis. For example, sociologists can study the relations among coalitions of nations, compare and contrast individual countries, examine relationships among multinational organizations, engage in analyses of various social institutions, make inter- and intraorganizational comparisons, study group interaction patterns, or analyze individual attitudes and behavior.

Different levels of analysis focus on different aspects of behavior, and usually call on different types of data. Consequently, as in the preceding example on individual change and societal stability, it is important to realize that what may apply to one level of analysis cannot be directly applied to another (see Robinson, 1950). In Box 2-2, **Death by Dieselization**, I have provided an example of how one sociological problem, that is, the social impact of a technological innovation (the introduction of diesel-powered locomotives in the railroad industry) might be studied using different levels of analysis.

Units of Analysis

By now it should be apparent that while we can point to examples of change all around us, it is an extremely difficult concept to measure precisely. As well as deciding at what level to measure change (e.g., societal, organizational, group, individual), it is also necessary to specify the units by which we will record these measurements.

As a concept, change implies an altered state from one time to another; and so it is possible, assuming that we are measuring the same thing in the same way from Time 1 to Time 2, to measure the *direction* of change. That is, at Time 2 we may record a value (e.g., on per capita energy consumption) as higher or lower or unchanged from Time 1. Also, provided that we have calibrated our measuring instrument, we may record the *magnitude* of this change.

As a process, we demand two things from measurement: (1) that it is valid and reliable; and (2) that we can make sense of what we are recording. For example, can we be sure that our two measurements (Time 1 and Time 2) are accurate? Are the direction and magnitude of change from Time 1 to Time 2 indicative of what is to come? Is the difference between Time 2 and Time 1 "normal"? Given only two measurements, it is impossible to answer any of these questions; but with a number of measurements taken over a sufficiently long period of time, one can be better informed with regard to both reliability of measurement and its interpretation. With many measurements over time, it is possible to compare magnitudes and thus establish *rates* of change. Also, serial measurement permits one to discern the *form* of change (e.g., linear or cyclical). However, caution must be taken to ensure that the interval of time is of adequate duration such that one can correctly identify the pattern being manifested. For example, what at first glance may appear as linear can upon more extended observation turn out to be cyclical.[4]

Finally, one can conceive of (and sometimes measure) the *duration* of change, particularly if it is cyclical and it is therefore possible to record the length of time or duration of the completed cycle before it repeats itself. One can also think of deviations from the normal state of affairs in this regard, as for example the duration of a strike or lockout. For an illustration of various types of social changes cross-classified by duration and magnitude of change, see Table 2.4.

An important point to keep in mind with regard to the measurement of social change is that it is severely hampered by the absence of a sufficiently detailed and long historical record. Recorded history reflects only a tiny fraction of the total history of humankind, and even now, relatively sophisticated and refined data are primarily limited to the more developed nations (see Haupt and Kane, 1980, pp. 16–17). Consequently, to the extent that we are concerned with the measurement of long-term, global changes, we must be extremely cautious both in our interpretations of what has happened and in our projections of what is likely to occur (see Davis, 1949, p. 629).

THEORIES OF SOCIAL CHANGE

Theories, which consist of sets of interrelated propositions or general statements of relationship, provide a focus for discerning and examining complex phenomena such that we can make sense of the myriad changes that have taken place and are still occurring. Without this focus, we would be employed in mindless recording without knowing what was important and not important. Theories provide lenses to "see," permitting us to assemble "like" bits of information or data into the same category, and thus afford us the ability to generalize and to predict.

Notwithstanding these beneficial features, it is important to keep in mind that different theories, like different lenses (e.g., microscope versus telescope), offer us different vantage points or ways of seeing the world. For example, what one theorist may see as evidence of social change, another may very well interpret as indicating stability within a social system. One is not right, and the other wrong.

Box 2-2   # Death by Dieselization

In 1951, W. F. Cottrell wrote about Caliente, a little one-industry railroad town located in the desert midway between two major terminals 600 miles apart. With the replacement of steam by diesel locomotives, the rationale for Caliente as a division point along the railroad line ceased to exist, and the company abandoned its operations there, thus consigning the town to oblivion.

Cottrell's analysis involves a description of the death throes of this small town with its complement of the usual amenities (e.g., school, hospital, four churches, hotel, theater, park and playing field, water system, shops, restaurants, and so on). It is an analysis of a small social system facing impending doom as it attempts to rally last-minute labor movement, government, and commercial investment support. Its demise is placed within the context of social disruptions caused by technological "progress." Cottrell concludes with a cost–benefit analysis of this technological innovation for the railroad company, its employees, the town, its citizens, and the structure and values of social life in America.

Cottrell's analysis is at the community level—the impact of dieselization on the town of Caliente. Although he indicates that this scene is typical of what is happening more generally in the country, his data are restricted to this one town. Also, while he speaks of the reactions of particular groups of individuals to dieselization, he does not in fact present any direct data on their reactions.

In what follows, I will present the same research problem with which Cottrell was concerned at both higher and lower levels of analysis in order to illustrate the variety of ways in which a general relationship (the impact of technological innovation on social structure and process) might be studied.

LARGE-SCALE, MACRO LEVELS OF ANALYSIS

With national data (e.g., government, industry, and union records), determine the impact over time of the switchover from steam to diesel on factors such as:

- employment in the railroad industry (e.g., specific occupations, occupational groupings, total numbers employed, unemployment rates, and so on);
- labor relations in the railroad industry (e.g., numerical strength of railroad unions, changes in the collective agreement, transfer and retraining policies, severance pay, organized resistance, and so on);
- structure of the railroad industry (e.g., number and size of division points, division points incorporated/phased out, ratio of operating to nonoperating employees, ratio of administrative and supervisory personnel to wage-earning employees, and so on);
- financial status of the railroad industry (e.g., inventory of rolling stock, real estate holdings, freight and passenger rates, productivity indices, profit-and-loss statements, and so on).

SMALL-SCALE, MICRO LEVELS OF ANALYSIS

With survey or participant observational data, determine the impact of the switchover from steam to diesel in terms of livelihood, work satisfaction, employment prospects, reactions to change, and advantages and disadvantages (costs and benefits) on populations such as:

- railroad employees (by job type and length of service with the company)
- railroad union personnel
- railroad managerial personnel
- citizens in one-industry railroad towns
- customers of railroad services
- elected officials and civil servants involved with transportation
- general public

It may be seen that depending upon the level of analysis employed in a research problem, different kinds of data (and conclusions) will be forthcoming.

Depending upon what each is seeking to explain, and given the logical considerations involved in the two theories and the units and levels of analysis employed, each may be making valid, if somewhat different, points about the world. As Einstein once remarked, "The categories are not inherent in the phenomena." They are employed by human observers (theorists) to simplify the vast complexity they are witnessing. Consequently, in order to gain a broad and hopefully balanced overview, we will examine several theories of social change involving a variety of theoretical orientations or perspectives.

Before I present these theories, let us consider some basic and fundamental limiting conditions or universal constants. First, all members of the human species have the same basic needs for food, water, and shelter in order to survive. Also, we all have physiological and anatomical limits that we cannot exceed. For example, while we have increased our life expectancy as a species, we have not increased our life span.[5] And whereas we have invented airplanes and submarines, we ourselves can neither fly in the air nor live in the oceans. In this regard, from our earliest beginnings humankind has experienced no change.

Second, as a species we are bound by the limiting conditions of the planet we are inhabiting. Again, while we can artificially insulate ourselves from the elements, we must nevertheless accept whatever the forces of nature dispense, whether this be feast or famine. Here too, at least until the prospect of interstellar travel actually materializes, we continue to be bound by the same basic ground rules as our early ancestors.

If we now look at the changes we *have* implemented, very generally most of them were instituted to improve humankind's odds against nature, or as was more

Table 2.4   SOCIAL CHANGES CLASSIFIED BY DURATION AND MAGNITUDE

Duration of change	Magnitude of change	
	Small scale	Large scale
Short term	Periodic cycles Group and organizational dynamics (e.g., strikes)	Revolutions Inventions
Long term	Individual life cycles Cumulative changes	Civilization "life cycles" Social evolution

Source: Adapted from Moore, 1963, p. 49. The arrows in the table point to some of the consequences of cumulative changes.

usual, a select portion of humankind. The impetus for many of the changes that have occurred and are taking place around us is control—control over our individual and collective (however this is defined) destinies.

Very closely tied to the striving for control is the pursuit of the possible. In part, the history of social change can also be interpreted as the attempt to reduce the distance between the actual and the ideal. As Cantril (1965, p. 273) noted in summarizing his 13-nation research on *The Pattern of Human Concerns*: "Our data confirm the truth of Aristotle's observation that happiness comes from 'the exercise of vital powers along lines of excellence in a life affording them scope'." Or, as Moore (1963, p. 19) has stated: "anything less than total control of human biology and the nonhuman environment leaves ample opportunities for strain and innovation."

To lay bare the conditions by which we are all constrained and to specify the human agenda that universally motivates us is important; however, what is more intriguing to the sociologist is to unravel the myriad differences that now characterize us and explain how they came about. In our earliest history, the limiting conditions more narrowly constrained our behavior and aspirations, thus minimizing individual and group differences. However, over time as we have adapted individually and socially to the environment, it is the differences that have become disproportionately apparent. The explanation of these differences directly involves us in the study of varying types and patterns of social change.

In considering types of social change, I will restrict the examination to those types that are humanly induced as opposed to naturally occurring, and to those that have implications for society (large social systems) rather than for individuals. Thus, whereas earthquakes, floods, and tornados can produce substantial changes for those experiencing them, these changes fall outside the purview of this analysis. However, changes in the ability of the atmosphere, land, and water to sustain life as a result of humankind's interference are changes that we will consider. Similarly, whereas the decision of a family to limit the number of children it will produce does result in a changed pattern of life for this family, only when this decision is made by a significant proportion of families, and thus has implications for society at large, will the resulting structural changes be included for analysis.

With these caveats in mind, let us now examine briefly two major perspectives in sociology—structural functionalism and conflict theory—to determine how each handles the concept of change, and then deal with other important theoretical formulations that have attempted specifically to explain various social changes which have occurred.

Structural Functionalism

Structural functional theory is more often thought of as a perspective that explains stability, order, control, and continuity rather than change; however, it does treat the dynamic as well as the static elements of society. Before we examine how this perspective contends with social change, it is necessary first to set out the assumptions that underlie it:

1. Societies or other large social groupings are conceived of as organismlike social systems;
2. Social systems are assumed to be relatively stable, integrated, and self-perpetuating, being held together through value consensus;
3. Social systems are differentiated, that is, they are comprised of interrelated and interdependent elements (functions) which contribute toward and maintain equilibrium within these systems;
4. Although there is strain among elements within social systems, and some elements may be dysfunctional, equilibrium is maintained or restored through the processes of reintegration, institutionalization, and social control;
5. Social change within systems is both gradual and orderly. (For summaries of structural functionalism, see Martindale, 1960, pp. 441–500; Strasser, 1981).

Given these assumptions, it may be seen that structural functionalism is a perspective that is more concerned with explaining how structural forms persist and perpetuate themselves rather than with how they change or are transformed (see Dahrendorf, 1958a). Nevertheless, because change is a fact of life and structural functionalists are interested in describing and explaining the social world, it is incumbent upon them to account for the changes that do occur.

According to structural functional theory, change is an evolutionary and cumulative process, "the unfolding of what is potential in societies and cultures" (Strasser, 1981, p. 156). The mechanism by which it occurs is differentiation, or the continual specialization and refinement of elements within a system to meet more adequately the requisite system needs. Also, because differentiation sometimes proceeds unevenly across elements within a social system, strain can arise among the elements, thus causing more change as the system itself attempts to reestablish or maintain equilibrium. And finally, the greater the social differentiation within a society (i.e., the more specialized elements there are), the greater the rate of change will be in that there is a higher probability of strain among elements (i.e., there are more of them), and there are a greater number and variety of ways to fulfill the functional requisites of the system.

To illustrate the above with an example, one significant and very topical social change that has occurred over the past two or three decades in all postindustrial nations is the substantial increase in female labor force participation, particularly among women with children at home. In the United States, over half of all women with children under 6 years and nearly three-quarters of women whose youngest child is from age 6 to 17 are in the labor force (U.S. Bureau of the Census, 1987, p. 374). This fact in turn has resulted in emotionally charged debates, both official and unofficial, on who will take care of the nation's children. Within the framework of structural functionalism, how can we make sense of these issues?

The economic institution in society is responsible for the production and distribution of goods and services essential to societal maintenance. From the industrial revolution onward, an increasing occupational division of labor (differentiation) has taken place within industrialized economies, with one result being a disproportionately high demand for female workers owing to the fact that traditional female occupations have grown at a faster rate (i.e., jobs in the services or tertiary sector). In taking on paid employment in the labor force, women with young children have experienced considerable role strain: As mothers, they were responsible for nurturing, caring for, and socializing their children (essential functional elements of the family institution) at the same time that, as workers, they were required to absent themselves from the home environment (see Hedley and Adams, 1982).

Over time, the strain between the social institutions of the economy and the family has been partially reduced as the functions traditionally performed by women in particular and families in general have become more differentiated owing to labor market pressures. The following additional changes have consequently taken place: (1) There has been a substantial increase in institutionalized day care facilities; (2) schools (the educational institution) now offer more courses in "life skills"; and (3) there is a societal shift in values occurring toward more equality between the sexes and, therefore, a more equitable household division of labor.

From a structural functional point of view, whereas there has been strain within the social system owing to increased differentiation within the economy, equilibrium is being reestablished with these other changes, and as a result there are now more ways in which families can fulfill both their economic and familial responsibilities. Families may adopt traditional male and female roles (husband-provider and wife-nurturer), or mothers may enter the labor force and use informal (kinship and neighborhood) day care facilities, or they may take paid employment in the highly differentiated labor market and rely on equally differentiated (day care and educational) institutional facilities elsewhere within the social system.

In summary, structural functionalists view change as an evolutionary and, for the most part, orderly process that is brought about through increasing social differentiation. Although strains can and do occur among the elements of a highly differentiated society, they are resolved through time as the system reestablishes a new dynamic equilibrium.

Social Conflict Theory

Whereas structural functionalism emphasizes the features of society that promote order and stability, social conflict theory focuses on social characteristics that produce conflict and change. The underlying assumptions of this model of society are as follows:

1. Within any society there are scarce and valued resources (e.g., power, authority, status, prestige, wealth).
2. Depending upon whether people have access to or are excluded from these resources, opposing interests are formed, which may or may not be organized (i.e., manifest and latent interest groupings).
3. Conflict occurs when organized interest groups are at odds with respect to the division of valued resources.
4. The opposition of interests, with conflict as its vehicle, is thus the source of change within social systems. (For summaries of social conflict theory, see Dahrendorf, 1958b; Martindale, 1960, pp. 127–207; Randall and Strasser, 1981, pp. 41–53.)

Because there is always contention concerning the allocation of scarce and valued resources, conflict and thus change are endemic to social systems as various interest groups attempt either to preserve or to change the status quo. Whatever stability there is arises either from the temporary domination of one group by another or from a transitory balance of power.

In order to compare the implications of social conflict theory with those of structural functionalism, let us examine again the issues surrounding increased female labor force participation, but this time from a conflict perspective. The specific data to which I will refer are American although, as I have mentioned, these data are generally indicative of all postindustrial countries.

As I will discuss in more detail in Chapter 6, the traditional pattern of women's participation in the labor force throughout most of the twentieth century was that they became employed during their late teens in typically "female" occupations that they then held until just prior to the birth of their first child, whereupon most of them left the labor force never to return. They were regarded by (male) employers as a temporary and auxiliary labor pool and consequently were treated as such, receiving only a fraction of men's earnings. Also, because of their presumed transitory and ancillary attachment to the labor force, they were largely considered to be unorganizable by the (male) trade union movement. In short, they constituted a useful but basically powerless adjunct to the (male) labor market.

In 1980, for the first time, there were more women employed in the labor force as opposed to out of it, and furthermore they comprised almost half of all workers (U.S. Bureau of the Census, 1987, p. 366). With these increases in their numbers and proportions came a consequent increase in their bargaining power. "Women's issues" (e.g., equal pay for work of comparable worth, affirmative action in employment and postsecondary/vocational institutions, maternal benefits, day care, and even the household division of labor), all raised earlier by previous generations of laboring women and subsequently disregarded, were finally being heeded and acted upon. At long last, women were (and are) becoming an economic (and political) force to be reckoned with.

From a conflict perspective, two opposed interest groupings based on gender were formed with men enjoying privileged access to certain scarce and valued resources (e.g., more pay, authority, prestige, influence, occupational choice and variety—in one word, power!). Regardless of the legitimate claims of women regarding the equitable division of these resources, men largely ignored their protests. Women had few means to enforce their will. Only when their numbers and proportions reached a critical mass did they begin to acquire the power necessary to effect changes that will improve significantly the conditions under which they work and live. Furthermore, the gains that women are achieving at work are being extended into other social arenas as the impact of their numerical clout is being felt in the trade union movement, state and federal ballot boxes, the courts, and vocational institutions, and in the allocation of male and female rights and responsibilities at home. The cumulative effect of all these changes is a basic change in the norms and values of society (see Table 2.4).

For the conflict theorist, changes do not evolve naturally; they are a prize of conflict. For centuries women have been denied their due, and consequently the male–female status quo has remained intact. Only when women themselves developed sufficient means (numbers) to win their struggle did significant changes begin to occur in the male–female relationship. According to the conflict theorist, it is the opposition of interests that is at the basis of all change.

In both the structural functional and conflict analyses of the changes arising out of the increased rate of female labor force participation, the facts remain the same. Only the interpretations of these facts are different as various aspects and features are given different emphasis. As I have mentioned in the section on "Dichotomies and Continua," it is important to recognize that stability and change are simply two ways of describing the same dimension. Where the structural functionalist can see evidence that supports a "stability" interpretation, the conflict theorist can point to evidence within the same constellation of facts to justify "change." Theoretical perspectives provide a systematic focus by which we can make sense of the world. Depending upon which focus we use, we will be concentrating our attention on different aspects of the same thing. (See Box 2-3, **Consensus and Conflict: Two World Views.**)

Cultural Lag

We will now examine three other theories that have social change as their major focus. They are cultural lag, demographic transition, and cultural convergence, and each takes industrialization or some aspect of it as the major independent variable or causal set of forces that produces change.

The standard dictionary definition of **cultural lag** is "the failure of one aspect of a cultural complex to keep pace with the changes in some other related aspect, as the failure of social institutions to keep pace with the rapid advances in science" (*Webster's New World Dictionary*, 1984). This term was coined by William F. Ogburn

Box 2-3 **CONSENSUS AND CONFLICT: TWO WORLD VIEWS**

In 1958, Ralf Dahrendorf juxtaposed the essential elements of the structural functional (consensus) and conflict models of society that I have reproduced below. You will note that each element in one characterization of society is the polar opposite of its counterpart element in the other societal perspective: stability versus change; integration versus conflict; functional versus dysfunctional elements; consensus versus constraint. Although they are polar opposites, they are not mutually exclusive. In every society at any time, one can find evidence of both stability *and* change operating in dynamic coexistence. They are different ways of looking at the same thing. As we are living, so also at the same time are we dying. What we see is in large part determined by what we are looking for.

Models of Society

Consensus	Conflict
1. Every society is a relatively persisting configuration of elements.	1. Every society is subjected at every moment to change . . .
2. Every society is a well-integrated configuration of elements.	2. Every society experiences at every moment social conflict.
3. Every element in a society contributes to its functioning.	3. Every element in a society contributes to its change.
4. Every society rests on the consensus of its members.	4. Every society rests on constraint of some of its members by others.

Source: Dahrendorf, 1958b, p. 174

(1922) in his book *Social Change.* Ogburn conceived the theory of cultural lag by observing the uneven pace of development within society and the corresponding unequal rates of change that produced maladjustment and strain. Through a variety of systematic empirical investigations, he developed the thesis that changes in material culture or "the applications of scientific discovery and the material products of technology" (Ogburn, 1956, p. 79) occur at a faster rate than do changes in the nonmaterial, adaptive culture (values, norms, patterns of social organization, and so on), thereby causing maladjustment in the nonmaterial culture, or cultural lag.

According to Ogburn, the material culture changes at a faster rate than the nonmaterial culture, thus increasing cultural lags because of three principal factors. First, science and technology as opposed to the arts, religion, and ritual, for example, are cumulative enterprises that build upon knowledge acquired through previous generations. Consequently, "the number of patents, discoveries in applied science, and inventions has been increasing in something like an exponential curve" (Ogburn, 1957, p. 92). Second, there is resistance to change or cultural inertia in the nonmaterial culture operating in the form of vested interests preserving the status quo; predispositions toward familiar routines, habits, custom, and tradition; social pressures to conform; and anxiety regarding uncertainty and change that provokes a conservative reaction (see Ogburn, 1922, pp. 143–196). And finally, Ogburn notes that although changes in the nonmaterial culture could conceivably precede changes in the material, it is unlikely because of the very high degree of planning, prediction, and control that this would entail (see Ogburn, 1922, pp. 211–213).

In order to test his theory of cultural lag, Ogburn examined a wide range of changes occurring within society. For example, he looked at the relation between industrial accidents and the introduction of workers' compensation legislation. With the onset of factory production in the United States in the nineteenth century, accidents caused by the less than ideal match between worker and machine rose dramatically (changes in the material culture); yet it was not until the first part of the twentieth century that worker compensation laws were instituted (i.e., change in the nonmaterial, adaptive culture), thereby distributing the cost of accidents to employers as well as workers, and, not incidentally, causing a reduction in the accident rates owing to increased safety standards instituted by employers. From his careful analysis of industrial and legislative records, Ogburn estimated that the cultural lag in this case was approximately half a century (see Ogburn, 1922, pp. 213–236).

One important conclusion that Ogburn drew from his work on cultural lag is that with ever-increasing technological accumulation and change, our major adjustment as a culture is to the technological environment we have created rather than to the nonhuman environment and biological limitations that have previously served as our major constraints. His words ring with remarkable clarity today:

> Unlike the natural environment, the technological environment is a huge mass in rapid motion. It is no wonder then that our society with its numerous institutions and organizations has an almost impossible task in adjusting to this whirling technological environment. It should be no surprise to sociologists that the various forms and shapes which our social institutions take and the many shifts in their function are the result of adjustments—not to a changing natural environment, not to a changing biological heritage—but adaptations to a changing technology. (Ogburn, 1956, p. 85)

Demographic Transition

In 1650, the world's population was approximately 500 million (Gee, 1986, p. 204); in 1988, we numbered well over five billion (*1988 World Population Data Sheet*). Figure 2.1 presents these figures schematically. In order to grasp the significance of these numbers, imagine that each human being represents a second of time. In 1650, the population of Earth corresponded to almost 16 years of seconds; but in 1988, *we need 163 years of seconds in order to represent the number of human beings currently inhabiting the world.* Given that it took tens of thousands of years for the world's population to reach 500 million, a tenfold increase in the last 300 years is change of the highest order of magnitude. Demographic transition theory attempts to explain how this change occurred and what lies in store for us in the future.

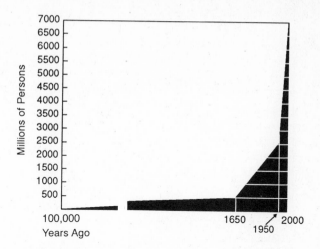

Figure 2.1 Schematic Representation of the Increase in Human Population

The demographic transition refers to the relationship between a population's birth and death rates, with the transition following four pronounced stages: (1) a high constant birth rate and a high fluctuating death rate; (2) a high birth rate and a high but rapidly declining death rate; (3) a declining birth rate and a low death rate; and (4) a low fluctuating birth rate and a low constant death rate (see Figure 2.2). This transition is descriptive of the experience of the so-called Western nations and Japan, which are now in or entering the fourth stage (see *1988 World Population Data Sheet*). Originally formulated by Thompson (1929), demographic transition theory postulates that industrialization, economic development, and urbanization (i.e., modernization) are the major independent or causal variables that produce the transition, and that eventually all nations in the world will experience the transition and the world population will again stabilize, albeit at a previously unimaginably high level.[6]

According to demographic transition theory, in the first stage of the transition the population is in precarious equilibrium as human beings reproduce themselves at a rate close to their biological limits so that they may survive as a species the relentless vagaries of the harsh environment (e.g., floods, drought, and pestilence). During the second stage, modified death control is introduced as humans learn to deal more successfully with the environment through refined agricultural techniques, the establishment of food and water reserves, and improved housing, sanitation, and public health measures. Particularly significant in the second stage is the dramatic decline in the infant mortality rate, although the previously high birth rate continues unabated, thus producing rapid population increase. During the third stage, the death rate declines further owing to continuing technological innovations in agriculture, nutrition, medicine, and life-style, while the birth rate also begins to drop as "insurance" births are no longer necessary. Population growth

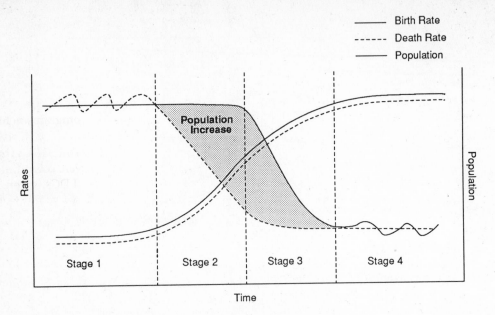

Figure 2.2   Four Stages of the Demographic Transition

during this stage is also high, although declining. In the fourth stage, the death rate stabilizes as life expectancy approximates the life span,[7] and the birth rate is similarly low as social values and norms finally fall in line with empirical reality. The population is once more in equilibrium (for a summary, see Coale, 1974).

To explain the rapid increase in population around 1650, demographers point to technological innovations in Europe, particularly in agriculture, which preceded the industrial revolution. These heralded the second stage of the demographic transition as death rates plummeted. However, fertility, a matter of choice and therefore value, did not change, thus resulting in dramatic population increases. With the industrial revolution and the general exodus from rural life came further technological improvements in the standard of living, and also, for the first time, the realization that it was no longer necessary to produce large families, and that furthermore in the cities they constituted an economic liability. In other words, the values surrounding childbirth began to change to fit the altered material circumstances, and consequently the birth rates followed the death rates in their decline, but not before recording an exponential increase on a substantially enlarged population base. Today, the developed countries are at or near zero population growth as their birth rates now parallel their death rates.

A major point of contention with demographic transition theory is whether it is descriptive only of the particular history of the more-developed countries (MDCs) or whether it may also be applied to the less-developed countries (LDCs) that presently constitute 77 percent of the world's population and are now in either the second or third stages of the transition (*1988 World Population Data Sheet*). Most notably, there are two major differences between the experiences of the MDCs and the LDCs.

First, in the case of the MDCs, technological innovations instrumental in reducing mortality rates were introduced gradually as they were invented or discovered over a period of 300 years. Consequently, the decline in mortality was much less dramatic than is now occurring in the LDCs, which have through widespread technology transfers and international aid programs achieved comparable death rates in a fraction of the time.

Second, and more important, it also took 300 years in the MDCs for the values surrounding procreation to change such that birth rates were comparable to death rates, thus completing the transition. In the case of the LDCs, given their rapid reduction in death rates and their huge population base, the world simply cannot wait for childbearing values to change of their own accord. Already, overpopulation constitutes one of the most pressing problems as population increases are nullifying the effects of any productivity gain or economic growth that is being achieved in many LDCs (see Hedley, 1985). For the world to survive, it is absolutely imperative that the second and third stages of the demographic transition be foreshortened and that world population once more enters into a state of equilibrium.

The question for demographers is: How much of what has been learned in the demographic transition of the MDCs can be applied to the similar but different circumstances of the LDCs? Demographic transition theory has tremendous practical implications as demographers refine their theoretical models in the search for key independent variables that are instrumental in achieving value change and thus fertility decline. Some of these causal variables include national economic and rural development, more equal distribution of income within countries, increased literacy rates, and established family planning programs (see Murdoch, 1980). How soon the transition is achieved is dependent upon these and other factors; but it is encouraging to note that through historical time fertility decline among nations in transition is occurring more quickly (Murdoch, 1980, pp. 86–90).

Cultural Convergence

In 1960, Clark Kerr and his colleagues wrote a book in which they set out "the logic or imperatives of industrialization," that is, those uniformities (universals) that appear in social structures and social processes regardless of where in the world or in what cultural context industrialization is introduced (see Kerr et al., 1964). In their words:

> Industrialization came into a most varied world; a world with many cultures, at many stages of development from the primitiveness of quasi-animal life to high levels of civilization. It was a world marked by great diversity; in terms of the contrast between the least and the most civilized societies; a world more diverse than at any other time during the history of mankind on this planet. In the midst of this disparity of systems there intruded a new and vastly superior technique of production; a technique which by its very nature was bound to spur imitation, since the more modern was always superior. This technique knew no geographical limits; recognized no elites or ideologies. Once unleashed on the world, the new technique kept spreading and kept advancing. (Kerr et al., 1964, p. 223).

Because the results of technology or a technique of production can be precisely measured in terms of quantity and quality of output, it is possible to determine which technology is superior in accomplishing specific objectives, and consequently the superior technology becomes widely adopted. Such was the fate of specialized and mechanized factory production as it was enthusiastically endorsed first in Europe and North America and then later in Japan, the Soviet Union, India, Latin America, and southeast Asia.

The central tenet of the convergence hypothesis is that upon the introduction of technologically superior factory production, structural adaptations are made that in turn have repercussions on other aspects of society until eventually all industrialized societies, no matter how dissimilar they were initially, converge in certain patterns of social organization and behavior. Some of the direct or first-order consequences include "an open and mobile society that assigns occupations to workers on universalistic grounds, an educational system that serves the needs of industry, a hierarchically differentiated and disciplined work force, a consensual web of rules regulating industrial social life, and increasing governmental involvement in industrial relations" (Form, 1979, p. 4). Other more far ranging or second-order consequences include the trends toward urbanization, bureaucratization, secularization, smaller nuclear families, greater female labor force participation, and more societal and international interdependence. In other words, industrialization as a process provokes both immediate and widespread social changes such that all nations, East and West, North and South, in adapting to this uniform process themselves become more standardized.

Not only do social structures and processes become adapted to industrialization, but also there occurs a manifest change in human personality and behavior. In an ambitious study of working men in six developing countries, Inkeles and Smith (1974) attempted to discover whether the nature of the work these men performed (i.e., industrial or nonindustrial) influenced what they valued and how they acted in society.[8] The researchers found in *all* countries that experienced factory hands, more than traditional urban (i.e., nonindustrial) workers, more than rural-urban migrants, more than cultivators of the land, scored highly on an "overall modernity" scale. With respect to values, the "modern" man was more likely to

- be open to new experience and accept change;
- be oriented toward the present and future rather than the past;
- be concerned with being on time and planning in advance;
- believe in self-determination and reject fatalism;
- be independent of traditional authority figures;
- believe in the efficacy of education, science, and technology;
- be ambitious for self and children;
- be tolerant of social differences; and
- be interested in civic and community affairs and broader social issues.

Behaviorally, the experienced factory worker was more apt to

- read the newspaper every day;
- discuss politics with his wife;

- join voluntary organizations;
- communicate with officials about public issues;
- vote; and
- be knowledgeable in political, community, and social issues.

This research and others (see, for example, Kahl, 1968) point strongly to the conclusion that the technological forces involved in industrialization contain within them the potent seeds of revolutionary societal and individual transformation.

While the proponents of cultural convergence state that the overwhelming impetus of industrialization is toward uniformity, nevertheless they also acknowledge that there are differences in its adoption worldwide. This diversity arises from a number of sources, principally the ideological predispositions of the indigenous elite classes, existing cultural traditions, key resources and central industries, and the actual historical period (e.g., early or late) in which industrialization is introduced, as well as its rate of introduction (see Kerr et al., 1964). However, overall they assert that it is changes in technology that produce social change, and that because particular superior technological innovations have been almost universally adopted, the result will be a convergence in social structure and behavior.

Overview

All the theories of social change that I have presented, either explicitly or implicitly, assign industrialization in general and technology in particular as the principal causal forces in the explanation of the large-scale changes that we have witnessed over the past three centuries.

Structural functionalism posits that change is produced by increasing societal differentiation. This initially occurred in the economic sector through the introduction of a complex occupational division of labor brought about by the industrial revolution. Subsequently, differentiation, and thus change, increased in other sectors of society.

Social conflict theory proposes that change occurs because of conflict over the division of valued resources. In industrial societies, the allocation of resources is principally determined by one's position in the occupational structure. Consequently, conflict, and therefore change, are manifestations of the industrialization process.

Cultural lag theory explicitly states that change occurs first in the material culture through technological innovations. This produces maladjustment in the nonmaterial culture (social structure and process) until it responds by adapting to these technologically induced changes.

Demographic transition theory explains the process by which initially high birth and death rates have declined over time. The decline in death rates, occurring first, can be explained principally by technological variables; the decline in birth rates, which came later, occurred because of changing values in response to changed material circumstances. Ogburn would call this an example of cultural lag.[9]

Cultural convergence theory postulates that change occurs through the introduction of superior technological methods, which upon worldwide diffusion and adoption causes hitherto diverse cultures and peoples to respond similarly. Over

Box 2-4 Fill in the Blanks

In Chapter 1, I brought to your attention some very substantial changes that have oc-curred in just two generations (**When I Was Your Age . . .**). In this chapter, we have examined various theories of social change and some of the factors that produce change. Now, I want to demonstrate in a slightly different way the forces of change and their impact.

Psychologically, all of us have a tendency to bestow some degree of permanence on our own social worlds. Regardless of how receptive we are to change, we also have a need for stability, routine, and predictability. In order to exist and to plan our lives, it is necessary to assume that tomorrow will be essentially unchanged from today. But what about 10 or 20 or . . . 50 years from now?

The year is 2040, that is, two generations hence, and *you* are the grandparents. Using the material presented thus far together with your own creative imaginations, try to think of some of the changes (concepts, things, processes, ways of living, inventions, occupations, and so on) that will have occurred when it is you who say, "When I was your age . . . ."

I have provided 60 spaces below, because that is how many innovations I recorded in Chapter 1. But that listing was incomplete, and the rate of change is increasing! Ob-viously, you will not be able to complete this mission impossible; however, it is a forceful way to illustrate the many changes that are occurring around us.

_____   _____

_____   _____

_____   _____

_____   _____

_____   _____

_____   _____

_____   _____

_____   _____

_____   _____

time, given the common stimulus of industrialization, there occurs a convergence in patterns of social organization and individual values and behavior.

Taking into consideration the tremendous impact of industrialization upon all our social institutions, and considering also the fact that technological innovation is cumulative and is increasing exponentially, we do have "an almost impossible task in adjusting to this whirling technological environment" (Ogburn, 1956, p. 85). However, it is also true that "technological revolutions are not something that 'happen' to us. We make them . . . . Our task is not to peer into the future . . ., but to shape the future we want to have" (Simon, 1987, p. 11).

SUMMARY

2.1 Early social theorists described the changes brought about by the industrial revolution in qualitative terms. They conceived of agricultural and industrial societies as polar opposites, and characterized the features of each social system as dichotomies (see Table 2.1).

2.2 Later theorists, while acknowledging that vast changes had indeed taken place, nevertheless also argued that these changes were a matter of degree. Prominent features in agricultural societies did not disappear in industrial societies; they received less emphasis. Gusfield identified seven common fallacies associated with "the great dichotomy."

2.3 Dichotomies (i.e., the division of phenomena into two mutually exclusive, contrasting categories) are crude representations of reality compared to continua that reflect gradients or degrees along specified dimensions or variables.

2.4 Industrialization is a complex multidimensional variable that reflects what people do for a living, how the wealth of a nation is earned, how economic activity is organized, how much energy is required to drive factories and machines, and what kinds of technological skills and methods are employed to produce the national product (see Table 2.3).

2.5 Social change may be studied on different levels of analysis. At the broadest level, sociologists can investigate change among and within societies; or they can conduct more limited research in organizations, or in groups, or even among individuals. Different levels of analysis focus on different aspects of behavior, and consequently what may be an instance of change at one level may be indicative of stability at another.

2.6 The units of analysis by which we can record change include direction, magnitude, rate, form, and duration of change.

2.7 Structural functionalism and social conflict theory present two opposing yet complementary perspectives of society. Structural functionalism states that society is based on the consensus of its members, and that change occurs through increasing social differentiation. Social conflict theory argues that society is based on the constraint of some of its members by others, and that change takes place as a result of conflict over the division of valued resources (see Box 2-3, **Consensus and Conflict: Two World Views**).

2.8 Cultural lag arises because technological innovations occur at a faster rate than our structural and behavioral adaptations to them.

2.9 Demographic transition theory describes and explains the factors responsible for differential declines in the death and birth rates.

2.10 Cultural convergence theory states that worldwide industrialization will result in increasing uniformity in social structure and social process.

NOTES

1. These early theorists also labeled agricultural and industrial societies according to what they considered were their dominant features. The list that follows presents some of these characterizations.

		Mode of social life	
Theorist		Agricultural	Industrial
Maine	(1861)	Rural-traditional	Urban-impersonal
Tonnies	(1887)	Gemeinschaft (based on togetherness)	Gesellschaft (based on rational design)
Durkheim	(1893)	Mechanical solidarity	Organic solidarity
MacIver	(1937)	Community	Society
Redfield	(1941)	Folk	Urban
Becker	(1957)	Sacred	Secular
Lerner	(1958)	Traditional	Modern

2. Value added in manufacturing is the "value derived by subtracting the cost of materials, supplies, containers, fuel, purchased electric energy, and contract work from the value of shipments" (Hagedorn et al., 1971, p. 186). It is the value added to raw materials as a result of the manufacturing process.
3. Wallace (1969, p. 45) notes: "It should be emphasized . . . that although I shall speak of only two levels—'micro' and 'macro'—this is merely for analytical convenience, since variation in level is to be thought of as continuous and therefore many-leveled."
4. One subfield of economics (long-wave theory), in order to minimize the effects of short-term anomalous fluctuations analyzes economic activity and events by placing them in as long a historical period as possible. See, for example, Freeman, 1983.
5. Life expectancy is defined as "the average number of additional years a person would live if current mortality trends were to continue." It is most often cited as life expectancy at birth. Life span is "the maximum age that human beings could reach under optimum conditions. The human life span appears to be about 100 years" (Haupt and Kane, 1980, p. 9).
6. According to current United Nations projections, stabilization of the world's population will be reached between 2010 and 2065 at which time, depending upon which of several projections is used, the "ultimate" world population will range between 7.5 and 14.2 billion people. The "best guess" projection is 10.2 billion (i.e., *twice* the world's present population) by the year 2035 (see *1988 World Population Data Sheet*).
7. See note 5.
8. The countries they investigated were: Argentina, Chile, East Pakistan (now Bangladesh), India, Israel, and Nigeria.
9. As a matter of fact, Ogburn (1957) in the closing remarks to his essay on "Cultural Lag as Theory" does allude to the demographic transition as an instance of cultural lag.

Chapter
3

The Industrial Revolution

The imperatives of technology and organization, not the images of ideology, are what determine the shape of economic society.

Galbraith, 1985, p. 7

Many reasons have been advanced as to how the industrial revolution began and why it occurred in Great Britain in the late-eighteenth century. Increases in technological knowledge, expansion of national and international trade, discovery and exploitation of the "New World," improvements in agriculture, developments in the textile industry, extension of the transportation network, mechanical motive power, and ideological changes (first the Protestant Reformation and later the establishment of a money-based capitalist economy)—all of these developments, both simultaneous and sequential, have been attributed as major causes of the transformation of Great Britain into an industrially based economy and world leader (see Lenski and Lenski, 1982, pp. 235–265; Mantoux, 1961; World Bank, 1987, pp. 38–57). Figure 3.1 presents in schematic form the interrelationship of these developments that together produced the revolutionary change.

In this chapter, applying the dimensions of industrialization identified in Chapter 2, we will first establish the extent of industrialization in Great Britain and the United States at various points during this period. Then, continuing with the British–American comparison, we will examine the period as two separate revolutions: first, a technological revolution in which the processes of invention and innovation are

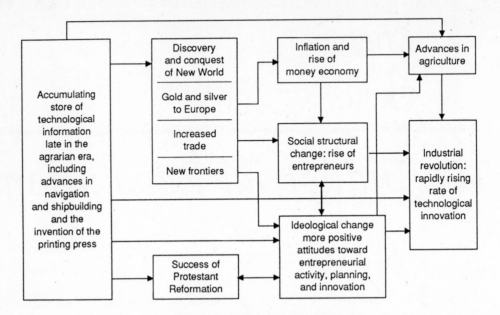

Figure 3.1   Model of the Causes of the Industrial Revolution

elaborated upon; and second, a social revolution in which we concentrate on the important consequences that emanated directly out of the industrial transformation.

DIMENSIONS OF INDUSTRIALIZATION

Of primary consideration in the industrial revolution was first establishing a sufficient agricultural surplus whereby the excess labor freed from farming could be recruited into industry. The manufacture of textiles represented a major channel of entry. Here was a traditional industry in which demand for its goods was already established, and which could be mechanized by relatively simple procedures. "The same factors also explain the early importance of leather goods, food processing, furniture, ceramics, building materials, and household utensils" (World Bank, 1987, p. 54).

With increasing mechanization came the demand for basic metals (first iron and then steel), machinery, equipment, engineering products, and coal as a source of heat and power. Also important was the growing chemical industry whose products were used to improve agricultural yield as well as to enhance production processes. Later, the implementation of the steam engine, electricity, and the internal combustion engine spawned their own industries. Consequently, how people earned their living and what they produced changed substantially during this period.

Table 3.1 reflects these changes along each of the dimensions of industrialization presented in Chapter 2 (see Table 2.3). The data compiled in 1899 by Michael Mulhall,

Table 3.1 MEASURES OF INDUSTRIALIZATION IN THE UNITED KINGDOM AND THE UNITED STATES AT VARIOUS STAGES IN THE INDUSTRIAL REVOLUTION

3.1.1 Economic Activity/Labor

Labor force distribution (percent employed)	UK		US	
	1841	1881	1840	1880
Agriculture	30%	16%	78%	44%
Manufactures	28	33	16	22
Commerce etc.[a]	42	51	6	34
Total	100%	100%	100%	100%
(Total number employed—000s)	(11,362)	(15,735)	(4,797)	(17,392)

[a]Includes professions, domestics, and various.

Data source: Adapted from Mulhall, 1899, pp. 419, 422, 432.

3.1.2 Economic Output/Productivity

Industrial distribution of gross national income	UK 1895	US 1895
Agriculture	10%	15%
Mines	6	8
Manufactures	31	31
Trade	11	10
Transport	12	11
Professions	13	11
Domestics	7	6
House rent	10	8
Total	100%	100%
(Millions of pounds sterling)	(1421)	(3178)

Data source: Adapted from Mulhall, 1899, p. 747

3.1.3 Factory System/Machine Production/Mechanization

UK—Factory Production and Mechanization In The Textiles Industry

Year	Number of factories	Number of operatives	Steam horsepower	Power looms	No. of spindles
1840	4,213	424,000	69,000	—	—
1850	4,601	596,000	108,000	302,000	31,000,000
1860	6,378	776,000	375,000	499,000	36,000,000
1870	6,258	907,000	473,000	606,000	42,000,000
1880	7,105	976,000	570,000	725,000	47,000,000
1885	7,465	1,034,000	—	774,000	48,800,000

Table 3.1   MEASURES OF INDUSTRIALIZATION IN THE UNITED KINGDOM AND THE UNITED STATES AT VARIOUS STAGES IN THE INDUSTRIAL REVOLUTION *(continued)*

US—Factory Production and Productivity, All Industry

Year	No. of factory operatives	Productivity perfactory hand (pounds sterling)
1840	596,000	160
1850	957,000	220
1860	1,311,000	301
1870	2,054,000	344
1880	2,733,000	408

Data source: Adapted from Mulhall, 1899, pp. 255, 379.

3.1.4   Energy Source/Use

	National Steam Power			
	UK		US	
Year	Total horsepower	Horsepower per 100 inhabitants	Total horsepower	Horsepower per 100 inhabitants
1840	620,000	2	760,000	4
1850	1,290,000	5	1,680,000	7
1860	2,450,000	8	3,470,000	11
1870	4,040,000	13	5,590,000	14
1880	7,600,000	22	9,110,000	18
1888	9,200,000	24	14,400,000	23
1896	13,700,000	34	18,060,000	25

Data source: Adapted from Mulhall, 1899, pp. 444, 450, 545, 787, 789, 807.

3.1.5   Technology/Skills/Techniques

	Patents Applied for and Granted				
	UK			US	
Year	Applications/granted		Year	Applications/granted	
1860–69	34,870	21,910	1840	735	473
1870–79	44,950	30,360	1850	2,193	993
1880–87	91,940	53,040	1860	7,653	4,778
			1870	19,171	13,333
			1880	23,021	13,917
			1889	40,575	24,158

Data source: Adapted from Mulhall, 1899, pp. 438, 439.

a Fellow of the Royal Statistical Society in London, represent a systematic and painstaking effort to provide statistical snapshots of these dimensions for both Great Britain and the United States at succeeding points in time during the industrial revolution.

With regard to how people earned their living (see 3.1.1 in Table 3.1), the first dimension of industrialization, you will note that there is a diminishing emphasis over time on agriculture, with corresponding increases in manufacturing and commerce. In the United Kingdom, fewer workers were engaged in agriculture in 1841 and 1881 than in the United States at comparable periods because the industrialization process occurred earlier in Britain. In any event, by 1880 fewer than half the workers in both countries were employed in agriculture.

The figures on labor force distribution (3.1.1) correlate with those on gross national income (3.1.2), or what the nations produced, even though there is only one time series presented. In another compilation, Mitchell (1962, p. 366), reporting on Britain, notes that while agriculture accounted for one-third of the national income in 1801, it produced only 6% of the total revenue in 1901, the comparable figures for manufacturing being 23% and 40%, respectively. Also of importance was the over 600% increase in total national income during this 100-year period, which exceeded by far the 153% growth in population.

With respect to the complex dimension involving the growth of the factory system, machine production, and mechanization (3.1.3), the third dimension of industrialization, it is difficult to find data that explicitly measure it, even though a large part of this chapter is devoted to describing its evolution. However, the data for Great Britain, dealing only with the textile industry, do portray the substantial increases both in factories and number of operatives, as well as mechanization in terms of energy source and operating equipment and machines.[1] Similar though less manifest data are presented for the entire spectrum of American industry over the same period. In describing the increases in productivity per factory hand in America, Mulhall (1899, p. 378) observed that it was "mainly due to improved machinery, enabling two men now [1880] to produce as much as five did in 1840."

The data on energy source/use (3.1.4) reveal the tremendous impact of steam power on both these industrializing nations during the late-nineteenth century. Comparing the two countries, both registered similar vast increases in total horsepower (just over 2000% in the 60-year interval); but Great Britain had a greater, more spectacular growth per capita than did the United States. This discrepancy is explained in large part by the phenomenal increase in America's population (326%) during this period compared with Britain (48%), a result of both large-scale immigration and the incorporation of less developed territories into the Union.

Mulhall (1899, p. 807) also provides a more detailed classification of the use of steam power, which gives a fuller picture of the period and further distinguishes the two countries. Whereas both nations in 1896 devoted similar proportions of their total steam power to the running of factories and other stationary installations (17% in the United Kingdom and 22% in the United States), almost two-thirds of American steam power ran the vast national railroad system, compared with just over one-third in Great Britain. By contrast, the United Kingdom, a small island nation, used almost half of its steam to power ships compared to only 13% for the United States.

For the final dimension of industrialization—technology/skills/techniques—the most relevant data available are the patents applied for and granted in the two countries (3.1.5 in Table 3.1). Although tabulated somewhat differently in Great Britain and the United States, both sets of statistics reflect the increasingly great number of innovative activities that occurred during this time.

As the term implies, the industrial revolution produced radical changes in what people did for a living, how their national wealth was created, and the manner in which they performed and organized their work. Let us now compare and contrast how this process unfolded in both these early industrializing countries.

THE TECHNOLOGICAL REVOLUTION

Technology is a term originally coined by an American physician and Renaissance man, Jacob Bigelow, upon his appointment to Harvard in 1816 "for the instruction of 'the application of the sciences to the useful arts,' a first attempt to create a meeting ground for self-made inventors and academic scientists" (Struik, 1962, pp. 224–225). Up until that time, and particularly in the beginning stages of the industrial revolution, technological innovations arose out of "practical necessity and professional experience" (Mantoux, 1961, p. 311).

> Every technical question is first and foremost a practical question. Before it ever becomes a problem to be solved by men with theoretic knowledge, it forces itself upon the men in the trade as a difficulty to overcome, or a material advantage to be gained. There is, as it were, an instinctive effort which not only precedes but is a necessary condition to the appearance of conscious effort. . . .
>
> The history of inventions is not only that of inventors but that of collective experience, which gradually solves the problems set by collective needs. (Mantoux, 1961, p. 206).

Invention and Innovation

During the time of the industrial revolution and before, most inventions came about through temporary imbalances among the stages of a technical process and a consequent innovative combination of known elements to correct these imbalances. The history of the textile industry is a classic case in point. The manufacture of textiles involves two main technical stages: the spinning of animal or vegetable fiber into yarn and the weaving of yarn into cloth. In the early 1700s, five or six spinning wheels were required to provide sufficient yarn for the work of one loom. However, in 1733 a weaver-cum-mechanic named John Kay invented the flying shuttle that increased both the speed and the efficiency of his loom, thereby creating a severe and intolerable imbalance between spinning and weaving. There was an immediate and disastrous shortage of thread, plus a sharp rise in its price.

Kay's invention was countered five years later by two men, one a self-made inventor and the other a self-styled entrepreneur, through the invention of the spinning machine, which corrected somewhat the imbalance created by Kay. Subsequent development by Hargreaves, a weaver and carpenter, in 1765 produced the spinning jenny, a machine that performed the work of eight spinning wheels and later much more. Also, Hargreaves and his contemporary Arkwright, who it is claimed invented the water frame and thus established the first spinning mills, introduced machine industry and the factory system into England (see Mantoux, 1961, pp. 189–270).

Even in the rare instances where invention occurred as the result of systematic scientific study, as was the case with James Watt's steam engine, the invention itself was largely a combination, albeit ingenious, of already known elements. As Thurston has observed in *A History of the Growth of the Steam Engine*, "At the beginning of the eighteenth century every element of the modern type of steam engine had been separately invented and practically applied" (Thurston, 1878, p. 55). However, as you will note in Box 3-1, **From Invention to Application: James Watt and the Steam Engine**, it was not until the end of the eighteenth century (1781) that Watt filed his final patent, his most important auxiliary invention that converted the power of the engine into rotary driving motion and thus launched the steam engine as the propelling force of the industrial revolution. Incidentally, you will also note that Watt was greatly assisted in this invention by William Murdock, a working foreman at Matthew Boulton's factory, who came up with the key idea underlying rotary motion (Mantoux, 1961, pp. 332–333).

According to Ogburn (1926), inventions are a result of three factors—the mental ability of the inventor, the existing state of accumulated cultural knowledge, and the social values predominant in a society. Of these, he attributes more importance to the latter two in that ability is sufficiently well distributed within society whereby any number of highly intelligent people could invent, for example, a steam engine or an automobile given appropriate conditions (accumulated knowledge) and reasonable encouragement (social values). As a test of this assertion, he and a colleague searched through histories of science and practical mechanical inventions to identify independently duplicated inventions, that is, areas of work in which two or more investigators, each unknown to the other, arrived at the same result (see Ogburn and Thomas, 1922). The search yielded 148 inventions reached independently and more or less simultaneously by multiple inventors.[2] A partial listing of these inventions relevant to industrialization and taking place largely in the time period under discussion is contained in Table 3.2.

As Ogburn and others have stated, the period of the industrial revolution was opportune for invention and discovery in that the base of accumulated historical and current knowledge was substantial, and the hitherto rigid societal value structure was also becoming increasingly supportive of innovation.[3] In addition, given certain fundamental inventions such as the steam engine and electricity, it does not stretch credulity too much to expect that several people independently might begin work simultaneously on spin-offs such as a steam boat or an electric railroad. As Benjamin has stated in *The Age of Electricity*, "It is a singular fact that probably not an electrical invention of major importance has ever been made but that the honor of its origin has been claimed by more than one person" (cited in Ogburn and Thomas, 1922, p. 88). In other words, great though particular inventors may have been, the conditions and the values of the time itself contained the seeds of invention.

Box 3-1   From Invention to Application: James Watt and the Steam Engine

Popular conceptions of inspirational light bulbs turning on in inventors' heads and scientists shrieking "Eureka!" notwithstanding, the process of invention and subsequent application is often slow, painstaking, tedious, and fraught with immanent roadblocks and potential oblivion. Consider the long and laborious development of the steam engine from its earliest glimmerings to its major role in the industrial revolution.

700–300 BC	The Greeks of the Hellenic period invented a steam engine, but made no practical application of it.
1601	Giovanni Battista Della Porta—an Italian mathematician, chemist, and physicist—invented a machine in which the pressure of steam was used to raise a column of water.
1605	Florence Rivault, a Frenchman, published a treatise on artillery in which he described heating water in a sealed bombshell to make it explode.
1615	Salomon de Caus, another French experimenter, constructed an apparatus similar to Porta's. He also expounded upon the possible practical use of steam.
1629	Giovanni Branca constructed a contrivance "in which . . . steam, issuing from a boiler, impinged upon the vanes of a horizontal wheel" (Thurston, 1878, p. 16).
1630	David Ramseye patented a steam engine in England mainly for use as a pump.
1660	The Marquis of Worcester used steam pressure to raise water in tanks to power ceremonial fountains.
1678	Jean Hautefille proposed the use of a piston in a steam engine. Huygens applied Hautefille's principle.
1690	Denys Papin constructed a steam engine and wrote a treatise on the use of steam for motive power.
1698	Thomas Savery, an officer in the British Army, patented " 'a new invention for raising of water and occasioning motion of all sorts of mill work by the impellant forces of fire, which will be of great use and advantage for draining mines, serving towns with water, and for the working of all sorts of mills where they have not the benefit of water nor constant winds' " (Mantoux, 1961, p. 313).
1705–1706	Thomas Newcomen, a blacksmith and locksmith in Devonshire, developed a more efficient, powerful, and safe steam (atmospheric) engine that largely superseded Savery's earlier effort.
1711	Newcomen and associates formed a company to build and sell the new steam engine which was being continually refined. Many were sold throughout England and Europe for use as atmospheric pumps in mines, reservoirs and locks, and to raise water to power factory and mill water wheels.

1718	Desaguliers in France also developed a steam engine that improved on Savery's design.
1761–1762	James Watt, at this time a maker of scientific instruments at the University of Glasgow and 25 years of age, began a series of systematic experiments on steam pressure, starting first with Papin's model (see 1690).
1765	Watt received financial backing from John Roebuck, a mine owner, to develop the steam engine for commercial application.
1769	Watt's first patented steam engine, named Beelzebub, remedied the major defects in Newcomen's relatively inefficient atmospheric engine. In his patent submission, Watt noted "the really new and fruitful result of his researches, which was the use of steam, not as an auxiliary power to create a vacuum in the barrel of a pump [as it had hitherto been used up to this time] but as an active motive power" (Mantoux, 1961, p. 321).
1773	John Roebuck declared bankruptcy before Watt's invention was sufficiently perfected. Matthew Boulton, a Birmingham metals trade manufacturer who for several years was interested in the development of steam as the motive power for his workshops, and who also had anticipated establishing a factory to manufacture Watt's perfected steam engine, entered into partnership with Watt. Watt moved to Birmingham to take advantage of Boulton's top-notch factory facilities.
1774	Watt, in a letter to his father, wrote: "'The business I am here about has turned out rather successful, that is to say, the fire engine I have invented is now going and answers much better than any other that has yet been made, and I expect that the invention will be very beneficial to me'" (Mantoux, 1961, p. 327).
1775	Watt applied to Parliament and received a 25-year extension on his 1769 patent.
1775–1786	Although Watt continued to refine, improve, and adapt the steam engine, and the Boulton works was receiving many orders in Britain and from the continent, early development costs and failures did not permit the two partners to realize any profits until 1786 or 1787, that is, 25 years after Watt began his first experiments. Also, many purchasers of the steam engine refused to pay the royalties for its use which consisted of "a third of the economy in fuel obtained by its use, in comparison with the consumption of coal made by a Newcomen engine of the same power" (Mantoux, 1961, p. 330).
1781	Watt patented auxiliary inventions associated with his steam engine, the most important of which, conceived in collaboration with a foreman at the Boulton works, converted the power of the engine into rotary driving motion. For the first time, the steam engine was generally applicable as a source of power.
1775–1800	During the last quarter of the eighteenth century, Boulton and Watt, with a labor force of over one thousand, constructed 321 steam engines for use in Britain and Ireland alone. These were used in the mines, metal trades industry, iron works, flour and malt mills, breweries, sugar refineries, textile factories, and in the first automatic mint.

"With this great new event, the invention of the steam engine, the final and most decisive stage of the industrial revolution opened. By liberating it from its last shackles, steam enabled the immense and rapid development of large-scale industry to take place. For the use of steam was not, like that of water, dependent on geographical position and local resources. Wherever coal could be bought at a reasonable price a steam engine could be erected. England had plenty of coal, and by the end of the eighteenth century it was already applied to many different uses, while a network of waterways, made on purpose, enabled it to be carried everywhere very cheaply: the whole country became a privileged land suitable above all others for the growth of industry. Factories were now no longer bound to

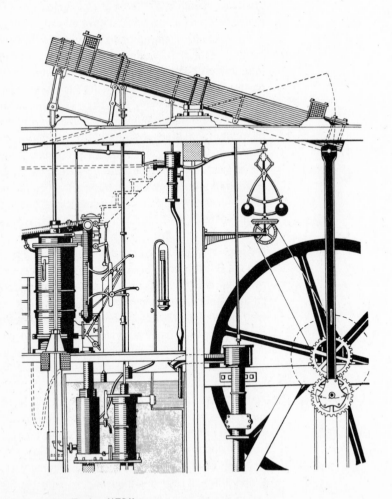

James Watt's Steam Engine (1781)

Source: Thurston, 1878, p. 104.

the valleys, where they had grown up in solitude by the side of rapid-flowing streams. It became possible to bring them nearer the markets where their raw materials were bought and their finished products sold, and nearer the centres of population where their labour was recruited. They sprang up near one another, and thus huddled together gave rise to those huge black industrial cities which the steam engine surrounded with a perpetual cloud of smoke. . . .

"Steam did not create the modern factory system, but it lent that system its power and gave it a force of expansion as irresistible as itself. Above all, it gave it unity. Up till that time the various industries were much less interdependent than they are now. From the technical point of view they had little in common, and they developed separately along their own lines. The use of a common motive power, and especially of an artificial one, thenceforward imposed general laws upon the development of all industries. The successive improvements in the steam engine reacted equally on the working of mines and of metals, on weaving and on transport. The industrial world came to resemble one huge factory, in which the acceleration, the slowing down, and the stoppage of the main engine determines the activities of the workers and regulates the rates of production." (Mantoux, 1961, pp. 337–338).

Sources: Mantoux, 1961, pp. 311–338; Thurston, 1878.

Great inventions are never, and great discoveries are seldom, the work of any one mind. Every great invention is really either an aggregation of minor inventions or the final step of a progression. It is not a creation, but a *growth*—as truly so as is that of the trees in the forest. Hence, the same invention is frequently brought out in several countries, and by several individuals, simultaneously. Frequently, an important invention is made before the world is ready to receive it, and the unhappy inventor is taught, by his failure, that it is as unfortunate to be in advance of his age as to be behind it. Inventions only become successful when they are not only needed, but when mankind is so far advanced in intelligence as to appreciate and to express the necessity for them, and to at once make use of them. (Thurston, 1878, pp. 2–3)

Inventions and innovations were not limited only to machinery and tools. They were applied also to the procedures and organization of industrial enterprises, and in these endeavors the early American capitalists and entrepreneurs excelled over their British counterparts.

While it may be asserted that industrialization is comprised of common features, it is also true that it is not uniformly introduced into all physical, cultural, demographic, social, and economic contexts in exactly the same way. Also important is the rate of industrialization as well as the actual period of history when it is introduced. Great Britain, first to industrialize in the mid- to late-eighteenth century, did not have the opportunity to choose from a variety of aspects those most advantageous to its industrial and economic development. It just grew and

Table 3.2   INVENTIONS ACHIEVED INDEPENDENTLY BY MULTIPLE INVENTORS, ARRANGED CHRONOLOGICALLY

Invention	Year (approx.)	Multiple inventors	Nationality
Printing	1420–1423	Coster	Dutch
	1443	Gutenberg	German
Pendulum clock	1583	Galileo	Italian
	1612	Burgi	Czechoslovakian
	1657	Huygens	Dutch
Steam boat	1802	Jouffroy	French
	1802	Rumsey	American
	1802	Stevens	American
	1802	Symmington	Scottish
	1807	Fulton	American
Typewriter	1714	Mill	British
	1829	Burt	American
	1833	Projean	French
	1867	Sholes	American
Cylinder printing press	1812–1813	Koenig	German
	1830	Napier	British
Reaping machine	1827–1828	Bell	Scottish
	1831	McCormick	American
	1833	Hussey	American
	1843	Ridley	Australian
Sewing machine	1830	Thimonnier	French
	1840s	Hunt	American
	1840s	Wilson	American
	1846	Howe	American
	1851	Singer	American
Electric motor	1830	dal Negro	Italian
	1831	Henry	American
	1835	Bourbouze	French
	1835	Davenport	American
Electromagnetic telegraph	1822–1837	Schilling	Russian
	1835	Morse	American
	1836	Cook & Wheatstone	British
Photography	1839	Daguerre-Niepe	French
	1839	Talbot	British

Table 3.2 INVENTIONS ACHIEVED INDEPENDENTLY BY MULTIPLE INVENTORS, ARRANGED CHRONOLOGICALLY *(continued)*

Invention	Year (approx.)	Multiple ventors	Nationality
Electric railroad	1838	Davidson	Scottish
	1847	Jacobi	German
	1847	Lilly-Colton	American
	1850	Page	American
	1850–1851	Hall	American
Self-exciting dynamo	1831	Faraday	British
	1832	Pixii	French
	1855	Hjorth	Danish
	1860	Pacinotti	Italian
	1861	Jedlik	Hungarian
	1863–1866	Wilde	British
	1866	Farmer	American
	1866–1867	Varley	British
	1866–1867	von Siemens	German
	1867	Wheatstone	British
Incandescent electric light	1845	Starr	American
	1848–1878	Swan	British
	1878	Lane-Fox	British
	1878–1880	Edison	American
Internal combustion engine	1859–60	Lenoir	French
	1862	De Rochas	French
	1867	Otto	German
	1884	Daimler	German
Telephone	1861	Reis	German
	1876	Bell	American
	1876	Gray	American
Phonograph	1877	Cros	French
	1877	Edison	American
	1877	Scott	French
Microphone	1877	Berliner	American
	1877–1878	Edison	American
	1878	Blake	American
	1878	Hughes	American
Trolley car	1881	von Siemens	German
	1884–1885	van Doeple	American
	1888	Sprague	American

Sources: Original list of multiple inventions provided by Ogburn and Thomas, 1992. Inventors, their nationalities, and the dates of invention were independently corroborated from the following sources: Abbott, 1985; de Bono, 1974; Carter, 1978; Jones, 1979; Singer et al., 1958a and b; Usher, 1929.

"I see by the current issue of 'Lab News,' Ridgeway, that you've been working for the last twenty years on the same problem I've been working on for the last twenty years."

Figure 3.2 Drawing by Opie. © 1976 The New Yorker Magazine, Inc.

evolved, all the time attempting to adjust and rationalize new and innovative practices into its old and established socioeconomic structure.

In contrast, the United States, which did not industrialize until the early to mid-nineteenth century, was a brand new nation eager to grow and to establish its own unique imprint on human history. Consequently, it had the advantage of being able to select those features, not to mention actual tools, machinery, and processes already gained from the British experience, which were most conducive to its development. As a result, it grew more rapidly. Also, since it was an emerging nation, it did not have to contend with the cultural overlay and time-honored customs and tradition that at times plagued British progress (see Habakkuk, 1962).

Comparing the British and American experiences, and returning for the moment to the argument advanced by Ogburn and Thomas (1922), it may be asserted that whereas both Great Britain and the United States had the requisite human inventive skills and talent within their populations, and both nations had similar access to the accumulated knowledge base, they differed substantially with respect to their prevailing social values.

> ... the structure of industry imposed more severe restraints on the choice of techniques in Britain than in the U.S.A. British industry was longer established and the entrepreneur more limited by history and by the need to shape his investments 'to fit the inherited structure of complementary assets.' ...
>
> A society in which existing habits and institutions were widely accepted and freedom slowly broadened down from precedent to precedent found it easier to maintain political and social stability; but it was also likely to grow more slowly than a society where individuals were bent on rising in the world and were ready to break with old ties and customs in order to do so. The restlessness of American life was favourable to economic achievement. (Habakkuk, 1962, pp. 218–219).

Mass Production

As an example of the differences in value and condition of Britain and America, let us examine the industrialization process in the United States in the early 1800s. At first, Americans were imitators rather than innovators, industrial knowledge at that time not being sufficiently broadly based. Most major equipment and machinery, including steam engines, were purchased directly from England. At this time, what few skilled workers there were in the United States did not have the requisite competence to operate machine valves, pistons, and chambers to the close tolerances required. Over the ensuing decades, given the scarcity of skilled labor, the whole process of manufacturing came under close scrutiny, with the result that both the machinery used to produce goods as well as the actual goods produced were manufactured by mass production methods by semiskilled machine operatives.

Mass production, the so-called "American system" of manufacture, involves a complex division of labor whereby simple product components are manufactured independently from one another, being assembled at a later stage in the process. Also, because the operations are so specialized, they can be performed by relatively unskilled workers. Crucial to the mass production system is the standardization of production such that each component made is completely interchangeable with all other components of the same type.

Eli Whitney, an American inventor and manufacturer, is credited with perfecting interchangeable components. Prior to his innovative efforts, machine and product parts were not interchangeable because each part was idiosyncratically handcrafted. There is a story about Whitney going to the nation's capital in 1801 to sell the Secretary of War mass-produced standardized muskets. In order to demonstrate his principles to the assembled audience, Whitney set out "ten separate piles each containing identical parts of a musket. To the amazement of the audience he was able to select parts indiscriminately from each of the piles, and put ten muskets together. The fact that this story has anecdotic value shows how dissimilar the ancient handmade guns had been and how much for granted we now take mass production" (Struik, 1962, p. 186).

Another essential feature of mass production is that it occurs on a sufficiently large scale to justify the initial capital cost of constructing all the special-purpose machinery that the semiskilled workers operate and still make a profit for the industrial capitalist. In other words, there must be economies of scale such that greater volumes of output are produced at a reduced cost per *unit* of output. This required large factories employing thousands of workers to produce the goods, and the opening of vast hitherto untapped markets to sell the goods; and in these two endeavors the Americans were in the vanguard.

Early systems and strategies of organization evolved to meet the demands imposed by large-scale industrial manufacture. Whereas the division of labor and the establishing of a hierarchy of command were early organization principles, never before had production tasks been ordered systematically within explicitly defined time frames. Box 3-2, **Time is Money,** describes how the emphasis on time has become a signature feature of industrial America.

As a result of all these technological and organizational innovations that were accomplished in the name of progress and the fulfillment (appropriate to one's socioeconomic level) of the American dream, the United States by the mid-nineteenth century, just 100 years after the industrial revolution had begun, had usurped Great Britain's place as world economic leader. In 1888, the United States produced 32% of world manufacturing output compared to Great Britain's 18% share (Lenski and Lenski, 1982, p. 249).

To complete the description of the American system of manufacture and mass production, we need to add what is now regarded as its quintessential element—the continuously moving automatic assembly line. This story begins with Henry Ford in the early twentieth century, although once again what Ford accomplished was the bringing together of already known elements. As Ford's chief of manufacturing stated:

> Mass production is simply focusing on accuracy, which means standardization and interchangeability of parts; continuity, the meshing of the moving assembly line and its component and subassembly lines; and speed, the result of a carefully timed correlation of manufacture, material handling and assembly. . . . All the elements of mass production were known before we combined them. (Gelderman, 1981, p. 88)

Not only did Ford perfect mass production, he was a pioneer in mass marketing. As Box 3-3, **Taking the Work to the Men,** describes, he established branch assembly plants and dealerships all across the country to promote the sale of his "universal car," the Model T. In discussing this, at the time, bold marketing strategy, Ford remarked, "We actually changed from making automobiles to making parts" (Ford, 1922, p. 41). Parts could be shipped more cheaply, and spare parts formed the beginnings of the automobile repair business.

Ford's universal car was almost universally adopted, as the sales figures indicate. In 1908, the first year of production of the Model T, 5986 automobiles were sold; 10 years later (1917), sales had increased more than 134 times to 802,771 units (Federal Trade Commission, 1964, pp. 33–34).

Invention of the Automobile

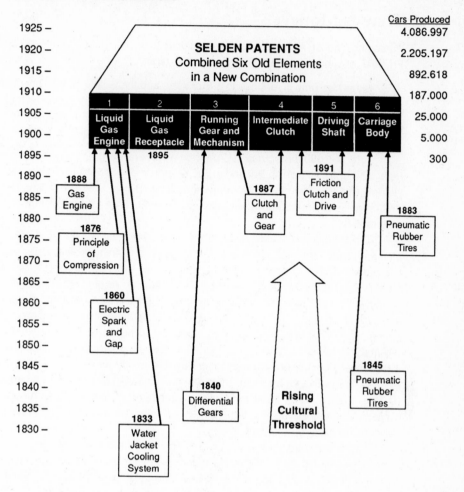

Figure 3.3 Invention of the Automobile: A Combination of Known Elements by Multiple Inventors

Source: Chapin, 1928, p. 336.

As a final note on the technological revolution, it is interesting to observe that the automobile, similar to the steam engine and many other inventions of this revolution, was not the product of one person but many people working independently. It too came about in final form as a new combination of known elements when in 1895 George B. Selden patented a working model of an automobile (see Chapin, 1928, pp. 334–337). Figure 3.3 presents the six major elements that comprise an automobile and indicates how they were differentially developed in the 60-year interval prior to Selden's final patent.

Box 3-2   Time is Money

Presaging one of America's major contributions to the industrial revolution, Benjamin Franklin, expanding on his famous aphorism, wrote:

> Since our Time is reduced to a Standard, and the Bullion of the Day minted out into Hours, the Industrious know how to employ every Piece of Time to a real Advantage in their different Professions: And he that is prodigal of his Hours, is, in effect, a Squanderer of Money (cited in E. P. Thompson, 1967, p. 89).

Prior to 1820, timepieces in America were a rarity, being limited primarily to town halls and church towers. For example, a survey of ten well-to-do houses of the era yielded close to 500 chairs, but only one clock (Brown, 1976, p. 134). The pace and rhythm of life in preindustrial America was very much geared to the sun and the evolving seasons.

Clocks, along with arms and textiles, were among the first goods to be manufactured by mass production methods in America. Owing to a scarcity of skilled artisans to produce the precision components comprising clocks and watches, early New England clock-makers such as Eli Terry, Seth Thomas, and Chauncey Jerome redesigned their manufacture (Struik, 1962, pp. 198–199). They introduced a minute division of labor such that semiskilled workers could machine and assemble standardized, and therefore interchangeable, components making up these complex mechanisms. By these methods, Chauncey Jerome, for example, was able to manufacture clocks for less than ten percent of what it traditionally cost skilled cabinetmakers to produce by hand (Brown, 1976, p. 129). "By the late 1850s five Connecticut factories were manufacturing 500,000 clocks annually" (Brown, 1976, p. 129). Mass production methods enabled virtually all Americans to own a clock or watch for the first time, and in so doing, changed the very character, not to mention the pace, of American life.

The railroad industry was an early convert to the strict enforcement of and rigid adherence to a time schedule. Clocks and voluminous timetables permitted the railroad to transport both thousands of passengers and tons of freight at high speed through an extensive and intricate network of lines with safety and dependability.

> All those who have direct responsibility for the actual operations of trains must carry a fine timepiece which will gain or lose not more than forty seconds in two weeks and which must be cleaned and regulated twice a year by a railroad watch inspector. A delay of thirty seconds in leaving a terminal calls for explanation, five minutes' delay means investigation, and a half hour gives apoplexy to every official from the superintendent to the lowest foreman. On single track roads where trains meet at passing tracks, a thirty seconds' delay means that one of the trains will be almost a half mile from a passing track when the other reaches it, and that means delay of a second train, with possible misunderstanding and resultant disaster. (Cottrell, 1939, pp. 190–191).

It was not coincidental that the manufacture of arms and textiles and clocks were subjected early to mass production methods. Armaments were necessary to defend the new Republic; textiles to clothe it; and clocks to coordinate, synchronize, and regulate the division of labor and work tasks of the emerging industrial nation. On this latter point, the work of Frederick W. Taylor and his *Principles of Scientific Management* (1911) figure prominently. He was the father of time and motion study and was largely responsible for the whole industrial engineering movement. As Daniel Bell (1962, pp. 231–232) has noted,

> One of the prophets of modern work was Frederick W. Taylor, and his stop watch was his bible. If any such social upheaval can ever be attributed to one man, the logic of efficiency as a mode of life is due to him. With "scientific management," as enunciated by Taylor, we pass far beyond the old rough computations of the division of labor; we go into the division of time itself.

Taylor, an engineer at the Bethlehem Steel Company at the end of the nineteenth century, converted the old rule-of-thumb procedures of workers into specific time-designated tasks and task elements, which then became standardized operating procedures dictated by management. Taylor was convinced that managers should become responsible for planning to the tiniest detail all the elements that comprised workers' jobs, establish a time limit for each task element, and then pay workers according to the actual number of work units completed (i.e., piece work instead of day work).

An application of Taylor's principles is cited by Bell (1962, p. 236) in the collective agreement signed between the U.S. Steel Corporation and the CIO Steel Workers in 1946. A "fair day's work" is defined as "that amount of work that can be produced by a qualified employee when working at a normal pace. A normal pace is equivalent to a man walking, without load, on smooth, level ground at a rate of three miles per hour." When this "normal pace" benchmark is applied to "shoveling sand," the following formula goes into effect:

> 'Material: River sand, moisture 5.5% approx., weight per cu. ft. 100–110 pounds.
> Equipment: Materials handling bos (steel) effective height above floor—32" shovel—No. 2 furnace.
> Working conditions: Under roof: smooth concrete floor, all other conditions normal.
> Production rate: For shoveling sand from pile to box—average weight sand on shovel—15 lbs; 12.5 shovelfuls per minute.' (Bell, 1962, p. 236)

Little did Benjamin Franklin realize that when he said "Time is money," some worker 200 years later would have to hoist a 15-pound shovelful of sand every 4.8 seconds for an entire working day in order to earn his money.

Box 3-3   Taking the Work to the Men

In 1908, just five years after he had established his now profitable automobile manufacturing enterprise, Henry Ford put out the Model T, the "universal car" which he continued to manufacture to the exclusion of all other models for eighteen years (Federal Trade Commission, 1964, p. 27).

> From the day the first motor car appeared on the streets it had to me appeared a necessity. It was this knowledge and assurance that led me to build to the one end—a car that would meet the wants of the multitudes. All my efforts were then and still are turned to the production of one car—one model. And, year following year, the pressure was, and still is, to improve and refine and make better, with an increasing reduction in price. (Ford, 1922, pp. 67–68)

In his decision to limit production to only one model, although with several body styles, Ford applied the principles of standardization and specialization, thus reducing substantially production costs at the same time increasing product quality. For example, the layout of the factory floor was designed exclusively for the most efficient handling and construction of only one type of engine and one type of chassis, and single-purpose machines were designed specifically to work on the standardized model T components flowing through the plant. Also, because these machines were restricted in function, they could be operated by less skilled and therefore less costly labor.

> Among these special machines were multiple drilling machines, which drilled simultaneously 45 holes in one cylinder block from four directions in $1\frac{1}{2}$ minutes. With these machines, it was not necessary to take a casting out and turn it bottom side up or around in order to continue the drilling process, as would be required if a standard general-purpose drill press were used. The use of these machines secured accuracy in drilling, avoided loss of castings, minimized the time of operation, and economized floor space. This particular machine as built could be used only on model T motors. (Federal Trade Commission, 1964, p. 30)

Other types of specialized, single-purpose machines abounded. Because of their standardized operations at very high levels of tolerance, this meant that each component was interchangeable with other similar components, a feature made possible only as a result of standardized machine operations.

In April 1913, Ford began his most famous set of engineering experiments—the design and construction of the automatic, continuously moving assembly line.

> A Ford car contains about five-thousand parts—that is counting screws, nuts, and all. Some of the parts are fairly bulky and others are almost the size of watch parts. In our first assembling we simply started to put a car together at a spot on the floor and workmen brought to it the parts as they were needed in exactly the same way that one builds a house. When we started to make parts it was natural to create a single department of the factory to make that part, but usually one workman performed all of the operations necessary on a small part. The rapid press of produc-

Assembling the Ford Model T.

Source: Lenski and Lenski, 1982, p. 250.

tion made it necessary to devise plans of production that would avoid having the workers falling over one another. The undirected worker spends more of his time walking about for materials and tools than he does in working; he gets small pay because pedestrianism is not a highly paid line.

The first step forward in assembly came when we began taking the work to the men instead of the men to the work. We now have two general principles in all operations—that a man shall never have to take more than one step, if possibly it can be avoided, and that no man need ever stoop over.

The principles of assembly are these:

1. Place the tools and the men in the sequence of the operation so that each component part shall travel the least possible distance while in the process of finishing.
2. Use work slides or some other form of carrier so that when a workman completes his operation, he drops the part always in the same place—which place

must always be the most convenient place to his hand—and if possible have gravity carry the part to the next workman for his operation.

3. Use sliding assembling lines by which the parts to be assembled are delivered at convenient distances.

The net result of the application of these principles is the reduction of the necessity for thought on the part of the worker and the reduction of his movements to a minimum. He does as nearly as possible only one thing with only one movement (Ford, 1922, pp. 79–80).

Prior to the introduction of the assembly line, it took an average of 12 hours and 28 minutes to assemble a stationary chassis in the Ford plant. The first experiment on a moving chassis assembly, accomplished by drawing the chassis with a rope and windlass down a line 250-feet long, resulted in a completed assembly in only 5 hours and 50 minutes, a reduction of more than half. In October of the same year, assembly on a continuously moving line was carried out in 2 hours and 57 minutes; and in April 1914, less than one year later, with the introduction of an elevated line (a waist-high $26\frac{3}{4}$ inches for the tall crew and $24\frac{1}{2}$ inches for shorter workers), chassis assembly averaged an astounding 1 hour and 33 minutes (see Arnold and Faurote, 1964).

The result of these technological and organizational innovations was an increase in the quality and quantity of output at substantially reduced costs. With these savings, Ford reinvested in his company, thus gaining an ever larger share of a rapidly expanding market, enlarged his growing network of branch assembly plants and dealerships located strategically across the country, paid out large dividends to his stockholders (including his 58% share), reduced substantially the price of his car to consumers (his model T Touring Car, which sold for $850 in 1908, was selling for $310 in 1926), and increased by more than double the wages of his workers (see Chandler, 1964, pp. 3–7; Federal Trade Commission, 1964; Gelderman, 1981). As one biographer later summed it up, "Henry Ford is an apt symbol of the transition from an agricultural to an industrial America" (Gelderman, 1981, p. 1).

THE SOCIAL REVOLUTION

Direct social consequences of the technological revolution were both quantitatively and qualitatively extensive. In this section, we will discuss the great rural–urban migration and the formation of super cities; the demographic transition, including population growth, increased life expectancy, labor force participation, and changes in family form, function, and life-style; the development of a national infrastructure to accommodate the demands and problems raised by industrialization; and the changing relationship of individual to society. No solutions will be forthcoming from this analysis in that, with respect to each of these social issues, we are still very much caught up in the social revolution, particularly if this revolution is viewed from its most general vantage point, that is, the human race attempting to adapt to and, at the same time, mold its environment. It is this latter point that makes the industrial revolution so historically and sociologically significant in that it marked the first time that human beings on a massive scale attempted to reconstruct the world in which they live.

Urbanization

One of the most visible social changes brought about by, or at least exacerbated by, the technological revolution was the large-scale movement of people to towns and cities. Whereas cities existed prior to this period (e.g., Rome during the time of Christ had a population of approximately 650,000 [Lenski and Lenski, 1982, p. 280]), never before were they so numerous or so large. The urbanization of Great Britain was in direct response to the demands of industrialism, which required massive labor reserves from which to recruit its industrial army. Also, it required population bases sufficiently varied and complex to coordinate the interdependent functions of acquiring raw materials and equipment, recruiting labor, and distributing and marketing manufactured goods. Large factories were extremely dependent upon their surrounding environment in order to maintain their complex organizations in peak operating condition. The early industrial cities which sprung up in the north of England largely fulfilled the insistent demands of this new industrial order.

Table 3.3 illustrates the phenomenal growth of these burgeoning cities in both England and the United States during the industrializing nineteenth century. Increases of nearly tenfold were recorded among historically established English towns, while in new and expanding America, New York City during the same period increased its size 42 times!

In order to understand and appreciate what urban growth of this magnitude means, I have included an excerpt on Manchester written in 1835 by Alexis de Tocqueville, a peripatetic and astute observer of both England and America during the 1800s (see Box 3-4). Tocqueville's narrative fleshes out the skeletal statistics, and

Table 3.3 POPULATIONS OF MAJOR ENGLISH AND AMERICAN CITIES, 1800 AND 1895, IN THOUSANDS

English cities	1801	1895	American cities	1801	1895
London	959	4,460	New York	60	2,530
Liverpool	82	740	Chicago	—	1,090
Manchester	77	740	Philadelphia	69	1,050
Birmingham	71	510	Boston	25	450
Leeds	53	410	Baltimore	26	440
Sheffield	46	350	Cincinnati	—	300

Data source: Adapted from Mulhall, 1899, pp. 445, 450, 788.

Box 3-4 ## Manchester

2 July 1835

. . . Thirty or forty factories rise on the tops of the hills . . . . Their six stories tower up; their huge enclosures give notice from afar of the centralisation of industry. The wretched dwellings of the poor are scattered haphazard around them. Round them stretches land uncultivated but without the charm of rustic nature, and still without the amenities of a town. The soil has been taken away, scratched and torn up in a thousand places, but it is not yet covered with the habitations of men. The land is given over to industry's use. The roads which connect the still-disjointed limbs of the great city, show, like the rest, every sign of hurried and unfinished work; the incidental activity of a population bent on gain, which seeks to amass gold so as to have everything else all at once, and, in the interval, mistrusts all the niceties of life. Some of these roads are paved, but most of them are full of ruts and puddles into which foot or carriage wheel sinks deep. Heaps of dung, rubble from buildings, putrid, stagnant pools are found here and there among the houses and over the bumpy, pitted surfaces of the public places. No trace of surveyor's rod or spirit level. Amid this noisome labyrinth, this great sombre stretch of brickwork, from time to time one is astonished at the sight of fine stone buildings with Corinthian columns. It might be a medieval town with the marvels of the nineteenth century in the middle of it. But who could describe the interiors of these quarters set apart, home of vice and poverty, which surround the huge palaces of industry and clasp them in their hideous folds. On ground below the level of the river and overshadowed on every side by immense workshops, stretches marshy land which widely spaced ditches can neither drain nor cleanse. Narrow, twisting roads lead down to it. They are lined with one-story houses whose ill-fitting planks and broken windows show them up, even from a distance, as the last refuge a man might find between poverty and death. None-the-less the wretched people living in them can still inspire jealousy of their fellow-beings. Below some of their miserable dwellings is a row of cellars to which a sunken corridor leads. Twelve to fifteen human beings are crowded pell-mell into each of these damp, repulsive holes.

The fetid muddy waters, stained with a thousand colours by the factories they pass, of one of the streams I mentioned before, wander slowly round this refuge of poverty. They are nowhere kept in place by quays: houses are built haphazard on their banks. Often from the top of one of their steep banks one sees an attempt at a road opening out through the debris of earth, and the foundations of some houses or the debris of others. It is the Styx of this new Hades. Look up and all around this place and you will see the huge palaces of industry. You will hear the noise of furnaces, the whistle of steam. These vast structures keep air and light out of the human habitations which they dominate; they envelope them in perpetual fog; here is the slave, there the master; there is the wealth of some, here the poverty of most; there the organized efforts of thousands produce, to the profit of one man, what society has not yet learnt to give. Here the weakness of the individual seems more feeble and helpless even than in the middle of a wilderness.

A sort of black smoke covers the city. The sun seen through it is a disc without rays. Under this half-daylight 300,000 human beings are ceaselessly at work. A thousand noises disturb this dark, damp labyrinth, but they are not at all the ordinary sounds one hears in great cities.

The footsteps of a busy crowd, the crunching wheels of machinery, the shriek of steam from boilers, the regular beat of the looms, the heavy rumble of carts, those are the noises from which you can never escape in the sombre half-light of these streets. . . .

From this foul drain the greatest stream of human industry flows out to fertilise the whole world. From this filthy sewer pure gold flows. Here humanity attains its most complete development and its most brutish; here civilisation makes its miracles, and civilised man is turned back almost into a savage.

Source: Alexis de Tocqueville, *Journeys to England and Ireland* (Reprinted in Harvie et al., 1970, pp. 40–42).

describes in graphic detail the consequences of rapid unplanned urbanization in a society in which there is as yet an infrastructure insufficient to accommodate the voluminous rural–urban migration and indigenous natural increase. Unfortunately, his description of Manchester in 1835 applies with equal force to many of today's sprawling and teeming cities of the Third World.

Population Growth

Not only did the technological revolution produce large-scale rural–urban migration such that by 1850 half of Britain's population was living in towns of at least 20,000 inhabitants (Mulhall, 1899, p. 445), it also was largely responsible for a huge natural increase in population. Technological innovations not only took place in industry, but they also occurred in agriculture, housing, sanitation, and public health, which all contributed to a sharply declining death rate and increased life expectancy. However, the previously high birth rate continued unabated. Britain was in the second stage of the demographic transition (see Chapter 2).

The first official census of England and Wales was conducted in 1801, the population at that time being almost nine million (Mantoux, 1961, p. 347). Previous estimates[4] reveal that since 1750 (roughly the beginning of the industrial revolution) population increases had been in the order of 50,000 per year, but that from 1600 to 1750 annual growth was only 10,000 (Mantoux, 1961, p. 348). Britain was in the midst of a population explosion.

It was at this time (1798) that Thomas Malthus wrote his extremely influential book on the principle of population. Malthus argued that the rate of increase in human population exceeds people's ability to grow food in quantities sufficient to maintain this rate. His famous principle was that the rate of subsistence increases in arithmetic progression (i.e., 1, 2, 3, 4, 5, and so on), but that population increases in geometric progression (1, 2, 4, 8, 16). Whereas the Malthusian principle was later demonstrated to be faulty, nevertheless the fact that it was enunciated at this time did indicate that population growth was considered a significant social problem.

The population explosion in Britain and the rest of industrializing Europe was dealt with in two major ways. First, during the period from 1840 to 1930, at least 52 million Europeans emigrated to the far-flung colonies and former colonies (Davis, 1974). Thus, emigration, aided largely by the invention of the steamship, served as a major conduit to reduce the impact of rapid population increase. Second, the industrial and commercial expansion that was occurring in Britain and the continent during this period absorbed much of the population excess. This was in large part the labor pool from which industrial capitalism drew as its enterprises grew apace.

In time, the large-scale rural–urban migration that was produced by industrialization introduced its own reality as industrial workers adapted to their changed environment. Large families, formerly an economic asset in agricultural life, were now perceived more as liabilities. With the industrial revolution and the creation of a labor market to match supply against demand, those not formally in the labor force constituted a drain on meager family incomes. Even though many children were employed during the early stages of the revolution, they were paid only a fraction of what adults earned (see Table 3.6). Consequently, an indirect result of the industrial revolution was a restructuring of the family in both form and function. The extended (multigenerational) kinship unit was gradually replaced by the more mobile nuclear (two-generational) family, the number of children per family unit decreased, and female labor force participation increased. With these changes and adaptations (to technologically produced circumstances), Great Britain and other industrialized countries entered the third and eventually the final stage of the demographic transition as the birth rate fell into line with the already reduced death rate.

Developing Infrastructure

Two important consequences of the technological revolution were the expansion of the transportation and communication network to enable better access to markets, raw materials, and labor, and the institution of a multitiered educational system to ensure that the industrial labor force was adequately trained to assume the varied responsibilities introduced by the new division of labor and occupational specialization. Because of the growing interdependence among all sectors of society, the state became increasingly involved in the provision of "essential services."

Transportation and Communication   With regard to transportation, the development of the railroad in the first half of the nineteenth century largely replaced canals and carriages as the preferred mode of conveyance, both for freight and passengers. In Great Britain, the first regular railway for carrying passengers was opened in 1825; and two years later in America, the four-mile track from Boston to Quincey was inaugurated (Mulhall, 1899, pp. 500, 507). Table 3.4 provides details of this remarkable development through the last century such that by 1897 the rail-

Table 3.4 FEATURES OF THE RAILROAD INDUSTRY IN THE U.K., U.S., AND THE WORLD, 1840–1897

Features of the railroad industry		United Kingdom	United States	World
Miles of track	1840	838	2,820	4,515
	1860	10,430	30,630	66,290
	1880	17,930	93,670	228,440
	1897	21,280	182,600	442,200
Number of locomotives	1885	15,200	28,600	—
	1892	17,440	35,280	—
Passengers (millions)	1860	180	60	413
	1887	816	451	2,362
	1897	980	535	3,380
Freight (millions of tons)	1860	82	70	222
	1887	282	590	1,424
	1897	357	774	1,920

Source: Mulhall, 1899, pp. 495–499, 794–795.

road in the United States consisted of 182,600 miles of track and 35,280 steam locomotives that had carried 535 million passengers and 774 million tons of freight—and all of this within seventy years!

In America, the development of rail transportation proceeded relatively unimpeded, the major obstacles being the rough physical terrain encountered and the vast expanses of territory. In comparison, the British railway companies faced entrenched opposition from the long-established canal and carriage trades. At its height, a government committee was struck to investigate the so-called encroachment of the upstart industry (see Thurston, 1878, pp. 169–172).

Box 3-5, **Selling the Railroad**, provides an example of the opposition faced by the British railway companies of the time. In 1852, a period of rapid expansion in the industry (see Table 3.4), the Liverpool and Manchester Railroad Company put out a proposal for a line between the two cities. This was a preliminary step to introducing a Bill into British Parliament for approval. You will notice from the language and tone employed in the prospectus what a "hard sell" this proposition was. As well as appeals to savings in time and cost, and increased efficiency, dependability, and safety, there are references to unfair trade practices (i.e., monopolistic excesses) and the larger benefits to the public and to the nation. This item illustrates well an essential difference discussed earlier between Great Britain and the United States. Whereas industrialization in the United States proceeded within a generally supportive value structure, in Britain the forces for "progress" were in constant battle with the custodians of the traditional order.

Box 3-5   Selling the Railroad

"The Committee of the Liverpool and Manchester Railroad Company think it right to state, concisely, the grounds upon which they rest their claims to public encouragement and support.

"The importance, to a commercial state, of a safe and cheap mode of transit for merchandise from one part of the country to another, will be readily acknowledged. This was the plea, upon the first introduction of canals: It was for the public advantage; and although the new mode of conveyance interfered with existing and inferior modes, and was opposed to the feelings and prejudices of landholders, the great principle of the public good prevailed, and experience has justified the decision.

"It is upon the same principle that railroads are now proposed to be established; as a means of conveyance manifestly superior to existing modes: possessing moreover this recommendation, in addition to what could have been claimed in favour of canals, namely, that the railroad scheme holds out to the public not only a cheaper, but far more expeditious conveyance than any yet established. . . .

"The total quantity of merchandise passing between Liverpool and Manchester is estimated, by the lowest computation, at 1,000 tons per day. The bulk of this merchandise is transported either by the Duke of Bridgwater's Canal or the 'Mersey and Irwell Navigation.' By both of these conveyances goods must pass up the river Mersey, a distance of 16 or 18 miles, subject to serious delays from contrary winds and not infrequently to actual loss or damage from tempestuous weather. The average length of passage, by these conveyances, including the customary detention on the wharfs, may be taken at 36 hours. . . . The average charge upon merchandise for the last 14 years has been about 15s. a ton.

"By the projected railroad, the transit of merchandise between Liverpool and Manchester will be effected in four or five hours, and the charge to the merchant will be reduced at least one-third. Here, then, will be accomplished an immense pecuniary saving to the public, over and above what is perhaps still more important, *the economy of time.* . . . It will afford stimulus to the productive industry of the country; it will give a new impulse to the powers of accumulation, the value and importance of which can be fully understood only by those who are aware how seriously commerce may be impeded by petty restrictions, and how commercial enterprise is encouraged and promoted by an adherance to the principles of fair competition and free trade.

"The Committee are aware that it will not immediately be understood by the public how the proprietors of a railroad, requiring an invested capital of £400,000, can afford to carry goods at so great a reduction upon the charge of the present water companies. . . . It is not that the water companies have not been able to carry goods on more reasonable terms, but that strong in the enjoyment of their monopoly, they have not thought it proper to do so. . . . IT IS COMPETITION THAT IS WANTED. . . .

"But it is not altogether on account of the exorbitant charges of the watercarriers that a railroad is desirable. The present canal establishments are inadequate to . . . the

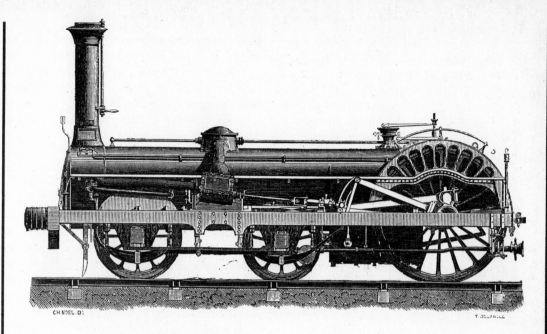

Crampton's Patent Express Engine, 1851

Source: Harvie et al., 1070, P. 59.

regular and punctual conveyance of goods at all periods and seasons. In summer time there is frequently a deficiency of water, obliging boats to go only half-loaded, while, in winter, they are sometimes locked up with frosts, for weeks together. . . .

"Merchandise is frequently brought across the Atlantic from New York to Liverpool in 21 days; while, owing to the various causes of delay above enumerated, goods have in some instances been longer on their passage from Liverpool to Manchester.

"The immediate and prominent advantages to be derived from the proposed railroad are, increased facilities to the general operations of commerce, arising out of that punctuality and dispatch which will attend the transit of merchandise between Liverpool and Manchester, as well as immense pecuniary saving to the trading community. . . . Moreover, as a cheap and expeditious means of conveyance for travellers, the railway holds out the fair prospect of a public accommodation, the magnitude and importance of which cannot be immediately ascertained. . . ."

Source: T. Baines, *History of Liverpool*, 1852 (Reprinted in Harvie et al., 1970, pp. 77–80).

The transportation and, later, communication systems established in industrialized countries were a result of the continuing technological revolution. Initially, it was industry that established its own extensive interdependent network, but the impact on society was enormous. For the first time, previously isolated and insulated boroughs, counties, states, and territories were woven into the national fabric. Transportation and communication linkages provided the social glue necessary to bind hitherto distinct and separate peoples together and, in so doing, developed a *national* consciousness. Nowhere was this more evident than in the United States, which was in the midst of a monumental effort to incorporate and consolidate vast territories into one political union. Were it not for the technological revolution, this may well have proved impossible.

Education   Another far-reaching, although not as immediately apparent, consequence of industrialization was the establishment of an integral and complex educational system. Not only did the institutionalization of education ensure an adequately trained industrial labor force, but also, particularly at the higher levels, it formalized and promoted innovation as a societal value. Whereas in the early stages of the technological revolution invention and innovation arose largely out of practical experience, increasingly, as industrial machinery and processes became more complex, innovative breakthroughs were achieved by organized teams of research scientists.

Comparative data for ten early industrial nations reveal that all but one had instituted at least four years of free compulsory education by 1900,[5] and that the number of years of schooling required was extended as the state assumed increasing responsibility for education (Mishra, 1973). Over time, the participation rates in all age categories increased, including the postsecondary level where the United States attained early supremacy (see Sanderson, 1988, pp. 364–366).

The American educational system merits special attention in that as well as being a product of the industrialization process, it also arose out of a post-Revolutionary zeal to democratize elite norms and to extend to all (free) Americans the means for economic independence and a better way of life (see Brown, 1976, p. 89). One obvious avenue to achieve this goal was education, and the participation rates of American children in the nineteenth century vis-à-vis their European counterparts attest to the fact that this avenue was well traveled.

> In 1850, for example, the United States ranked second only to Denmark in its ratio of students to the total population (even though more than 10 percent of its population were slaves, forcibly excluded from education). In spite of the endemic scarcity of labor in America, people in the United States were sending their offspring to school more than twice as often as was true in Germany and over one-third more than in England. New England, in fact, led the world in its percentage of student population. (Brown, 1976, p. 138)

Education in the United States was more instrumentally oriented than it was in Europe, which was steeped in the classics and bound up in metaphysics and the humanities. Based in large part on the "progressive education" of John Dewey (1900), American education began from the premise that all genuine thought grows out of real problems. Thus, "a key task of educators was to . . . present students with opportunities to become effective members of society. The objective was to form students' capacity for independent, critical social practice" (Bidwell and Friedkin, 1988, p. 450), and schools and universities emphasized practical concerns (e.g., natural and mechanical sciences, and mathematics) in their curricula.

Universal education, an important consequence of industrialization, in turn produced its own impact upon society. An educated citizenry develops different values and expectations, thereby changing in a fundamental manner the relationship of individual to society. For an educated populace, the social contract undergoes substantial revision to include the assurance of equal access for all to the rights and privileges that society makes available. Table 3.5, which presents data on the proportion of the British population eligible to vote over a one hundred year span demonstrates exactly this point. Education, the great equalizer, transforms society from its previous overriding emphasis on elite privilege to a more universalistic focus on participation, merit, and achievement.

Quality of Life

The technological revolution also had a profound impact upon the daily lives of the men, women, and children who constituted the industrial labor force. In general, it ushered in a new era of economic progress and an improved standard of living, but at a cost of extreme individual hardship and dislocation. Most of all, it necessitated a drastic restructuring of old, established customary patterns.

One of the most consistently supported empirical generalizations in the social sciences is people's resistance to change. No matter how convincing a case might be made, fear and anxiety most often greet the new, the untried, and the unknown, while fierce loyalty and attachment are reserved for the familiar and routine. Whereas many atrocities, particularly against children, were committed during this era in the name of industrial progress, nevertheless the most severe challenge was change itself. The inhumane treatment of one person by another was constant in its transition from an agricultural to an industrial society.

Table 3.5 PERCENTAGE OF THE BRITISH POPULATION AGED TWENTY-ONE AND OVER ELIGIBLE TO VOTE, 1831–1928

Year	% Eligible to vote
1831	5.0
1832 (after First Reform Act)	7.1
1867 (after Second Reform Act)	16.4
1884 (after Third Reform Act)	28.5
1918 (after women were enfranchised)	74.0
1928 (after Equal Franchise Act)	96.9

Source: Judith Ryder and H. Silver, *Modern English Society: History and Structure, 1850–1970*. London: Methuen, 1970, p. 74. (Reprinted in Lenski and Lenski, 1982, p. 305.)

The most active resistance to change was levied against those characteristics integral to the industrial process: machine production, the factory system, and the unrestrained power of the industrial capitalist (for an extended discussion, see Mantoux, 1961, pp. 399–477). Opposition to machinery was certainly understandable, at least in the short run, for its avowed purpose was to "save" or displace labor. Not only did the machine threaten worker employment, but also in many cases it made redundant hard-won skills. The case against the factory system was more complex. It represented a regime that stripped workers of their autonomy with respect to the time (including pace) and place of work, as well as how it should be performed (i.e., division of labor and formalized rules and procedures). With regard to the industrial capitalist, even though he had simply assumed the exalted position of the feudal landowner before him, nevertheless he was the more feared and reviled in that through technological and organizational means he had further consolidated his position and made unbroachable the gulf between master and servant. His power had virtually no bounds.

In Great Britain, resistance was both organized and of a more sporadic nature. In either case, however, it was violent and protracted, spanning several decades. Opposition took the form of organized protests; petitions to Parliament; strikes; the destruction of machinery, equipment, and products; the burning of mills and factories; and full-scale riots. Many people were killed, some of these being sentenced to the gallows for murder and sedition. The period of transition was far from easy.

At first, the government adopted a laissez-faire position, not wanting to usurp the lawful domain of the capitalist class to do as it pleased. However, two factors finally produced a policy of increasing government intervention into industrial relations. First, because hundreds of thousands of workers were controlled by a relatively few industrial capitalists, any changes in the administration of their factories (such as layoffs or wage cuts) could and sometimes did have devastating repercussions throughout society. Second, the government was becoming increasingly concerned about the treatment of one particular class of workers, namely children. Paupers, the first children to work in mines and factories, were sold in lots to these establishments by local parishes anxious to cut their expenses. These young children often received no wages whatsoever, being forced instead into a life of perpetual servitude.

In 1782, British parliament introduced a new Poor Law, which resulted in a more humane treatment of those unfortunate wretches who by dint of age (old and young), infirmity, famine, or other causes (natural and humanmade) could not find sufficient work or food to exist. In 1800, the Arbitration Act was signed into law providing government with the power to set minimum wages, and in 1802 the first Factory Act came into being. Legislated mainly for the protection of children, but also containing general provisions, this new act was a definite watershed marking the previous era from that which was to come. It contained clauses relating to workshop hygiene, hours and conditions of employment, and the care and compulsory education of children (including religious instruction). For the first time, the unrestrained power of the industrial capitalist was bridled as the state intervened to establish minimum conditions under which all would labor.

Table 3.6 **WAGES OF MALES AND FEMALES IN WOOL FACTORIES IN LEEDS AS A PROPORTION OF MALES AGED 31 TO 40 (1831)**

Ages	Workers	
	Male	Female
Under 11	.09	.11
11–15	.19	.20
16–20	.43	.29
21–30	.93	.32
31–40	1.00*	.33
41–50	.98	.31
51–60	.96	.31
Over 60	.82	.15

*1.00 represents 22 shillings and 6 pence per week.

Source: Adapted from Ure, 1835, p. 476.

Whereas government intervention did improve the conditions of the working poor, nevertheless great inequalities still persisted, particularly with regard to age and gender. As an example, Table 3.6 presents the wages of textile workers in Leeds (one of the most highly paid group of workers) in 1831 as a proportion of males aged 31 to 40. Women, who constituted more than half of all textile workers in Britain (Ure, 1835, p. 481), on average earned less than one-third of the wages paid to men, while children, comprising nearly two-fifths of the textile labor force, earned only 20% or even 10% of the adult male wage.

In presenting these data on wage inequities, the author (Ure, 1835) justified them in the following fashion:

> The small amount of the wages of the very young children employed in factories deserves notice, but should constitute a subject of satisfaction rather than of regret, because there will be less loss to the parents in withdrawing the youngest from the factories and sending them to school.
>
> Factory females have also in general much lower wages than males, and they have been pitied on this account with perhaps an injudicious sympathy, since the low price of their labour here tends to make household duties their most profitable as well as agreeable occupation, and prevents them from being tempted by the mill to abandon the care of their offspring at home. Thus Providence effects its purposes with a wisdom and efficacy, which should repress the short-sighted presumption of human devices. (Ure, 1835, p. 475)

More deserving of this English upper-class gentleman's concern was the fact that there were also gross inequities in men's wages depending upon where in the country they worked. He did not stop to consider that should women and children have heeded his advice and stayed at home or gone to school that the British textile industry, one of the mainstays of the industrial revolution, would have ground to a sudden halt.

The period of transition was marked by great turmoil and social upheaval. However, it is important to note that overall there was an improvement in the quality of life and standard of living of the entire citizenry (Gilboy, 1967). I have mentioned that from 1801 to 1901 there was an increase of over 600 percent in total national income in Britain (Mitchell, 1962, p. 366). At least part of this increase was distributed among all the populace, as Mantoux (1961, p. 421) notes that both before and after the introduction of the factory system, "the wages of industry were higher than those of agriculture," and that this difference increased over time. Also, I have indicated that life expectancy increased, and that in general people were fed, clothed, and housed better than in the previous era. The manufactured products of the industrial revolution were widely distributed. Moreover, all the people were being educated and increasingly being permitted to participate in the electoral process (see Table 3.5). There was beginning to occur a redistribution of power on a grand scale. Judged by contemporary standards, there were many injustices during this period, but evaluated against the era it was replacing, the industrial revolution marked a new stage in social and economic progress.

SUMMARY

3.1 The industrial revolution began in Great Britain in the late eighteenth century. Its essential features included machine production, the factory system of manufacture, and mechanical motive power.

3.2 Tracing the dimensions of industrialization during the nineteenth century, data for Great Britain and the United States show that by 1880 less than half of all workers were employed in agriculture; industry comprised a continually expanding proportion of national wealth; there were increases in factories, factory workers, energy consumption, and mechanization; and technological innovation as measured by the number of patents filed rose exponentially.

3.3 The technological revolution was the result of cumulative and interconnected inventions and innovations that arose largely out of practical necessity and experience.

3.4 Invention as a process is comprised of three factors: (1) the mental ability of the inventor; (2) the existing state of accumulated knowledge; and (3) predominant social values. The latter two factors were important in producing the industrial revolution.

3.5 Industrialization in America, occurring in the first half of the nineteenth century, proceeded rapidly because it drew upon the British experience and because the United States had a value structure supportive of innovation and progress.

3.6 Mass production, the American system of manufacture, involves a complex division of labor, standardized interchangeable components, and continuously moving assembly lines, all organized into precise time sequences. The result is a great volume of output at a reduced cost per unit of output. Henry Ford was one of the most successful pioneers of mass production techniques.

3.7 The technological revolution produced a social revolution, one consequence being a vast rural–urban migration. By 1850, more than half of Britain's population was living in cities numbering 20,000 or more.

3.8 Another facet of the social revolution was population growth brought about technologically through reduction of the death rate. To handle population excess, there was a large exodus of people to the New World, and expanding industry absorbed the remainder.

3.9 With increasing industrialization, there was an expansion of the societal infrastructure with the state becoming increasingly involved in the provision of social services. As a result of the invention of the steam locomotive, the railroad in both Great Britain and the United States formed the basis of the transportation network during the last half of the nineteenth century. Also, the state became responsible for the provision of universal education, in part to provide a technologically competent industrial labor force.

3.10 Central features of the technological revolution that were responsible for the great societal changes became the bases of widespread social protest. In Britain, workers revolted against the machine, the factory system of production, and the almost limitless power of the industrial capitalist. Because of the profound social repercussions of the technological revolution, the state became increasingly involved in industrial relations legislation. Although this period was marked by intense struggle and unrest, nevertheless there was an overall improvement in the standard of living of all.

NOTES

1. Reporting on factory size, Mulhall (1899, p. 767) did note that "two of the largest factories [steel] in the world are Armstrong's at Newcastle, with 27,000, and Krupp's at Essen, with 24,000, workmen."
2. With regard to multiple inventors, Ogburn and Thomas (1922, p. 85) make the additional point that "the records of the United States Patent Office show that about twice as many patents are applied for as are granted. Many of these applications are no doubt denied because the invention is already patented. This is further evidence that many inventions are made independently by more than one person." See Table 3.1.5.
3. As you will observe in Table 3.2, printing, a most important technology in the historical accumulation of knowledge, is a relatively recent invention given the total span of human history. This fact gives added impetus to the period of the industrial revolution as a time for invention, innovation, and application.
4. Prior to census enumeration, population estimates were made from taxation returns and from church records of christenings and burials.
5. Mishra (1973, p. 559) notes that compulsory education was in effect in 1900 for 32 out of 48 states in the United States, and that by 1918 such a law had been passed for the remaining states.

Chapter

4

Major Transformational Theories

During the early phase of industrialization a new way of life is in the making and an old way of life is on the defensive.

Bendix, 1963, p. 4

. . . industrialization disrupted traditional patterns of social life. It made available a new richness of individual experience in some directions but in others it imposed new constraints . . . .

Harvie, Martin, and Scharf, 1970, p. 11

. . . the industrial revolution . . . did not actually alter the legal form of society, yet it modified its very substance.

Mantoux, 1961, p. 476

*I*n the wake of the technological and social revolutions that constituted the great industrial transformation, various social theorists attempted to explain the myriad far-reaching changes that had taken place. This period also marked the beginnings of sociology as a formal and distinct discipline of study.[1] Karl Marx (1818–1883), a philosopher and self-proclaimed revolutionary, and Emile Durkheim (1858–1917) and Max Weber (1864–1920), both sociologists, were all concerned with the effects of the industrial revolution upon the structure of society and the relationship of individuals to society. Not only were their seminal works regarded as major accomplishments of the period, they were also instrumental in laying the theoretical and methodological foundations of sociology as it is practiced today.

In this chapter, we will focus on the scientific study of society as engaged in by these three theorists. First, we will examine some of the methodological problems that hampered early empirical social research. This will be followed by brief theoretical overviews of Marx, Durkheim, and Weber, including their explanations of how the industrial revolution came about and its consequences for individuals and society. The chapter will conclude by bringing together major themes common to the work of these great thinkers.

THE SCIENTIFIC STUDY OF SOCIETY

Similar to technological innovations, the promulgation of ideas is a cumulative enterprise, and each of these great thinkers owed an intellectual debt that spanned recorded history. As one of Marx's biographers put it, "The originality of Marx's thought lies in his immense efforts to synthesize, in a critical way, the entire legacy of social knowledge since Aristotle" (Rubel, 1968, p. 35). Notwithstanding the tremendous intellect of these theoretical giants, it was their particular historical vantage point that afforded them their claim to immortality. Rosenberg (1982), in describing Marx's study of inventions and technological change, reveals how Marx himself was aware that the individual inventor/creator is simply a cog, albeit an important one, in a larger complex machine:

> . . . although individual human beings are, inevitably, the actors, the *dramatis personae* of the historical process, the actual unfolding of the plot turns upon the larger social forces that shape their actions . . . what is really involved is a process of a cumulative accretion of useful knowledge, to which many people make essential contributions, even though the prizes and recognition are usually accorded to the one actor who happens to be on the stage at a critical moment. (Rosenberg, 1982, pp. 48–49)

Not only were these early sociologists strategically placed with respect to time, place, and historical circumstance, but also the methods that they employed were considered revolutionary for the period. Each adhered to the empirical method of data collection to support his argument rather than rely on traditional armchair speculation. For years, Marx went daily to the British Museum where he studied and analyzed the Blue Books of factory inspectors and documented through numerous records the structure and conditions of industrial life (Coser, 1971, p. 64). Durkheim and Weber both were instrumental in replacing personal observation and insight with painstaking systematic and comprehensive empirical investigation as the means to achieving valid social generalizations. As a result of their respective endeavors, each wrote methodological treatises specifying the problems and procedures involved in empirical social research (see Durkheim, 1964b; Shils and Finch, 1949).

By today's standards, it must be remarked how generally unavailable and inaccessible good factual information was 100–200 hundred years ago. The role of government as national record keeper had not assumed the prominence it has today, public bureaus and agencies being restricted to a limited number of fundamental endeavors such as taxation. Relatively speaking, what few records there were, both public and private, were neither systematic nor comprehensive in their coverage, nor uniform and standard in the information they contained. This lack of good data in combination with the enormity of the theoretical problems that Marx, Durkheim, and Weber were wrestling with, in a fledgling discipline without adequately developed social research techniques, makes their resulting accomplishments all the more phenomenal.

Another important methodological concern was the objectivity with which these writers initiated their investigations and reported their results, and on this point the revolutionary Marx stands apart from the two sociologists. From 1848, when he wrote *The Manifesto of the Communist Party* with Engels, until he died, Marx was waiting to lead the revolution that never occurred. Virtually all of his writing from the time he was thirty, notwithstanding its empirical documentation, was devoted to the impending overthrow of the ruling capitalist class, and was written in a polemical and impassioned vein.

On the other hand, Durkheim and particularly Weber were the "objective" social scientists. Each wrote on the role of personal values of the investigator in the research process—when they were likely to intrude and when they should not be permitted to interfere. For Weber, "value-free" social science was not only an ideal but absolutely essential in order that scientists "not inadvertently confuse their own values and ideas with those of the actors they are studying" (Bendix, 1968, p. 495). According to Weber, the only place where the values of scientists may legitimately enter the research process is in the initial selection of the problem to study.

For Durkheim, although social facts could and should be collected objectively and dispassionately, the values of the investigator could intrude in the *interpretation* of these facts. As I mentioned in Chapter 2, depending upon the theoretical orientation of the researchers, and depending also upon the emphases attributed to various aspects or features of the empirical domain, interpretations of facts may vary from one investigator to another. What we see is indeed determined in large part by what we are looking for.

Box 4-1, **Marx's Questionnaire Survey of Industrial Workers,** highlights the methodological issues I have been discussing. In 1880, Marx published a questionnaire comprised of 101 questions in the *Revue Socialiste*, a French socialist magazine. By all accounts, it represented the first independent effort to collect factual data from workers themselves since it was only they who could "describe with full knowledge the evils which they endure" (Marx, 1880 in Weiss, 1979, p. 178). Thus, Marx was concerned with empirical documentation; but as the phrase above implies, together with some of his actual questions, he was not merely asking for information. By the very nature of his questions, he was attempting to inform workers of the injustices inherent in the capitalist system in which they labored.

In scanning the only partial listing of Marx's questions, you will be struck by their complexity. Although Marx was desirous of obtaining such information, it was clearly beyond the grasp of ordinary and, in many cases, illiterate factory workers to provide, even if they did take the excessive amount of time necessary

Box 4-1   Marx's Questionnaire Survey of Industrial Workers (1880)

PREFACE

No government—whether monarchical or bourgeois-republican—has dared to undertake a serious investigation of the condition of the French working class, although there have been many studies of agricultural, financial, commercial and political crises.

The odious acts of capitalist exploitation which the official surveys by the English government have revealed, and the legislative consequences of these revelations (limitation of the legal working day to ten hours, legislation concerning the labour of women and children, etc.), have inspired in the French bourgeoisie a still greater terror of the dangers which might result from an impartial and systematic inquiry.

While awaiting the time when the republican government can be induced to follow the example of the English monarchical government and inaugurate a comprehensive survey of the deeds and misdeeds of capitalist exploitation, we shall attempt a preliminary investigation with the modest resources at our disposal. We hope that our undertaking will be supported by all those workers in town and country who realize that only they can describe with full knowledge the evils which they endure, and that only they—not any providential saviours—can remedy the social ills from which they suffer. We count also upon the socialists of all schools, who, desiring social reform, must also desire *exact* and *positive* knowledge of the conditions in which the working class, the class to which the future belongs, lives and works. . . .

The following hundred questions are the most important ones. The replies should follow the order of the questions. It is not necessary to answer all the questions, but respondents are asked to make their answers as comprehensive and detailed as possible. The name of the respondent will not be published unless specifically authorized, but it should be given together with the address, so that we can establish contact with him. . . .

Section 1. Division of Labor and Working Conditions

1. What is your occupation?

2. Does the workshop in which you are employed belong to a capitalist or to a joint-stock company? Give the names of the capitalist employers or of the directors of the company.

3. State the number of persons employed.

4. State their ages and sex.

5. What is the minimum age at which children (boys or girls) are employed?

12. Is your work done by hand or with the aid of machinery?

13. Give details of the division of labor in your industry.

20. Are the machines, the transmission system, and the engines supplying power, protected so as to avoid any accidents?

21. Enumerate the accidents which have occurred in your personal experience.

26. In case of accidents, is the employer obliged *by law* to pay compensation to the worker or his family?

27. If not, has he ever paid compensation to those who have met with an accident while working to enrich him?

Section 2. Hours of Work and Child Labor

30. State your daily hours of work, and working days in the week.

37. State the hours of work of children and of young persons below the age of 16.

39. Are the laws concerning the employment of children enforced by the government or the municipality? Are they respected by the employer?

Section 3. Employment Contract, Wages, and Cost of Living

46. What kind of work contract do you have with your employer? Are you engaged by the day, by the week, by the month, etc.?

53. Are you paid time rates or piece rates?

56. If you are paid piece rates, how are the rates fixed? If you are employed in an industry in which the work performed is measured by quantity or weight, as is the case in the mines, does your employer or his representatives resort to trickery in order to defraud you of a part of your earnings?

57. If you are paid piece rates, is the quality of the article made a pretext for fraudulent deductions from your wages?

58. Whether you are paid piece rates or time rates, when are you paid, or in other words how long is the credit which you extend to your master before receiving the price of the work carried out? Are you paid at the end of a week, a month, etc.?

63. What are the wages of women and children working with you in the same workshop?

71. Have you noticed, in your personal experience, a greater rise in the price of the necessities of life, such as food and shelter, than in wages?

76. Compare *the price of the article you produce*, or of the services you provide, with the price of your labor.

Section 4. Industrial Relations

82. Are there any defense organizations in your trade, and how are they conducted? Send their statutes and rules.

90. Give an account of the rules and penalties instituted by your employer for the government of his wage earners.

91. Have there been any combinations of employers for the purpose of imposing wage reductions, increasing working hours, or preventing strikes or, in general, for getting their own way?

92. Do you know any instances in which the Government has misused the forces of the State, in order to place them at the disposal of employers against their employees?

100. What is the general physical, intellectual, and moral conditions of men and women workers employed in your trade?

Source: Marx, cited in Weiss, 1979, pp. 178–184.

to complete the questionnaire. It is small wonder that only a few responses were ever received.

Through Marx's questionnaire survey we can summarize some of the important problems encountered by early social investigators in conducting research on the effects of the industrial revolution: (1) There was a severe lack of systematically accumulated social data; (2) given the social conditions of the period, it was extremely difficult and in some cases impossible to collect data representative of the bulk of the population; (3) the predilections of many early observers interfered with their objective descriptions of the social scene; (4) the methods of social scientific research were in their infancy; and (5) societal values were not supportive of *social* research. Whereas Durkheim and Weber were considerably more observant of the scientific principles underlying the research process than was Marx, nevertheless they too suffered from these constraints. The following is a brief examination of each theorist presented in chronological order.

MAKING SENSE OF THE GREAT TRANSFORMATION

Karl Marx

In the Preface to *A Contribution to the Critique of Political Economy* written in 1859, Marx set out "the general conclusion" of his work, which constituted the "leading thread" in his studies:

> In the social production which men carry on they enter into definite relations that are indispensable and independent of their will; these relations of production correspond to a definite stage of development of their material powers of production. The sum total of these relations of production constitutes the economic structure of society—the

real foundation, on which rise legal and political superstructures and to which correspond definite forms of social consciousness. The mode of production in material life determines the general character of the social, political, and spiritual processes of life. It is not the consciousness of men that determines their existence, but, on the contrary, their social existence determines their consciousness. (Marx, 1859 in Feuer, 1959, p. 43)

In simplified form, Marx asserted that it is the mode of economic production that determines the structure of society and the character of social life. Whether it be the present industrial capitalist society or the Asiatic, ancient, or feudal types of societies that preceded it, an individual's position is fixed by his or her relationship to the means of production. In bourgeois capitalist society, two major classes are formed on the basis of who owns the means of production. On the one hand are the numerically few ruling bourgeoisie who own the factories, mines, and railroads,

Figure 4.1 Karl Marx (1818–1883)

while on the other there are the vast oppressed proletariat who have only their own labor to sell to the industrial capitalists.

In Marx's materialistic and dialectic conception of history, he posited that over time human beings have achieved growing success in mastering the natural environment and in eking out a living, but that in the process our relationship to our fellow human beings has become increasingly exploitive. According to the theory, each successive stage of history produces classes based on the prevailing "material powers of production," that is, how people make their living. Depending upon changes and growth in the productive capacity of society, there develop challenges to the traditional order that in turn produce revolutionary social changes, and a new type of society based on different material powers of production emerges (see Coser, 1971, pp. 55–57). However, paradoxically, given the success of the industrial capitalists with their machine-based factory system of production to control the environment, and thereby to concentrate their own power, the next revolution by the proletariat who because they constitute the overwhelming majority of society will be the last. "'The prehistory of human society will have come to an end'" (Marx, cited in Coser, 1971, p. 57). The rule of the proletariat, because it comprises all of humankind, will usher in a new classless and therefore harmonious society.

An important by-product of Marx's analysis of history was the concept of alienation. Increasingly, as humankind has exerted control over nature, it has lost touch with its own humanity (Coser, 1971, p. 50). Alienation or dehumanization occurs when "the producer is divorced from the means of production and when 'dead labor' (capital) dominates 'living labor' (the worker)" (Rubel, 1968, p. 36). "Formally free, man has been converted into a commodity, whose labor power, talents, and personality are for sale on the free market" (Meyer, 1968, p. 41). According to Marx, the industrial revolution institutionalized alienation as the prevailing human condition.

Workers no longer able to compete economically with the factory system of production had to give up their tools and yield to the dictates of the industrial capitalist in order to earn a livelihood. In the factory, because of the division of labor, workers could not create entire products; and because of mass production methods, they were only appendages to the machines that controlled them. Finally, they were subject to the impersonal rules and regulations of the factory organization that specified precisely what they were to do, where and when it was to be performed, by what methods, and in how much time. Through these means, workers lost their own identities as individual creators and producers in society.

Whereas Marx documented the ills of the capitalist system and prophesied its ultimate demise, he nevertheless marveled at its accomplishments:

> The bourgeoisie, during its rule of scarce 100 years, has created more massive and more colossal productive powers than have all preceding generations together. Subjection of nature's forces to man, machinery, application of chemistry to industry and agriculture, steam navigation, railways, electric telegraphs, clearing of whole continents for cultivation, canalization of rivers, whole populations conjured out of the ground—what earlier century had even a presentiment that such productive forces slumbered in the lap of social labor? (Marx and Engels, 1848 in Feuer, 1959, p. 12)

It was Marx's thesis that the industrial revolution had produced the potential for the emancipation of humankind from the precarious and burdensome hand to mouth existence of previous eras, but that this potential could not be realized until the oppressive capitalist class was expunged through revolutionary means. Marx argued that the capitalists themselves would ultimately be responsible for the destruction of the unjust class system they had created and that the benefits produced by this system would be distributed equally amongst all. "Modern bourgeois society with its relations of production, of exchange, and of property, a society that has conjured up such gigantic means of production and of exchange, is like the sorcerer who is no longer able to control the powers of the nether world whom he has called up by his spells" (Marx and Engels, 1848, in Feuer, 1959, pp. 12–13).

The seeds of destruction of the capitalist system lay in the continual erosion of its base, thus inexorably diminishing the ranks of the bourgeoisie at the same time that the proletariat were being augmented by disaffected and disenfranchised capitalists. According to Marx, two principal means by which this erosion of the ruling class was occurring were the concentration of capital and the centralization of power (see Bottomore, 1985, pp. 4–21). First, as a result of the growing productivity of modern industry, more and more surplus value (i.e., profit) was accruing to the capitalists, thus producing ever-increasing disparities in income within society. And second, as a result of competition amongst capitalists themselves, some inevitably were being bought out, amalgamated, or forced out of business, thus producing more profit for fewer capitalists.

Marx proposed that the logical conclusion of these two processes would be the untenable position wherein fewer and fewer capitalists would divide an ever-larger economic pie. Eventually, because of their reduced numbers, they would be unable to defend themselves against the organized revolt by the rightful heirs to the benefits of capitalism. The capitalists' own greed would ultimately catapult them from power and thus lay the foundation for the classless society.

In summary, for Marx, the industrial revolution introduced new material powers of production, that is, a different economic system that was responsible for the demise of the previous feudal society. These new material powers of production (mechanically driven, machine-based technology) were qualitatively different from those of earlier eras. For the first time, productive capacity could exceed the physiological and psychological limitations of human beings (see Rosenberg, 1982, pp. 34–51). Aided by science, the new technology of production could be applied systematically and continuously to wrest an almost limitless bounty from a previously hostile environment. However, before all humankind could enjoy the just fruits of their labor, the relations of production, that is, the exploitive and oppressive class system based on the ownership of the means of production, must be dispensed with.

Part of Marx's failure to predict accurately the outcome of the industrial revolution lay in his overwhelming urge to "liberate mankind forever from the curse of property and class" (Meyer, 1968, p. 41), to provide an "association, in which the free development of each is the condition for the free development of all" (Marx, 1848 in Rubel, 1968, p. 35).[2] Despite his voluminous empirical documentation of the social ills brought about by the industrial revolution, his sense of mission oftentimes overrode his scientific perception in objectively setting out and explaining the actual effects upon individual and society caused by the industrial revolution.

Emile Durkheim

Durkheim's first major work, *The Division of Labor in Society*, his doctoral dissertation published in 1893, is concerned directly with the antecedents and consequences of the industrial revolution. It is in this book that he maps out his agenda for his life's work in that the ideas for his subsequent books on sociological method, suicide, and religion are all contained here (Schnore, 1958, p. 622). In fact, his later concerns may be said to be derivative of the two major themes (and dilemma) he introduces in the *Division of Labor*, that is, the differentiation and cohesion of society.

Like Marx, Durkheim concentrated on the structural aspects of society rather than individuals' concerns within it. Also like Marx, "he wanted to devote himself to a discipline that would contribute to the clarification of the great moral questions that agitated the age, as well as to practical guidance of the affairs of contemporary society" (Coser, 1971, p. 145). However, here the similarities end. Marx was a fervent critic of an unjust system that he wished to change through revolutionary means; Durkheim was an ardent supporter of an evolving society based on mutual interdependence. Marx's legacy to sociology was a concern with those structural aspects of society which could produce its eventual demise (e.g., inequality, constraint, and conflict). Durkheim, on the other hand, provided sociology with a functionalist orientation, a theoretical rationale that explains how the various elements and features of society contribute to a cohesive and integrated whole.

Prior to the industrial revolution, according to Durkheim, society by and large consisted of small isolated communities in which there was little division of labor. In the constant struggle for survival against a harsh environment, most people engaged collectively in a relatively small variety of tasks (e.g., hunting, fishing, gathering, herding, and farming). What little differentiation there was in the assignment of tasks occurred along traditional gender and age lines. Because everybody was working at similar occupations for survival, the resulting social system was based upon and emphasized what they shared and had in common. Durkheim called this *mechanical solidarity*, "a more or less organized totality of beliefs and sentiments common to all the members of the group" (Durkheim, 1964a, p. 129). Because of the unitary character and constitution of the group, uniqueness and individuality were minimized. "Solidarity which comes from likenesses is at its maximum when the collective conscience completely envelops our whole conscience and coincides in all points with it" (Durkheim, 1964a, p. 130). Thus, mechanical solidarity is also repressive.

In developing the case for increased differentiation (i.e., division of labor) within society, Durkheim argued that it was caused by humankind's ever-growing technological expertise and therefore its ability to deal effectively with the environment. He hypothesized that the following factors were instrumental in producing

Figure 4.2   Emile Durkheim (1858–1917)

increasing differentiation: (1) population growth achieved through technological death control; (2) increased population density arising out of urbanization; and (3) increased human interaction ("moral or dynamic density") due to the above two factors plus technologically improved means of transportation and communication (see Durkheim, 1964a, pp. 256–263).[3]

All these factors together led to the penetration of and encroachment upon the isolated small communities that he had earlier described. These hitherto self-sufficient and insulated enclaves were now forced into direct competition with each other. Consequently, specialization or a division of labor (i.e., cooperation and mutual interdependence) occurred as a result of like units competing for limited resources.

> We say, not that the growth and condensation of societies *permit*, but that they *necessitate* a greater division of labor. It is not an instrument by which the latter is realized; it is its determining cause. . . .

One need not add that, if society effectively includes more members at the same time as they are more closely in relation to each other, the struggle is still more acute and the resulting specialization more rapid and complete. (Durkheim, 1964a, pp. 262, 269)

For Durkheim, the division of labor or the increasing differentiation of functions in society, both within and outside the economic sector, constituted the major independent variable that caused other profound social changes—changes in the structure of social relationships and in the manner individuals were linked to and participated in society. He argued that while a rudimentary division of labor emphasizes likenesses, and consequently produces a society in which individuals are diminished through their total adherence to unwavering social custom, a highly differentiated society presumes differences. A complex society encourages individuality as a result of the distinct and functionally interdependent contributions that autonomous individuals make in order to maintain it. In Durkheim's words, the basis for social integration, that is, individual cohesion within society, changes from mechanical to *organic solidarity*.

There are in each of us . . . two consciences: one which is common to our group in its entirety, which, consequently, is not ourself, but society living and acting within us [i.e., the basis of mechanical solidarity]; the other, on the contrary, represents that in us which is personal and distinct, that which makes us an individual [i.e., the basis of organic solidarity]. . . . There are, here, two contrary forces, one centripetal, and the other centrifugal, which cannot flourish at the same time. We cannot, at one and the same time, develop ourselves in two opposite senses. If we have a lively desire to think and act for ourselves, we cannot be strongly inclined to think and act as others do. If our ideal is to present a singular and personal appearance, we do not want to resemble everybody else. (Durkheim, 1964a, pp. 129–130)

Not only is individuality emphasized in a highly differentiated society, but here are other important consequences that result in a notably different social system. Durkheim dealt at length with the changing constitution of societal norms (and law) as a result of specialization. In a society with little division of labor, and therefore based on mechanical solidarity, a crime against one is a crime against all, and consequently calls forth strong and swift punishment of the deviant. On the other hand, in an occupationally diverse society based upon organic solidarity, "a new motive enters the law—the restoration of the social system to a workable state and the repair, insofar as possible, of any damage done to the injured parties" (Martindale, 1960, p. 88). Thus, Durkheim distinguished between mechanically repressive, penal law on the one hand and organically restitutive, civil law on the other. In detailed historical and comparative studies, he demonstrated how increasing differentiation results in greater proportional weight being placed on restitutive law (i.e., domestic, contract, commercial, procedural, administrative, and constitutional law), thus qualitatively changing the relationship between individual and society.

Another important consequence of differentiation for Durkheim was the changed structure of social interaction. Because of increased moral density (i.e., an increase in the level of social interaction) and the fact that people engaged by and large in different but mutually interdependent tasks, the bases of social interaction perforce became more explicit and circumscribed. These two conditions, the increasing density and interdependence of social interaction, necessitated a new structural arrangement in order for society to function effectively. For Durkheim, the contract became "*par excellence*, the juridical expression of cooperation" (1964a, p. 123). In relations between buyers and sellers, employers and workers, tenants and landlords, lenders and borrowers, principals and agents, in short, between all parties convened to achieve defined and limited objectives, "the contract is the symbol of exchange" (1964a, p. 125). Thus, an important consequence of the division of labor was a shift toward more impersonal formal social relationships.

A significant, partially unresolved problem for Durkheim was the extremes to which differentiation or the division of labor could occur in society and the possible consequences this had for social cohesion. While he stated that in a highly differentiated society individuals were integrated through their mutual interdependence upon one another, and therefore it was necessary to cooperate contractually, nevertheless he foresaw the case where "the division of labor could not be pushed farther without becoming a source of disintegration" (1964a, p. 357).

> Functional diversity induces a moral diversity that nothing can prevent, and it is inevitable that one should grow as the other does. We know, moreover, why these two phenomena develop in parallel fashion. Collective sentiments become more and more impotent in holding together the centrifugal tendencies that the division of labor is said to engender, for these tendencies increase as labor is more divided, and, at the same time, collective sentiments are weakened. (Durkheim, 1964a, p. 361).

One consequence of moral diversity is what Durkheim called *anomie*, a state of normlessness wherein society no longer provides a common moral imperative for individual action, and individual citizens are consequently left to their own devices. Thus, differentiation can lead to the atomization and individuation of society.

Durkheim's solution to the dilemma of achieving societal cohesion within the condition of increasing differentiation may be found in his Preface to the second edition of the *Division of Labor* written in 1902. Here he sought to establish an intermediary social institution that would perform the same cohesive role of binding individuals to society in a complex differentiated society as the family and kinship group performed in simple traditional social systems.

Durkheim proposed that because of the functional importance of the economic sector to modern society, and because the division of labor is most pronounced in this area of social life, occupational groups or associations organized according to industry be instituted to provide "a moral power capable of containing individual egos, of maintaining a spirited sentiment of common solidarity in the consciousness of all the workers, [and] of preventing the law of the strongest from being brutally applied to industrial and commercial relations" (1964a, p. 10). Thus would a "community of interests" (i.e., occupational associations) replace the "community of blood" (i.e., the family) in preserving the overarching ethical and moral principles of society. Occupational associations would provide common reference points for autonomous individuals to coalesce around, and thereby to function lawfully and morally in society.[4] Durkheim argued further that as the economic division of labor increased, occupational associations, because they would be an integral part of this process and thus would have "a perpetuity at least equal to the family," would continue to serve as cohesive sources of individual attachment and solidarity.

It was Durkheim's thesis that as a result of the process of differentiation and the structural changes that it engendered, the lot of all individuals in society had improved greatly. Whereas the change from mechanical to organic solidarity stripped individuals of sure and certain knowledge of what was morally legitimate, at the same time it encouraged them to develop their own unique personalities and thus decide for themselves the difference between right and wrong. While Durkheim acknowledged potentially anomic factors being produced as a logical consequence of differentiation, he nevertheless contended that contractual duties and responsibilities mutually agreed upon in successive divisions of labor together with the moral force of occupational associations would permit the ideal of worldwide human solidarity to be realized.

Although it may be contended that Durkheim never did resolve satisfactorily the dilemma of a simultaneously coexisting differentiated *and* cohesive social system, nevertheless his scientific approach to the study of society as a constellation of social facts, which exert external constraints upon individuals is a central defining aspect of contemporary sociology. Also, as Box 4-2, **Urbanization, Technology, and the Division of Labor,** indicates, the issues that he originally raised remain an integral part of the discipline today.

Max Weber

The major question that directed Max Weber's sociological research was "Which social factors have brought about the rationalization of Western civilization?" (Mannheim, cited in Coser, 1971, p. 218). His most famous work, *The Protestant Ethic and the Spirit of Capitalism*, written in 1904–1905, was an attempt to identify those elements responsible for producing the industrial capitalist revolution and the highly organized and urbanized society in which he lived.

Unlike Marx and Durkheim, Weber sought the explanation for these vast changes in the ideas, thoughts, and values of his fellow human beings rather than in the structural conditions that constituted preindustrial societies. It was Weber's conviction that social conditions in many parts of the world were conducive to the rise of industrial capitalism, and yet it occurred in northern Europe and the United States. Why? He argued that while objective conditions are important, it is the attitudes and orientation of people and how they interpret these conditions that determine social action.

For Weber, the explanation lay in the particular religious orientation and way of life of certain "ascetic" branches of Protestantism (e.g., Calvinists, Baptists, Quakers, and Methodists). In contrast to other denominations, Weber contended that these sects had a common ethical approach to life that developed within their adherents both attitudinal and behavioral characteristics, which led fortuitously to

Figure 4.3 Max Weber (1864–1920)

the rise of capitalism (see Gerth and Mills, 1958, pp. 61–65; Parsons, 1966, pp. 249–256). For example, although these ascetic Protestants believed that ultimate salvation lay in the hands of an all-powerful God, nevertheless through word and deed (i.e., hard work, self-denial, and unwavering devotion to God) they could place themselves in a state of grace. Thus, they came to conceive of secular work as a "calling" in much the same way as they attributed importance to God's work, and consequently they approached their worldly activities with single-minded, methodical dedication. An extremely important by-product of this hard work, thrift, and devotion to "duty" was the accumulation of capital. In fact, one's piety

Box 4-2   # Urbanization, Technology, and the Division of Labor

As already described in this chapter, Durkheim hypothesized that a complex division of labor is caused by an increase in the rate of human interaction which in turn is produced by or related to increases in population size, population density (urbanization), transportation and communication networks, and technological development. In a partial test of this assertion, Gibbs and Martin (1962) assembled data on 45 countries in various stages of economic development throughout the world in order to examine the empirical foundation of the relationships involved. The measures they used are what follows:

Division of Labor   The proportional representation of the labor force in each of nine industrial groupings: (1) agriculture, forestry, hunting and fishing; (2) mining and quarrying; (3) manufacturing; (4) construction; (5) electricity, gas, water, and sanitary services; (6) commerce; (7) transportation, storage, and communication; (8) services; and (9) not classifiable elsewhere. The more even the distribution of workers across industrial groupings, the greater is the division of labor.* Of the 45 countries Gibbs and Martin examined, Australia had the highest division of labor (.83 on their scale) and Thailand the lowest (.27). The United States (.81) was seventh in the rank order and the United Kingdom (.77) was fifteenth.

Urbanization   The percentage of the total population in each country who live in standard metropolitan areas. The data (c. 1950) indicate that the United Kingdom was most urbanized (71.5%) and Pakistan the least (5.1%). The United States was the second most urbanized country (55.9%).

Technological development   Based on previous research studies, Gibbs and Martin claimed that "the best indicator of the level of technological development would appear to be the per capita consumption of energy" (1962, p. 672). Consequently, they used the estimated commercial consumption of energy expressed in metric tons of coal per capita. The highest consumer was the United States (7.74) and three countries (Haiti, Paraguay, and Thailand) were tied as the lowest commercial consumers (.02). The United Kingdom, third on the list, consumed 4.42 tons per capita.

Transportation and communication networks   Gibbs and Martin argued that while residents of rural areas and small towns may be more or less self-sufficient with regard to essential goods and services, a city "cannot possibly develop, within its own limits, [all] the materials necessary for its inhabitants to survive" (1962, p. 668). Consequently, its lifeline is the transportation and communication network that it establishes to provide these necessities. In attempting to measure both the extent of this network as well as the frequency with which it was used, the two researchers recorded the total dollar value of imports of a given country from all other countries (i.e., volume or frequency of use) and

*Gibbs and Martin note that although the categories are too gross to measure precisely the division of labor in each country, they are the best data available for making international comparisons.

the distance of these exporting countries from the importing country (i.e., extent of the network). The formula they developed revealed that remote New Zealand and Australia had the most extensive and utilized networks (3310 and 1457, respectively) while India's was least developed (34). The United Kingdom was fourth in the overall rank order (1188) and the United States was eighteenth (381).*

Gibbs and Martin found relatively high direct relationships among all the above variables. For example, the rank order correlation (rho) between urbanization and division of labor was .91, that is, the greater the urbanization of countries, the greater their division of labor. Similarly, the relationship between technological development and division of labor was .85, and between transportation and communication network development and division of labor it was .83.

In an attempt to control for the size of the urban units being compared, (and thus indirectly both population size and the rate of human interaction), the two sociologists further classified all of the countries according to city size. Thus, for each of the relationships described, they were able to compare the large cities of all countries to the medium-sized cities as well as to small towns and villages. The table that follows shows one result of this analysis. It indicates that the relationship between urbanization and division of labor is much stronger in large urban centers than it is in smaller localities. For example, in 1950, Australia, Israel, and the United States each had more than 40 percent of their populations living in cities of more than 100,000 inhabitants, while Costa Rica and Honduras did not have any cities of this size. Consequently, the larger the urban center, the greater is the impact of the overall national urbanization rate upon the division of labor.

RANK ORDER CORRELATIONS OF URBANIZATION AND DIVISION OF LABOR, CONTROLLING ON CITY SIZE

City size range	Correlations
100,000+	.87
50,000 to 99,999	.47
20,000 to 49,999	.66
10,000 to 19,999	.58
5,000 to 9,999	.29
2,000 to 4,999	.22

Source: Adapted from Gibbs and Martin, 1962, p. 676.

Gibbs and Martin, through their careful and systematic examination of all countries for which relevant and adequate data existed, empirically documented an important part of Durkheim's earlier theoretical work. Though the relationships they uncovered were correlational rather than causal, their analysis reveals that not only was Durkheim's reasoning theoretically sound but also that the issues he raised are still vitally important today.

*Gibbs and Martin state that one important weakness of their indicator is that it measures only networks *external* to countries, and therefore does not reveal the internal dispersion of goods and services that occurs *within* national boundaries. This deficiency, incidentally, may explain the relative position of the United States in the overall standing. However, once again they are limited in their international comparisons by the data available for this purpose.

came to be measured by one's prosperity. Gerth and Mills (1958, p. 447) summarize Weber's theory in a similar fashion:

> Ideas place premiums upon special psychic traits; through these premiums, and through habitual (and hence socially controlled) conduct, a special personality type is produced. Once fixed, sustained, and selected by organizations (sects), this personality type acts out conduct patterns. These patterns are religiously oriented but they lead to unforeseen economic results, namely, methodical workaday capitalism with its constant reinvestment of profits in productive enterprises.

While Weber did not deny that other factors were also important in the genesis of capitalism, he did claim that the Protestant ethic was a necessary condition (Parsons, 1966, p. 251). To demonstrate this point, he engaged in an extensive comparative analysis of the world's major religions in order to isolate those factors unique to Protestantism and thus instrumental to the development of capitalism. He discovered that with the exception of Protestantism each of the different theological doctrines in their pursuit of "salvation" had an interpretation that was not conducive to the rational exploitation of economic resources (see Bendix, 1968, pp. 496–497). Only Protestantism encouraged active resolution of mundane matters in the most efficient and systematic manner possible. For example, in comparing Protestantism with Confucianism, Weber stated that "while Calvinism was a doctrine of rational *mastery over* the world, Confucianism was a doctrine of rational *adaptation to* the world" (cited in Parsons, 1966, p. 254).

As a result of his cross-cultural and historical analyses, Weber was impressed with the variety of institutional arrangements by which people conducted their lives and the manner in which power was exercised within societies. However, once again he was struck by what appeared to him as the unique rationality of the capitalist system and the particular authority relations that characterized it. In his formal study of authority, Weber discerned three basic grounds of legitimacy to govern: rational-legal, traditional, and charismatic. Of these, he wrote at length about rational-legal authority, how it had largely replaced traditional authority as the basis of Western civilization, and how it pervaded most social institutions and associations that comprised capitalist society.

> In the case of legal authority, obedience is owed to the legally established impersonal order. It extends to the persons exercising the authority of office under it only by virtue of the formal legality of their commands and only within the scope of authority of the office. (Weber, in Parsons, 1964, p. 328)

For Weber, the organizational apparatus most suited to the administration of rational-legal authority was a bureaucracy.

> ... the purely bureaucratic type of administrative organization ... is, from a purely technical point of view, capable of attaining the highest degree of efficiency and is in this sense formally the most rational known means of carrying out imperative control [i.e., authority][5] over human beings. It is superior to any other form in precision, in stability, in the stringency of its discipline, and in its reliability. It thus makes possible a particularly high degree of calculability of results for the heads of the organization and for those acting in relation to it. ...

> However much people may complain about the 'evils of bureaucracy,' it would be sheer illusion to think for a moment that continuous administrative work can be carried out in any field except by means of officials working in offices. The whole pattern of everyday life is cut to fit this framework. For bureaucratic administration is, other things being equal, always from a formal technical point of view, the most rational type. For the needs of mass administration today, it is completely indispensable. The choice is only that between bureaucracy and dilettantism in the field of administration. (Weber in Parsons, 1964, p. 337)

Weber was convinced of the technical superiority of bureaucracy to accomplish explicitly defined complex goals, yet his prognosis for bureaucratized society was considerably less glowing. He speculated that "cumulative technological rationalization" (Gerth and Mills, 1958, p. 51) through its oppressive might will eat away at and ultimately erode completely idiosyncratic individual freedom. In this sense, he struck a chord similar to Marx's theme of alienation. However, whereas Marx contended that the capitalist system had expropriated workers from the means of production and thereby was responsible for their alienation, Weber argued that it is not capitalism *per se* that produces this estrangement but "any system of rationalized and centrally coordinated production" (Coser, 1971, p. 232). Thus, for Weber, Marx's "alienation" is simply a special case of a more general phenomenon—the rationalization and bureaucratization of *all* aspects of society (be it capitalist or socialist), including not only economic and political institutions but also science, law, religion, and even music (see Coser, 1971, pp. 230–234).

> The world of modernity, Weber stressed over and over again, has been deserted by the gods. Man has chased them away and has rationalized and made calculable and predictable what in an earlier age had seemed governed by chance, but also by feeling, passion, and commitment, by personal appeal and personal fealty, by grace and by the ethics of charismatic heroes. (Coser, 1971, p. 233)

Thus, Weber posed what appears to be an insoluble dilemma for individuals in contemporary bureaucratized and rationalized society. On the one hand, modern citizenry, through their rejection of a traditional, yet stable and secure, institutional framework based on "the sanctity of immemorial traditions," have achieved a system in which benefit and opportunity theoretically are available to all, and individual rights are protected under an objective and universalistic rational-legal constitution. However, the necessarily impersonalized and formalized manner by which these benefits, opportunities, and rights are extended strips individuals of their integrity as individuals. Instead, they are evaluated and treated within a rational system according to various relevant, functionally specific attributes and characteristics which they possess. According to Weber, it is highly likely that the impartial, "just," and very disciplined system that we have created will result in the disintegration of our own humanity.

As a result of this structural dilemma of a system that is rationally designed to protect individual freedom at the same time that it diminishes individuality and thereby freedom, Weber argued that the system itself is inherently unstable (see Parsons, 1964, pp. 78–86). He foresaw the possibility of a charismatic (and therefore uniquely individual) leader sparking a large-scale social movement away from rationality and toward eventually a more traditionally based mode of life. Whereas Weber thought that contemporary bureaucratized society was technically and organizationally superior, nevertheless because of the reasons advanced above he also acknowledged that it was subject to severe structural strain.

To summarize, for Max Weber industrial capitalism was a highly rationalized and organized system of production and consumption that arose almost serendipitously as a result of the ethical predispositions and life-style of certain ascetic Protestant sects. It was Weber's thesis that these Protestants through their particular interpretation of what constituted morally appropriate behavior devoted themselves systematically and rationally to master their environment, and in the process accumulated capital, technological expertise, and an organizational apparatus, that transformed society and brought about the industrial revolution.

While Weber was tremendously impressed by the many accomplishments achieved as a result of rationalization and bureaucratization, and by the fact that the institutionalized administrative framework of society was technically superior to any other form previously known, nevertheless he was pessimistic in his outlook as far as the consequences that this type of society would have for the expression of individual free will.

Weber's impact on contemporary sociology is ongoing. Although his analyses were incomplete at the time of his death, and certainly not correct in every respect (see Box 4-3, **The Unintended Consequences of Bureaucracy**), nevertheless his overall theory of the structural problems underlying contemporary society is more accurate in its determination than either of those offered by Marx or Durkheim. Perhaps part of the reason for this lies in Weber's assiduous concern with method. As a sociologist, it was his foremost goal to provide an objective yet interpretive understanding and causal explanation of social structure and process.

RATIONAL ORGANIZATION, TECHNOLOGICAL MASTERY, AND THE INDIVIDUAL IN INDUSTRIAL SOCIETY

From the foregoing analyses, several common elements and themes emerge. Although Marx, Durkheim, and Weber focused on different aspects of the industrial revolution and proposed different underlying causal models, nevertheless each was most concerned to explain what had happened, how it had come about, and what consequences these widespread technological and social changes would have for both individual and society. Therefore, in an attempt to distil the cumulative wisdom of these three great theorists, it is instructive to concentrate on those points and issues on which they converged. On the assumption that if a particular theme was raised by each of the three, then that theme is crucial to our understanding of the great transformation, we will now try to lay bare these commonalities.

Box 4-3 # The Unintended Consequences of Bureaucracy

In his extensive historical study and analysis of bureaucracy, Weber concluded that while this organizational form ultimately may be dysfunctional for society in which individuals would be trapped in an "iron cage" of their own creation (i.e., "each man becomes a little cog in the machine"), nevertheless he was unwavering in his assessment of bureaucracy as the most technically superior organizational form to accomplish complex goals.

Specifying precisely the criteria that characterize the "ideal type" of bureaucracy, Weber argued that this particular constellation of organizational characteristics was "the most rational known means of carrying out imperative control over human beings." To the extent that an organization has a specialized division of labor, hierarchical levels of authority, written documentation and record keeping, selection based on expert qualifications and training, commitment to office, and general rules and regulations designed to apply to any exigency that might arise, Weber asserted that it has "technical superiority over any other form of organization. The fully developed bureaucratic mechanism compares with other organizations exactly as does the machine with the nonmechanical modes of production" (Weber in Gerth and Mills, 1958, p. 214).*

Subsequent to Weber's death in 1920, other sociologists, trained in the principles of classical Weberian bureaucracy, researched in detail actual bureaucratic organizations in action in an attempt to determine the empirical foundation of Weber's theory (see, for example, Blau, 1955; Gouldner, 1954; Merton, 1969 [1940]; Selznick, 1949). What they found permitted this new generation of sociologists not only to document the technical merits of functioning bureaucracies but also to identify the structural weaknesses inherent in this organizational form. Following is a description of Robert Merton's research on "Bureaucratic Structure and Personality" (1969 [1940]) and some of the unintended consequences of bureaucracy.

According to Merton's interpretation of Weber, bureaucratic organizational control is achieved through the implementation of and strict adherence to a systematic code of rules and regulations designed to accomplish organizational objectives.

> Within the structure of hierarchically arranged authority, the activities of "trained and salaried experts" are governed by general, abstract, and clearly defined rules which preclude the necessity for the issuance of specific instructions for each specific case. The generality of the rules requires the constant use of *categorization*, whereby individual problems and cases are classified on the basis of designated criteria and are treated accordingly (Merton, 1969, p. 48).

The *intended consequences* of this body of rules are reliability and predictability of organizational behavior wherein members perform their roles according to impersonal, standardized operating procedures. Furthermore, to the extent that bureaucrats follow

*See Gerth and Mills, 1958, pp. 196–198, for Weber's specification of the characteristics that constitute an "ideal type" of bureaucracy.

these general rules, they can justify their individual actions, which in turn increases reliability and predictability. Thus is the loop closed in continual and mutually reinforcing behavior.

However, in seeking empirical corroboration for these theoretically intended consequences of bureaucracy as described by Weber, Merton also discovered a complex set of *unintended consequences* in operation.

If the bureaucracy is to operate successfully, it must attain a high degree of reliability of behavior, an unusual degree of conformity with prescribed patterns of action. Hence, the fundamental importance of discipline which may be as highly developed in a religious or economic bureaucracy as in the army. Discipline can be effective only if the ideal patterns are buttressed by strong sentiments which entail devotion to one's duties, a keen sense of the limitation of one's authority and competence, and methodical performance of routine activities. . . .

At the moment, it suffices to observe that in order to ensure discipline (the necessary reliability of response), these sentiments are often more intense than is technically necessary. . . . Adherence to the rules, originally conceived as a means, becomes transformed into an end-in-itself; there occurs the familiar process of *displacement of goals* whereby "an instrumental value becomes a terminal value." Discipline, readily interpreted as conformance with regulations, whatever the situation, is seen not as a measure designed for specific purposes but becomes an immediate value in the life-organization of the bureaucrat. This emphasis, resulting from the displacement of the original goals, develops into rigidities and an inability to adjust readily. Formalism, even ritualism, ensues with an unchallenged insistence upon punctilious adherence to formalized procedures. This may be exaggerated to the point where primary concern with conformity to the rules interferes with the achievement of the purposes of the organization, in which case we have the familiar phenomenon of the technicism or red tape of the official. An extreme product of this process of displacement of goals is the bureaucratic virtuoso, who never forgets a single rule binding his action and hence is unable to assist many of his clients. (Merton, 1969, pp. 51–52)

According to March and Simon (1958, pp. 37–41), who reanalyzed the work of Merton, the unintended (and undesirable) consequences of bureaucracy also form a self-perpetuating closed loop, thus providing a structurally inherent dysfunctional counterpart to the functional loop initially proposed by Weber. Their schematic representation of these two loops is reproduced on the next page.

As a result of careful and systematic empirical observation of actual private and public bureaucracies in action, Merton and other sociologists who followed Weber were able to demonstrate both the intended as well as the unintended results of bureaucratic organization. While much of their work supported Weber's earlier analysis, it also revealed that there are structural contradictions inherent in bureaucracy as an organizational type. The uncritical assessment provided by Weber required substantial modification, as those of us who have confronted Merton's ritualistic bureaucratic official will testify.

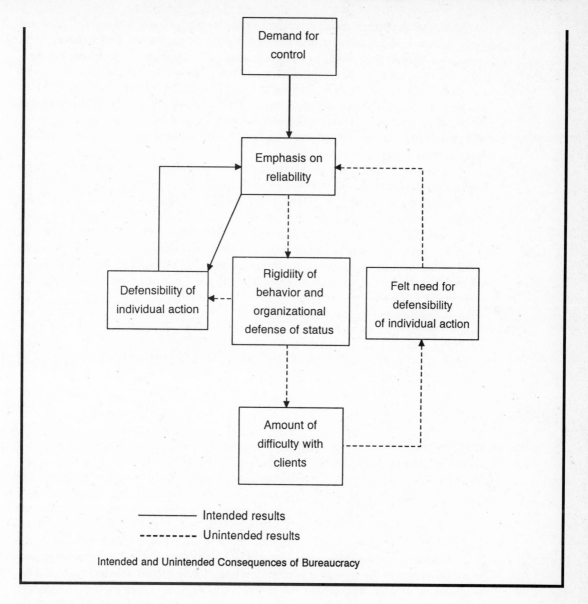

Intended and Unintended Consequences of Bureaucracy

Rational Organization

It is widely acknowledged that the move toward the systematic organization of society in all of its aspects preceded the major technological innovations that have been associated with the industrial revolution (Mantoux, 1961). Whether it was the expansion of maritime navigation and consequently commercial trade, the establishment of a money economy in the mid-seventeenth century, the increasing democratization of the political and legal structures, agricultural reform and enclosure, the systematic organization of the institutions of science and education, the continual economic differentiation of society, particularly among the growing middle classes, the expansion and improvement in transportation systems and the mass rural–urban migration, or the development of the factory system of production, the rational application of organizational principles in all sectors of society resulted in the development of a more or less integrated infrastructure capable of sustaining and promoting the additional vast changes that were to follow. On this point, all three theorists were in agreement and wrote extensively, although Marx did give particular weight to the economic sector in bringing about these wider organizational developments.

The overall theme of rational organization as a major factor in the distinctive evolution of Western civilization is explicit in the work of Durkheim and Weber. For Durkheim, increased horizontal differentiation (division of labor), and for Weber, increased horizontal and vertical differentiation (bureaucratization) produced qualitative changes within society (see Table 2.1). Emphasis on the rational organization of social structures and processes to accomplish specific goals resulted in a more centralized, interdependent, and formalized society wherein there were numerical as well as proportional increases in contractually limited secondary relationships. Various courses of action were objectively evaluated against the norms of utility, efficiency, and control. Predictability of outcome expanded beyond tomorrow and next season to the more distant forseeable future as planning and a future orientation become major preoccupations. In short, the industrial revolution saw the coordination of human activity within specified space and time parameters on a scale never before even imagined.

Technological Mastery

Closely interwoven with the theme of rational organization is the equally important feature of technological mastery. Central in the writings of Marx, Durkheim, and Weber is the continual struggle of humankind against a harsh and hostile natural environment. For each theorist, the industrial revolution marked a technological threshold in which for the first time the outcome of this human–environment struggle was not a foregone conclusion. Self-determination and expanding horizons replaced fatalistic acceptance as artisans, entrepreneurs, and practitioners of all types achieved technical feats previously deemed impossible. Marx marveled at the technological accomplishments of the capitalist system; Durkheim maintained that technological expertise was largely responsible for the division of labor; and Weber analytically detailed the process of "cumulative technological rationalization." Each of them greeted with awe the technological mastery of the age.

Reduced mortality rates, an improved standard of living, higher agricultural yields through chemistry, mechanically driven machine-based systems of manufacture, even the shrinking of the earth's surface through increasingly efficient and novel networks of transportation and communication: This was the evidence that verified the technoscientific might of modern humanity. And when this newly won technical power was channeled into the equally powerful conduit of rational administrative organization, the impact upon individual and society was truly revolutionary.

The Individual in Industrial Society

While Marx was critical of capitalist industrial society and sought its overthrow, Durkheim was enthusiastic about the changes brought about by the great transformation, and Weber simply chronicled these changes with the detached view of the scientist. Nevertheless, each was most concerned about the impact the industrial revolution (i.e., rational organization and technological mastery) had upon the relationship between individuals and society. Each posed severe structural problems that would have to be confronted if individual and society were to function in mutually supportive interaction. In large part, we are faced with these same structural problems today.

At the heart of the problem is a profound paradox. On one hand, the forces of rational organization and technological mastery have empowered individuals, freeing them from their physiological limitations and, consequently, there has been improvement for all. The overall yield of the industrial revolution, both tangible and intangible, was not only greater than that experienced in any other social system, it also, in part because of the size of the yield, was more widely diffused throughout society than in any other time in recorded history. Whether one looks at the actual products produced, the wages and salaries received, the working conditions experienced, or the general all-encompassing legislative and judicial rights and freedoms extended, there was a comprehensive improvement, both absolutely and relatively, in the quality of life of individuals in society.

On the other hand, the forces of rational organization and technological mastery have enfeebled individuals, subjecting them to the dictates of impersonal mechanistic systems designed to accomplish objectives over which they have little control or understanding. A constant theme, particularly in the writings of Marx and Weber, is that individuals in industrial society are alienated. They do not participate as unique beings; instead, they are standardized, interchangeable cogs in a well-oiled, efficient machine.

Hence the paradox and the dilemma. Through rational organization and technological mastery, we have achieved greater control over the natural environment and have improved our material well-being, but in the process we have simply substituted one set of dependences for another. While we have decreased our dependence upon the natural environment, we have become increasingly dependent upon the artificial (i.e., organizational and technological) environment we have created. The costs of this dependence for individuals include loss of intimacy, spontaneity, idiosyncrasy, heterogeneity, and individuality, because the by-products of industrialization are predictability, control, standardization, formalization, and centralization. Thus, while there are benefits for individuals in an industrialized society, there are also substantial measurable costs.

Marx, Durkheim, and Weber were among the first to document, empirically and systematically, the origins, conditions, and consequences of the industrial revolution. While they differed in their ideologies, conceptions, and modes of analysis, they did agree on certain themes. What they revealed indicated that the great transformation was both quantitative and qualitative in its impact upon individual and society.

While each highlighted the problems engendered by industrial society, none proposed an adequate solution. Consequently, the problems remain.

Throughout the remainder of this book, as we now focus on the contemporary scene, we will be reminded of these problems as they are manifested at all levels of society. As a concluding note, perhaps it is appropriate once more to reflect upon what Herbert Simon (1987, p. 11) had to say about technological revolutions:

> Technological revolutions are not something that "happen" to us. We make them for better or for worse. Our task is not to peer into the future . . . , but to shape the future that we want to have—a future that will create new possibilities for human learning, including, perhaps most important of all, new possibilities for learning to understand ourselves.

SUMMARY

4.1 After the technological and social revolutions, there was an attempt by various social theorists to investigate, understand, and explain the great industrial transformation. This period marked the beginning of sociology as a discipline of study.

4.2 Important problems hindering the scientific study of society by early social investigators included: (a) a severe lack of systematically accumulated social data; (b) the virtual absence of any data (aside from births, deaths, and marriages) on the large majority of the population; (c) the interference of investigators' values in the "objective" description of events; (d) crude methods of social scientific research; and (e) lack of public support.

4.3 For Karl Marx (1818–1883), the industrial revolution ushered in a new type of capitalist society in which two major classes were formed based on ownership of the means of production. The numerically small bourgeoisie owned the machine-based factory system of production while the vast, oppressed proletariat had only their own labor to sell.

4.4 According to Marx, the proletariat were alienated or dehumanized because they were forced to yield to the dictates of the capitalists; to suffer the division of labor in which they were appendages to industrial machinery and not responsible for creating entire products; and to endure the factory system of discipline and regulation.

4.5 The final revolution in which the proletariat would overthrow the capitalists and form a classless society would come about through the increasing concentration of capital and the centralization of power. Whereas both these latter conditions have occurred, the revolution that Marx so desperately supported has yet to happen.

4.6 For Emile Durkheim (1858–1917), the industrial revolution, sparked by *The Division of Labor in Society*, came about as a result of population growth and increased population density and social interaction. These factors caused formerly self-sufficient and insulated homogeneous communities to become organized into interdependent, cooperative, occupationally diverse regional networks.

4.7 In turn, Durkheim argued, increasing differentiation or division of labor resulted in other structural changes. For example, individuals were now linked to society through their unique, individual contributions (organic solidarity); societal norms were supportive of individual differences (restitutive law); and the bases of social interaction became increasingly explicit and circumscribed (contractual).

4.8   A major problem for Durkheim was that functional diversity led to moral diversity or *anomie* (normlessness), a condition under which society could no longer provide a common moral imperative for individual action. To prevent this from occurring, Durkheim proposed the establishment of various occupational associations whose purpose would be to provide common reference points and thus serve as cohesive sources of individual attachment and solidarity.

4.9   For Max Weber (1864–1920), the industrial revolution arose almost fortuitously as a result of the values and ethical approach to life of certain Protestant sects. The adherents believed that if they worked hard and were thrifty and dutiful in their obligations they would place themselves in a state of grace. Their highly disciplined and organized behavior resulted in them accumulating so much capital and technological expertise that they caused the industrial revolution.

4.10   Weber devoted most of his working life to determining which factors brought about the rationalization of Western civilization. To this end, he engaged in a massive study of bureaucracy. For Weber, a bureaucratic organization was the most efficient rational means of achieving complex objectives.

4.11   Although Weber was convinced of the technical superiority of bureaucracy, his outlook for contemporary bureaucratized society was pessimistic. He thought that ultimately the rationalization and bureaucratization of *all* aspects of society would erode individuality and free will, resulting in the disintegration of our own humanity.

4.12   This chapter concluded with a presentation of those features common to the work of Marx, Durkheim, and Weber in their respective examinations of the industrial revolution. Each theorist dwelled at length on the twin themes of rational organization and technological mastery as the principal elements of the industrial revolution. Each noted also that while these factors contributed substantially to the material well-being of both individuals and society, they also were a major source of individual estrangement and alienation.

NOTES

1. It was Auguste Comte (1798–1857) who formally coined the term *sociology* to describe the area of "social physics" in which he was currently working. See Coser, 1971, pp. 2–41, for a biography.
2. Recent events in the Communist-bloc countries (e.g., the introduction of a market economy) forcefully demonstrate Marx's basically utopian conception of human nature.
3. For an excellent discussion of the *Division of Labor* and the process of differentiation see Schnore, 1958. This article is contained in a special commemorative issue of the *American Journal of Sociology* marking the 100th anniversary of Durkheim's birth.
4. Durkheim's conception of occupational association does not correspond to contemporary trade or industrial unions whose main task is to secure fair wages and working conditions for their members. Rather Durkheim was referring more to historical guilds that in addition to establishing the contractual relations surrounding work also provided a source of social solidarity (e.g., "safeguarding their common interests" through religious observances, celebratory ritual, and mutual aid and support).
5. The actual term that Weber used was *Herrschaft*. It has been variously translated as "imperative control" or "authority." See Parsons, 1964, p. 152, fn 83.

Chapter
5

Industrialization in the World Today

The gap between them (the "South") and us is so wide that we had better manage a change in our economic relations with them before we find it thrust upon us.

Pierre Trudeau, Canadian Prime Minister, at the Western Economic Summit meeting, 1981.
Cited in Crow and Thomas, 1983, p. 71

*I*n the 200 years since the industrial revolution in England, the process of industrialization has had perhaps more impact upon all the nations in the world than any other complex set of forces. In this chapter, we will apply the dimensions and measures of industrialization developed in Chapter 2 to all countries for which there are sufficient data. Similar to the exercise in Chapter 3 in which we measured the extent of industrialization at various times in Great Britain and the United States, this examination will allow us to establish a rank ordering of the industrial status of all countries in the world today. Then, using this industrial rank order, we will look at the degree to which industrialization is related to other structural features of society (e.g., national output, urbanization, the development of an infrastructure, and the quality of life for individual citizens). Similar to the social revolution described in Chapter 3, we will note that there are strong relationships between industrialization and these structural correlates. The inescapable conclusion is that industrialization has produced inequities among nations and among people on a scale never before experienced.

In the latter part of the chapter, we will examine various theories of economic and social development. Following the formulations initially put forward by Marx, Durkheim, and Weber (see Chapter 4), modern theorists have attempted to explain and to place in perspective the process of industrialization as it has evolved in the interim period. This examination also highlights current barriers to industrialization in less-developed countries and strategies of development as these nations attempt to reap the material advantages that accompany this complex process.

DIMENSIONS AND MEASURES OF INDUSTRIALIZATION

Table 5.1 is a rank ordering of 49 countries according to four explicit measures of industrialization. Derived from the dimensions of industrialization discussed in Chapter 2 (see Table 2.3), these four indicators permit us to make a composite national assessment of industrialization in the world today. The four indicators measure the proportion of national output that is contributed by manufacturing, the percent of a country's labor force involved in industrial production, the technological skill and organizational base of national labor forces, and the amount of energy consumed in each country is devoted to commercial purposes.[1]

The 49 countries were selected from the 128 listed in the *1987 World Development Report* (see World Bank, 1987) for which it was possible to locate data on each of these four measures.[2] Usually it is true that the more developed the nation, the more available and adequate are the data pertaining to it; however, the listing in Table 5.1 is fairly representative of all countries with the exception of the Eastern-bloc, nonmarket economies, for which data are extremely limited.

You will note that not only are the countries individually rank ordered from highly industrialized to nonindustrialized, but also there are five separate groups of nations based on how many of the criteria of industrialization each country satisfies. For example, all of the 10 countries in Group 1 are industrialized according to each of the four measures of industrialization specified, while none of the nine countries listed in Group 5 satisfies any of these same requirements.

Measure 1, Manufacturing as a Percent of Gross Domestic Product (GDP), reflects the proportional contribution of the manufacturing sector to national output. The range is from a high of 31% in West Germany to a low of 5% in Nepal; the median value or center point of the distribution is 18%. For a country to be industrialized on this dimension, at least 15% of its gross domestic product must come from manufacturing. This arbitrary though reasonable cutoff point is derived from an analysis conducted by Müller (1988, pp. 69–70). For 128 countries over three separate time periods (1970, 1975, 1980), Müller found that on average (mean and median) the percentage share of manufacturing to the GDP was between 14 and 16%. Thus, given these figures and the premise that manufacturing is an integral aspect of industrialization, 15% represents a reasonable operational criterion.

Table. 5.1 SELECTED COUNTRIES RANKED ACCORDING TO FOUR MEASURES OF INDUSTRIALIZATION

	Measures of industrialization			
	1	2	3	4
	Manufacturing as a percent of GDP (1985)[1]	Percent of labor force in industry (1980)[2]	Percent of professional & technical workers in labor force (c. 1980)[3]	Commercial energy consumption (kg) per capita (1985)[4]
Group 1. Countries industrialized according to all four measures				
West Germany	31%	44%	14%	4451 kg
Sweden	21	33	27	6482
Finland	23	35	17	4589
France	25	35	16	3673
Belgium	23	36	12[5]	4666
United States	20	31	15	7278
Austria	28	41	12	3217
New Zealand	24	33	15	3823
Australia	17	32	15	5116
United Kingdom	22	38	12[5]	3603
Group 2. Countries industrialized according to three of four measures				
Canada	16%	29%	15%	9224 kg
Kuwait	8	32	16	4569
Trinidad and Tobago	7	39	10	3641
Japan	30	34	9	3116
Singapore	24	38	9	2165
South Africa	23	35	4[5]	2184
Venezuela	21	28	10	2409
Group 3. Countries industrialized according to two of four measures				
Norway	14%	29%	20%	8920 kg
Greece	18	29	10	1841
Libya	5	29	11[5]	3042
Group 4. Countries industrialized according to one of four measures				
South Korea	28%	27%	5%	1241 kg
Jordan	12	26	12	771
Peru	20	18	8	543
Ecuador	19	20	6[5]	720
Turkey	25	17	4	712
Philippines	25	16	6	255
Panama	9	18	11	634

Table. 5.1   SELECTED COUNTRIES RANKED ACCORDING TO FOUR MEASURES OF INDUSTRIALIZATION
(continued)

	Measures of industrialization			
	1	**2**	**3**	**4**
	Manufacturing as a percent of GDP (1985)[1]	**Percent of labor force in industry (1980)[2]**	**Percent of professional & technical workers in labor force (c. 1980)[3]**	**Commercial energy consumption (kg) per capita (1985)[4]**
Nicaragua	27	16	5[5]	259
Morocco	17	25	6	237
Colombia	18	24	2	755
Dominican Republic	19	15	6	372
Zimbabwe	29	11	4	427
Paraguay	16	21	5	281
Tunisia	14	36	2	546
Pakistan	20	16	3	218
Thailand	20	10	2	343
El Salvador	16	19	4	186
Sri Lanka	15	14	6	139
India	17	13	3	201
Rwanda	16	3	1	43

Group 5. Countries not industrialized according to four measures

Hondurus	14%	16%	4%[5]	201 kg
Indonesia	14	13	3	219
Ghana	11	18	4[5]	131
North Yemen	7	9	4	117
Cameroon	12	8	2	145
Sudan	9	8	3[5]	61
Bangladesh	8	6	2	43
Nepal	5	1	4	17
Mali	7	2	2	25

		1	**2**	**3**	**4**
Median Values	*(N)*				
Group 1	(10)	23%	35%	15%	4520 kg
Group 2	(7)	21 ⎫ 17	34 ⎫ 30	10 ⎫ 10	3116 ⎫ 3079
Group 3	(3)	14 ⎭	29 ⎭	11 ⎭	3042 ⎭
Group 4	(20)	18	18	5	358
Group 5	(9)	9	8	3	117
All countries	(49)	18%	24%	6%	712 kg.

Notes for Table 5.1 on next page.

Examination of Table 5.1 reveals that two-thirds of the countries listed (33 of 49) meet this criterion of industrialization, yet only one-fifth (10) are fully industrialized according to all four measures. Of those 20 countries which are industrialized on only one of the four measures (Group 4), fully 85% (17) achieve industrial status based on this criterion. A casual scanning of the countries in Group 4 indicates that although manufacturing contributes to the GDP in proportions similar to the countries listed in Group 1, most Group 4 nations are not industrialized in the usual sense attributed to this term.

Manufacture, according to the dictionary definition, is "the making of goods and articles by hand *or* by machinery" (emphasis added). Most of the countries listed in Group 4 manufacture goods by traditional methods, which have varied little over successive generations. Consequently, although manufacture is indeed an essential component of industrialization, there is considerably more involved in the process. Because industrialization is multidimensional, it therefore cannot be measured by only one indicator.[3]

Measure 2, Percent of Labor Force in Industry, indicates the proportion of all workers who are engaged in industrial activity. Industry, according to the World Bank (1987, p. 272), includes the manufacturing sector as well as mining, construction, and those employed in providing utilities. Again, West Germany has the highest percentage (44%) and Nepal the lowest (1%), with the median for all countries listed being 24%. For a country to be industrialized on this measure, at least 30% of its labor force must be involved in industry. The rationale for this particular cutoff point also comes from Müller's analysis (1988, pp. 44–45). He found that over the same three time periods he measured previously, the mean percentage of industrial workers in all nations was slightly below 30% while the median was marginally above (32%). Thus, 30% would ppear to be a reasonable point to distinguish between industrial and nonindustrial status on this measure.

Measure 2 is the most stringent indicator of industrialization in that only 16 of the 49 countries (33%) have at least 30% of industrial workers in their labor forces. For example, Canada, a member of the group of seven leading Western industrial nations,[4] has only 29% of its labor force in industry, and thus, according to

---

[1]World Bank, 1987, pp. 206–207. For a country to be industrialized according to this measure, manufacturing must contribute at least 15 percent toward the gross domestic product (GDP).

[2]World Bank, 1987, pp. 264–265. According to the World Bank (1987, p. 272), "industry comprises mining, manufacturing, construction, and electricity, water, and gas." For a country to be industrialized according to this measure, at least 30 percent of the labor force must be in industry.

[3]Müller, 1988. "The professional, technical, and related workers are defined as the categories 0–1 of the *International Standard Classification of Occupations* (ISCO-1968)" (Müller, 1988, p. 47). For a country to be industrialized according to this measure, at least 10 percent of the labor force must be professional and technical workers.

[4]World Bank, 1987, pp. 218–219. The figures in this column include all commercial types of energy consumption converted into kilograms of oil equivalent. For a country to be industrialized according to this measure, at least 2000 kilograms per capita must be consumed annually.

[5]Figures are for c.1970.

the four measures applied here, falls just short of full industrial status (Group 2). Part of the reason for this no doubt can be attributed to the fact that while Canada is resource rich and heavily involved in the primary sector, its manufacturing base is relatively weak as the data on Measure 1 indicate. However, another factor to be considered is that industrial nations such as the United States and Canada are becoming increasingly less involved in the manufacture of goods and more active in the provision of services and the production and distribution of information. This is the move toward postindustrialism that was mentioned in Chapter 1 and that we will discuss more fully in Chapter 6.

Measure 3, Percent of Professional and Technical Workers in the Labor Force, is an indicator of the increasing specialization and technoscientific development that is an important part of the industrialization process. It is also indicative of an organizational support structure. Again following Müller's analysis, the lower limit established on this measure in order to merit industrial status is 10% (see Müller, 1988, pp. 47–48). Nineteen of the 49 countries (39%) meet this criterion, although surprisingly Japan at 8.6% is not among them and thus falls into Group 2.[5] In industrialized Sweden, fully 27% of the labor force is in this highly educated and specialized group of workers, while in less technically developed nations barely 1 or 2% make up this category. The median for all 49 countries is only 6%.

Measure 4, Commercial Energy Consumption per Capita, reflects the driving force of industrial activity as well as its technical and organizational base. Consequently, it has become the single most used measure of industrialization. Given that "total worldwide energy consumption in 1980 was 8,705,911,000 tons of coal equivalent, or 2,019 kg per capita" (Kurian, 1984, p. 226), and that "85 per cent of the world's oil consumption takes place in the industrialized world" (Brandt Report, 1980, p. 226), countries in which per capita consumption is at least 2000 kilograms of oil equivalent per year are operationally defined here as being industrial according to this measure.

With the exception of Greece, all countries in Groups 1 to 3 are industrialized on this measure, while none is industrialized in the remaining two groups. The highest per capita consumption is in Canada (9224 kg), and Nepal, with 17 kilograms per capita, consumes the least amount of commercial energy. As the Report of the Independent Commission on International Development Issues (see Brandt Report, 1980) has documented, the use of energy throughout the world is tremendously uneven.

> The consumption of energy per head in industrialized countries compared to middle-income and low-income countries is in the proportion of 100:10:1. One American uses as much commercial energy as two Germans or Australians, three Swiss or Japanese, six Yugoslavs, nine Mexicans or Cubans, 16 Chinese, 19 Malaysians, 53 Indians or Indonesians, 109 Sri Lankans, 438 Malians, or 1072 Nepalese. All the fuel used by the Third World for all purposes is only slightly more than the amount of gasoline the North burns to move its automobiles. (Brandt Report, 1980, p. 162)

The bottom portion of Table 5.1 presents the median values on each measure of industrialization for all five groups of nations. On average, for the 10 fully industrialized nations in Group 1, manufacturing contributes 23% to their gross domestic products; 35% of their labor forces are in industry; 15% are professional and technical workers; and they use 4520 kilograms of oil equivalent per capita for commercial purposes. These fully industrialized countries are located in northern Europe, North America, and Oceania.

As well as presenting the separate medians for Groups 2 and 3, I have also computed their combined medians in that there are only ten countries in both groups, and thus the medians of these groups individually, particularly Group 3, are unstable. The combined medians indicate that on average the countries in Groups 2 and 3 achieve industrial status on each of the measures of industrialization, although not to the same degree as the countries in Group 1. The countries in Groups 2 and 3 consist of nations generally acknowledged as being industrialized (e.g., Japan, Canada, and Norway), newly industrializing countries (e.g., Singapore, South Africa, Venezuela, and Greece), and high-income, oil exporting countries (e.g., Kuwait, Trinidad and Tobago, and Libya).[6]

The medians for Group 4 reveal that only on one measure (manufacturing as a percent of GDP) are these countries industrialized. Aside from the traditional manufacturing base of these nations, there is little indication for the most part that their economies are geared to industrial activity.[7] Compared to Group 1, these 20 countries have only half the percentage of industrial workers in the labor force, one-third as many professional and technical workers, and they consume less than one-tenth as much commercial energy. Group 4 nations are located predominantly in Latin America, Asia, and Africa.

The nine countries comprising Group 5 are not industrialized on any of the four measures presented, their median values being only approximately half of the Group 4 nations. These rural economies have anywhere from 56% to 93% of their labor forces employed in agriculture, and from one-quarter to one-half of their gross domestic products are gained from agricultural commodities (World Bank, 1987, pp. 206, 264). They are located primarily in Africa and southern Asia.

As we discussed in Chapter 3, the original industrial revolution was revolutionary not only because of the radical changes it produced in what people did for a living and how their national wealth was created, but also because it transformed the broader social structure. During the 200 years since the industrial revolution, the process of industrialization has expanded and developed in some countries while barely being noticeable in others. Consequently, the impact of this complex process has produced changes within the world on a scale never before even imagined, and at the same time it has resulted in structural inequalities among nations that, although already monumentally large, are still increasing. It is to these social structural repercussions of industrialization that we now turn.

STRUCTURAL CORRELATES OF INDUSTRIALIZATION

In describing various countries and regions of the world, certain terms have come to be adopted, first by official agencies such as the United Nations and national governments, and then more generally by scholars, journalists, and those interested in making sense out of international relations. For example, the terms "North" and "South" were coined by Willy Brandt in his Report of the Independent Commission on International Development Issues (see Brandt Report, 1980). In the report is a map of the world with a bold line dividing it into two parts. In Chapter 1, I introduced the terms "more-developed countries" (MDCs) and "less-developed countries" (LDCs) which are categories created by the United Nations to classify all countries in the world. The resulting classification scheme mirrors the North–South divide. Following World War II, the term *Third World* was coined by the movement for Afro-Asian solidarity to distinguish nonaligned countries from the capitalist Western nations (First World) and the Communist Eastern-bloc countries (Second World) (Crow & Thomas, 1983, p. 8). Today, the First and Second World countries form the "North," or MDCs, and the Third World comprises the "South," or LDCs.

The terms I have just described are used as convenient labels to dichotomize the world into two basic camps—rich and poor. In some cases, the underlying variable upon which this distinction is made is economic; in other cases it is political; and in still others, the underlying dimension is left unspecified. As mentioned in Chapter 2, dichotomies are shorthand techniques employed to simplify and emphasize one or more features that are perceived to be important. However, in order to understand and explain complex social phenomena, it is necessary first to specify precisely the dimensions or variables being analyzed, and then to establish appropriate gradients along these dimensions against which comparable units of analysis can be measured.

In the preceding section of this chapter, 49 countries were placed on an overall rank order of industrialization based on four explicit measures of this concept which reflect its essential dimensions. Now, in order to assess the impact of industrialization on these countries, this same rank ordering is reproduced together with other structural features that have previously been found to be related to industrialization. Table 5.2 presents industrialization in relation to national output (GNP per capita), urbanization (percent living in urban areas), three measures of the presence and extent of an infrastructure (communication, education, and health), and five measures that reflect the quality of life at the structural level. Thus, we are in a better position to evaluate the extent to which industrialization contributes to the distinctions between North and South, more developed and less developed, and rich and poor.

National Output

Table 5.2 reveals that gross national products per capita range from $17,500 in the industrialized United States to $160 in nonindustrialized Bangladesh and Nepal. The median values at the bottom of the table indicate that the rank order of gross national product is identical to industrialization. In other words, the fully industrialized Group 1 countries have the highest per capita output while the nonindustrialized Group 5 nations have the lowest. This direct relation between industrialization and national output was noted previously in Chapter 3 where in

Great Britain between 1801 and 1901, largely due to the effects of industrialization, total national income increased over 600% (Mitchell, 1962, p. 366). However, as Murdoch (1980) and others have pointed out, the relationship is even stronger today. The conditions and terms of international trade, established primarily by the now rich developed nations, have steadily depreciated the value of agricultural commodities and other raw materials and primary products in relation to finished manufactured goods. The consequence is that the gap in earnings is increasing between the industrialized developed countries, which export primarily manufactured goods, and the nonindustrialized developing countries which, export mainly agricultural commodities.

> ... by 1973 the LDCs were exporting the equivalent of more than twice as much (in constant dollar value) to obtain the same amount (in constant dollar value) as they had obtained in 1913 (Murdoch, 1980, pp. 251–252).

Not only do these changed conditions of international trade and commerce incur disproportionate disadvantage on the less-developed countries as a whole, they also translate directly into reduced earning power on the part of individuals in these countries. For example, in 1850 when the industrial revolution was well under way, per capita income in the industrialized nations was 70% higher than in the nonindustrialized developing countries (Murdoch, 1980, p. 246), but 100 years later the difference had grown to over 2000%, and by 1980, just 30 years later, the average citizen in the developed countries was earning almost 4000%, or 40 times more than his or her counterpart in the less developed countries (Seligson, 1984).[8] Consequently, for a variety of reasons, the direct relationship between industrialization and national individual income is increasing.

Urbanization

Table 5.2 also shows a strong direct relationship between industrialization and urbanization. On average, at least three-quarters of the population in the industrialized countries of Groups 1 to 3 are urbanized, while slightly less than half the people in Group 4 and only one-fifth of those in Group 5 live in urban centers. Again, you will recall from the discussion in Chapter 3 that industrialization and urbanization covary in that with the increasing growth and specialized development of industry, population bases sufficiently large and varied are required in order to satisfy its complex needs and demands. However, as you will learn later in this chapter, the pattern of urbanization that is presently occurring in the LDCs is markedly different from that which has traditionally taken place in the MDCs.

Infrastructure

Also discussed in Chapter 3 (on the industrial revolution) was how an institutionalized framework or infrastructure arose and was developed in response to the novel and complex problems faced by industrial society. The establishment of national transportation and communication networks, the introduction of state-run

Table 5.2   INDUSTRIALIZATION IN RELATION TO NATIONAL OUTPUT, URBANIZATION, INFRASTRUCTURE, AND QUALITY OF LIFE

Selected countries ranked by industrialization[1]	National output (GNP per capita US $) 1986	Urbanization (Percent urban population[2]) 1986	Communication (Telephones per 100 population) c.1981	Education (% Enrolled in sec. schools[3]) 1984 Boys	Education Girls	Health (Population per physician) 1981
Group 1						
West Germany	12,080	94	40.4	72	76	420
Sweden	13,170	83	74.4	79	88	410
Finland	12,180	62	44.7	94	109	460
France	10,740	73	37.2	84	96	460
Belgium	9,230	95	33.2	89	89	370
United States	17,500	74	77.0	95	95	500
Austria	10,000	55	32.5	73	79	440
New Zealand	7,110	84	54.5	84	86	610
Australia	11,910	86	44.0	92	95	500
United Kingdom	8,920	91	41.5	80	84	680
Group 2						
Canada	14,100	76	64.8	102	102	550
Kuwait	13,890	80	14.3	85	79	700
Trinidad and Tobago	5,120	34	6.7	75	78	1,500
Japan	12,850	77	42.4	94	94	740
Singapore	7,410	100	20.4	70	73	1,100
South Africa	1,800	56	9.8	80	72	2,016
Venezuela	2,930	82	6.5	40	49	1,000
Group 3						
Norway	15,480	71	40.2	93	95	460
Greece	3,680	58	26.6	86	74	400
Libya	7,170	76	2.1	64	22	620
Group 4						
South Korea	2,370	65	6.5	94	88	1,390
Jordan	1,540	59	1.8	80	78	1,200
Peru	1,130	69	2.7	58	53	1,571
Ecuador	1,160	52	3.0	51	53	1,621
Turkey	1,110	53	3.2	47	28	1,530
Philippines	570	41	1.3	65	71	6,710
Panama	2,330	51	8.6	56	63	1,010
Nicaragua	790	57	1.9	39	48	2,230
Morocco	590	43	1.1	37	25	18,600
Colombia	1,230	65	5.4	48	49	1,969
Dominican Republic	710	52	2.8	31	33	1,400
Zimbabwe	620	24	2.9	46	31	7,100
Paraguay	880	43	1.7	26	26	1,750
Tunisia	1,140	53	2.7	37	26	3,900
Pakistan	350	28	0.3	20	8	2,910
Thailand	810	17	0.9	31	27	6,870

Table 5.2 **INDUSTRIALIZATION IN RELATION TO NATIONAL OUTPUT, URBANIZATION, INFRASTRUCTURE, AND QUALITY OF LIFE** *(continued)*

Selected countries ranked by industrialization[1]	National output (GNP per capita US $) 1986	Urbanization (Percent urban population[2]) 1986	Communication (Telephones per 100 population) c.1981	Education (% Enrolled in sec. schools[3]) 1984 Boys	Education Girls	Health (Population per physician) 1981
El Salvador	820	43	1.8	23	26	2,720
Sri Lanka	400	22	0.5	58	64	7,460
India	270	25	0.3	44	23	3,700
Rwanda	290	6	0.1	3	1	32,100
Group 5						
Honduras	740	40	0.7	31	36	3,120
Indonesia	500	22	0.3	45	34	12,300
Ghana	390	31	0.7	45	27	7,250
North Yemen	550	15	0.1	17	3	7,100
Cameroon	910	42	—[8]	29	18	15,820
Sudan	320	20	0.3	23	16	9,800
Bangladesh	160	16	0.1	26	11	9,700
Nepal	160	7	0.1	35	11	28,770
Mali	170	18	0.1	12	5	26,450
Median Values						
Group 1	11,325	83.5	42.8	84	88	460
Group 2	7,410 } 7,290	77 } 76	14.3 } 17.4	80 } 82	78 } 76	1,00 } 720
Group 3	7,170	71	26.6	86	74	460
Group 4	815	47	1.8	45	32	2,475
Group 5	390	20	0.2	29	16	9,800
All countries	1,160	53%	3.0	56	53	1,571

	Quality of life				
	Infant mortality rate[4] 1986	Life expectancy at birth (yrs)[5] 1986	Population "doubling time" (yrs)[6] 1986	Population density of persons/room 1980	Human suffering index[7] c. 1985
Group 1					
West Germany	8.6	75	∞[9]	1.5	5
Sweden	5.9	77	673	0.7	12
Finland	5.8	74	247	1.0	16
France	8.0	75	166	1.3	14
Belgium	9.7	75	1034	0.6	9
United States	10.0	75	99	0.6	8
Austria	10.3	75	∞[9]	0.9	9
New Zealand	10.8	74	87	0.7	16

Table 5.2   INDUSTRIALIZATION IN RELATION TO NATIONAL OUTPUT, URBANIZATION, INFRASTRUCTURE, AND QUALITY OF LIFE *(continued)*

	Quality of life				
	Infant mortality rate[4] 1986	Life expectancy at birth (yrs)[5] 1986	Population "doubling time" (yrs)[6] 1986	Population density of persons/room 1980	Human suffering index[7] c. 1985
Australia	9.8	76	88	0.7	16
United Kingdom	9.5	75	408	0.7	12
Group 2					
Canada	7.9	76	94	0.6	9
Kuwait	18.4	72	24	2.1	35
Trinidad & Tobago	12.7	70	31	1.7	21
Japan	5.2	78	133	1.1	11
Singapore	9.4	73	71	2.9	18
South Africa	66	60	31	1.3	52
Venezuela	36	70	28	1.5	44
Group 3					
Norway	8.5	76	33	0.6	14
Greece	12.3	74	330	0.9	25
Libya	74	65	22	—	53
Group 4					
South Korea	30	68	52	2.3	44
Jordan	56	69	19	—	53
Peru	88	61	28	1.9	61
Ecuador	66	65	25	2.3	54
Turkey	95	63	32	2.2	55
Philippines	51	66	25	2.3	55
Panama	25	71	32	2.2	47
Nicaragua	69	62	20	2.8	67
Morocco	90	61	27	2.4	66
Colombia	48	64	34	1.8	44
Dominican Republic	70	65	28	2.0	53
Zimbabwe	76	57	20	2.0	69
Paraguay	45	66	24	2.4	53
Tunisia	71	63	31	3.2	56
Pakistan	121	54	24	2.8	73
Thailand	52	64	33	—	47
El Salvador	65	66	25	3.1	65
Sri Lanka	31	70	38	2.5	58
India	104	54	35	2.8	61
Rwanda	122	49	19	—	80

Table 5.2 INDUSTRIALIZATION IN RELATION TO NATIONAL OUTPUT, URBANIZATION, INFRASTRUCTURE, AND QUALITY OF LIFE *(continued)*

	Quality of life				
	Infant mortality rate[4] 1986	Life expectancy at birth (yrs)[5] 1986	Population "doubling time" (yrs)[6] 1986	Population density of persons/room 1980	Human suffering index[7] c. 1985
Group 5					
Honduras	69	63	22	2.4	62
Indonesia	88	58	40	1.5	62
Ghana	72	58	22	—	87
North Yemen	175	45	21	—	78
Cameroon	126	50	26	—	78
Sudan	112	49	24	2.5	77
Bangladesh	135	50	26	—	79
Nepal	112	52	28	2.0	81
Mali	175	43	24	—	88
Median Values					
Group 1	9.6	75	328	0.7	12
Group 2	12.7 } 12.5	72 } 72	31 } 51	1.5 } 1.3	21 } 23
Group 3	12.3	74	176	0.8	25
Group 4	67.5	64	28	2.3	55.5
Group 5	112.0	50	25	2.2	78
All countries	52.0	66	31	2.0	53

Sources: Kurlan, 1984; Population Crisis Committee, 1987; World Bank, 1987, *1988 World Population Data Sheet.*

[1]See Table 5.1 for the determination of how countries are ranked.

[2]"Percent of total population in areas termed urban by that country" *(1988 World Population Data Sheet).*

[3]Figures computed as numbers enrolled in secondary school as a percentage of the age group, most commonly 12–17 years. Percentages for Finland and Canada are greater than 100, indicating that enrollment in secondary school is not limited only to this age group, and thus can exceed the total of the group.

[4]"The annual number of deaths of infants under age 1 year per 1,000 births" *(1988 World Population Data Sheet).*

[5]"The average number of years a newborn infant can expect to live under *current* mortality levels" *(ibid.).*

[6]"The number of years until the population will double assuming a *constant* rate of natural increase" *(ibid.).*

[7]The International Human Suffering Index, created by the Population Crisis Committee (1987), is comprised of 10 measures: (1) per capita gross national product; (2) average annual rate of inflation; (3) average annual growth of labor force; (4) average annual growth of urban population; (5) infant mortality rate; (6) daily per capita calorie supply; (7) access to clean drinking water; (8) per capita energy consumption; (9) adult literacy rate; and (10) personal freedom/governance. The Index has a possible range of 0 (no suffering) to 100 (extreme).

[8]Data not available.

[9]Because the current birth rates in West Germany and Austria do not exceed the death rates, their populations will never double; hence the sign for infinity.

compulsory education to prepare citizens to enter an industrial labor force, and the increasing provision of various health and welfare benefits related to work and industry were among the first notable features of a developing infrastructure. In Table 5.2, I have selected measures that reflect each of these three major domains of an industrial infrastructure.

One indication of an infrastructure is how well the social system is interconnected such that people living and working in different areas can easily communicate and interact with one another. Since its invention in 1876 (see Table 3.2), the telephone has become the symbol par excellence of human communication and exchange. The fact that there is almost one telephone for every two people in the industrialized countries of the world (there are considerably more in North America) reveals how much these symbols have become taken for granted. However, outside this industrial enclave, the telephone is notable for its absence. The median for Group 4 countries is almost two telephones per 100 people, while in the nonindustrial Group 5 nations these same two telephones must service 1000 inhabitants. Clearly, as far as this indicator is concerned, there is not a well-developed, interconnected infrastructure operating in these latter two groups of countries.

Table 5.2 also illustrates how important formal education is as a correlate of industrialization. In the fully industrialized Group 1 countries, 84% of 12- to 17-year-old boys and an even larger percentage of similarly aged girls (88%) are enrolled in secondary school.[9] In Groups 2 and 3, the percentages are similar, although the attendance rate of boys is higher than of girls. However in Group 4, not only is enrollment less than half the relevant population, but the disparity between boys and girls increases. While slightly less than half the boys in this group of nations attend secondary school, not even one-third of the girls have this same opportunity. In Group 5 countries, there is a further decline in overall participation, with differential enrollment by gender becoming even more significant. In this nonindustrial group of nations, secondary school attendance does not appear to be a viable option for the overwhelming majority of school-aged children, most particularly girls. The establishment of nationally sponsored universal education does not extend for the most part beyond the primary school system (see World Bank, 1987, pp. 262–263). These data together suggest that industrialization is a powerful and important impetus in the creation of an educated citizenry, both women and men alike.

The third and final measure of the presence and extent of an infrastructure is in the area of health—the number of inhabitants per physician. While it is a specific indicator, it also more generally reflects the extent of the health and medical establishment throughout the various countries listed. Once again, the industrialized countries of Group 1 are most well endowed. On average, each practicing physician has a caseload of 460 patients; in Groups 2 and 3, this extends to 720. However, in some Group 4 countries and all of those in Group 5, clearly many individuals do not have access to medical doctors. They continue to care for themselves through the use of traditional folk customs practiced over centuries. Occasionally, due to widespread famine or pestilence, formal medical practitioners may intervene on their behalf. However, in countries where on average there are

10,000 (and in some cases 20,000 and 30,000) inhabitants per doctor, it is obvious that the medical infrastructure does not extend to all.

Quality of Life

There are five columns in Table 5.2 that are devoted to different structural indicators of the quality of life in these 49 countries. The first measure, the number of deaths of infants under one year per 1000 births, is commonly used as an indicator of development or modernization. It also reflects the extent of the medical infrastructure. On average in the industrialized countries of the world, there is only one chance in a hundred that an infant will not live to celebrate its first birthday. However, in the more populous nonindustrial nations, the odds for survival are severely diminished; for every 100 children born, more than 10 will not survive their first year.

Life expectancy at birth, the second quality of life measure, illustrates essentially the same set of conditions. Predicated on current national mortality rates, demographers and actuaries project the number of years a newborn girl or boy can expect to live. On average a child born in 1986 in any of the industrialized countries can expect to live between 72 and 75 years; but a child born in one of the Group 4 nations has a life expectancy of only 64 years, and in the nonindustrial countries it is statistically improbable that a newly born infant will surpass 50 years. Given that the average child born in Sierra Leone may expect to live only 35 years, and that the average child in Japan may claim 78 years (i.e., 2.23 Sierra Leone lifetimes), life expectancy is indeed a measure of the quality of life (see *1988 World Population Data Sheet*).

Also contributing both directly and indirectly to the quality of life of a nation and its people is the rate of population growth or natural increase. As noted in Chapter 2, the industrially developed nations are either in or just entering the fourth stage of the demographic transition and thus have relatively stable populations, while the nonindustrial and industrializing nations are in the second and third stages of the transition and consequently are experiencing rapid population growth (see Figure 2.2). The figures on population "doubling time" reflect the differences between fertility and mortality rates, which is the basis for computing how rapidly a particular population is expanding.

Among the fully industrialized countries listed in Table 5.2, West Germany is actually experiencing "negative growth." Given its present birth rate of 10 (per 1000 population) and death rate of 11, its present population will never double.[10] Similarly, Austria cannot double in that its birth and death rates equal 12. These countries are in stage four of the demographic transition. Overall, given current rates, it will take Group 1 328 years to double its population; Groups 2 and 3 require 51 years to replace themselves; and Groups 4 and 5 will double in a scant 28 and 25 years, respectively.

One of the direct consequences of population growth is an increase in population density, which can be measured in a variety of ways. One such indicator, number of persons per room, reflects the relative ability of populations to house themselves. Among the Group 1 nations, one person on average has two rooms at his or her disposal. For Groups 2 and 3, space is at more of a premium as each person generally has only one room to claim personally. However, in the less-developed countries, which constitute Groups 4 and 5, there are two to two and a half people per room. Given that there are missing data for eight countries in these latter two groups, there could actually be more crowding than is presently indicated. However, particularly in tropical and semitropical countries, the common use of outdoor space does serve as an alleviating factor (Kurian, 1984, pp. 319–320).

The final measure of quality of life is the 10-item International Human Suffering Index constructed by the Population Crisis Committee (1987). As indicated in Chapter 1 (Table 1.5), this index is ranked on a scale from 0 (no suffering) to 100 (extreme) and is comprised of measures "judged to be the best of those available according to the team that assembled the Human Suffering Index." Broadly ranged to reflect economic, demographic, health, educational, and political aspects of life, the Human Suffering Index provides independent corroboration of the conclusions already drawn: "The majority of the world's people must endure lives of poverty and human misery." Once again there is a strong relationship between industrialization and the quality of life. According to the classification system developed by the Population Crisis Committee, on average the industrialized countries listed in Groups 1, 2, and 3 experience "minimal human suffering"; Group 4 nations are faced with "high human suffering"; and the nonindustrial countries in Group 5 live under conditions of "extreme human suffering." Not only are the countries of the "North" more industrialized and richer than those of the "South," but they enjoy a more fully developed quality of life in virtually all spheres of their existence.

Box 5–1, **The Social Progress of Nations,** provides yet another research example of this same conclusion. Furthermore, the researcher Richard Estes (1984, 1988) found that while the industrialized market economies of the First World made "progress" between 1970 and 1983 on nearly all of the 36 measures for which he collected data, the initially most disadvantaged, nonindustrial countries actually lost ground during this same period.

All the social structural measures in Table 5.2 are highly correlated to national levels of industrialization. Whether it be gross national product, urbanization, the ability of the infrastructure to provide essential services, or a wide variety of quality of life indicators, these data show that the level of industrialization explains much of the variation among countries. The median correlation between industrialization and each of the 11 social structural measures presented in Table 5.2 is .87.[11] To put it another way, there are gross inequities between MDCs and LDCs as measured by industrialization. These disparities are further compounded by the fact that *within* countries there are also differences in how the resources of a nation are distributed among its citizens, these differences again being related to the level of national development.

Income Distribution

Felix Paukert's landmark study (1973) of the effect of national development on income distribution within nations reveals that there is a curvilinear relationship between development and the equality with which individual income is distributed. Paukert grouped the 56 countries for which he could find data into seven levels of national income (GDP) per capita. Then within each level, he determined what proportion of total national income the top and bottom earners received. For example, in those countries with the highest national income (Group 1), Paukert found the distribution of individual income to be least unequal. The 20% of families earning the highest incomes received a smaller proportion of total national income (42.7%) than did the top 20% in the next most developed group of countries (46.6%). This trend of increasing inequality with the top earners receiving progressively greater shares of total income continued through the next three levels of development (50.1%, 57.4%, 57.7%). Only in the two least-developed groups of nations was this trend reversed, with the top earners in Group 6 receiving 56.5% of the total and those in Group 7 earning 50.5%.

These results, which have been reproduced in other studies, highlight the two-pronged effect of the level of economic and industrial development upon individuals in society. In the most-developed countries, not only is there greater bounty to share, it is shared more equally among all citizens. Conversely, in less (but not the least) developed countries, there is less initially to share and it is divided more unequally. Consequently, to be poor in a less developed country means that one suffers from the combined effects of both international *and* national stratification systems.[12]

Table 5.3 provides an illustration of income distribution over two time periods in the United States, which has a relatively low level of inequality compared to the countries of Latin America, in which inequality of income distribution is among the highest in the world (Paukert, 1973). As well as indicating what share of total income the highest and lowest groups of earners receive, this table also provides data on income in constant 1970 dollars. Consequently, you can observe how the percentage shares of total income translate into the amount of actual income earned per household.

Aside from the fact that income distribution in Latin America is grossly unequal compared to the United States, which also has an unequal distribution, it is interesting to note the effect of this greater Latin American inequality when different strata are compared to their counterparts in the United States. For example, even though total income is considerably less in Latin America than it is in the United States, the richest 10% in Latin America still receive almost three-quarters of what the richest 10% of Americans receive. Contrast this with what the poorest 40% in Latin America earn in relation to the same group in the United States. The fact that the poorest 40% of Latin Americans earn only ten percent of what the poorest 40% of Americans earn illustrates the two-pronged effect I discussed earlier. Not only is there less initial total income to divide, but given the system of grossly unequal allocation, the poor in the developing countries receive proportionately less than do the poor in the developed nations.

Some summary figures for Latin America give an idea of the tremendous inequalities that persist on the continent where economic growth has been greatest. In 1974 average per capita income on the continent was almost $900. Yet, of the roughly 300

Box 5-1 # The Social Progress of Nations

In a comprehensive worldwide study of 124 countries, Richard Estes (1984, 1988) examined the relationship between national economic development and the "capacity of nations to provide for the basic social and material needs of their populations." From 1970 to 1983, he measured the progress of these nations using 36 indicators grouped into 10 dimensions of national well-being. His detailed and exhaustive list of measures is presented in the accompanying table.

In order to determine the effect of national development on these indicators of progress, Estes classified nations into four major groups: (1) 24 First World countries; (2) 8 Second World countries; (3) 67 Third World countries; and (4) 25 Fourth World countries (i.e., the least developed Third World countries officially "designated by the United Nations as LDCs . . . targeted for priority international development assistance"). Thus, the first two categories represent MDCs and the latter two are LDCs (the Fourth World countries correspond approximately to the nonindustrial Group 5 nations described in the text).

Index of Social Progress Indicators by Subindex

1. *Education Subindex*
   School enrollment ratio, first level (+)*
   Pupil–teacher ratio, first level (-)
   Percent adult illiteracy (-)
   Percent GNP in education (+)

2. *Health Status Subindex*
   Male life expectancy at 1 year (+)
   Rate of infant mortality (-)
   Population in thousands per physician (-)
   Per capita daily calorie supply (+)

3. *Women Status Subindex*
   Percent eligible girls in first level schools (+)
   Percent adult female illiteracy (-)
   Length of time legislation in effect
     protecting legal rights of women (+)

4. *Defense Report Subindex*
   Military expenditures as percent of GNP (-)

5. *Economic Subindex*
   Per capita gross national product (+)
   GNP per capita annual growth rate (+)
   Average annual rate of inflation (-)
   Per capita food production index (+)
   External public debt as percent of GNP (-)

6. *Demography Subindex*
   Total population (-)
   Crude birth rate (-)
   Crude death rate (-)
   Rate of population increase (-)
   Percent of population under 15 years (-)

7. *Geography Subindex*
   Percent arable land mass (+)
   Natural disaster vulnerability index (-)
   Average death rate from natural
     disasters (-)

8. *Political Participation Subindex*
   Violations of political rights index (-)
   Violations of civil liberties index (-)
   Composite violations of human
     freedoms (-)

9. *Cultural Diversity Subindex*
   Largest percent sharing same mother
     tongue (+)
   Largest percent sharing same
     religious beliefs (+)
   Largest percent with same
     racial/ethnic origin (+)

10. *Welfare Effort Subindex*
    Years since first law:
      Old age, invalidity, death (+)
      Sickness and maternity (+)
      Work injury (+)
      Unemployment (+)
      Family allowance (+)

*The + or - sign specifies the direction of "progress."
Source: Estes, 1988, pp. 2–3.

From the scores on each of the 10 dimensions or subindexes, Estes constructed a cumulative Index of Social Progress for each country that ranged between -8 (Ethiopia) to +208 (Denmark). The table that follows presents the values on this index for each of the above group of countries, first in 1970 and then in 1983. The extreme differences in total scores between MDCs and LDCs are indicative of how poorly off people living in less-developed countries are relative to their fellow human beings in the more prosperous developed nations. With the exception of the defense, geography, and cultural diversity subindexes, LDCs at best score only half as well as MDCs in providing for the basic needs of their citizens; and in the most disadvantaged Fourth World countries, the differences are even greater.

With respect to changes in the Index of Social Progress over the 14-year period represented in the table that follows, the developed market economies of the First World registered the greatest advance. Thus, even in this brief interval, the evidence indicates that the gap between MDCs and LDCs is increasing. The least-developed Fourth World countries actually declined in what little "progress" they had initially achieved. As Estes (1988, p. 43) states: "Increased militarism and internal political oppression—coupled with *decreased* government expenditures for health, education, fertility control, and related programs—are only suggestive of the high level of 'mal-development' that characterizes current social trends occurring in [these countries]."

Index of Social Progress by Developmental Status of Country, 1970 and 1983

Developmental status of country	Number of countries	Social progress score		Percentage change 1970–1983
		1970	1983	
First World	24	163	172	+ 5.5
Second World	8	158	142	-10.1
Third World	67	87	91	+ 4.6
Fourth World	25	45	43	- 4.4

Source: Adapted from Estes, 1988, pp. 40–41.

million population, 100 million had a per capita income of about $70, and half of the population lived on $120 per year, or less. The new consumerism is restricted to a tiny fraction of the population: the top 10% eat 41% of the meat and get 44% of the clothes, 85% of the motor vehicles, 74% of the furniture, and half of the electrical appliances. The bottom half gets 12% of the meat, 13% of the clothes, 1% of the motor vehicles, 5% of the furniture, and 5% of the electrical appliances. (Murdoch, 1980, p. 244)

Table 5.3   INCOME DISTRIBUTION IN THE UNITED STATES AND LATIN AMERICA, 1960 AND 1975

Income strata	Share of total income (%)		Income per household (1970 dollars)		(% of U.S. income)
	1960	1975	1960	1975	
United States					
Richest 10%	28.6	28.3	15,538	21,488	
Poorest 40%	17.0	17.2	4,976	6,635	
Latin America					
Richest 10%	46.6	47.3	11,142	15,829	(74)
Poorest 40%	8.7	7.7	520	648	(10)

Source: Adapted from Portes, 1985, p. 25.

The two-pronged effect of disparity *between* and *within* nations essentially underscores the fact that there are two separate sectors operating within LDCs today: a small modern "have" sector that makes a relatively high per capita income, benefits from the services provided by the limited infrastructure, and enjoys a quality of life comparable to that in the MDCs; and a large traditional "have-not" sector that ekes out a subsistence living, does not have access to the infrastructure, and is more concerned with survival than with quality of life (see Figure 5.1). Labeled the "modern dual economy" by Murdoch (1980), its existence means that while the "average" statistics used to reflect the structural conditions operating in the MDCs are reasonably accurate portrayals, the same "averages" used to describe the LDCs are statistical artifacts, which mask *two* separate realities. Whereas the figures reported in Table 5.2 for the less-developed (Group 4) and nonindustrial (Group 5) countries are grim according to Western standards, in fact they are inflated for the vast majority of the population in the LDCs who live and work in the traditional sector.

PATHS OF DEVELOPMENT

The evidence presented so far reveals a direct relationship between industrialization and national development. Whether the data involve cross-national comparisons of countries at different levels of industrialization (as in the present chapter) or historical comparisons of the industrialization of nations over time (as in Chapter 3), the results are consonant. Industrialized countries have higher economic returns, are more urbanized, have a more well-developed infrastructure, provide a better quality of life for their citizens, and have a less unequal distribution of income than nonindustrial nations.

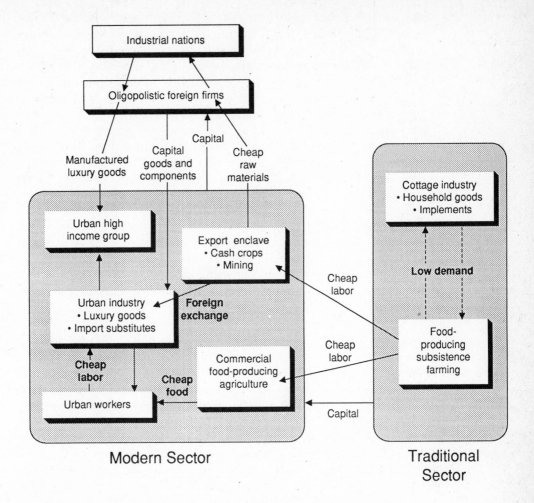

Figure 5.1 The Modern Dual Economy of the Less Developed Countries
Source: Murdoch, 1980, p. 238

While it has been empirically established that these correlations exist, it would be erroneous to conclude that there is something about industrialization that necessarily causes or produces an improvement in national living standards. Whereas we have determined that industrialization improved the material well being of the first nations to undergo this process, we cannot say that industrialization by itself will result in a similar improvement for the now developing nations. The conditions that the LDCs presently face are vastly different from those that the MDCs originally confronted, and therefore might well produce different outcomes. For example, the MDCs currently enjoy substantial comparative advantage over the LDCs, not only in material circumstance but also in the fact that by and large it was they who established the rules, procedures, and administrative practices under which world trade, industry, and commerce now operate. Thus, there are many vested interests in maintaining the status quo. Also, while both the MDCs, and the LDCs have experienced population pressure during initial industrialization, this pressure is far more intense in the LDCs. They have a larger initial population base, a higher rate of growth, and less room for expansion (emigration). Consequently, population growth represents a more serious problem for the LDCs, and can interact with the industrialization process in such a way as to nullify its main effects.

Furthermore, while we have noted the uniformities in the industrialization process, at the same time we have also observed that there are large differences with respect to how it is introduced. Depending upon the time and rate of introduction, the natural and human resources of the particular country involved, and the type of social structure and governing elite, the process may be different and therefore have different results. Given the multifaceted dimensions that are involved in industrialization and the fact that it takes place within a complex set of social forces, it is virtually impossible to make causal assertions. All we can do is try to note the relevant similarities and differences as we attempt to understand and explain this very important process and its consequences.

Theories of Development

Similar to Marx, Durkheim, and Weber, modern theorists of development have attempted to explain the process of industrialization and its results during the two hundred years following the industrial revolution. Like their predecessors, they differ widely in their interpretations. Following is a brief description of the major theoretical perspectives that have been developed to make sense out of industrialization from a world view.

The earliest systematic attempts to explain patterns of development were put forward by proponents of "modernization theory." Borrowing heavily from the work of Durkheim and Weber, modernization theorists proposed that industrialization and urbanization were forces that would eventually become diffused throughout the world regardless of historical period, cultural circumstance, or indigenous natural resources. Ultimate cultural convergence (i.e., modernization) would be accomplished through the increasing rationalization of the functions of production, distribution, and consumption. The twin processes of bureaucratization and the systematic division of labor would result in the less-developed countries emulating more or less the same pattern of development experienced earlier by the European nations and North America. While temporary strains and maladjustments were to be expected, the overall unilinear path of development was clear (see Kerr et al., 1964).

Early Marxist interpretations of this developmental process were not so sanguine. They argued that the facts were contrary to the theory, and that as a result of the international division of labor capitalists the world over were concentrating and centralizing their power by exploiting the industrial underclass. The "temporary strains" and "maladjustments" were in point of fact full-blown class warfare. Marxists, like the modernization theorists, viewed this process as being uniform and constant regardless of where in the world and under what circumstances it occurred. "The country that is more developed industrially only shows, to the less developed, the image of its own future" (Marx, cited in Evans and Stephens, 1988, p. 743). Only with the emergence of "dependency theory" and later "world system theory," both offshoots of Marxist theory, did analysts begin to realize that the process of development was not universally constant, and that how it occurred depended upon a whole variety of complex factors.

Dependency theory, which originated in the Third World (see Cardoso and Faletto, 1979), and world system theory (Wallerstein, 1979) both view the process of development within the world context. The "center" or "core" nations constitute the industrialized developed nations; they are the powerful actors on the world scene. The "periphery" is populated by the LDCs, which are in various stages of development. Not only do the MDCs exert an influence on the rate of progress of these nations, at times they actually impede development through the use of various strategies at their disposal (e.g., terms of trade, finance, and aid; transnational corporate practices; covert operations, and so on). Consequently, how a Third World country is situated within the core–periphery configuration and the kind of relationship it has with major core actors can influence dramatically its path of development. Development in this context is very much based on the interaction between and among states and on the interactional networks established by elites in the core and various parts of the periphery. Viewed from the dependency and world system perspectives, economic development is in large measure a matter of political "progress" (see Evans and Stephens, 1988).

Barriers to Development

Regardless of the theoretical perspective employed, there are empirical realities to face. Although technically it is more feasible to introduce industrialization today, there are other factors which, when taken into consideration, make it more difficult now for the developing nations to become industrialized. Following is a discussion of the barriers or constraints to industrialization.[13]

Population Growth and Migration As I mentioned previously, the present rate of population growth in the LDCs serves as an impediment to economic growth and industrialization. Particularly for the LDCs, high population growth rates place additional burdens on already low levels of national income and inadequate, over-taxed social services (i.e., the infrastructure). Furthermore, just in order to stay even, less-developed countries must achieve economic growth rates that are at least comparable to their population growth rates. Currently, the annual rate of natural increase in the LDCs is 2.1% (*1988 World Population Data Sheet*). Given current birth and death rates, this means its population will double in only 33 years. These figures illustrate how constraining population growth can be on economic growth. In the developed nations, the annual natural increase is a modest 0.6% and thus has far less impact on economic development.

When the now developed nations were industrializing, they too experienced high population growth rates, thereby potentially reducing much of the productivity gains achieved through industrialization. One solution to this problem was emigration. As mentioned in Chapter 3, during the period from 1840 to 1930 at least 52 million Europeans emigrated to form settlements in the temperate regions of the world, thus providing an important safety valve in the control of European population growth. Today, even though the world migration pattern has changed such that there is a general population movement from the poor to the rich nations, it is insufficient to absorb the excess growth. Given the present population of the LDCs—almost four billion—and their annual rate of growth (2.1%), the MDCs would have to accept over 82 million immigrants per year, or an annual increase of 6.8%. Thus, the escape value of emigration that existed for the industrializing European countries cannot be used by the LDCs.

Another solution to population growth for the now developed countries was the absorption of the excess into the areas of expansion—trade, industry, and commerce. Thus, there occurred the now familiar process of rural–urban migration and the eventual urbanization of the MDCs. This was a very accommodating process, both for the rural and the urban components. For the rural component, population excesses were siphoned off by the city, thus allowing adequate agricultural use of the land. For the urban component, population excesses from the country were required in order to operate the factories and to provide the services so essential to a large urban complex.

In the LDCs, while a similar rural–urban migration has taken place, it has occurred in the context of substantial overall population increase. Consequently, much of the fantastic growth of Third World cities is a result more of natural increase within the urban population rather than of rural–urban migration. With the cities creating their own population surpluses, they become less attractive as places of opportunity and employment, thus reducing rural–urban migration. In turn, this results in increasing rural densities such that more people work on reduced agricultural preserves to produce less food for a larger, ever growing population (see Davis, 1965). Consequently, because the option of large-scale emigration from the LDCs is blocked, rural–urban migration as a complementary strategy is no longer viable, and the LDCs increasingly work themselves into a deteriorating position vis-à-vis the MDCs.

Capital Costs and Debts   Another major obstacle to industrialization is the financing of this increasingly expensive process. In the original industrial revolution, this was achieved largely through colonial exploitation of the tropical and semitropical regions of the world, or what today is called the "South." Labeled "the pillage of the Third World" by one author (Jalée, 1968), colonial administrations were established for the sole purpose of acquiring raw materials (gold, silver, diamonds, and other goods not indigenous to Europe) that helped to finance the industrialization process in Europe. The forced takeover of these countries varied quite substantially, from almost complete extermination of the indigenous population to trading and manipulation of the infrastructure; but the result generally was the same. The basic social structure and primary activities were completely remolded to fit European interests (see Murdoch, 1980).

While some academics and politicians in the developed nations have suggested that it is now only fair for the industrialized countries to repay their debt to the developing nations and financially assist in their industrialization, generally this support has not been forthcoming in amounts sufficient to bring about a new international economic order (see Tinbergen, 1976). Loans to the developing countries have resulted in massive debt—close to $800 billion according to recent World Bank estimates—such that now the ratio of debt to exports in the LDCs is 144.5%, with the debt load constituting 35.4% of the total gross national product (World Bank, 1987, p. 18).

One reason why international loan and aid programs have failed to bring about the desired changes is that as a result of increasing technological development, the cost of industrializing is far more expensive now than it was originally. As Galbraith (1985, p. 14) has stated, "There is an increase in the capital that is committed to production aside from that occasioned by increased output." This increase in capital cost arises from greater emphasis on planning and design, more specialized knowledge and manpower, more complex and intricate machinery, and the resulting coordination and organization that all of this entails. Box 5-2, **Technology and Capital Costs**, is a comparative example provided by Galbraith to illustrate how technological development incurs greater capital cost. To put it simply, it is more expensive now for the LDCs to industrialize than it was for the MDCs during their industrialization.

Economic Structure: Internal and External One of the legacies of European colonization was the establishment of limited product economies throughout most of the LDCs in the world (see Murdoch, 1980). Previously, many of these countries had well-developed, diversified agricultural economies, some in fact more sophisticated than their European counterparts. The colonial powers set up limited product economies to provide the raw resources, including minerals and semi-finished manufactures (e.g., textiles), that were not grown or produced in Europe. The result today is that the exports of each LDC are restricted to only a few, mainly agricultural, products. Murdoch (1980, pp. 248–249) provides some examples:

> Cuba and other Caribbean islands are almost totally dependent upon sugar exports. In Africa, copper supplies 90 percent of Zambia's foreign earnings and three-quarters of Zaire's. Ghana gets two-thirds of its foreign earnings from cocoa, Chad three-quarters from cotton, Uganda three-quarters from coffee and cotton, Malawi three-fifths from tobacco and tea, Kenya one-half from coffee and tea, Ivory Coast over one-half from cocoa and coffee. Five commodities (cocoa, coffee, oilseeds, cotton, and copper) make up half of the export earnings of Sub-Saharan Africa. In Asia, Sri Lanka gets over 60 percent of its foreign earnings from tea and natural rubber, and Burma earns over 70 percent from rice and wood.

The point is that the economies of most of the LDCs today are not sufficiently balanced to accommodate the industrialization process. Furthermore, examination of the listing above reveals that there is a good deal of regional specialization such

---

Box 5-2   Technology and Capital Costs

On June 16, 1903, after some months of preparation which included negotiation of contracts for various components, the Ford Motor Company was formed for the manufacture of automobiles. Production was to be whatever number could be sold. The first car reached the market that October. The firm had an authorized capital of $150,000. However, only $100,000 worth of stock was issued, and only $28,000 of this was for cash. Although it does not bear on the present discussion, the company made a handsome profit that year and did not fail to do so for many years thereafter. Employment in 1903 averaged 125 men.

Sixty-one years later, in the spring of 1964, the Ford Motor Company introduced what is now called a new automobile. In accordance with current fashion in automobile nomenclature, it was called, one assumes inappropriately, a Mustang. The public was well-prepared for the new vehicle. Plans carefully specified prospective output and sales; they erred, as plans do, and in this case by being too modest. These preparations required three and a half years. From late in the autumn of 1962, when the design was settled, until the spring of 1964, there was a fairly firm commitment to the particular car that eventually emerged. Engineering and "styling" costs were $9 million; the cost of tooling up for the production of the Mustang was $50 million. In 1964, employment in the Ford Motor Company averaged 317,000. Assets at that time were approximately $6 billion. In the autumn of 1977, Ford brought out two new models—the Zephyr and the Fairmont. For these the cost was roughly $600 million, although part of the increase reflected the diminution of the dollar. By then, Ford's assets were approximately $16 billion, and employment worldwide was around 445,000.

Source: Galbraith, 1985, pp. 11–12.

---

that LDCs are placed in direct competition with one another. Because there are alternate suppliers of the same goods, or because total supply often exceeds demand, the buyers or importers of these goods (i.e., the MDCs) are placed in the advantageous position of being able to set their own price. In view of the fact that the LDCs have unbalanced economies and are limited to a very few exports, they are thereby forced to accept virtually whatever offer is made.[14]

As well as internal barriers to industrialization operating in the form of limited product economies, the LDCs also face external barriers—the existing structure of world trade. Overwhelmingly, the LDCs export agricultural commodities and other primary goods, while the MDCs export finished manufactured products. Not only has there been a recent "significant deterioration" in the terms of trade for primary producers (World Bank, 1987, p. 14ff), but also the LDCs are extremely dependent upon the developed countries who constitute their principal market. The developed economies trade primarily among themselves, and consequently established markets and trading lines are already in place. To the extent that the LDCs industrialize and thus produce manufactured goods, they are still dependent upon the developed economies for their market. Many barriers in the form of tariffs, quotas, preferred status, and other trade restrictions serve to make it extremely difficult for industrialized newcomers to break into this established trading network.

Human Resources: Education   A further problem to achieving industrial status in the LDCs is the fact that the population by and large does not have the necessary level of education and technical expertise to operate satisfactorily in an *industrial* labor force. As Table 5.2 illustrates, less than half of the relevant population are enrolled in secondary school in the Group 4 developing countries, and less than one-quarter in Group 5. By extension, the illiteracy rates are even more extreme (see Kurian, 1984, pp. 356–359). Particularly, given the rate and level of technological development and innovation over the past 200 years, possession of basic language and computational skills by most of the population is requisite to the industrialization process.

Natural Resources: Limits to Growth   The industrial revolution marked a technological threshold in which for the first time the outcome of the struggle of humankind against a harsh and hostile environment was not a foregone conclusion. With technological assistance, human beings could exceed their physiological and psychological limitations and exert their will upon the previous unrelenting state of nature. The processes of industrialization and urbanization were testimony to the change in relationship between individuals and their environment. Now, 200 years later, with one-quarter of the world population classified as industrialized and almost one-half urbanized, we are beginning to realize that our human interventions are taking a toll upon the surrounding biophysical system, and that we can no longer ignore the consequences.

Table 5.4 illustrates the consumption patterns by the more-developed and less-developed countries of some of the world's renewable and nonrenewable resources. For each commodity listed, the developed countries consume considerably more than their proportional share when their population is compared to the developing countries. Given this disproportionate consumption pattern, a question raised by many concerned with the future of the earth is: Can the world sustain universal industrialization, or, in other words, are there limits to growth? The LDCs, in their bid to industrialize now, find themselves in a much different ecological situation than did the MDCs when they became industrialized. Consequently, the ability of the environment to sustain yet more industrialization represents another potential barrier for the LDCs.[15]

According to the World Commission on Environment and Development (1987), world industrial production has increased more than fiftyfold in the past 100 years, and we produce seven times more than we did in 1950. However, given population growth rates and the period in the middle of the next century when we may expect world population to stabilize at approximately twice our present num-

Table 5.4   DISTRIBUTION OF WORLD CONSUMPTION BY DEVELOPED AND DEVELOPING
COUNTRIES, 1980–1982

Commodity	Units of per capita consumption	Developed countries (26 % of population)		Developing countries (74 % of population)	
		Share in world consumption (%)	Per capita	Share in world consumption (%)	Per capita
Food:					
Calories	kcal/day	34	3395	66	2389
Protein	gm/day	38	99	62	58
Fat	gm/day	53	127	47	40
Paper	kg/year	85	123	15	8
Steel	kg/year	79	455	21	43
Other Metals	kg/year	86	26	14	2
Commercial energy	mtce/year	80	5.8	20	0.5

Source: World Commission on Environment and Development, 1987, p. 33.

ber, the Commission (1987, p. 15) projects that we will have to surpass our present manufacturing output five to ten times more in order to raise total world consumption of manufactured goods to the level presently enjoyed by the developed countries. Clearly, the problems that we are now experiencing with environmental degradation (e.g. pollution, deforestation, desertification, resource depletion, and toxic waste disposal), as well as our inability to regulate the non-nationally controlled environment (e.g., oceans, seabed, airwaves, sky, space), will intensify as more nations begin to industrialize.

Strategies of Development

These five general sets of constraints or barriers to industrialization severely curtail opportunities for the LDCs to industrialize and therefore to reduce the ever widening gap between the rich and poor nations. However, while these hurdles are massive in their combined impact, they are not insurmountable. Various schemes, proposals, and strategies have been suggested whereby the LDCs can begin to share the same advantages as those presently enjoyed by the MDCs. For example, two World Bank commissions under the direction of former Prime Minister of Canada Lester Pearson (1969) and ex-Chancellor of West Germany Willy Brandt (1980) have made recommendations concerning things such as the institution of a modified and more equitable world financial structure, the liberalization of international trading policy, increased agricultural and energy production, and the establishment of a more workable international negotiating process. Similarly, the Third World nations themselves have made various proposals regarding what has come to be known as the New International Economic Order (see Tinbergen, 1976). In a slightly different vein, the World Commission on Environment and Development (1987) has presented various options and strategies whereby economic development can occur in ecologically sound ways.

Generally, there are two dominant strategies of economic development—inwardly focused import substitution and outwardly oriented export promotion (see Balassa, 1981, pp. 1–26). Countries employing import substitution attempt to industrialize by manufacturing for their own domestic markets the majority of those products they normally import. According to this strategy, not only do these countries become industrialized, they become economically self-sufficient, thus diminishing their heavy reliance upon MDCs for expensive manufactured imports. India and many Latin American countries have established economies that are illustrative of this approach. On the other hand, countries emphasizing export promotion concentrate on those goods, both primary and manufactured, that have traditionally contributed to their economies, and that therefore can earn export income. Successful pursuit of this strategy results in more profitable manufactured goods making up an increasing share of total exports, and consequently there occurs both industrial and economic development. Taiwan, South Korea, Hong Kong, and Singapore exemplify this approach.

While the viability of either of these strategies obviously depends upon many factors (e.g., size of domestic market, natural resources, education and skills of the labor force, presence and type of foreign investment, and sociopolitical conditions), the evidence to date favors the outward orientation as the preferred path of development (see Syrquin and Chenery, 1989). According to the World Bank (1987, pp. 92–94), "Outward orientation encourages efficient firms and discourages inefficient ones. And by creating a more competitive environment for both the private and public sectors, it also promotes higher productivity and hence faster economic growth."

Consequently, although there are barriers to industrialization for the less-developed countries, they can be overcome. To the extent that nothing is done and the gap between the rich and the poor continues to widen, dire predictions have been made as to the possible consequences. In fact, already we are witnessing an increase in world disorder. Manifestations of this deterioration include increasing acts of terrorism and civil disobedience, illegal migration, an increase in crime, widespread famine, and internal disputes that escalate into international conflicts. Further instability may be introduced through large-scale default on debt repayment, expropriation and the curtailment of the activities of transnational corporations, the formation of cartels among the LDCs to limit the supply of goods necessary to the developed nations, the breakdown of international bodies and diplomatic communication, and finally, revolution and war.

While it is clear that the LDCs will not "modernize" in the same fashion as the MDCs, it is also apparent that increasingly we live in an interdependent world system. To the extent that the now industrialized countries are not cognizant of the difficulties faced by the LDCs and act to ameliorate them, the rich nations along with the poor will suffer the calamitous consequences.

Before long, in our affluent, industrial, computerized jet society, we shall feel the wrath of the wretched people of the world. There will be no peace. (Lester Pearson, cited in Tinbergen, 1976, p. 59)

SUMMARY

5.1 It is possible to rank all countries in the world according to various generally accepted measures of industrialization, which include manufacturing as a percent of gross domestic product, percent of the labor force in industry, percent of professional and technical workers in the labor force, and commercial energy consumption per capita. These measures together form an index of industrialization in which it is possible to assign each country to one of five groups based on how many criteria of industrialization it meets or satisfies. See Table 5.1.

5.2 By popular convention, the countries in Western Europe, the United States, Canada, Japan, Australia, and New Zealand have been variously termed the "North," more developed, First World, and rich. Excluding the U.S.S.R. and the Eastern-bloc European countries which are termed Second World but are also the North, developed, and rich, the remaining nations of the world have been labeled the "South," less developed, Third World, and poor.

5.3 Table 5.2 reveals that there are direct relations between a country's level of industrialization and national income per capita, rate of urbanization, the development of its infrastructure (communication, education, and health), and the quality of life of its citizens. Furthermore, the gap between the industrialized and the developing nations is increasing.

5.4 Rich, industrialized, First World countries of the North score significantly higher on the Index of Social Progress than do poor, developing, Third World nations of the South. The Index measures the progress of nations from 1970 to 1983 in education, health, the status of women, defense spending, economic growth, population growth, ecological balance, political stability and participation, cultural diversity, and provision of welfare benefits.

5.5 Income distribution within countries is least unequal among the richest nations of the world. Consequently, to be poor in a less-developed country means that not only is there less initial total income to share, but also it that it is divided more unequally than it is in the most developed countries. The poor in the developing countries receive proportionately less than do the poor in the developed nations.

5.6 Generally, it is expected that while there will be some similarities to the developed nations in how the less-developed countries industrialize, there will also be major differences. These differences arise from the fact that many of the conditions that the LDCs now face bear little resemblance to what the MDCs experienced 200 years earlier.

5.7 Theories of development presented include the following: (1) modernization theory, which states that the less-developed countries will industrialize in a fashion similar to the now developed countries; (2) Marxist theory, which postulates that industrial capitalists throughout the world are exploiting the alienated international proletariat in much the same way as in the original industrial revolution; (3) dependency and world system theories which examine the relationship between the powerful "core" nations and the developing nations on the periphery.

5.8 Barriers to industrialization in the less-developed countries include rapid population growth that consumes much of any economic growth that is achieved, the increasing cost of industrialization and the staggering debt load, the limited product economies of the LDCs, the restrictive international trade structure, lack of a sufficiently educated and technically trained work force, limited availability of strategic natural resources, and the decreasing ability of the world environment to sustain even more industrial growth.

5.9 Two general strategies of economic development that have been used in the less-developed countries are inwardly focused import substitution and outwardly oriented export promotion. The evidence to date favors outward orientation as the preferred path of development.

5.10 The chapter concluded that because of the growing interdependence among all nations of the world, it is in the enlightened self-interest of MDCs to assist in the economic development of LDCs.

NOTES

1. While it is possible to use other indicators of industrialization, and thus also quite possible to end up with a slightly different rank order of industrialization, these measures were chosen because data are readily available on them and because they have been used as measures of industrialization in the past (see Hagedorn et al., 1971). Based on the rankings presented in Table 5.1, the correlation matrix (Pearson's correlation coefficients) below reveals how strongly these four indicators of industrialization are related to each other:

	1	2	3	4
1. Manufacturing as a percent of GDP	—			
2. Percent of labor force in industry	.42	—		
3. Percent professional and technical workers	.27	.71	—	
4. Per capita energy consumption	.42	.85	.84	—

2. These 128 countries represent a complete enumeration of all nations in the world with populations of at least one million.
3. Because of the fact that manufacturing occurs by hand *and* by machinery, and consequently many of the 49 countries listed in Table 5.1 are industrialized according to this indicator, "manufacturing as a percent of GDP" is therefore not highly related to the other three measures of industrialization. See the correlation matrix in Note 1 above.
4. The other countries in this group are: France, Italy, Japan, United Kingdom, United States, and West Germany.
5. In the 10 years between 1978 and 1987, the fastest growth experienced in Japan's labor force was in the professional and technical sector. By 1987, one out of every ten Japanese workers was a professional or technician (see ILO, 1988, p. 476).
6. Venezuela, as well as being a newly industrializing country, is also one of the world's leading oil producers (see Banks, 1986, p. 616).
7. The data for South Korea on all four measures of industrialization prove the one clear exception to this statement.
8. Seligson (1984) notes that in 1980, per capita income in the LDCs was US $245, while in the MDCs it was US $9,648. It should be noted that this difference of 3838% is modified

somewhat by the fact that the economies of the LDCs are geared to subsistence living, and hence a significant proportion of income is produced in kind via the barter system and consequently is not reported in dollar terms. However, the gap in per capita income between the LDCs and the MDCs is still very large and is increasing.

9. See footnote 3, Table 5.2.

10. Hence the sign for infinity ∞ in Table 5.2.

11. The actual correlation coefficients (Pearson's *r*) of industrialization in relation to each of these social structural measures were computed as follows:

> .93   Telephones per 100 population
> −.92   Human suffering index
> .91   GNP per capita
> −.91   Population per physician
> .87   Percent in secondary school—girls
> .87   Life expectancy at birth
> −.86   Percent urban population
> .86   Infant mortality rate
> .84   Percent in secondary school—boys
> −.71   Number of persons per room
> .67   Population "doubling time"

12. The distribution of wealth (i.e., accumulated income) is even more unequal than the distribution of income (see Murdoch, 1980).

13. These barriers to industrialization were first identified in one of my previous articles. See Hedley, 1985.

14. Only among the oil-producing exporting countries (OPEC) has a cartel been established to fix prices.

15. Currently, newly industrializing countries such as Mexico, Brazil, South Korea, and Taiwan have *higher* rates of pollution than do the United States, Japan, and the industrialized Western European nations. See, for example, the cover feature on the environment in *Newsweek*, 24 July 1989.

Chapter

6

Occupational and Labor Force Structure

It is important to acknowledge the kind of work we do because we are what we do, and what we do shapes society.

Naisbitt, 1982, p. 14

*T*he preceding chapters have laid the groundwork for a more detailed analysis of fully industrialized, more-developed countries. First, after a brief introduction to the features characteristic of industrialized societies (Chapter 1), we examined the various theoretical dimensions that comprise industrialization together with empirical indicators that have been used to measure these (Chapter 2). This formed the basis for an historical comparison of Great Britain, the first nation to become industrialized, and the United States, the leading industrial economy since the mid-nineteenth century (Chapter 3). This historical overview also detailed several of the important structural changes that occurred as a result of industrialization. Then, after outlining major theories that were proposed to explain the great transformation (Chapter 4), we first determined the extent to which all countries are industrialized today and then, similar to the historical analysis, examined various social correlates of industrialization (Chapter 5).

In the remaining chapters, in an attempt to identify both common and unique features of industrialization and its consequences, we will continue with the British–American comparison and introduce Japan into the analysis. The addition of Japan makes sense on a number of grounds. First, it is the only industrialized country without a European heritage. Thus, it serves as an important theoretical case to determine whether characteristics normally associated with industrialization are actually integral to the process or whether they are merely artifacts produced as common cultural (i.e., Western) responses. As we will note, researchers have compared many facets of industrialization in Japan and the West solely to assess just how robust the thesis for cultural convergence is. Consequently, the introduction of Japan into the remainder of the book will permit us to distinguish more precisely those aspects of industrialization that may be universal from those that represent idiosyncratic cultural adaptations.

Second, the addition of Japan into the analysis at this point is justified on substantive grounds. Currently, Japan is seriously challenging the position of the United States as world industrial leader. Regardless of competing claims both in academe and the popular press as to whether or not it has already achieved this feat, its economic preeminence and the fact that it appears to have taken an alternative route certainly warrants its inclusion in any comparative study of industrialization.

Finally, and following from the point above, Japan is very topical. Hardly a week passes without a major economic, trade, or business story about Japan that directly affects American interests. Whether it be high-profile commercial acquisitions, continuing trade imbalances, the deteriorating market share of American automobile manufacturers, or stories about Japanese-style management and the work ethic, Japan as an industrial nation is interesting as well as theoretically and substantively relevant.[1] Hence, on these grounds we will, where data permit, extend the analysis to include a three-nation comparison of Great Britain, the United States, and Japan.

In the present chapter, we will establish a comparative base for these countries by setting out in historical detail the dimensions of industrialization already identified. In determining how initially similar these countries are, we are in a better position in subsequent chapters to note any differences that do appear. In the latter part of the chapter, we will begin the analysis by comparatively examining the composition of the labor force in each country, noting how the personal attributes of workers themselves (e.g., sex, age, and race) are important determinants of the work they do. The chapter will conclude with a presentation of two major theoretical perspectives on labor markets and a projection of labor force trends into the twenty-first century.

STRUCTURAL FEATURES OF WORK

Sectors of Employment and Income

As mentioned in previous chapters, how people make their living is an important indicator of the industrial status of a country. One very general way to classify work is to group all jobs into one of three broad sectors of employment—primary, secondary, and tertiary. According to standard convention, jobs in the primary sector involve the harvesting of natural resources; there is no transformation of raw materials into finished goods. People in the primary sector work in agriculture, forestry, fishing, and hunting, although the vast majority of workers in this sector are usually employed in agriculture. Again by common convention, if at least half the workers are in the primary sector, the society is termed agricultural.

Work in the secondary sector involves the transformation of basic raw materials into semifinished or finished products. Thus, by this definition, those workers in the logging industry (i.e., harvesting trees) are in the primary sector, but those working in sawmills (i.e., transforming trees into lumber) are in the secondary sector. Work in the secondary sector includes manufacturing, construction, the provision of utilities, and mining and quarrying.[2] Most jobs in this sector are in manufacturing. When less than half the workers in the labor force are in the primary sector, the society is termed industrial.

In 1967, Daniel Bell noted what appeared to be a common feature of mature industrial societies. Increasingly, work in these societies involves providing services rather than raw or manufactured goods. For Bell, this constituted a qualitative change in the division of labor, which he termed "postindustrial." Expanding employment in the areas of wholesale and retail trade, restaurants and hotels; transport, storage, and communication; financing, insurance, real estate, and business services; and community, social, and personal services accounted for this change. To the extent that at least half the labor force of a country is employed in the provision of services, that is, the tertiary sector, it is defined as postindustrial.

Table 6.1 presents data on primary, secondary, and tertiary sector employment in the United Kingdom, United States, and Japan in five-year periods from 1965 to 1985. While there are differences to be observed among these three nations, the major conclusion to be drawn is one of similarity. Overall, in each of the three countries there is a systematic decline in primary sector employment over time and an increase in jobs in the tertiary sector. The increasing concentration in the provision of services is due in large part to mechanization of both the primary and secondary sectors, which results in greater productivity, thus freeing workers to move into the less easily mechanized tertiary sector of the labor force. According to Bell's definition, each of these countries is now postindustrial, Japan achieving this status by 1975, Great Britain by 1970, and the United States in the 1950s (Miller and Form, 1980, p. 75).[3]

Table 6.2, Average Percent Contribution of Industrial Sectors to Gross Domestic Product, complements the employment data provided in Table 6.1. Generally, the income earned by sector in these three countries is commensurate with the proportion of the labor force working in these sectors. Once more there is a decline over the three decades represented in the percent of the gross domestic product provided by the primary sector, and an increase in the contribution of the tertiary sector. However, in the secondary (manufacturing) sector, the percentage share of the GDP in Japan is considerably higher than the employment figures would suggest, while in Britain earnings from this sector are somewhat lower than the proportional representation of workers. This in part reflects the greater industrial

Table 6.1   PERCENT OF LABOR FORCE EMPLOYED IN PRIMARY, SECONDARY, AND
TERTIARY SECTORS IN THE UNITED KINGDOM, THE UNITED STATES, AND
JAPAN, 1965–1985

Country	Year	Sector of employment (%)			Total
		Primary[1]	Secondary[2]	Tertiary[3]	
United Kingdom	1985	2.6	32.3	65.1	100.0
	1980	2.6	37.7	59.7	100.0
	1975	2.7	40.5	56.8	100.0
	1970	3.2	44.8	52.0	100.0
	1965	3.8	46.6	49.6	100.0
United States	1985	3.1	28.0	68.8	99.9
	1980	3.6	30.5	65.9	100.0
	1975	4.1	30.6	65.3	100.0
	1970	4.5	34.4	61.1	100.0
	1965	6.3	35.5	58.2	100.0
Japan	1985	8.8	34.9	56.4	100.1
	1980	10.4	35.3	54.2	99.9
	1975	12.7	35.9	51.5	100.1
	1970	17.4	35.7	46.9	100.0
	1965	23.5	32.4	44.1	100.0

[1]Primary sector includes agriculture, hunting, forestry, and fishing.

[2]Secondary sector includes manufacturing; mining and quarrying; utilities; and construction.

[3]Tertiary sector includes wholesale and retail trade; restaurant and hotels; transport, storage and communication; financing, insurance, real estate, and business services; and community, social, and personal services.

Source: Adapted from OECD, 1987, pp. 90–91, 106–107, 450–451.

productivity of Japan over the United Kingdom, a subject we will treat in more detail later in the chapter.

While these two tables reflect broad trends of occupational change in the labor force arising from industrialization, and indicate in general terms the sources of employment and income within highly developed economies, they do not begin to portray the tremendous horizontal and vertical differentiation that is now characteristic of these modern complex postindustrial societies. The division of labor or occupational specialization that Durkheim wrote about has developed to such an extent that it is now almost impossible to measure in precise ways the kinds and degrees of change that have taken place. Particularly when researchers are attempting to compare and contrast changes between countries, it is problematic whether in fact they are focusing on the same aspects or features in the different nations they are examining.

One solution to this problem, and also an indication of the complexities involved, is described in Box 6-1, **ISCO and ISIC**. Given that it is necessary to

Table 6.2   AVERAGE PERCENT CONTRIBUTION OF INDUSTRIAL SECTORS TO GROSS
DOMESTIC PRODUCT IN THE UNITED KINGDOM, THE UNITED STATES, AND
JAPAN, 1950—1981

Country	Period	Sectoral contribution to GDP (%)			
		Primary	Secondary	Tertiary	Total
United Kingdom	1970–81	2.2	35.9	61.8	99.9
	1960–70	2.8	39.8	57.4	100.0
	1950–60	3.4	42.8	53.9	100.1
United States	1970–81	3.0	34.2	62.9	100.1
	1960–70	3.1	37.1	59.8	100.0
	1950–60	4.0	38.3	57.7	100.0
Japan	1970–81	5.0	43.2	51.8	100.0
	1960–70	8.5	45.0	46.5	100.0
	1950–60	12.6	44.6	42.9	100.1

Source: Adapted from World Bank, 1983, pp. 239, 255, 257.

measure the same thing in the same way from Time 1 to Time 2 in order to assess the direction, magnitude, rate, and form of change (see "Units of Analysis," Chapter 2), labor statisticians have over the past 40 years attempted to devise standard and at the same time valid labor force classification systems that reflect the actual detail of the innumerable tasks and empirical contexts that constitute the world of work. Although the solution is not perfect, it does permit researchers and policymakers alike to make relatively informed decisions about labor force changes that are occurring in both national and international contexts.

Organizational Base

Another important feature of contemporary postindustrial societies is their organizational base. Not only was Durkheim astute in selecting out the division of labor as a key independent variable responsible for producing vast structural changes in society, but also Weber was prophetic in identifying bureaucracy as a continuing force in the rationalization of work and society. Actually, it can be argued that in an important way the work of Weber subsumes Durkheim's earlier notion in that two principal features of bureaucracy are horizontal and vertical differentiation (see Chapter 7 for further elaboration). Thus, in describing the bureaucratization of society, Weber was most attentive to the division of labor, or horizontal/functional differentiation, as well as to the hierarchical ordering of rational-legal authority (i.e., vertical differentiation).

Modern industrial societies have labor forces that overwhelmingly are comprised of wage and salary earners or, in other words, organizational employees. Notwithstanding the common reference to Britain as a nation of shopkeepers, over 90% of its labor force for at least the past two decades has been made up of wage

Box 6-1 ISCO AND ISIC

In 1958, the International Conference of Labour Statisticians approved two classification systems designed to act as models or standards for national classification systems, and thereby to promote international comparability of labor statistics. The International Standard Classification of Occupations (ISCO) and the International Standard Industrial Classification (ISIC), both published by the International Labor Office in Geneva, were revised in 1968 and are currently under revision again.

In order to provide a standard and uniform base to describe the increasingly complex and specialized world of work, two basic principles of classification were adopted: (1) the type of work performed (occupation), and (2) its setting or context (industry). Thus, theoretically it is possible to cross-classify any job in the world according to these two dimensions, although practical problems do arise in that no empirical classification system is ever perfect.

Both ISCO and ISIC are comprised of four levels, each one providing successively finer descriptive detail (definition) of occupations and industrial contexts. While the first level classifies occupational groupings and industrial divisions on a very broad basis (i.e., seven major occupational groups and nine major industrial divisions), the fourth level succeeds in categorizing essentially similar jobs (i.e., over 1500 occupational categories and close to 1000 industrial groups). Depending upon the purpose of analysis and the availability of data, one may operate at any of these four levels. The first levels of ISCO and ISIC are reproduced as follows:

International Standard Classifications of Occupations (ISCO) and Industries (ISIC)—Level 1

ISCO	ISIC
1. Professional, technical, and related workers	1. Agriculture, hunting, forestry, and fishing
2. Administrative and managerial workers	2. Mining and quarrying
3. Clerical and related workers	3. Manufacturing
4. Sales workers	4. Electricity, gas, and water
5. Service workers	5. Construction
6. Agricultural, animal husbandry and forestry workers, fishermen, and hunters	6. Wholesale and retail trade, and restaurants and hotels
7. Production and related workers, and transport equipment opertors and laborers	7. Transport, storage, and communication
	8. Financing, insurance, real estate, and business services
	9. Community, social, and personal services

Sources: ILO, 1968; United Nations, 1968.

and salary earners. Similarly in the United States, despite the writings of Horatio Alger and the American dream of individualistic free enterprise, currently (1985) 91% of the labor force work in organizations (86% in 1965). Only in Japan, the last of these three countries to industrialize, is there a significant proportion of the labor force (26%) who are not employees. However, consonant with the trend of increasing bureaucratization, this proportion is greatly reduced from that of 20 years earlier (39%) (see OECD, 1987, pp. 90–91; 106–107; 450–451). Nissan, Matsushita, Toyota, Hitachi, and Nippon are becoming household words and increasingly changing the structure of Japanese society.

Table 6.3 presents World Bank data on the structure and organization of manufacturing in Great Britain, the United States, and Japan. Because there are more production units (establishments) in Japan than there are in the United States and Great Britain combined, this means that on average Japanese manufacturing establishments employ fewer workers per organizational unit than is true in either Great Britain or the United States, which have had a longer period in which to build their industrial organizational base (see Granovetter, 1984). It should be noted that the figures pertaining to the number of manufacturing establishments include branch plants and individual operating sites of employing organizations. Therefore, the actual number of employees per manufacturer is considerably higher than what is reported in this table.

The last three rows in Table 6.3 contain measures of productivity in British, American, and Japanese industry (c. 1980). Whereas the determinants of productivity are very complex and are comprised of many factors including level of technological development, the volume and unit costs of production, the labor–capital

Table 6.3 ORGANIZATIONAL STRUCTURE, PRODUCTIVITY MEASURES, AND LABOR COSTS IN BRITISH, AMERICAN, AND JAPANESE MANUFACTURING, C. 1980

Manufacturing sector	United Kingdom	United States	Japan
Number of employees[1]	6,462,000	19,210,000	10,252,000
Number of establishments[2]	107,920	335,288	735,183
Average number of employees per establishment	60	57	14
Gross output per employee (US $)[3]	65,069	96,674	94,467
Value added per employee (US $)[4]	25,318	40,078	32,905
Wages and salary per employee (US $)	12,363	16,406	11,523

[1] Average number of regular workers employed in manufacturing.

[2] Number of production units that engage in one or predominantly one kind of activity at a single location (e.g., an individual workshop or factory).

[3] Average contribution of each employee to the total gross value of all production.

[4] Average contribution per worker to the total value added to raw materials as a result of the manufacturing process.

Source: Adapted from World Bank, 1983, pp. 470, 477, 478.

ratio, managerial expertise, exchange rates, and other conditions affecting supply and demand (see Wohlers and Weinhart, 1988, pp. 74–82), it would appear that manufacturing in the United States and Japan generally is more productive than it is in the United Kingdom. At least part of the reason for this difference lies in the fact that Britain, being the first nation to industrialize, in general has an older and therefore less efficient manufacturing base than the United States and particularly Japan, which has recently (1988) been acknowledged as being slightly more productive than the United States (see Bednarzik and Shiells, 1989; *Monthly Labor Review*, 1989, p. 102).

All these data attest to the substantial and still growing organizational base of mature industrial societies. Although the figures for Japan reveal that it has not yet achieved the level of organizational development found in the United States and Great Britain, nevertheless all of the evidence available indicates that it is moving in this direction. Marx's prediction of the growing concentration and centralization of capital is in part manifested by this continual organizational consolidation.

Technological Expertise

The final structural dimension of work we will discuss concerns the technological component of industrialization. Owing to the expansion of accumulated knowledge such that now it consists of a plethora of highly complex disciplines and subdisciplines, the process of invention, discovery, and innovation is achieved more by organized teams of specialized scientists and technicians than by individuals working independently. Consequently, bureaucratization provides the organizational support necessary to underwrite the increasingly expensive and complicated process of research and development. As noted in Table 5.1, at least 10% of the labor forces of industrialized countries (in 1981) are comprised of professional and technical workers (11.7%, 15.4%, and 8.6% in the United Kingdom, United States, and Japan, respectively).[4] In Japan over the past decade (1978–1987), this occupational category has gained a remarkable 52% making it by far the fastest growing sector of employment. Now, one out of every ten Japanese workers is a professional or technician (see ILO, 1988, p. 476).

Technological development is reflected not only in the category of workers who contribute directly to the process of invention and innovation but also in the labor force as a whole. Increasingly, those employed in mature industrial societies have a wide range of technical skills and general expertise. For example, from 1970 to 1980, the mean years of schooling of the United States labor force climbed from 10.6 to 12.6, while in Japan the comparable figures were 7.6 and 9.8 (Psacharopoulis and Arriagada, 1986, p. 573).[5] Other data indicate that the largest and still growing tertiary sector is considerably more educated than either the secondary or primary sectors (Bednarzik and Shiells, 1989, p. 37). These statistics in turn are attributable in large part to the amount of money devoted to formal education by these countries. In the United Kingdom (1983), 5.3% of the gross national product is spent on education, while in the United States the equivalent figure is 6.7%, and in Japan it is 5.7% (United Nations, 1988, Table 51).

This general description of the structural features common to mature industrial societies as exemplified by Great Britain, the United States, and Japan has revealed that diminishing proportions of the labor force make their living in the primary sector, which for the most part is compensated for by complementary increases in the services-providing tertiary sector. With the advent of industrialism, there is also an expansion in the secondary (manufacturing) sector, which gradually peaks as more productive capital-intensive technology is substituted for human labor. Generally, national income figures mirror those in employment. The growth of the secondary and tertiary sectors is aided very largely by the organizational development of modern capitalism, the growth of public enterprise, and the bureaucratization of the labor force, which constantly displaces both independent entrepreneurs and craft workers. The increased horizontal and vertical differentiation of the labor force results in occupational titles and job descriptions expanding exponentially. Technological development, an integral feature of industrialization, occurs through organizational sponsorship of the scientific and technical elite and through a general upgrading of the labor force as a result of expanding educational and vocational training opportunities.

While the foregoing is descriptive of industrial development at the broad national level, it does not indicate that the attributes of workers themselves are important determinants of how they will participate in the labor force. Obviously, individual educational and vocational achievement serves as an important channeling mechanism, which determines the type and level of labor force entry. However, there are other attributes that have also been important in defining the labor market experience of individual workers. It is to these attributes that we now turn our attention.

THE DIVISION OF LABOR BY SEX

Labor Force Participation

The labor force participation rate is the percentage of people of working age who are either employed or formally registered as seeking employment. Table 6.4, which presents the labor force participation rates for men and women of various age groups in the United Kingdom, United States, and Japan over a 20-year span, reveals that there are vast differences in these rates by gender, but that over time these differences have diminished substantially, particularly in Great Britain and the United States.

The bottom row of Table 6.4 presents the combined labor force participation rates for men and women in each country for 1967 and 1986. In general, these rates do not vary materially over the 20 years in any of these countries. In both 1967 and 1986, approximately three-quarters of all those eligible to work in the population were either employed or actively seeking work. However, these figures mask the very real changes that have occurred during these two decades. When the par-

Table 6.4   LABOR FORCE PARTICIPATION RATES BY AGE GROUPS OF MALES AND FEMALES IN THE UNITED KINGDOM, THE UNITED STATES, AND JAPAN, 1967 AND 1986

| | Participation rates (%) United Kingdom | | | |
| | 1967 | | 1986 | |
Age	M	F	M	F
16–19[1]	73.7	69.6	73.7	71.1
20–24	93.9	61.8	84.5	69.2
25–34	98.3	41.8	93.4	62.8
35–44	98.7	53.7	94.5	71.8
45–54	97.6	55.9	91.7	70.2
55–64	91.8	37.5	67.0	35.0
65 and over	22.6	6.7	7.4	2.7
Totals	97.5	52.7	87.3	63.5
Total male and female	74.9		75.4	

| | Participation rates (%) United States | | | |
| | 1967 | | 1986 | |
Age	M	F	M	F
16–19[1]	58.5	41.4	56.8	52.9
20–24	85.4	52.5	85.4	72.5
25–34	96.0	41.5	93.5	71.6
35–44	96.0	47.6	94.1	72.9
45–54	94.5	51.8	90.3	65.7
55–64	82.2	41.4	66.7	42.0
65 and over	26.0	9.0	24.5	10.0
Totals	91.2	47.8	87.2	66.5
Total male and female	69.2		76.7	

| | Participation rates (%) Japan | | | |
| | 1967 | | 1986 | |
Age	M	F	M	F
16–19[1]	36.9	38.8	18.0	17.2
20–24	83.6	70.0	70.8	73.7
25–34	97.0	50.1	96.4	52.1
35–44	97.3	60.5	97.3	64.4
45–54	96.4	60.7	96.0	64.9
55–64	86.6	46.7	82.9	44.7
65 and over	54.5	21.6	36.2	15.2
Totals	88.7	56.5	87.5	57.4
Total male and female	72.3		72.4	

[1] In Japan, the participation rates are for 15- to 19-year olds.

Source: Adapted from O.E.C.D., 1987, pp. 474–77; 500–501.

ticipation rates of males and females are presented separately (see the next row up), you will note that men who constitute the majority of the working population have reduced somewhat their labor force participation over these 20 years, while women who comprise an expanding proportion of the labor force have dramatically increased their participation rates, both absolutely and relative to men.[6] Let us now examine separately in more detail male and female labor force participation in each country.

For men in each of the three countries and for both of the years represented, ages 25 to 54 are years of virtual full employment. Participation rates average around 95 percent, and are even higher in the modal 35 to 44 age range. The most significant changes in participation rates occur in the age groups at either end of this uniformly high participating group. You will note that in 1967 men's participation was also relatively high in the 20 to 24 and 55 to 64 age ranges, but dropped, in some cases dramatically, by the time the 1986 rates were recorded. With regard to the younger of these two age groups, the drop in participation is largely due to retarded labor force entry owing to increased educational and vocational training demands made of labor force participants. Only in the United States is there no decline in participation between these two periods. This is explained by the fact that the United States, currently the world leader with respect to postsecondary enrollment, has occupied this position for some decades (see Kurian, 1984, pp. 368–371; Sanderson, 1988, pp. 364–366). Consequently, the effect of these increased educational demands on American labor force participation occurred prior to 1967 (see Moore, 1969, pp. 119–122).[7] Comparison of the 1967 participation rates of American men aged 20 to 24 with the 1986 rates of similarly aged Britons gives further credence to this explanation.

The reduced labor force participation of older men in 1986, particularly in Great Britain and the United States, is explained by increased access to public social security programs and private pension schemes. Furthermore, according to one American study of the provisions and stipulations contained in 187 private pension plans, requirements have been relaxed in recent years making it easier for older workers to retire before age 65 (see Bell and Marclay, 1987). Another American study found that as well as the creation of explicit Early Retirement Incentive Plans (ERIPs), the rules of both public and private pension plans often encourage early retirement (Herz and Rones, 1989). Most industrialized European countries, including Great Britain, also have enacted a variety of early retirement and disability options in an attempt to deal with high rates of unemployment (see Mirkin, 1987).

These provisions, which are all part of the expanded infrastructure, permit older workers now to exercise more options with regard to how they live their lives than were available to previous generations whose circumstances forced them to work while they were still able (see, for example, Friedmann and Havighurst, 1954). However, it is important to note that for a variety of reasons not all older workers are eligible to receive either public or private pensions, and therefore cannot exercise the options available to the majority (see ILO, 1984). As Table 6.4 indicates, this is particularly true for Japanese men aged 55 to 64 who by and large do not yet have this luxury of choice.

Consequently, while male labor force participation has decreased over the past few decades owing to increased educational demands made on the young and more universal social security coverage of older workers, the major bulk of male workers labors on as before. The changes that have occurred represent refinements to a general pattern that has persisted throughout the whole industrialization process. On the other hand, the recent changes in female labor force participation represent a fundamental alteration in women's pattern of behavior and have resulted in a basic restructuring of societal values regarding appropriate male and female roles.

The traditional pattern of female labor force participation through the first half of this century consisted of large numbers of young single women entering the labor market. Here they worked until either they got married or just prior to the birth of their first child, whereupon they left their paid employment and assumed housewife/mother roles in the community. Consequently, after the initial influx of female workers aged 16 to 24, participation rates dropped off dramatically and consistently with each succeeding age level. Although each new decade revealed higher participation rates for every age category, the overall pattern remained the same (see Oppenheimer, 1970).

With the 1960s came the first break in the traditional pattern. Whereas, consistent with the previous era, participation was highest in the youngest age groups, it did not decline consistently thereafter. Participation rates rose in the 35 to 44 age range as women began to reenter the labor force in increasing numbers. The figures for 1967 in all three countries reflect this change in pattern. Following 1960, female participation rates continued to rise, but particularly in the 25 to 54 age categories, with the consequence that not only was the previous decline in participation upon marriage and childbirth no longer immediately discernible but also the highest participation was now occurring among women aged 35 to 44. The form of female participation at present is beginning to approximate that of men. The 1986 figures for Great Britain and the United States demonstrate this new configuration.

The dramatic increase in female employment has occurred as a result of a variety of interrelated factors. As mentioned previously, the process of industrialization involves the creation of a labor market to match labor supply with demand. Those not in the labor market (traditionally women and children) constitute economic liabilities. Consequently, one of the results of industrialization was a decrease in the birth rate and an increase in female labor force participation. With fewer children more closely spaced (plus an increase in life expectancy), women certainly have more time to resume their labor force activity. As Moore (1969, p. 113) so succinctly states it, "As far as release of married women from domestic household functions is concerned, it is clear that the major, and perhaps the only important labor-saving device has been the contraceptive, which permits limiting the number and especially the duration of childbearing."

Another important set of factors affecting female employment concerns the occupational structure itself. As we will determine below, women are primarily concentrated in tertiary sector employment. Traditionally, employers could meet their demands for female labor in their preferred recruiting pool—young, single women. These were preferred because they were more "manageable" and had fewer external ties and demands placed on them. However, with the tremendous expansion of the tertiary sector that ensued, demand exceeded preferred supply, and consequently employers were forced to hire older and married women (see Oppenheimer, 1973).

Other factors explaining increased female labor force participation, especially older women, include the resurgence of the feminist movement during the 1960s and the demand for more equality of treatment of the sexes. This movement can be seen as part of a larger concern, which emanates from an increasingly educated populace that advocates the eradication of *all* special privilege based on ascribed rather than achieved status. The feminist movement proposed that the freeing of women from their economic dependence on men and thus their subordination to them could only be achieved by women entering the labor force and thereby gaining their own sense of personhood. Not incidentally, two wage earners in one family also contribute substantially to the overall quality of family life.

A final reason underlying greater female labor force participation is the increase in the separation and divorce statistics, particularly in the United States, which has the third highest divorce rate in the world (Kurian, 1984, pp. 32–33).[8] More and more women are working because they have no other choice. As a result of either separation, divorce, widowhood, or husband unemployment, it is estimated that fully one-third of the American female labor force are the sole supporters of their families (Ford, 1988, p. 54).

Occupational Segregation

Not only is the pattern of women's participation in the labor force different from that of men, but also women and men tend to have quite separate and distinct work experiences. As one researcher put it, a "woman's work is never done—by men" (Power, 1975). Although women are being employed in increasing numbers such that by 1985 in Great Britain, the United States, and Japan they constituted 42.1%, 44.1%, and 39.7% of the labor forces, respectively (OECD, 1987), nevertheless both the history and contemporary situation of women and men is that they are segregated into two separate work divisions in which they labor more or less independently.

One commonly accepted measure of occupational segregation by sex is the index of segregation or dissimilarity (Duncan and Duncan, 1955). Varying from zero (complete interchangeability of jobs between the sexes) to 100 (complete segregation such that no man's job is ever performed by a woman and vice versa), one recent cross-national study of occupational segregation in 12 industrialized nations found that most countries ranged between 40 and 50 on the index of segregation (Roos, 1985). This means that for there to be complete occupational integration between the sexes, 40% to 50% of either men or women would need to change occupations. Furthermore, although there have been slight, recent reductions in this index over the past two decades, sex segregation of occupations can be documented throughout the history of industrialization (see, for example, Aldrich and Buchele, 1986, pp. 1–39; Jacobs, 1989).

Table 6.5 presents the general pattern of occupational segregation occurring in industrialized countries. Based on previously conducted nationally representative sample surveys (Roos, 1985), it shows how men and women are distributed among various broad occupational groupings that have been ranked by the relative prestige accorded to them. Thus, it is possible to determine the amount of segregation not only by function or the type of work that men and women do, but also by status or the general esteem in which this work is held. The international prestige scale was developed by Treiman (1977). It is based on his analysis of the prestige scores of 509 separate occupations gained through national surveys conducted in 60 countries. Because Treiman found that "occupational prestige hierarchies are essentially similar throughout the world (1977, p. 166), he consequently felt confident in devising a composite scale based on the earlier surveys.[9]

With regard to the functional division of labor by sex, Table 6.5 reveals that close to three times as many men as women work in production and related activities, while women predominate in clerical and service occupations. Concerning the prestige dimension, men far outnumber women in high-prestige professional and managerial activities, while women form the bulk of low-prestige professional and technical workers. Similarly, men are in the majority in high-prestige sales but form a distinct minority in low-prestige sales. Consequently, with regard to both function and status, these data indicate that there are essential differences in the work that men and women perform. The index of dissimilarity (segregation) at the bottom of each country's listing confirms in general the particular distinctions contained in the body of the table.

While the conclusions drawn are appropriate to Great Britain and the United States, they do not apply as well to Japan. The major reason for this, as Roos (1985, pp. 48–49) explains, is that the survey upon which the Japanese data are based was conducted in 1967. Consequently, rather than being fully industrialized, Japan was an emerging industrial nation. The large percentages of both women (37%) and men (19%) in agricultural activities attest to this fact. Subsequent developments that have occurred in Japan, for example, the increasing concentration of women in clerical occupations, now makes it more similar to the patterns displayed by postindustrial Great Britain and the United States. No doubt its index of segregation would also reflect this if it were recomputed now.

While this table indicates in a general way the type of occupational segregation experienced by women and men in industrial society, it is not precise in describing the actual amount or degree. Because of the broad occupational categories, men and women may be classified as the same and yet be employed in very different jobs with different responsibilities, conditions of work, and rates of pay. For example, of the occupations grouped under "high-prestige clerical and related" in the United States, women's jobs include bookkeepers, secretaries, typists, and miscellaneous clerical workers, while men's jobs do not list secretaries and typists, but do include bookkeepers and miscellaneous clerical workers. In addition, the following categories are also listed for men: inspectors; office managers; officials and administrators; public administration; clerical supervisors; and peripheral equipment operators (see Roos, 1985, Appendix A). Consequently, to the extent that one wishes to be precise in measuring occupational segregation, it

Table 6.5 PERCENT DISTRIBUTION OF BRITISH, AMERICAN, AND JAPANESE MEN AND WOMEN IN OCCUPATIONS RANKED BY THE STANDARD INTERNATIONAL OCCUPATIONAL PRESTIGE SCALE

Occupational Category	United Kingdom		United States		Japan	
	Men (%)	Women (%)	Men (%)	Women (%)	Men (%)	Women (%)
1. High-prestige professional and technical	4.8	2.3	11.1	6.7	5.4	4.8
2. Administrative and managerial	6.1	0.9	10.4	3.0	8.4	1.0
3. High-prestige clerical and related	5.5	29.4	2.4	22.9	15.5	15.2
4. High-prestige sales	4.9	3.5	4.4	1.5	6.2	6.3
5. Low-prestige professional and technical	7.2	12.6	6.5	15.6	3.3	2.5
6. High-prestige agricultural	2.5	0.0	3.4	0.1	16.8	30.4
7. High-prestige production and related	17.3	4.7	18.4	4.5	17.8	7.3
8. High-prestige service	5.5	7.3	5.0	8.8	2.0	2.8
9. Medium-prestige production and related	24.9	10.4	19.1	8.5	12.7	9.8
10. Low-prestige clerical and related	4.5	0.4	4.7	10.3	1.0	0.5
11. Low-prestige sales	2.2	8.3	5.1	5.3	2.0	4.9
12. Low-prestige agricultural	3.0	1.3	1.7	0.4	2.1	6.2
13. Low-prestige service	1.5	15.4	2.9	10.4	2.0	8.1
14. Low-prestige production & related	10.0	3.4	5.0	2.0	4.9	0.2
Totals	99.9	99.9	100.1	100.0	100.1	100.0
Number of cases	(545)	(314)	(1939)	(1298)	(719)	(454)
Index of dissimilarity	51.1		46.8		27.6	

Source: Roos, 1985, pp. 50–52

is necessary to get down to the detail of the actual job or occupation. It should also be noted that the more types of jobs or categories there are, the greater will be the index of segregation. (See Box 6-2, **Clerical Workers**.)

Table 6.6 provides another approach to measuring the extent of occupational segregation of the sexes. Employing 1980 census data for the United States, it is a listing of those occupations (based on three levels of classification) that are the largest sources of employment for men and women. The right-hand column of the table indicates that the top 10 occupations of men are almost exclusively the preserve of men, while similarly the largest occupations of women are virtually a female domain. All of the ten occupations listed for men are at least 70% male, while seven of them are dominated by upwards of 80% men. Likewise, seven of the leading female occupations employ at least 80% women. Only one occupation, managers not elsewhere classified, is common to both lists. These more detailed data indicate not only the type but also the extent of occupational segregation.[10] In the labor force overall, 53.2% of American men work in occupations that are at least 80% male-dominated, and 46.3% of American women have occupations in which 80% or more are female (Rytina and Bianchi, 1984, p. 14). In essence, then, there are two labor forces, one for men and one for women.

Box 6-2   Clerical Workers

Who is a clerical worker? Secretaries, typists, stenographers, filing clerks, bookkeepers, bank tellers, computer operators, and telephone operators are all clerical workers. But so is a mail carrier and even a postmaster! Also included are air traffic controllers, railway station masters, sleeping car attendants, government executive officials, proofreaders, office managers, bus conductors, hotel receptionists, radio officers on ships and aircraft, messengers, and automatic data-processing machine operators.

According to the International Standard Classification of Occupations (ISCO), "clerical and related workers" represent one of seven major occupational groups. In turn, there are 10 minor groups of clerical and related workers, 20 unit groups, and 81 separate occupational categories of clerks (see ILO, 1968, pp. 274–275). Only when you get down to the fourth classification level of ISCO is it possible to make meaningful distinctions about actual occupations. However, even on this most detailed level, there is still a great deal of variability among clerical jobs with the same occupational title. For example, variation in rates of pay, areas of responsibility, and work context all serve to make "the same job" different. Consequently, on national or international levels of comparison, it is possible to draw only the most general of conclusions. "A rose is a rose," but a clerk may not necessarily be "a clerk."

While the first right-hand column of Table 6.6 indicates the degree of segregation, the other two columns reflect the occupational concentration of men and women. Of the 312 occupations classified, the top ten male occupations account for just over one-quarter of all men employed, whereas the 10 most populous female occupations comprise fully two-fifths of the female labor force. Just 16 occupations encompass half of all women working in America (see Rytina and Bianchi, 1984, p. 16). Note also that of these leading female occupations, four (comprising more than one-fifth of all employed women) are classified as clerical. Consequently, not only are women segregated (like men), but also they are concentrated (unlike men) into a relatively small collection of "female" occupations.

Researchers and writers in this field have observed that most of the work that women do in the labor force is simply an extension of what they have traditionally done in the home—being a help mate to man. Secretarial and clerical work, cooking, waiting tables, hosting, teaching and caring for small children, nursing, cleaning, and sewing are all chores that women have done since time immemorial. The only difference between what most women are doing now and what they traditionally did is that they are being paid directly for their labor. Whereas it is true that in the decade of the seventies women have made modest inroads into "male" occupations, it is also true that traditional "female" occupations continue to be predominantly "woman's work" (see Rytina and Bianchi, 1984, pp. 15–16).

Table 6.6   TOP TEN OCCUPATIONS OF AMERICAN MEN AND WOMEN, 1980

Top ten occupations for men	Occupations as a % of men employed	Cumulative percent	Percent male in occupation
1. Managers, NEC[1]	6.7	6.7	73.1
2. Truckdrivers, heavy	3.2	9.9	97.7
3. Janitors and cleaners	2.9	12.8	76.6
4. Supervisors production	2.8	15.6	85.0
5. Carpenters	2.2	17.8	98.4
6. Supervisors, sales	2.0	19.8	71.8
7. Laborers	2.0	21.8	80.6
8. Sales representatives	1.9	23.7	85.1
9. Farmers	1.8	25.5	90.2
10. Auto mechanics	1.7	27.2	98.7

Top ten occupations for women	Occupation as a % of total women employed	Cumulative percent	Percent female in occupation
1. Secretaries	9.4	9.4	98.8
2. Teachers, elementary school	4.2	13.6	75.4
3. Bookkeepers	4.0	17.6	89.7
4. Cashiers	3.7	21.3	83.5
5. Office clerks	3.4	24.7	82.1
6. Managers, NEC[1]	3.3	28.0	26.9
7. Waitresses and waiters	3.1	31.1	88.0
8. Salesworkers	2.9	34.0	72.7
9. Registered nurses	2.9	36.9	95.9
10. Nursing aides	2.9	39.8	87.8

[1]NEC stands for "not elsewhere classified."

Sources: Adapted from OECD, 1987, pp. 92–25, and Rytina and Bianchi, 1984, pp. 15–16.

Wage and Salary Discrimination

The occupational segregation and concentration of women has one other important consequence. Because women and men for the most part are employed in different occupations, it is very difficult to make precise comparative assessments of the work that they do in relation to the income that they earn. In comparing women's and men's earnings, factors that should be taken into account include different job types and levels, required qualifications, previous experience, and length of time at work and with the same employer. However, when all these variables are controlled or taken into account, there remains a substantial residual factor that cannot be explained away (see Ferber and Lowry, 1976; Reskin and Hartmann, 1986, pp. 10–13; Staines et al., 1976). Throughout the industrialized nations of the world, women earn less than men (see Hedley, 1986b, p. 504).

According to the U.S. Bureau of Labor Statistics, in 1986 women earned on average 69% of men's earnings (see Mellor, 1987, p. 42). This is similar to a 1982 study of British workers in which women earn 74% of what men earn, and considerably higher than 1983 Japanese data that report that women make only 53% of men's earnings (see Ford, 1988, p. 53). In his study of Japanese companies, Clark (1979, p. 234) observes that "it is admittedly true that no industrial society gives women genuine parity with men in economic affairs, but Japanese women are more rigidly discriminated against than their Western counterparts." (See also Box 6-3, **The Power of Japanese Women.**)

One of the most significant factors explaining the sex differential in earnings is occupational sex composition. In general, the greater the proportion of females in an occupation, the lower is the income received by both women *and* men. Reskin and Hartmann (1986, p. 10) report on one American census study, which made a detailed analysis of 499 occupational categories:

> ... the correlation between median annual wage and salary earnings (adjusted for time spent working) and the percentage female among occupational incumbents is -.45: The higher the percentage female, the less an occupation paid. Employment in a female-dominated occupation depressed wages of workers of both sexes; each additional percentage point female in an occupation was associated with $42 less in median annual income.

Consequently, occupational segregation has the effect not only of creating two separate labor forces but also of undervaluing women's work relative to that of men.

Further income disparity is experienced by those women most advantageously placed in the occupational hierarchy. A cross-national study by Swafford (1978) reports an inverse relation between occupational level and women's earnings relative to men's. For example, in Britain, female manual workers earned 71 percent of male manual workers, but female nonmanual workers received only 62% of what their male counterparts made. A similar result may be gained by examining the relative earnings of female to male blue collar workers in the United States (see Mellor, 1987, Table 1). Unskilled female handlers, equipment cleaners, helpers, and laborers on average earn 83% (i.e., $226 per week) of what males earn ($271) in this same occupational category; semiskilled female operators, fabricators, and laborers make 68% ($225) of the average semiskilled male wage ($332); and skilled female precision production and craft workers earn 66% ($277) of males ($418) in the skilled trades. Consequently, given this inverse relationship and as these particular figures indicate, it is possible for a semiskilled female machine operator to be paid actually less than an unskilled female laborer.[11]

These data appear to indicate that when a case for uniqueness of job or occupation can be made, as is more probable at the higher occupational levels, income differentials between the sexes will be greatest. Conversely, in those

Box 6-3 The Power of Japanese Women

The following excerpt comes from an article entitled "The Power of Japanese Women." It was written by Kimindo Kusaka who, according to the biographical note accompanying the article, was born in 1930 and graduated from the University of Tokyo where he majored in economics. Currently, he is adviser to the Long-Term Credit Bank of Japan, managing director of the Softnomics Center, and a Wilson Center fellow.

To the extent that the argument Kusaka presents is characteristic of male-dominated Japanese corporate society, it is likely that women will continue to occupy traditional roles in the economy and have relatively low occupational status.

In evaluating the place of women, we need to distinguish between status and power. It is the former Western observers have in mind when they assert that women have a relatively low place in Japanese society. They are thinking of the dearth of female political leaders, executives, professors, and ambassadors.

But Westerners fail to notice Japanese women's power. They generally hold the family purse strings; they are responsible for 60% of the money spent in the country and even make the decisions on most housing purchases. Japanese women outvote men and therefore have a greater say in elections. They have a strong influence on what gets shown on television and printed in newspapers since they are the media's main consumers. Because fathers are tucked away behind their desks at work, mothers wind up making the decisions on children's education and jobs.

Should women be given status when they already have this much influence? It can be argued that since women are already the real power behind the throne in so many fields, men should at least be given fancy titles as a sort of consolation prize. Indeed, to strip men of this privilege might destroy their self-confidence. Wives already joke that their husbands, when at home, are about as useful as a bag of rubbish. If women take over the top jobs in work as well as at home, rubbish is what many men will become. Surely, then, it makes more sense to get some use out of this refuse by leaving it in command at work. . . .

Women as a whole will, we may safely say, not be seeking to exchange places with men. Some will, however, be seeking a slight improvement in their social standing, and accommodating this should not be hard. Since such minor gains can be accomplished at any time, however, the great majority of women will probably conclude that they need not make a fuss about thrusting themselves forward.

What about the other women, especially those who want to get ahead in society and have little interest in rearing children? Frankly I believe that their temperament, like that of similarly inclined men, has a genetic foundation. People of this type will not be bearing many children, and their genes will gradually disappear from the genetic pool. Perhaps by the middle of the next century the child-oriented type will have become so dominant that society ranks homemaker at the top of the social hierarchy. (Kusaka, 1989) occupations for which there are explicit job descriptions and objective qualifications for entry, there is less latitude to assign differential rates of pay based on extra-job characteristics. Job holders, regardless of sex and other nonrelevant criteria, are more likely to receive identical remuneration. However, all of the data presented in this section point to the irrefutable fact that, no matter what the circumstance, men and women are not paid equally for equal work.

Because men and women are occupationally segregated, legislation requiring men and women to be paid equally for equal work has not been hugely successful in reducing wage and salary discrimination (see Aldrich and Buchele, 1986). In some cases, equal pay legislation has had the opposite effect in that employers have introduced more segregation in a concerted effort to avoid direct wage comparisons between the sexes. In turn, a new reform movement has arisen with the much more difficult objective of legislating equal pay for jobs of comparable worth. The idea of comparable worth involves the analysis and evaluation of all jobs with respect to certain specified characteristics or dimensions (e.g., educational qualifications, skill level, responsibility, and so on) such that it is possible to assign points and thereby to determine equitable wages and salaries.

Comparable worth laws have been enacted in Australia and Sweden, and many job evaluation studies have been undertaken in the United States with the purpose of establishing comparable worth (see Aldrich and Buchele, 1986, pp. 64–69 for a listing). It is estimated that should comparable worth legislation come into force in the United States, wages in female-dominated occupations (i.e., at least 70% female) would rise by 10 to 15% (Aldrich and Buchele, 1986). Put another way, on average, most women in the labor force are currently receiving 10 to 15% less than they are worth.

Figure 6.1 provides a schematic representation of the status and function of women in the labor forces of industrialized countries today. Due to a variety of factors, female labor force participation has increased dramatically over the past few decades, particularly among married women with children, such that now women constitute at least two-fifths of the industrial labor force. However, for the most part they tend to be segregated and concentrated into a relatively few occupations (hence their smaller proportional representation), which involve most of the same duties and responsibilities associated with the traditional woman's role, that of a supportive nurturer. Furthermore, they predominate at the middle to lower end of the occupational hierarchy, in many cases not even being responsible for the direction and supervision of their own "female" occupations.

Because there are in essence two labor forces, one for women and one for men, and because women have been unable to assume control of their own occupational destinies, "women's work" is significantly undervalued compared to the work that men perform. Whereas one of the hallmarks of an industrial society is the systematic replacement of ascribed for achieved criteria in the assessment and evaluation of individual worth, the data on the relatively undifferentiated position of women and other disadvantaged groups in the labor force would indicate that we have a long way to go in attaining this goal.

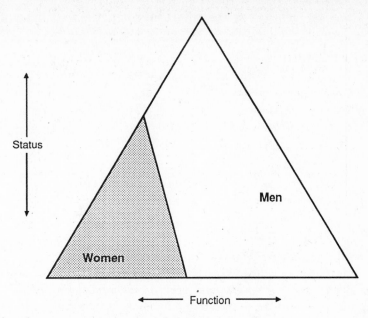

Figure 6.1 Women and Men in the Occupational Hierarchy

THE DIVISION OF LABOR BY RACE

Another ascribed characteristic that influences individual life chances is race. Particularly in the United States, but also in other industrialized countries, there has developed an informal but nonetheless powerful pecking order in which those jobs and occupations deemed to be least desirable are allotted to the least advantaged racial and ethnic groups, while the more prized occupations become the almost exclusive preserve of those most advantaged in society. Whereas various laws have been instituted to counteract this informal institutionalized discrimination, nevertheless it does still persist. Blacks are paid less than whites for the same jobs and for essentially the same reasons as are women paid less than men (Aldrich and Buchele, 1986).

Table 6.7 indicates the percentages of Black and white men and women who have the most prestigious and sought after managerial and professional occupations in the United States today. It also controls on level of education attained, as this serves as a very important criterion of entry. Overall, the bottom line of this table reveals that a far greater percentage of white men and women are managers and professionals than are either Black women or particularly Black men. Proportionately, twice as many white men and women hold these jobs as black men. The major reason for the large differences is the fact that a greater percentage of whites than blacks have college or university degrees, an important qualifying condition for these jobs. For example, of all managers and professionals included in the table, 61 percent have had four years of college or more, and 80 percent have had at least some college.

Table 6.7   PERCENT OF AMERICAN LABOR FORCE IN MANAGERIAL/PROFESSIONAL
OCCUPATIONS BY SEX, RACE, AND EDUCATIONAL ATTAINMENT (1988)*

Educational attainment	Males (%)		Females (%)	
	White	Black	White	Black
4 years of college or more	67.6	58.5	68.9	63.9
1 to 3 years of college	27.1	16.8	30.0	23.1
4 years of high school only	12.8	5.4	13.6	9.2
Less than 4 years of high school	6.4	2.8	6.2	3.8
Total managerial/professional	30.6	15.0	29.6	20.5

*These data refer to the civilian noninstitutional population 25 to 64 years of age.

Source: Adapted from *Statistical Abstracts of the United States 1989*, p. 390.

When we examine those Black and white men and women who have at least four years of college, the initial large differences in the percentage of whites and Blacks who are managers and professionals are substantially reduced. This demonstrates the impact that educational qualifications have on gaining entry to these jobs. However, significant differences do remain, particularly between Black men on the one hand and white men and women on the other. Whereas over two-thirds of whites with four years of college are managers or professionals, only 58.5% of Black men with similar credentials are. This demonstrates the impact of race on occupational attainment.

In order to appreciate fully the data presented in Table 6.7, it is necessary to examine also the differential rates between the races of educational level achieved. For example, whereas 29.5% and 24.0% of white males and females, respectively, have at least four years of college, only 15.2% of Black men and 17.3% of Black women are college graduates (*Statistical Abstracts*, 1989, p. 390). Consequently, not only do smaller percentages of Black than white college graduates become managers and professionals, but also there are proportionately fewer blacks than whites who complete college. Thus, Blacks suffer the main and interaction effects of both occupational and educational stratification by race.

It is also important to remember from the discussion in the previous section that the managerial/professional category is very broad and therefore encompasses a wide variety of levels and types of managers and professionals. This means that a more detailed analysis of white and Black managerial/professional jobs would reveal substantial qualitative differences between the races which in addition to the quantitative differences already revealed indicate that blacks and whites occupy separate labor forces in much the same way as do women and men (see Feagin and Feagin, 1978).

THEORETICAL PERSPECTIVES

During the twentieth century, structural changes of vast proportion have occurred among now industrially developed societies. The types of jobs that we perform, the organization of work, and cumulative technological innovations all have greatly altered how we make a living. Based on the evidence available, sociological theorists have attempted to explain how labor markets in modern, highly complex societies are organized both to accomplish overall societal objectives and to attend to the well-being of individual citizens. Below are descriptions of the most prominent of these labor market theories.

Human Capital Theory

In 1945, Davis and Moore proposed a functional theory of stratification which attempted to explain both how a society meets its needs for survival and why social inequality exists. In any society, while certain needs are important, the human talents available to fulfill these needs are scarce and consequently must be more highly rewarded in order that society may survive. For example, there is a need in society to maintain the public health of its citizenry. Thus, the collection of garbage and the preservation of human life are both important functions. However, because the qualifications required of a garbage collector are widely distributed throughout the population and because there is minimal training involved, the rewards attached to this position are relatively small. On the other hand, the talents required of a physician are not widely found, and many years of training during which the incumbent receives little or no remuneration are required in order to develop these talents. Consequently, the position is highly rewarded. Thus, society meets its needs by establishing a system of differential rewards to ensure that enough individual citizens are motivated to invest sufficiently in their talents to accomplish those tasks that only a few are qualified to perform. Through these means, there are adequate supplies of requisite talents to meet societal demands.

This theoretical model is a precursor to human capital theory (see Becker, 1964), which specifies that job rewards are basically a function of the contribution that jobs make to society. The greater the contribution, the higher is the reward. In turn, the theory proposes that job rewards (i.e., income, status, fringe benefits, and intrinsic satisfaction) are commensurate with the human capital (i.e., education, training, skill, experience, and commitment) invested by workers. The labor market is simply an impersonal and impartial mechanism that matches in the most efficient manner possible human capital supply with appropriate job demands. To the extent that workers make the most of their inherent human capital, they will be rewarded accordingly. Conversely, if they do not invest sufficiently in themselves, they must then be content with the least rewarded and therefore least desirable jobs in society.

Labor Market Segmentation Theory

While human capital theory proposes an ideal match between effort and reward, in fact, as the previous sections on the division of labor by sex and race have demonstrated, empirical reality falls somewhat short of the ideal. Although there are moderately high correlations between education on the one hand and occupational status and income on the other, they are by no means perfect (see, for example, Treiman, 1977). Depending upon various ascribed criteria and social class origins, the amount of human capital invested may be more or less effective in achieving desired occupational goals.

Labor market segmentation theory, a conflict perspective, argues that human capital investment is an insufficient explanation of how people end up with the jobs that they have. The structure of the labor market is a far more important determinant of individual life chances. Based on descriptive empirical studies, segmentation theorists propose that instead of one homogeneous labor market which impartially matches supply with demand along universally standard gradients of ability, the labor market is divided into virtually separate primary and secondary sectors.

> The former (i.e., primary sector) offers jobs with relatively high wages, good working conditions, chances of advancement, equity and due process in the administration of work rules, and above all, employment stability. Jobs in the secondary sector, by contrast, tend to be low-paying, with poorer working conditions and little chance of advancement; to have a highly personalized relationship between workers and supervisors, which leaves wide latitude for favoritism and is conducive to harsh and capricious work discipline; and to be characterized by considerable instability in jobs and a high turnover among the labor force. (Piore, cited in Kalleberg and Sorensen, 1979, pp. 356–357)

Similar to dependency theory discussed in Chapter 5, labor market segmentation advances the notion of a powerful core sector in which the most important industries, employing organizations, and occupational groups operate. Restrictive barriers function both to limit mobility between sectors and to place the secondary sector in a dependent relationship. Within the dominant primary sector, studies have found that human capital variables tend to have their expected effects (Kalleberg and Sorenson, 1979, p. 364). In other words, given the structural conditions previously outlined, there is a stronger relationship between effort and reward in the stable primary sector than is found in the more volatile secondary sector.

According to one interpretation of segmentation theory, the primary or core sector of the economy recruits workers primarily through internal labor markets, while the secondary peripheral sector relies overwhelmingly on the traditional external labor market (see Hodson and Kaufman, 1982). Internal labor markets are limited to, and therefore controlled by, the firms that use them. Typically, recruitment takes place at several lower-level points of entry within the organization and involves heavy screening of applicants. Upon being hired, employees learn the skills and procedures specific to the firm through on-the-job training, and thus advance through the organizational ranks as their ability dictates. Consequently, internal labor markets offer employment security and reasonable prospects for workers and, in return, employers end up with knowledgeable and loyal work forces. By contrast, firms relying on the external labor market do not make such an initial heavy investment in their workers. They pick and choose from the talent available in the open market those skills required to meet organizational needs.

Because there is no understanding of job security, there is no reciprocal commitment of employer to employee, and consequently labor turnover is high.

Segmentation theorists have used Japan to corroborate this interpretation of a dual economy (see Kalleberg and Sorenson, 1979). Japanese workers in the primary sector (i.e., almost one-third of the labor force who work in large manufacturing corporations) enjoy relatively high wages, good fringe benefits, and lifetime employment in one firm. In contrast, secondary sector workers (i.e., the remaining two-thirds of the labor force who work in small, largely family-owned enterprises) earn considerably less money, have few benefits, and are not assured of permanent employment (see Bednarzik and Shiells, 1989). However, this interpretation is less applicable to the more complex American economy. Critics have charged that the model is too simplistic and therefore distorts the reality it is attempting to explain (see Hodson and Kaufman, 1982).

Part of the difficulty with segmentation theory is that because it has been empirically derived through descriptive studies, there are no clear theoretical guidelines on how to divide the labor market into primary and secondary sectors. Some researchers have defined the sectors according to occupational groupings, while others have used industrial classifications, and still others have examined organizational characteristics. Depending upon what criteria are used, different sectors are formed, and there is not always a great deal of overlap in sectors between studies employing different criteria. As Hodson and Kaufman (1982, p. 727) have stated, "Unfortunately, a well-defined theoretical model of the dual economy does not exist in the literature."

The complex structure of the labor market with many variables operating simultaneously, together with the fact that it is in continual dynamic process, makes it extremely difficult to construct theoretical models that accurately portray and account for the myriad actions of individual workers, labor unions, employing organizations, and governments. Because of this, both the human capital and labor market segmentation models have been criticized as being conceptually underdeveloped. We have yet to come up with a theory that fully incorporates all of these forces in action. No doubt, any new theory will have to employ features from both the human capital and labor market segmentation models in order to explain adequately the participation, segregation, concentration, and discrimination that are presently ongoing processes of industrialized labor markets.

LABOR FORCE TRENDS AND PROJECTIONS

From the above introduction to some of the changes that reflect the industrialization process in Britain, the United States, and Japan, it is possible to make limited projections of the composition of the occupational and labor force structure in the twenty-first century. First, we consider broad trends with respect to all three countries, and then make a more detailed examination of the occupational outlook for the United States.

Broad Trends

Perhaps the most far-reaching set of changes experienced in Great Britain, the United States, and Japan is the increasing concentration of employment in the tertiary sector and the growing contribution of services to national income (see Tables 6.1 and 6.2). This trend is expected to continue such that in the United States by the year 2000, almost four out of five jobs will be in this services-producing sector (Bureau of Labor Statistics, 1988).[12] Contributing greatly to this growth in all three countries will be the expansion of professional and technical workers (ILO, 1988) and, in the United States, this will be supplemented by substantial increases in the managerial ranks. Also, services associated with the information revolution will expand as will employment in the many leisure industries and health services (Koseki, 1989; Rajan and Pearson, 1986).

In the United States and Japan, increases in tertiary sector employment will on average be matched by overall increases in the labor force; thus employment in the primary and secondary sectors should remain relatively stable (*Statistical Survey of Japan's Economy*, 1986, p. 8). However, in Britain, it is anticipated that there will be real declines in these goods-producing sectors as tertiary sector growth outstrips labor force increases (Rajan and Pearson, 1986). In general, this reflects the direct relationships operating between productivity indices, economic growth, and labor force growth.

In all three countries the composition of manufacturing will change, with losses being registered in traditional industries such as basic steel and textiles, and gains being achieved in emerging "modern" industries (e.g., electronic computing equipment, plastics, and medical instruments and supplies). (See Table 8.4 and the accompanying text.) Also, multifunctional craftworkers and technicians will be in demand "due to the growing use of new technologies; lessening job demarcations; and diversification into the selling of technical expertise" (Rajan and Pearson, 1986, p. xxi). Associated with these changes and reflecting the growing demand for greater flexibility in the allocation of work, there will also be an increase in part-time employment, large organizations will continue their practice of contracting out part of their work to smaller specialized firms, and telecommuters (workers electronically attached to their employing organizations) will constitute a large proportion of the labor force (see Cordell, 1985; Herteaux, 1985).[13]

With regard to the characteristics of labor force participants themselves, women will continue to increase their participation rate such that by the year 2000 they will comprise close to half the labor forces in each of these three countries. Also, the median age of workers will increase slightly, reflecting the general demographic trends in the larger population. Finally, given all of the changes described, greater educational and vocational qualifications will be required for labor force entry in the twenty-first century.

Occupational Outlook for the United States

Every two years, the U.S. Bureau of Labor Statistics publishes occupational and labor force projections based on emerging demographic trends and characteristics of the American labor market (see Bureau of Labor Statistics, 1988). Figure 6.2 provides a broad overview of its analysis. Although the labor force is expected to grow relatively slowly during the last part of the century due to the decrease in the birth rate, nevertheless the Bureau projects a 19 percent increase which will add more than 21 million new people to the labor force between 1986 and 2000.

Figure 6.2 reveals that all of the eight occupational groups that will experience larger than average percentage gains in the labor force are in the tertiary sector. Furthermore, the top four groups generally require college degrees, are all part of the larger category of professional, technical, and related workers, and are directly involved with the technological development of society. In some cases, these jobs will be on the leading edges of technology. For example, for natural, computer, and mathematical scientists, who are expected to register the highest percentage increases, the Bureau cites "substantial growth in computer and data processing ser-

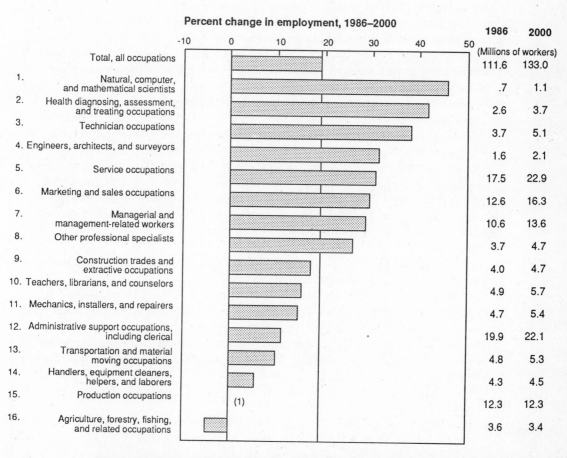

Figure 6.2 Projected Employment Growth in the United States by Occupational Group
(1) No change.

Source: Adapted from Bureau of Labor Statistics, 1988, pp. 10–13.

vices," "genetic research," and "development efforts in the fields of lasers, super-conducters, and other areas of advanced science" (Bureau of Labor Statistics, 1988, p. 11).

While it is extremely likely that these four top occupational groups will incur the largest percentage increases (46%, 42%, 38%, and 32%, respectively) during the last part of the century, it is important to keep in mind that their total combined contribution to the labor force will not equal the numerical increases that are expected in either the fifth-ranked service or the sixth-ranked marketing and sales occupations (see the two columns on the right side of Figure 6.2). In absolute numbers, the top four occupations will account for only 16% of the expected labor force increase, while the next three occupations (service, marketing, and management) are expected to make up well over half (57%) of this labor force growth. Consequently, in terms of numerical growth, these latter three occupational groups will attract the majority of new workers.

Within the service occupations, most growth is expected in the areas of health (increased care of the elderly), food (more people dining out), security (more commercial and personal use of protective services), and building maintenance (increased number of office buildings, commercial outlets, and so on). Increases in marketing and sales occupations will occur predominantly in real estate, travel, and finance, as well as retail sales in general, while the growth in managerial and related occupations will take place precisely in those areas in which the largest numbers of new workers will be employed (see above).

Table 6.8 provides a listing of those specific occupations that are expected to record the highest relative rates of growth (i.e., percentage increases) and those that will make the greatest absolute gains (i.e., numerical increases). Together, these two lists indicate the particular directions in which the labor force may be expected to change. The occupations with the highest projected rates of growth are new wave jobs that are on the frontiers of labor force expansion, while the occupations with the greatest projected increases in size are more established jobs which nevertheless reflect the look of things to come and also are likely to be instrumental in the general transformation from industrial to postindustrial activities. All of the 20 occupations listed will grow faster than the labor force in general, and all of them are part of the continually expanding tertiary sector.[14]

By the beginning of the twenty-first century, there will be relatively few occupational reminders of what work was like in the industrial revolution 200 years earlier. The labor force of the new era will in very large part be comprised of highly educated professionals and technicians involved with the production, manipulation, recording, and distribution of knowledge, thus consolidating the information revolution that we are currently experiencing.

SUMMARY

6.1 Work is divided into three sectors: primary, secondary, and tertiary. Work in the primary sector involves the harvesting of natural resources, agriculture being the prime example. Work in the secondary sector concerns the transformation of raw

Table 6.8 TOP TEN AMERICAN OCCUPATIONS IN TERMS OF PROJECTED PERCENTAGE AND NUMERICAL INCREASES, 1986–2000[1]

	Actual employment in 1986 (000s)	Projected employment in 2000 (000s)	1986–2000	
			Numerical increase (000s)	Percentage increase (%)
A. *Occupations with Highest Projected Rates of Growth*				
1. Medical assistants	132	251	119	90
2. Home health aides	138	249	111	80
3. Computer systems analysts, EDP	331	582	251	76
4. Computer programmers	479	813	334	70
5. Radiologic technologists and technicians	115	190	75	65
6. Legal assistants and technicians, exc. clerical	170	272	102	60
7. Dental assistants	155	244	89	57
8. Guards	794	1,177	383	48
9. Electrical and electronic engineers	401	592	191	48
10. Computer operators, exc. peripheral equipment	263	387	124	47
B. *Occupations with Greatest Projected Increases in Size*				
1. Salespersons, retail	3,579	4,780	1,201	34
2. Waiters and waitresses	1,702	2,454	752	44
3. Registered nurses	1,406	2,018	612	44
4. Janitors and cleaners	2,676	3,280	604	23
5. General managers and top executives	2,383	2,965	582	24
6. Cashiers	2,165	2,740	575	27
7. Truck drivers, light and heavy	2,211	2,736	525	24
8. General office clerks	2,361	2,824	463	20
9. Food counter, fountain, and related workers	1,500	1,949	449	30
10. Nursing aides, orderlies, and attendants	1,224	1,658	434	35

[1] The Bureau of Labor Statistics computed three projections from 1986 to 2000: low, moderate, and high. The data reported in this table are based on the "moderate" projections.

Source: Adapted from *Statistical Abstracts of the United States* 1989, p. 387.

materials into semifinished or finished products. Most work in the secondary sector is in manufacturing. Work in the tertiary sector entails the provision of services rather than the production of goods. The administration of government is an example of tertiary sector work.

6.2   The majority of the labor forces in Great Britain, the United States, Japan, and other industrially developed countries work in the tertiary sector. They are employed in sales, the administration of private and public enterprises, transportation and communication, and the provision of a variety of community, business, social, and personal services. When more than half the labor force work in the tertiary sector, the society is defined as "postindustrial." Generally, national income figures mirror those in employment.

6.3   An important feature of modern postindustrial societies is their bureaucratic organizational base. Approximately 90 percent of all workers in the United States and Great Britain are employees of organizations; that is, they are wage and salary earners as opposed to self-employed workers. Organizational support structures are necessary for the complex research and development programs that lead to invention, discovery, and innovation in today's society.

6.4   Participation in the labor force varies by sex. For men, particularly from ages 25 to 54, virtually all are employed. For women, participation rates have risen dramatically in the past three decades. Increasingly, married women with children are now also members of the labor force. In industrially developed countries, women constitute at least 40 percent of all those employed. Demographic, economic, occupational, and social factors all explain the increase in female labor force participation.

6.5   Within the labor force, women and men tend to be employed in separate occupations. Women predominate in clerical and service occupations, while men make up the bulk of production workers. Comparatively few women are employed as managers and high-prestige professionals. In general, women are segregated and concentrated into jobs, that have traditionally been defined as "women's work."

6.6   Women are paid less than men, even when factors such as type and level of job, qualifications, experience, and length of service are taken into consideration. One of the most significant factors explaining the sex differential in earnings is occupational sex composition. In general, the greater the proportion of females in an occupation, the lower is the income received by both women and men. Also, the male–female discrepancy in earnings is greater at the higher occupational levels. These pay inequities have sparked a movement to legislate equal pay for jobs of comparable worth.

6.7   Participation in the labor force also varies by race. Data for the United States indicate that not only do smaller percentages of black than white college graduates become managers and professionals, but also there are proportionately fewer blacks than whites who complete college, an important avenue to higher labor force entry. Consequently, there exists occupational segregation and discrimination by race as well as by sex.

6.8   Human capital theory explains the labor market as a mechanism whereby individual qualifications, experience, and commitment (i.e., human capital) are matched to particular job demands. The greater the human capital, the greater will be the extrinsic and intrinsic job rewards. Job rewards are directly related to the functional contribution that jobs make to society.

6.9   Labor market segmentation theory proposes that the labor market is divided into primary and secondary sectors. Within the primary sector are the core industries and employing organizations that employ workers through internal labor markets. These workers receive relatively high wages, good fringe benefits, and secure careers. In contrast, work in the secondary sector is peripheral to and dependent upon what transpires in the primary sector. Jobs in the secondary sector, contracted via the external labor market, are poorly paid and there is little security of employment. Neither human capital theory nor labor market segmentation theory explains fully the intricacies that characterize complex modern labor forces.

6.10 Recent labor force projections in Great Britain, the United States, and Japan indicate that by the beginning of the twenty-first century, almost 80% of all jobs will be in the services-providing tertiary sector. Because the greatest area of job growth will be in the professional and technical fields, higher educational qualifications will generally be required for labor force entry. Increasingly, work will be comprised of the generation and transmission of information, and women will comprise close to half the labor force. More detailed data indicating these trends is provided for the United States.

NOTES

1. For a recent best-seller on "the parallel stories of the Japanese ascent and the American malaise," see David Halberstam's *The Reckoning* (1986, p. 279).
2. According to some classifications, mining and quarrying is defined as "extractive," and therefore workers in this industry are placed in the primary sector. Similarly, the provision of utilities is sometimes defined as a "service," and consequently workers in this industry are assigned to the tertiary sector. Yet according to the OECD (1987) upon whose figures Table 6.1 is based, both mining and quarrying and the provision of utilities are placed in the secondary sector. However, because the numbers employed in these particular industries are relatively small, their placement does not affect in any significant way the proportional representation of the three sectors over time.
3. As MDCs become "postindustrial," that is, place greater emphasis on the tertiary sector, they also necessarily become less "industrial." Tables 6.1 and 6.2 reflect this diminishing relative importance of the secondary "industrial" sector over time for both employment and national income.
4. The figure reported for Great Britain is for 1971.
5. Comparable data for the United Kingdom are not available.
6. While it is true that female labor force participation has increased substantially during recent decades, a significant share of this increase has been in part-time employment. In Great Britain (1981), 37 percent of all jobs held by women are part-time; for men, the corresponding figure is 1.4 percent. Fully 94 percent of all part-time employment in the United Kingdom is taken up by women. In the United States also, women are overrepresented in part-time employment, although not to the same degree (almost one-quarter of women's jobs are part-time, and women constitute 70 percent of all part-time workers) (Bakker, 1988, p. 21). Comparable data for Japan are not available.
7. In 1965, labor force participation of American men aged 20 to 24 was 88.0%; in 1960, it was 90.2% (see *Historical Statistics*, 1975, pp. 131–132).
8. For 106 countries in which data were available, the United States (1980) had 5.3 divorces per 1000 population, the United Kingdom, ranked fourteenth, had 2.7 per 1000, and Japan (44th) had 1.2.
9. Treiman found that "the average intercountry occupational prestige correlation (computed over 55 countries) is .81" (Treiman, 1977, p. 166).
10. While it is true that these detailed occupational data permit a more precise comparative analysis of men and women, there are also disadvantages to consider. First, the very detail that is achieved can sometimes obscure the broader picture of what is happening generally. Second, this level of detail makes for very complex data analysis. And third, often data do not exist at this level of analysis, particularly when one is engaged in cross-national comparison. For example, comparable occupational data are not available in this form for Great Britain and Japan.

11. Aldrich and Buchele (1986, p. xix) report even greater inequities when the comparison is made *between* the sexes rather than within the same sex. In the United States (1980), "full-time, year-round female professionals earned less than male semiskilled blue-collar workers, and female college graduates earned less than male high school graduates who had never attended college."

12. All of the American data reported in this section are taken from the *Occupational Outlook Handbook 1988–1989* published by the Bureau of Labor Statistics (1988).

13. Herteaux (1985) reports that "since 1974 half of the new jobs in Europe have been part-time," and Rajan and Pearson (1986) point out that approximately 25 percent of total employment in Britain is part-time.

14. The Bureau of Labor Statistics (1988) cautions that its projections are for the country as a whole, and that there will be regional variations that do not conform to the overall pattern. In addition, as well as "new" jobs arising from labor force growth, there will also be "replacement" jobs that come available as various workers withdraw from the labor force.

Chapter
7
Formal Organizations

Organizations—producing goods, delivering services, maintaining order, challenging the established order—are the fundamental building blocks of modern societies, the basic vehicles through which collective action is undertaken.

Aldrich and Marsden, 1988, p. 361

*I*n Chapter 6, we examined what people do for a living in contemporary postindustrial nations and how these activities contribute to overall national income. This involved an analysis of the structure of occupations and the labor force. In the next two chapters, we will look at the context of work, the organizations in which most of us work. This involves a presentation of the defining characteristics of formal organizations, discussion of the theoretical perspectives that have arisen to explain how organizations function, an examination of various contingencies that produce organization variation, and an attempt to chart the path of future organizational development. In the following chapter, we will examine just one of these developments, the emergence of the transnational corporation on the world scene.

In keeping with our established practice, we will continue the strategy of focusing on cross-national studies of organizations in Great Britain, the United States, and Japan. In this way, we will be able to address the issue of whether complex organizations as they are found in modern postindustrial societies are "culture free" (i.e., essentially the same regardless of cultural circumstance) or "culture bound" (structurally determined according to prevailing cultural values and norms). Incidentally, the strategy will also permit us to evaluate comparatively the empirical bases of the so-called "Japanese miracle."

CHARACTERISTICS OF FORMAL ORGANIZATIONS

Like people, not all organizations are the same. As well as obvious differences such as size and the fact that organizations are established at different times, for a variety of purposes, and produce disparate goods and services, organizations also differ with respect to the various features that make up an organization's structure. As a result of research in organizations, particularly in the latter half of this century, sociologists have identified the most important of these features from the point of view of measuring significant differences among organizations. The following is a description of these structural characteristics.[1]

Complexity

According to Hall (1987, pp. 58–72), the determination of organizational complexity involves examining organizations with respect to how extensive their division of labor is (i.e., horizontal differentiation or specialization), their hierarchical structure (vertical differentiation), and the extent to which organizational subunits are physically separated geographically or regionally (spatial dispersion).

Horizontal Differentiation One prominent feature of organizations is a division of labor or horizontal differentiation whereby members participate collectively in the achievement of an organizational task. Depending upon the nature of the task being performed, the degree of horizontal differentiation may be extensive or slight. For example, in a modern university there is a widespread division of labor. Not only are there separate divisions for academic, administrative, and financial functions, but also within divisions there is extensive specialization. Each academic department represents a specialized discipline requiring many years of training in order to master. It is inconceivable that a professor of chemistry could also be expert in the areas of music, medicine, and political science, not to mention accounting, counseling, and campus security. Even within academic departments, there is considerable specialization in the subareas that comprise the disciplines that these departments represent.

Vertical Differentiation A corresponding feature of formal organizations is vertical differentiation or the establishment of a hierarchy to achieve the coordination necessary for completing a task. Almost as soon as there is a division of labor, it is likely that someone will assume a supervisory role. Again, the degree of vertical differentiation varies according to the nature of the task to be accomplished.

In the example of the university, the top organizational level is occupied by the president, who is the chief executive officer. On the next hierarchical level are vice presidents responsible for various functional divisions (e.g., academic, administrative, and financial). The academic vice president directs the activities of the registrar of students, the head librarian, and the deans of faculties who in turn supervise departmental chairpersons who manage the individual faculty and support personnel within their departments. The administrative vice president is in charge of areas such as buildings and grounds, purchasing (supplies), staff personnel, and various campus services (e.g., bookstore, counseling, food, health, housing, and so on), all of which have their own departmental managers, supervisors, and corresponding staff. The financial vice president heads operations in general accounting, payroll, student fees, financial aid, fund-raising, and institutional analysis, again each operation being comprised of several hierarchical levels. A partial, simplified organization chart or table of a university structure illustrating both horizontal and vertical differentiation is shown in Figure 7.1.[2] It may be characterized as being broad (i.e., much specialization or division of labor) but short (i.e., relatively few hierarchical levels).

Spatial Dispersion At times, organizations may find it advantageous to establish operations in two or more physical locations. Either separate functions are carried out at different sites (e.g., mining and smelting; production and sales; main university campus and satellite medical school located at a major hospital), or essentially similar organizational units are strategically located to take advantage of available resources and/or markets (e.g., mines, retail sales, state universities with multiple

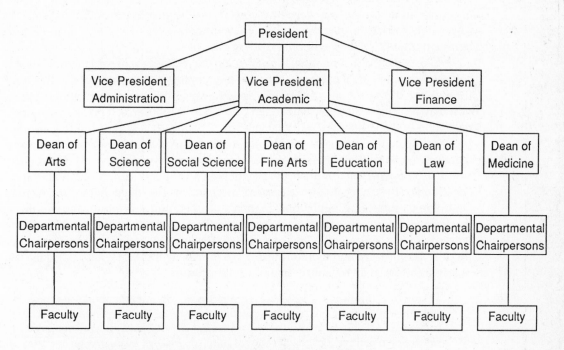

Figure 7.1 Partial Organization Chart of a University
Source: Hedley, 1986b, p. 211

campuses). Spatial dispersion may be seen as a physical manifestation of either horizontal or vertical differentiation (Hall, 1987, pp. 63–64). For example, to continue with the university illustration, whereas some academic programs must be located near strategic resources (e.g., medicine, oceanography, and marine biology), physical relocation is no more than horizontal differentiation occurring at different sites. Similarly, whereas several satellite campuses may be situated throughout a state in order to provide access to all population centers, they are still in effect subordinate academic units in relationship to the central campus which houses the senior administration and support staff of the entire university system. However, regardless of whether spatial dispersion occurs as a function of either horizontal or vertical differentiation, this fact alone does add to the complexity of an organization.

Formalization

Another characteristic of organizations is the degree of formalization or standardization, that is, the extent to which organizational operations are codified in terms of job descriptions, procedures, and rules and regulations. In those organizations with highly predictable operations and outcomes, a high degree of formalization may be introduced. For example, in some government bureaus responsible for processing many similar cases, job types and levels within jobs are defined in specific detail and procedures are rigidly standardized within an exhaustive system of rules and regulations. However, in bureaus where many dissimilar cases are encountered and there is uncertainty with respect to procedure and outcome, it is impossible to standardize operations. Instead, employees are given discretion to handle matters as they see fit on a case-by-case basis.

Like vertical differentiation, formalization is a means of achieving organizational control. When the level of formalization is low, control is exercised personally either through the direct use of verbal orders and requests from superiors to subordinates, or it may be achieved indirectly through prior socialization, which involves the internalization of the values and norms one learns through professional training and apprenticeship. In the latter case, the already socialized worker "knows" what to do and therefore requires little direct supervision. In an organization that is formalized, there is less need for personal human intervention as a means of control. Blau and Scott (1962) coined the term "impersonal control mechanisms" to refer either to bureaucratic control (e.g., rules and regulations, manuals of operating procedure, and so on) or mechanical control, in which work performance is dictated by the machinery one works with (e.g., an assembly line). Obviously, the introduction of sophisticated computerized equipment and monitoring devices into the workplace will increase the use of formalization as an organizational control procedure.

> Thanks to computers, for instance, managers now can monitor employees' business calls, their minute-by-minute work patterns, and the time they spend in contact with customers. Already today [in the United States], about 5 million workers, mostly in clerical or repetitive jobs, have some or all of their work evaluated on the basis of computer-generated data, and many more have computer-generated data collection but not currently used in evaluation. (Williams et al., 1989, p. 26)

Centralization

The final characteristic of organizations we shall consider is centralization or the delegation of authority. Power is the ability to influence the actions of others, and it may be located at the uppermost ranks of the organization (i.e., a centralized structure) or it may be diffused throughout (i.e., decentralized). Again the nature of the task (and other factors) influences whether an organization is centralized or decentralized with regard to its decision-making function.

Traditionally, centralization varies inversely with organizational complexity. The more differentiated an organization is in both function and location, the more difficult it is to maintain central control over key areas of decision making. A good example of a highly differentiated organization is a government state department with embassies located throughout the world. Embassies are charged with reflecting and acting upon official policies of the home government as these may apply in the countries in which they are situated. In a highly complex, nonstandardized situation such as this, it is extremely difficult for the chief executive officer of the state department to be sufficiently informed about all aspects of government policy (horizontal differentiation) as they might apply to particular countries (spatial dispersion). Consequently, ambassadors traditionally have been delegated a great deal of authority to deal with matters as they see fit.

As with formalization, the advent of powerful "real-time" computers has permitted a reformulation of the complexity–centralization relationship. Advances in information and communications technology now make it possible for managers geographically remote from their various operations to have instant access and up-to-the-minute information on all facets of their business simply by punching a few keys on their head-office terminals. Clearly, this new technology has important implications for the locus of power within organizations. For embassies in general and ambassadors in particular, they now exercise very limited authority in comparison to what they wielded in previous decades.

Formal Organizations Defined

A definition of formal organization is difficult because it must apply to all the many different social structures we characterize as organizations. In the United States, it is conservatively estimated that there are 4.6 million business organizations alone (Aldrich and Marsden, 1988, p. 365). These range from General Motors, with factories located throughout the world, dealerships in every American town of consequence, over 100,000 employees, and gross sales of $65 billion annually, to the local corner store (Crow and Thomas, 1983, p. 61). To these must be added universities, schools, hospitals, prisons, governments and their affiliated agencies, churches, labor unions, and armies. What do they all have in common?

Organizations are collectivities that are purposively and formally established on a more or less continuous basis to accomplish a defined set of goals. They are horizontally and vertically differentiated, the positions being connected by a communications system and bound by rules and regulations.

MAJOR PERSPECTIVES ON ORGANIZATIONS

Analyses of organizations as an integral feature of industrial society date back to the work of Max Weber at the beginning of the twentieth century. Generally, early perspectives characterized organizations as constant structural units within society that were systematic in their impact upon both individuals and society itself (Scott, 1975; 1987). These perspectives assumed that there was a perfect or ideal organizational form which, if attained empirically, would result in various predictable outcomes. Organizations were perceived as rational mechanisms capable of attaining the most complex of human objectives with maximal efficiency and effectiveness. If only the ideal structural conditions could be established, then the result was a foregone conclusion. Consequently, early theorists were convinced that there was a "one best way" to establish and administer formal complex organizations.

Subsequent theoretical perspectives, based increasingly on systematic, comparative empirical research in diverse organizational settings began to question the notion of one ideal type of organization that could handle any exigency that might arise. On a variety of fronts, organizational researchers introduced notes of uncertainty and variability into what had previously appeared to be simply a technical problem of organizational engineering. How does the informal social structure relate to formal organizational design? Do all members of organizations have the same interests and goals? Should organizations that produce different products under different technological circumstances be structured in the same way? What effect does size have upon organizational structure? How do various cultural and institutional factors impinge upon organizations? These and other questions have led organizational researchers to the conclusion that organizations, like their environments, are variable. Optimal structural features are contingent upon many factors both internal and external to the organization. Consequently, the research agenda of organizational researchers today is the identification and explanation of these factors or contingencies that are primarily responsible for structural variability.

Table 7.1 provides an overview of the most important of these theoretical perspectives on organizations, and the following pages present a more detailed descriptive chronology.

Rational-Economic Perspectives

Bureaucracy Max Weber was the pioneer in the modern study of organizations. As outlined in Chapter 4, he proposed that "the purely bureaucratic type of administrative organization . . . is, from a purely technical point of view, capable of attaining the highest degree of efficiency and is in this sense formally the most rational known means of carrying out imperative control over human beings" (Weber, in Parsons, 1964, p. 337). According to Weber (see Weber, in Parsons, 1964, pp. 329–341), all bureaucratic organizations should contain the following features:

Table 7.1   MAJOR PERSPECTIVES ON ORGANIZATIONS

Perspective	Major proponents	Approx. date of introduction	Critical features
Rational-economic	(a) Weber	1900	The ideal type of rational organization (bureaucracy) contains certain essential features: (1) hierarchical ranking (2) functional specialization (3) written records (4) rules (5) appointment based on merit
	(b) Taylor	1910	An engineering model of work organization wherein managers are responsbile for specifying precisely to workers: (1) the type of work to be done (2) the method of performance (3) the time necessary for completion
Human relations	Mayo	1930	A perspective that recognizes the importance of social relations and the informal social structure in the attainment of organizational goals.
Functional theory	Parsons	1950	A model that posits that organizations are social systems with requisite system needs. Organizations meet their needs through horizontal and vertical differentiation.
Conflict theory	Dahrendorf	1955	A model of organization that focuses on the inherent conflict among organizational participants, which arises from the unequal distribution of power and authority.
Open-systems theory	Thompson	1965	A perspective that recognizes the importance of the environment on the structure and operation of organizations. There is constant interaction and adjustment of an organization to its environment.
Contingency theory	Lawrence and Lorsch	1970	An open-systems theory derivative that asserts that there is no one best method of organization. Contingencies such as the kind of environment, technology, and organizational tasks and personnel all influence organizational structure.
Organizational climate and culture	Dore	1975	A perspective that focuses on cultural contexts both inside and outside organizations, and how these produce variation in how organizations are designed and how they function.
Population-ecology theory	Aldrich	1980	A model that stresses the impact of the environment on organizational survival. Environments select out those organizational characteristics that they are most likely to endure.

1. *A hierarchy.* All bureaucracies should have graded levels of authority, with each level reporting and being responsible to the level immediately above, and with the person at the apex of the hierarchy having ultimate authority for all dealings within the organization.
2. *Functional specialization (division of labor).* Tasks should be assigned on the basis of specialized competence. Thus, there should be clear areas of jurisdiction and delimited spheres of duty within all bureaucracies.
3. *Written records.* Ideally the life of a bureaucratic organization lasts longer than that of any one individual. Organizational continuity is maintained through reliance on written records or "the files," which constitute the lifeblood of the organization.
4. *Rules and regulations.* Bureaucratic organizations should establish rules and regulations that are exhaustive, and that will extend to any contingency that the organization may expect to confront.
5. *Appointment based on merit.* The sole criterion for appointment to a position or promotion within a bureaucracy should be based on merit or achievement.

Weber's analysis of organizations was more prescriptive than descriptive. In other words, he was concerned with identifying those characteristics he thought contributed most to bureaucratic effectiveness and control rather than assessing the extent to which these same characteristics were evident in functioning organizations. In the words of Scott (1975, p. 2), "If Weber can be credited with emphasizing the structural features of organizations, he can also be charged with having set back their systematic empirical analysis by his use of the ideal-type model which implied, or was interpreted as implying, that all modern (bureaucratic) organizations were quite similar in their structural characteristics." Weber's elaboration of the ideal bureaucracy came about through his cross-cultural and historical study of political and economic organizations. By this method, he abstracted what he believed to be the essential elements of a bureaucracy in the rational pursuit of its objectives.

Scientific Management   Frederick Taylor, an American engineer, was also concerned with devising the best system to accomplish organizational goals (Taylor, 1911). His approach, called scientific management, began from the principle that it is the duty of managers to assume responsibility for organizing *all* aspects of work—what workers do, how they do it, and how long it takes them. Furthermore, managers must organize the activities of all workers into a coordinated system of efficient output (see Box 3-2 in Chapter 3, **Time is Money**).

The basis of scientific management is task specialization, that is, the dividing and subdividing of work into its essential task elements, which can then be performed by individuals with a minimum of training and instruction. Each task element is explicitly defined in terms of workers' body movements, the time it takes to complete these movements, and then costed in terms of wages. Through these detailed time and motion studies, Taylor claimed to have established the most efficient means to achieve production quotas.

Both Taylor and Weber sought to establish systems of organization that could be universally applied to accomplish any limited set of objectives. Weber was a sociologist concerned with the total operation of complex organizations; Taylor was a manager interested in somewhat more limited endeavors, but both assumed that it was possible to arrive at the one best method of organization. The major difference between the two was that Taylor was interested in applying this knowledge to actual work organizations, whereas Weber devised general abstract principles of organization.

Human Relations

Elton Mayo (1960) and his colleagues at the Harvard Business School introduced the first note of uncertainty into the study of organizations. As a result of a number of experiments in a telephone assembly plant (the Hawthorne experiments) during the 1930s, they discovered both a formal and an informal structure within organizations.

The formal structure refers to the blueprint or design for organizational behavior, that is, what *should* take place according to the rules and regulations, prescribed channels of communication, stated operating procedures, and official chains of command. In other words, the formal structure is an empirical approximation of Weber's ideal bureaucracy.

The informal structure refers to what actually takes place within the organization that is not consistent with the formal structure; or in the words of the researchers, "the actual personal interrelations existing among members of the organization which are not represented by, or are inadequately represented by, the formal organization" (Roethlisberger and Dickson, 1964, p. 566). Thus, the informal structure may either complement or run counter to the formally specified goals of the organization.

Discovery of the informal structure meant that just because organizations are *designed* in a certain fashion (e.g., Weber's bureaucracy) does not mean that they will necessarily *operate* in this way. Examples of the informal structure running counter to organizational design are: (1) when friends are chosen for positions over more qualified candidates; (2) when rules are circumvented according to common operating procedure; and (3) when written records contain what is supposed to be on file, but not necessarily what actually occurred. In short, although many of the conclusions drawn by the Hawthorne researchers are still in doubt (see Franke and Kaul, 1978), their findings gave rise to the first questioning of whether we can assume an organization will operate in the way we specify it should.

Functional Theory

An outgrowth of the research on human relations in industry (which in turn was largely a reaction to the mechanistic model proposed by Taylor) was the development of functional models of organizations. Embedded within a larger abstract social theory (see Parsons, 1951), functionalists viewed organizations as social systems with various system needs, the most important being the need to survive.

In order to function (i.e., survive), organizations must acquire adequate resources (adaptation); establish and achieve organizational objectives (goal attainment); maintain effective coordination among all members and organizational subunits (integration); and promote loyalty and adherence to organizational values and purposes (latency) (see Scott, 1987, pp. 68–72). Vertical and horizontal differentiation occurs in response to these needs. For example, purchasing and personnel departments are set up to acquire necessary organizational inputs; production and sales divisions are instituted to accomplish manufacturing and marketing quotas; hierarchical levels are put in place to achieve coordination among functional subunits; and various instrumental and expressive mechanisms are established to foster organizational commitment.

Functional organization theory may be seen as a specific application of more general structural functionalist theory (see Chapter 2). According to this perspective, organizations are organic, naturally evolving social systems that are relatively stable and self-perpetuating owing to the fact that there is value consensus among organizational members. Differentiation occurs in order to meet system needs, and whereas this sometimes produces strain on the system, it is at least partially alleviated through the processes of reintegration, institutionalization, and social control.

In their studies of organizations, organizational functionalists were among the first to document empirically the structural weaknesses inherent in bureaucratic design. Whereas the rationalists were convinced of the technical superiority of this organizational form in achieving complex objectives, the functionalists identified several important unanticipated and dysfunctional consequences arising out of formal organizational expectations (see March and Simon, 1958, pp. 36–47). In Box 4-3, **The Unintended Consequences of Bureaucracy,** in Chapter 4, I have described one example in which bureaucatic rules and regulations, while being necessary to the functioning of the organization, also introduce rigidity and inflexibility, which can impede the achievement of organizational goals. Thus, the functionalist school raised serious objections to the notion that the ideal type of bureaucracy represents the "one best way" to administer organizations.

Conflict Theory

Largely in response to functionalist theory that advocates value consensus among organizational members, conflict theory, a Marxist perspective, asserts that all members of an organization do not share the same interests and goals (see Dahrendorf, 1959). Specifically, conflicts of interest occur between ranks within an organization. For example, managers and owners do not have the same objectives as do workers on the shop floor; often their objectives are antithetical to each other. Because of the unequal distribution of power and authority within organizations, conflict is endemic. Recognition of this fact strengthens the contention that the formally stated goals of an organization (i.e., management objectives) are not the goals of all organizational members. An obvious and dramatic example of this fact is a prison. Prison officials have different goals than the inmates. A researcher who studies both groups will come away with very different accounts as to how the prison (organization) actually functions. Consequently, in presenting the organization as an arena of competing interests, conflict theorists upset even more the mechanistic model of integrated rational design.

Open Systems Theory

A relatively recent perspective introduces still more uncertainty into the study of organizations. Originating out of more general theoretical developments within sociology (see, for example, Buckley, 1967), open systems theory asserts that organizations interact with their environment in crucial ways and therefore cannot be studied as closed systems impervious to the effects of the larger society of which they are a part (see J. D. Thompson, 1967). Thus, in their study of organizations, open systems researchers are concerned with such factors as labor supply, raw material, and competition as they affect organizational structure and process. For example, factories located near large available pools of labor employ a different recruitment strategy than do more isolated factories. Similarly, organizations in a highly competitive environment operate differently than organizations that have a monpoly over resources.

Open systems theory assumes a state of flux and uncertainty rather than certainty. Through complex feedback mechanisms, organizations must continually adjust and adapt to their environment. Because environmental conditions everywhere are different and are themselves in a state of flux, no one structure is assumed to be best for all organizations; rather, the structure evolves in response to a particular environment.

Contingency Theory

Originally coined by Lawrence and Lorsch (1967), contingency theory focuses on those factors both external and internal to the organization that contribute to task uncertainty: the nature of the environment, the type of technology employed to produce particular goods or services, organizational size, and the kind and level of information that must be processed in order to achieve adequate organizational performance. The nature of the structure and process is contingent upon these and other factors. No longer do researchers look for the one best way to organize; instead, they attempt to specify those variables that produce variation in structure and performance. In so doing, they hope to uncover complex relationships that both explain and predict the variance in organizational design.

Organizational Climate and Culture

Another perspective employing an open systems approach that explains the variation in otherwise similar organizations concentrates specifically upon the larger culture within which organizations operate as well as the particular cultural configurations created by organizations themselves. This approach has gained ascendacy with the emergence of Japan as a leading industrial nation (see Morgan, 1986, pp. 111–140). Despite earlier predictions of cultural convergence (see Abegglen, 1958), recent cross-national research suggests that cultural factors do play a significant role in producing different organizational outcomes (see Dore, 1973, who was a pioneer in this line of inquiry).

According to Morgan (1986, p. 112), culture as an explanatory concept can operate at four different levels of analysis: (1) "Organization is itself a cultural phenomenon that varies according to a society's stage of development"; (2) holding the stage of development constant, variation in cultural standards and practices (e.g., the United States and Japan) produces organizational variation; (3) holding culture constant, different organizational philosophies and values (i.e., different corporate cultures or organizational climates) result in different organizational structures and behavior; and (4) holding organization constant, different subcultures within the same organization (e.g., production and sales) may have their own ethos, which in turn produce different behavioral outcomes. Consequently, cultural variation on any of these levels implies a corresponding variation in organizational structure and process.

Population–Ecology Theory

The final perspective included in Table 7.1 is also an open systems derivative. Based on earlier theoretical work (see Campbell, 1969), the population-ecology or natural selection model asserts that the environment is crucial in determining what organizational characteristics are most likely to survive (see Aldrich, 1979; Aldrich and Pfeffer, 1976). This perspective proposes that "environments differentially select organizations for survival on the basis of the fit between organization structure (and activities) and environmental characteristics. Those organizations that have the appropriate social structure, for whatever reason, are selected over those that do not" (Aldrich and Pfeffer, 1976, pp. 80–81). As an example of this line of reasoning, population–ecology theorists would contend that only since the 1960s were environmental conditions conducive to the appearance of the transnational corporation (TNC) as an organizational form, and consequently from this time onward TNCs have become a regular and increasing feature of the organizational landscape (see Chapter 8).

The population–ecology perspective operates on the most general level of analysis. It attempts to discern broad organizational trends over time given significant variations in the environment. Where other perspectives emphasize how organizations themselves are important actors in their own determination and survival, the population–ecology model focuses more on features of the environment as being instrumental in organizational growth and dissolution.

Table 7.1 does not exhaust the number of perspectives that have been developed to study organizations. For example, Morgan (1986) has suggested a wide variety of ways in which organizations may be perceived—as political and holographic systems, and even as psychic prisons and instruments of domination. Similarly, other analysts (e.g., Hall, 1987; Scott, 1987) have provided still other conceptions. However, all the recent perspectives employ open systems models and all take a contingency approach. In other words, organizations, like people, are in a constant state of flux as they attempt to adjust and adapt to a similarly changing environment. While some aspects of the environment are highlighted as being crucial to organizational design and development, contemporary theorists differ from earlier generations of researchers who sought to identify the ideal type of organization.

In the following sections we will examine comparative studies of organizations in Great Britain, the United States, and Japan with the purpose of (1) identifying those contingencies found to be most strongly related to organization structure; and (2) determining the extent of variation in organization structure by culture. With respect to the latter of these two purposes, national culture in all its many ramifications is part of the environment within which organizations function. Thus, by comparing organization structure in three quite different cultural contexts, we will be able to determine whether similar types of organizations designed to achieve similar purposes have esssentially the same organization structures or whether there are significant differences among them that may be attributable to differences in national culture.

This issue, as well as being theoretically interesting, also has important practical implications. The economic successes of Japan in recent decades have academics and practitioners alike speculating whether at least part of the explanation lies in the organization of Japanese industry. Are there significant differences in the manner in which Japanese businesses are established and operate that give them a competitive edge, and if so, can these practices be applied to Western-style organizations, or do they only work because of certain aspects which are inherent in Japan's culture? While all the answers are not yet in, at least we will be able to broach this issue and arrive at some tentative conclusions.

CONTINGENCIES

Organizational Size

As indicated in Table 6.3, manufacturing organizations as measured by the number of employees are on average four times larger in Great Britain and the United States than in Japan. For Japanese industry as a whole, slightly more than three-quarters of all those employed work in establishments of less than 100 people, whereas in the United States the comparable figure is just over one-half (Granovetter, 1984). Consequently, notwithstanding the fact and the image of modern, large-scale corporate capitalism,[3] it is also true that most people, particularly in Japan, work in organizations of modest size. While some of these organizations are subsidiary to larger firms, nevertheless the daily working experience of most workers in industrialized nations takes place within an organizational context in which all employees, regardless of vertical and horizontal differentiation, are on a fairly familiar basis with one another. As a result, these workers are responding not only to *organizational* imperatives but also to the *people* who are responsible for administering them.

Research on size as it affects organizational structure has found that with increments in personnel, organizations, be they British, American, or Japanese, generally become more horizontally and vertically differentiated, have proportionately smaller administrative components (i.e., number of managers and supervisors in relation to the total number of employees), and are more formalized (Aldrich and Marsden, 1988, p. 373; Marsh and Mannari, 1981). In other words, large organizations are able to diversify and specialize their operations more than smaller units. In turn, the number of hierarchical levels is increased in order to achieve the additional coordination required for these specialized functions. Because of economies of scale, the increase in hierarchical differentiation does not translate into a larger administrative overhead. Rather proportionately more human resources can be directly focused on the attainment of organizational objectives. Finally, large organizations are by definition impersonal, and therefore they must rely more on formalized impersonal control mechanisms than small organizations in order to achieve effective administrative control.

On the other hand, research results differ with respect to the effects of size on centralization. In some studies of British and American organizations, researchers have found that delegation of authority increases with size, and have therefore argued that because larger organizations are also more structurally complex, it becomes increasingly difficult to maintain centralized control (Child, 1976). However, in other studies, two of which were carried out in Japan, centralization varies independently of organizational size (see Marsh and Mannari, 1981). These data suggest that while size is a significant contingency in its influence on organizational structure, there are other important factors, certainly with respect to centralization, that also exercise their effects.

Technology

The first large-scale comparative study of the effects of technology on organization structure was conducted by Woodward (1965) in approximately 100 British manufacturing firms. Woodward argued that the technical methods by which goods are produced rather than the particular goods themselves are important determinants of how organizations structure their operations. For example, the production technology involved in made-to-measure suits (i.e., unit production) is vastly different than off-the-rack suits (mass production) and therefore, according to Woodward, calls for a different organizational structure, regardless of the fact that in both instances suits are being made.

In unit and small-batch production, skilled workers (e.g., tailors) are involved in the unique specialized manufacture of one or several items according to individual customer specifications. In large-batch and mass production, semiskilled workers operate machines that produce standardized components, which are subsequently assembled into integral products for stock or inventory. At the most technically complex end of the production technology scale, Woodward identified process production which involves the manufacture of dimensional rather than integral products (e.g., chemicals, refined oil, and liquids). In this type of production, workers are responsible for overseeing highly complex equipment that automatically produces goods that are defined in terms of weight, capacity, or volume.

With regard to the scale of technical complexity, Woodward noted that at the unit production end, individual workers with the assistance of various tools and equipment are primarily responsible for product manufacture, whereas at the process end, machines predominate in the manufacturing operations, and workers perform only a monitoring function. Mass production methods fall in between these two extremes, with workers tending machinery that completes most but not all of the manufacturing (see Woodward, 1965, pp. 35–49). According to Woodward, these different worker–machine relationships require different organizational structures in order that production operations can be administered effectively.

Despite the difficulties in constructing standardized measures of techonology that can be applied across all organizations, including goal-producing and services-producing organizations (see Scott, 1987, p. 213), many of Woodward's original findings have been confirmed in subsequent replications in both Great Britain and the United States (see Aldrich and Marsden, 1988, p. 374). Scott (1987, p. 214) has summarized the most important of these enduring relationships between technology and organization structure:

1. The greater the technical complexity, the greater the structural complexity. The structural response to technical diversity is organizational differentiation.
2. The greater the technical uncertainty, the less formalization and centralization.
3. The greater the technical interdependence, the more resources must be devoted to coordination.

Confusion does exist in the research literature over whether technology or size is the more important determinant of organizational structure. Proponents of either side of the debate have launched extensive arguments as to the primacy of their particular independent variable. However, this problem may be resolved by asserting that both technology *and* size are important contingencies and by establishing a reasonable causal sequence between technology, size, and organization structure. On this latter point, Aldrich states:

> ... the development of an organization proceeds from its initial founding and capitalization in response to market opportunities, through its design based on copying and modifying an existing technology, on to the design of the organization's structure, and finally to the employment of a workforce to staff the nearly completed organization. .... Technology is causally prior to the size of the workforce ... and is also causally prior to organization structure. (cited in Marsh and Mannori, 1981:55).

While the impact of technology on organizational structure has been documented in Great Britain, the United States, and other Western industrial countries, its influence on Japanese organizations does not appear to be so strong. Lincoln and McBride (1987, pp. 303–304) suggest that this might be "because the institutional environment in that country [Japan] exerts a greater influence on organizing modes" than in the United States and other more "culturally heterogeneous and politically decentralized" countries. In other words, the impact of the environment on organization structure is another important contingency that must also be considered.

Environment

The environment of an organization constitutes everything that is *not* the organization—it consists of interrelated factors that are only now being examined systematically and comprehensively. Figure 7.2 presents the major components of the environment with which organizations interact. In order to survive, organizations adapt their structures to those environmental conditions that are crucial to their functioning. For example, during the early 1970s many organizations were seriously affected by the skyrocketing increases in the price of oil. In order to adjust to this significant change in the external environment, some organizations (e.g., automobile manufacturers) were forced to alter and in some cases curtail their operations, while others (e.g., oil exploration and public transport) expanded enormously. Historical events such as this obviously have an impact on organizational creation and dissolution rates. Currently, the annual birth and death rates of organizations in the United States runs at about 10% of the organizational population (Aldrich and Marsden, 1988). In other words, approximately as many organiza-

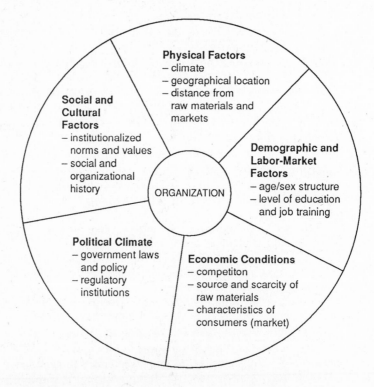

Figure 7.2 Organization and Environment
Source: Hedley, 1986b, p. 220.

tions are being created as are dissolving, with the result that the organizational landscape is in constant dynamic process.

Part of the organizational environment is other organizations many of which are in the immediate environment (e.g., suppliers, competitors, regulatory agencies, markets, and so on). Researachers are increasingly expanding their focus by studying these immediate environments that are also termed organizational networks. Box 7-1, **Black Monday,** describes one of these networks and what can happen when the environment is technologically enhanced.

Recent research attention has focused on the effects that social and cultural factors of the enviroment have on organizations, or to put it simply, does culture make a difference? Only during the past decade have a sufficient number of cross-national organizational studies been carried out whereby it is possible even to address this question. Certainly more research is required before it can be adequately answered. However, an increasing number of comparisons between American and Japanese business organizations have been made such that at least we can make some plausible conjecture with respect to these two nations.

The most popular of the United States–Japan comparisons was conducted by William Ouchi (1981) whose book, *Theory Z,* was on the best-seller list for months. Ouchi states that American and Japanese organizational modes are diametrically opposed in regard to each of the following seven important features:

American Organizations	Japanese Organizations
Short-term employment	Lifetime employment
Rapid evaluation and promotion	Slow evaluation and promotion
Specialized career paths	Nonspecialized career paths
Explicit control mechanisms	Implicit control mechanisms
Individual decision making	Collective decision making
Individual responsibility	Collective responsibility
Segmented concern	Wholistic concern

Source: Ouchi, 1981, p. 58

Ouchi argues that the more consensually based, less bureaucratic Japanense method of organization derives from more general aspects of Japanes culture. Given their geographical, topographical, and historical circumstances, the Japanese people found collective communal strategies to be most successful in their struggle for survival. As a result, the group has come to be valued more than the individual. This cultural pattern Ouchi contrasts with the individualistic ethos of self-reliance and independence, which is more characteristic of American cultural adaptation. Thus, whereas collectivism is the prevailing value upon which Japanese organizations are established, individual achievment and responsibility form the value underpinnings of American organizations. Ouchi goes on to claim that the Japanese style of organization results in greater productivity, which is why Japan is currently posing such an economic threat to the United States today.

Ouchi's description of the essential differences between Japanese and American organizations is supported by comparative studies that have been con-

Box 7-1 **Black Monday**

For the first time in recent memory on the floor of the New York Stock Exchange, the steady, dull roar of American capitalism faded, as if someone had slowly turned down the volume on a television set. Soon it was eerily quiet. The bustle of traders and brokers and clerks scurrying across the massive floor practically ceased. Eyes focused on the computer screens that hung above the floor's 17 trading kiosks, some of which were suddenly and inexplicably going blank. A few traders left the floor, unable to watch. "This is it," muttered one exchange clerk over and over.

"What is going on?" someone asked. "This is it," the clerk repeated, staring at the floor and dragging on a cigarette.

From 10:30 a.m. until 12:30 p.m., the Dow Jones industrial average fell as fast as anyone ever thought it could. Down 50 points in 15 minutes. Down 100 in 45. Down 167 in an hour. Down 200 in an hour and a half. . . .

It was "God tapping us on the shoulder," said Dallas billionaire H. Ross Perot.

Newsweek, 2 November 1987, p. 24.

ILLUSTRATION FOR TIME BY DAVID SUTER

Time, 2 November 1987.

On Monday, October 19, 1987, the unthinkable happened—stock prices plummeted more sharply and more deeply than in the benchmark crash of 1929. The Dow plunged 508 points (22.6%); U.S. securities declined by $500 billion. More than 600 million shares were traded.

Contributing to the swiftness and severity of the fall was our increasingly sophisticated and responsive technological expertise. The sudden and dramatic drop was at least in part caused by thousands of computers all similarly programmed, and all operating in electronically linked stock exchanges throughout the world in an interdependent global trading system. In New York, Toronto, London, Zurich, Tokyo, and Hong Kong the computers acted, and reacted almost immediately, to produce a self-perpetuating downward spiral.

Computer-generated Program Trading   It is ironical in a free enterprise system that the products and services offered to us have become increasingly similar in form and function. Whether it be automobiles, clothes, or professional services, a uniform standard emerges as various enterprises begin to emulate the industry leader. So it is with computer hardware and software despite the many competitors in the field. Performance standards are established and technological innovations are copied so much that, almost regardless of the manufacturer of the computer or the developer of the software, the end result is the same.

In computer program trading, large programs or portfolios of stocks are systematically bought and sold according to certain underlying principles of the stock market that form the bases of the computer programs. Operating like complex thermostats, the computers minutely monitor the market, automatically ordering trades when prices rise above or fall below a preestablished margin or gap.

On Black Monday, all the computers acted in concert responding to the same stimuli. Their ability to execute trades instantaneously and in overwhelming volume contributed to the panic and subsequent free fall of the market. "It was like trying to catch a falling knife," remarked one trader. The number of stocks traded on the New York Stock Exchange that day more than doubled the previous record high. Computer-driven trades were estimated to account for as much as 30% of this volume.

Although there is still debate on the actual direct impact of computers on the fall, restrictions were placed on computer-generated program trading for the three weeks following the fateful plunge, and one senior government official called for "hearings into the role of computerized trading programs that dump securities when the market falls." As one broker observed, "It was the ultimate video experience."

Electronically Connected Exchanges   Experts analyzing the crash placed its origin on the Friday previous when the Dow dropped a daily record of 108 points. By the time the New York Stock Exchange reopened on Monday morning at (9:30, the exchanges in Australia, the Orient, and Europe had been open for some hours. Nervousness over the decline in the Dow on Friday sent all these exchanges into a tailspin as they tried to anticipate the reaction of the North American market. The big money managers in New York armed with this information from their computer screens hit the New York exchange with bearish frenzy at the opening bell. In the first half hour, 50 million shares were sold and the rout was on.

One market's fear and panic fed on another. On Tuesday, triggered by New York's Black Monday, Tokyo registered a 15% loss on its Nikkei Dow Jones index, London dropped 12%, Paris 6%, Toronto 7%, and the Hong Kong Stock Exchange closed for the week. All these electronically linked exchanges provoked a cumulative chain reaction that intensified the impact on any one exchange. As one investment banker put it, "We really do not know what we've created. It's high tech and it's transnational and more powerful than anything we could ever have imagined."

Computer trading and computer networks did not cause Black Monday; other factors such as world trade imbalances, national debts, and shifting exchange rates and international investments precipitated the loss of confidence. However, our lightning-fast technological dexterity most certainly set the stage on which this world drama was to be played, and exacerbated the pervading sense of doom.

Technology influences behavior independently of the true causal variables in that it establishes the structural freedoms and constraints under which we operate. If we do not explicitly separate out the effects of technology, they can be mistakenly interpreted as causal, which in fact they can eventually become with the sometimes horrendous consequences that this entails. It was W. I. Thomas who stated that if a situation is perceived to be real, it is real in its consequences. Fortunately, some sane minds prevailed on that ominous Black Monday. Interconnected computer-driven drives were interpreted as "informationless trading" made without the benefit of experience or judgment. On Tuesday morning in New York, human intervention based on a sound appraisal of recent events managed to break the chain of technologically determined decline. The market would now rise or fall on its own merits.

Factual information and quotations taken from the November 2, 1987 issues of *Newsweek* and *Time*.

---

ducted with more methodological rigor. For example, Lincoln and his research associates (1986), reporting on their comparative survey of 55 American and 51 Japanese manufactuing plants, summarize the differences as follows:

> Compared with the U.S., Japanese manufacturing organizations have taller hierarchies, less functional specialization, less formal delegation of authority but more de facto participation in decisions at lower levels in the management hierarchy. These structures are consistent with the internal labor market processes (lifetime employment, seniority-based promotion) that characterize Japanese companies and the general emphasis on groups over individuals as the fundamental units of organization. (Lincoln et al., 1986, p. 361)

Dore's comparative study (1973) of two Japanese and two British factories arrives at essentially similar conclusions. Making the same basic contrast between the group and the individual as the underlying core upon which the organization is established, Dore found far less formal division of labor in Hitachi than in English Electric (the Japanese and British firms he studied). Instead of specific duties being functionally allocated to formally defined positions within the organization as was the case in English Electric, in Hitachi he observed that diffuse responsibilities were assigned to groups, and that these responsibilities could change from time to time. With regard to vertical differentiation, Dore noted a more finely graded, almost continuous hierarchy in Hitachi that offers a career ladder to Japanese managers, most of whom devote their entire working lives to the same organization. An important aspect of this hierarchical arrangement is that because there are so many gradients of authority, a gulf between "them and us" is not perceived as it was at English Electric. Finally, Dore concluded that while the Japanese factories were more formalized than their British counterparts (e.g., more formally prescribed procedures, written communication, and record keeping), responsibility for organizational performance was more widely diffused.

To these differences between Japanese and Western-type organizations, Abegglen and Stalk (1985) add various competitive strategies that leading Japanese corporations have adopted since the end of World War II. Because Japan is culturally homogeneous, a point made by Lincoln and McBride (1987), the impact of any national strategy is more uniform and therefore more strongly felt than in a more heterogeneous culture. Hence the term "Japan, Inc.," which has crept into common parlance when discussing the economic performance of this nation.

The first competitive advantage that Japan enjoyed vis-à-vis the Western industrial nations was relatively low wage rates. As this gap narrowed, the Japanese concentrated on high-volume, large-scale, capital-intensive production that permitted them to achieve economies of a scale that their Western competitors did not have. This was followed by what Abegglen and Stalk term "focused manufacturing," which involves limiting production to a relatively few product lines, which together with high-volume production gave Japanese corporations substantial cost advantage over their more broadly based competitors. Currently, many Japanese corporations are reversing themselves, opting for flexible rather than focused production. (See Box 1.1, **Flexible Manufacturing Systems**, in Chapter 1.) This is occurring at the same time that Western competitors are reducing product variability. Thus, by introducing various cost-saving innovations and reducing their inventories, Japanese manufacturers in offering greater product variety are able to capture ever-increasing shares of the international marketplace.

The general picture of Japanese organizations that emerges from all of this research may be summarized around two central themes: collaboration and task organization. The greater emphasis on the group in Japanese companies results in more consultation and collaboration than is typically found in traditional bureaucratic settings. Furthermore, because of the low levels of interfirm mobilitiy in Japan (see Bednarzik and Shiells, 1989, pp. 37–38), these organizational groups remain relatively intact over time, and there thus develops a strong sense of loyalty to and identification with the group. In fact, most workers develop their careers and have a sense of progression and commitment within one comparatively small organizational context.

Task organization involves the structuring of organizational activities according to the particular tasks or objectives that the organization is currently faced with as opposed to functional organization in which tasks are allotted to existing departments or divisions of functional expertise as is required. Task organization basically means fitting the organization to the task, whereas functional organization requires that the task be fitted into the existing structure. Consequently, task organization is more flexible and more responsive to the external environment.

Research in Japanese organizations indicates that they are more task oriented in their organizational structure than is found in American and British organizations, which tend to be organized around particular specialized functions. In other words, Japanese organizations are less horizontally differentiated. Instead of anticipating the tasks that they will be called upon to perform, and attempting to match these tasks within existing structural arrangements, Japanese managers respond to challenges by organizing task groups that they feel will be most capable of meeting these challenges. Consequently, the composition of these groups varies according to the particular tasks they are required to achieve. Given the strategic move toward flexible production discussed by Abegglen and Stalk, one may expect that task organization will become even more strongly emphasized in Japanese business organizations.

The question remains as to whether this picture of Japanese organizations that we have come up with is culturally unique to Japan. Whereas we have found similarities between Japanese and Western organizations in the effects of size and technology on organizational structure, nevertheless there do appear to be overall distinctive differences in how these two types of organizations are constituted. How can we explain these differences?

While it is true that organizations in which collaboration and task organization are encouraged are descriptive of the organization scene in Japan, and that this type of organization may even be culturally compatible with Japan's historical circumstances, at the same time there is nothing about these organizations that makes them uniquely Japanese. In fact, Ouchi (1981, pp. 57–70) points out that several prominent American corporations including IBM, Hewlett-Packard, Eastman-Kodak, and Procter and Gamble are currently structured in this fashion, having devised this type of structure in respose to their own organizational demands rather than emulating the "Japanese model." Furthermore, task organization is not a Japanese concept. It was first advanced by the Austrian-born American management consultant Peter Drucker (1954), who advocated "management by objective" as opposed to "management by control."

Marsh and Mannari (1981) caution against propounding culturally specific models of organization before every attempt has been made to identify universal contextual features which might be responsible for producing variation in organizational structure. Lincoln and McBride (1987) suggest that Japanese organization may not be so much "Japanese" as a prototype or organizational wave of the future. Dore (1973), emphasizing Japan's relatively late industrial development, argues that the differences in organizational structure between Great Britain and Japan may be more a function of the differences in the initial time and rate of industrialization rather than cultural factors per se.

While definitive answers cannot be provided at this stage, nevertheless there is evidence that suggests that the so-called Japanese model, or certainly the themes of collaboration and task organization, may indeed be indicative of what is to come. The following section deals with this prospect.

EMERGENT ORGANIZATIONAL FORMS

Over the past 30 years, researchers have been identifying and ascertaining the independent and combined effects of various contingencies upon organization structure. While we have briefly looked at three of these contingencies—organizational size, technology, and culture—there are many more, and their joint impact has resulted in what some researchers have identified as new organizational types. In this section, we will examine the evidence for and characteristics of these so-called emerging organizations, and then attempt to specify the underlying factors that explain their appearance at this time.

Professional Organization

Basically there are two ways in which an organization can achieve a complex goal: (1) by breaking the objective into its component parts with various individuals becoming responsible for the achievement of simple tasks; or (2) by training all persons in all the skills necessary to attain the objective independently. This is the underlying distinction between bureaucratic and professional organization. Bureaucracies are involved in the division and subdivision of goals such that with the appropriate coordination and control, the entire task can be accomplished with no one actually having all the requisite skills to achieve it on his or her own. In contrast, professions are comprised of workers each of whom is knowledgeable in the skills required for task completion. From this very simplified characterization, other implications follow. Table 7.2 juxtaposes the essential features of the bureaucratic and professional models of organization.

Given these different bases of work organization, the question arises as to what happens when increasing numbers of professionals are employed in traditional bureaucratic organizations (see Chapter 6). Notwithstanding the fact that professionals need organizations both as contexts of works and custodians of scarce resources (e.g., money and equipmen), and that organizations need professionals for their specialized knowledge and talents, conflict can and does occur (see Scott, 1966). The greatest source of conflict between the professional and bureaucractic modes of work is in determining who should exercise authority (see Hall, 1968). To the extent that hierarchical authority is imposed on professionals, there is an almost corresponding loss in their feeling of autonomy. Professionals strongly resist supervision from uninformed laypersons, regardless of the latter's rank within the organization. As indicated in Table 7.2, only professional colleagues with similar expertise are deemed competent to judge professional performance.

Although the potential for conflict between professionals and bureaucrats is strong, it does not necessarily occur. Depending upon the perceived costs and benefits to both, accommodation and adaptation do take place. But each side pays its price: for professionals, there is an erosion of (professional) autonomy; for organizations, an adjustment in structure and process. Out of the bargain that is struck develops the professional type of organization. Generally, what occurs is the carving out of an area of professional jurisdiction within an overall bureaucratic

Table 7.2   BUREAUCRATIC AND PROFESSIONAL MODELS OF ORGANIZATION

Bureaucratic model	Professional model
1. **Division of labor.** Assumes that complex objectives will be broken down into specific task elements; these elements are then assigned to participants according to their functional area of competence.	1. **Systemic theory.** Presumes mastery by all professionals of that body of knowledge that constitutes the profession's major focus of interest.
2. **Hierarchical authority.** The basis of control lies in the hierarchical level of the position; organizational rank rather than knowledge becomes the grounds for assuming authority.	2. **Professional authority.** Possession of a unique fund of knowledge, considered essential to society, places the professional in the logically necessary position either of being responsible for his or her own actions or of being controlled by other professionals who have the requisite knowledge upon which to judge performance.
3. **Rules and regulations.** The participant's actions are governed by a *specific* set of rules and regulations established by the organization which are designed to cover any exigency that may arise.	3. **Code of ethics.** The professional's actions are governed by a *general* code of ethics established by the profession, which is internalized during the long training period by the professional to the point where the professional code and the individual's code are one.
4. **Full working capacity of the official.** Involves participants in the notion of a career with, and loyalty to, the organization.	4. **Professional culture.** Arises out of the formal and informal social interaction among professionals and involves commitment to the profession and what it stands for.

Source: Hedley, 1986b, p. 223.

system of control. Within this defined area, professional norms of work organization are applied, provided that the outcome is consonant with bureaucratic expectations. In other words, both professional and bureaucratic models can be accommodated in a sort of uneasy alliance (see Hedley, 1977).

Compared with a traditional bureaucratic structure, a professional organization (1) is more flexible with regard to rules and procedures; (2) is more task oriented rather than being organized within strict functional jurisdictions; (3) engages more in horizontal, collaborative communication and decision making; and (4) is more responsive to changes in the environment.

Organic Organization

In 1961, Burns and Stalker published their research on 20 industrial firms in Britain in which they found that organization structure or, more properly, management style, appeared to be dependent upon the stability of the organizational environment. In organizations operating in relatively stable environments in which there was a great deal of certainty and predictability of outcome, Burns and Stalker concluded that management was "mechanistic," following closely the precepts of organization originally laid down by Weber.

> In mechanistic systems the problems and tasks facing the concern as a whole are broken down into specialisms. Each individual pursues his task as something distinct from the real tasks of the concern as a whole, as if it were the subject of a subcontract. "Somebody at the top" is responsible for seeing to its relevance. The technical methods, duties, and powers attached to each functional role are precisely defined. Interaction within managment tends to be vertical, that is, between superior and subordinate. (Burns and Stalker, 1961, p. 5)

However, in those organizations in rapidly changing environments in which technical and market conditions were uncertain, management was "organic" and functioned within a loosely defined organization structure.

> Organic systems are adapted to unstable conditions, when problems and requirements for action arise which cannot be broken down and distributed among specialist roles within a clearly defined hierarchy. Individuals have to perform their special tasks in the light of their knowledge of the tasks of the firm as a whole. Jobs lose much of their formal definition in terms of methods, duties and powers, which have to be redefined continually by interaction with others participating in a task. Interaction runs laterally as much as vertically. Communication between people of different ranks tends to resemble lateral consultation rather than vertical command. (Burns and Stalker, 1961, pp. 5–6)

Coincidental with the Burns and Stalker study, other researchers were also suggesting that all organizations are not bureaucratically monolithic (see, for example, Bennis, 1966; Litwak, 1961; Stinchcombe, 1959). Generally, the case that they made involved organizations characterized by a more flexible and task-oriented structure, with considerable responsibility and autonomy being given to organizational participants.

Flexible Organization

In the concluding chapter to their collection of international and interinstitutional studies of organizations, Lammers and Hickson (1979) provide a cross-national typology of organizations based on the diverse studies contained in their edited volume. They contend that most of the cross-national research of organizations supports the view that there are three (culturally) distinctive types of organizations: (1) traditional Third World; (2) classic Latin; and (3) flexible Anglo-Saxon.[4]

The traditional Third World type, characteristic of many organizations in developing nations, has an almost prebureaucratic structure. It is relatively underdeveloped in terms of both vertical and horizontal differentiation (i.e., organizations are "flat," with few specialized staff), and it is managed by a paternalistic leader in a highly centralized manner who resorts to "implicitly transmitted custom" rather than explicitly formalized bureaucratic controls. This type of organization also is not particularly adaptable to changes in its environment.

The classic Latin type of organization, found predominantly in southern European countries and Latin America, is most characteristic of classical Weberian bureaucracy. Its organization structure is typified by a rigid hierarchical system with clear lines of demarcation between ranks. Authoritarian leaders manage operations through a highly centralized decision-making structure and a relatively inflexible system of bureaucratic controls (i.e., highly formalized). This type of organization, not surprisingly, is not particularly innovative and does not adapt well to changes in the environment.

The flexible Anglo-Saxon type, more typical of organizations in northwestern Europe and North America, is considerably more flexible and responsive to its environment. It is less rigidly stratified and not as formalized as the classic type. Leaders engage more in consultative, democratic decision making, and the system is relatively decentralized.

While all the evidence that Lammers and Hickson bring to bear support the existence of these three general types of organization, they are also careful to point out that "it (almost) goes without saying that no type of organization is found exclusively in just one culture-area. . . . We are trying to trace broad patterns in which a good deal of overlapping must occur" (1979, p. 429).[5] However, implicit in their analysis is an evolutionary perspective on the development of organizations in response to environmental contingencies.

Consultative Organization

Between 1967 and 1969 and again between 1971 and 1973, Hofstede (1979) conducted a questionnaire survey of approximately 60,000 employees of a transnational corporation located in 40 countries. The employees and managers of each subsidiary were indigenous to the country in which business was conducted. Given that the organization structure, production technology, and composition of the labor force were similar from one country to another, Hofstede argued that any differences revealed in the survey would very likely be cultural differences.

Hofstede's main dependent variable was a "power distance index" that was comprised of the responses to three questions dealing with:

1. Subordinates' perceptions of the decision-making behavior of their superior [responses ranged from "autocratic" to "consultative"] . . . ;
2. Subordinates' perception that employees (their colleagues) are afraid to disagree with their managers [responses ranged on the degree of frequency];
3. Subordinates' own expressed preference for a certain type of decision-making behavior by their superior [responses same as 1 above] (Hofstede, 1979, p. 101).

The responses to each of these questions were combined and transformed to a scale that ranged from 0 (low-power distance) to 100 (high-power distance). A low score on the power distance index indicated that the respondent perceived his or her superior to be consultative in management style, that the respondent's peers were not afraid to disagree, and that the respondent preferred to be treated in just this fashion. On the other hand, a high score reflected autocratic management, constant fear to disagree, and an indication that this was appropriate and expected superior–subordinate interaction.

In that organizational life may be seen as a microcosm of what goes on in the larger society, Hofstede thought that any between-country differences in the power distance index would in effect be mirroring larger cultural differences with respect to how power is perceived in society and how it should be exercised. For example, he found in all countries that managers and professionals scored lowest on the index and that unskilled and semiskilled workers scored the highest. This finding reflects the universal notion that for managers and professionals of differing ranks it is seen as appropriate to interact in a consultative or collaborative fashion, but for interaction between manual workers and supervisor a more authoritarian manner is considered suitable.[6]

Hofstede's main findings on the differences between countries revealed extensive dissimilarities. "People working within the same multinational corporation, in the same occupations, but in different countries, experience vastly different power distances with their superiors" (Hofstede, 1979, p. 106). On average, workers from the Philippines scored highest on the power distance index (PDI = 94), Austrian employees measured lowest (11), and the median score dividing the 40 countries was 56. Of those countries with the highest power distance indices, most were from Asia and Latin America, while those with the lowest scores were from the developed countries of Europe, Oceania, and North America.[7] Great Britain averaged 35 on the power distance index; the United States scored 40; and Japan measured 54.

Another interesting result from Hofstede's research arises from his two separate time measurements of the employees from this transnational corporation. His analysis shows that while a decrease in *preference* for autocratic managers was recorded by employees in all countries from one time period to the next, only in those countries that had an initially low power distance index did workers perceive a decrease in *actual* autocratic behavior.

Table 7.3 presents the consequences of national differences in hierarchical power distance for organizations. Based on Hofstede's research and supported also by other studies (see Hofstede, 1979, pp. 113–115), this table shows that in countries in which power distances between superiors and subordinates are perceived to be small, organizations in general are less vertically differentiated, have a smaller proportion of supervisory personnel, and are less centralized than organizations in countries that manifest large power distances. Performance criteria rather than status form the bases for interaction, and consequently relationships among employees of differing rank, tend to be more consultative rather than autocratic or paternalistic.

Table 7.3   CONSEQUENCES OF HIERARCHICAL POWER DISTANCE FOR ORGANIZATIONS

Power distance index	
Large power differential (autocratic management)	**Small power differential (consultative management)**
Tall organization pyramids	Flatter organization pyramids
Large proportion of supervisory personnel	Smaller proportion of supervisory personnel
Greater centralization	Less centralization
Vertical communication	Vertical and lateral communication
Low qualification of lower strata	Higher qualification of lower strata
Large wage differentials	Smaller wage differentials
Promotion based on school education and seniority: gerontocracy	Promotion based on performance and shared values: meritocracy

Source: Adapted from Hofstede, 1979, p. 114.

Synopsis

Each of the four emergent organizational forms presented thus far shares basic similarities. Perhaps most important, professional, organic, flexible, and consultative organizations all may be seen as significantly departing from Weber's ideal type of bureaucracy. Rather than being deterministic and mechanical in form and function, they manifest the almost diametrically opposed properties of variability and responsiveness. From these four emergent types, it is possible to derive a composite model of organization.

First and foremost, the new type of organization is perforce attentive both to its surrounding environment and to the organizational climate it creates within its sphere of operations. Its very survival is dependent upon being cognizant of and attuned to these two sets of conditions. Consequently, rather than imposing an invariable structure and code of operating procedures from on high, it must adopt a more flexible, loosely defined operating system that will accommodate the many novel situations it constantly faces. Therefore, the new organization is less rigidly differentiated, both vertically and horizontally, and also it is not as rule bound as its predecessor.

Given that the new type of organization is highly responsive to its environment, it adapts its structure according to the tasks at hand rather than along traditional functional lines. Task groups of specialists are organized to accomplish specific projects, and are then disbanded to form again in different constellations as different projects require. Because organizational groups are constituted and reconstituted on a task basis, relationships formed tend to be more collaborative and consultative rather than purely hierarchical. The traditional model of vertical communication, that is, the flow of directives down and the transmission of information up the hierarchy, is supplemented by horizontal or lateral communication in an attempt to bring task expertise to various problems demanding immediate attention.

An organization's climate is in large part determined by the composition of its workforce. In that the nature of work has become more and more specialized, organizations increasingly are comprised of countless experts each of whom has highly technical knowledge in certain areas of competence. Because no one general manager can be conversant in all these specialties, authority to make certain decisions must rest with the expert rather than the generalist. As a result, the new organization is also relatively decentralized, and evaluation is based on performance rather than one's formal rank within the organizational hierarchy.

This composite model of organization is consistent with respect to all features of the four models from which it is derived. It is also remarkably similar to the "Japanese model" discussed in the preceding section. The fact that essentially one organizational form emerges from five very different avenues of research provides testimony that it is real and not just a theoretical abstraction. Furthermore, the diverse origins of this single organizational form is a strong argument that we are not dealing with a culturally specific type of organization. Despite the assertions of some of the original investigators, it would appear that noncultural explanations must be used to account for this emerging type of organization.

As a starting point, consider the world in which Weber wrote about organizations, and then contrast this with the contemporary world of work. What are the salient differences with respect to organizational structure and process? The evolution of organization theory discussed earlier in this chapter may in part be interpreted as the attempt by successive generations of scholars to deal with the growing indeterminacy in the world around them. Again in part, increasingly complex theories were devised in order to explain an increasingly complex world. In other words, Weber was not analyzing the same type of organizations that contemporary researchers and theorists are. The Weberian model of bureaucracy was more descriptive of organizations in Weber's time than it is today because organizations were operating in relatively stable environments with more or less uniform work forces. The mechanistic bureaucratic model is aptly suited to dealing with like cases in a constant environment.

In contrast, the organic flexible model is more appropriate to conditions in which change and our ability to deal with it constitute significant social problems (see Chapter 1). As open systems theorists have pointed out, organizations adapt to their environment. Since Weber's day, organizational environments have expanded enormously due to technological innovation; have become more densely populated in terms of both people and other organizations; have grown more complex and interdependent; and are in constant states of flux. As a result, organizations must be more flexible and less structured in order to survive.

Another factor underlying the emerging type of organization is the profound change that has occurred in the composition and variability of organizational employees. As indicated in Chapter 6, professional and technical workers comprise the fastest growing category of all occupational groups and, overall, the educational qualifications of all employees far surpass the educational levels achieved at the beginning of the century. When these facts are considered against the backdrop of social legislation that has limited the power of employers and guaranteed certain rights to individual workers, organizations again must adapt to these changed conditions.

Modern organizations are made up of a multitude of trained experts who do not respond well to the "principles of scientific management." Because they possess specialized skills that require judgment as well as performance, superior–subordinate interaction is characterized more by consultation than by command. Consequently, the professional organization is a viable substitute for the strictly bureaucratic model.

While the emergent type of organization just described is obviously not descriptive of all organizations in industrial society, it is likely to become a more characteristic form as more and more organizations confront uncertain environments and have to deal with highly educated, specialized work forces. It is important to note that the professional, organic, flexible, consultative organization is not one single type of organization. Rather it is more of an organizational stance, an orientation both to the outside world and to its own inner workings. Depending upon its environment and its climate, this type of organization is infinitely variable in action and reaction.

Given the research evidence to date, it would appear that this type of organization is a more prominent feature in the organizational landscape of Japan than it is in either Great Britain or the United States. This is not a "Japanese miracle." It could simply be that this form of organization that stresses group collaboration and task organization is more consonant with major aspects of Japanese culture, and therefore this represents a good organization—environment fit, or alternatively as Dore (1973) has suggested, given the earlier industrial development of both Great Britain and the United States, these countries may be somewhat reluctant to give up their traditional Weberian legacy. In any event, the evidence argues strongly that all organizations, East and West, are becoming more flexible and responsive in reaction to the environmental changes, including cultural changes, that are occurring around them. As we shall see in Chapter 8, organizations have become increasingly sophisticated and ingenious in their adaptability to this ever-changing environment.

SUMMARY

7.1   The principal variables of organization structure that sociologists study are complexity, formalization, and centralization. Complexity is comprised of three separate dimensions: (1) horizontal differentiation or division of labor; (2) vertical differentiation or the number of heirarchical levels; and (3) spatial dispersion or the extent to which organizational units are established in separate physical locations. Formalization refers to the degree to which organizational operations are codified in terms of operating procedures and rules and regulations. Centralization is a measure of how much and what type of authority is located throughout the organization.

7.2   Organizations are defined as collectivities that are purposively established on a more or less continuous basis to accomplish a defined set of goals. They are horizontally and vertically differentiated, the positions being connected by a communication system and bound by rules and regulations.

7.3 The modern study of organizations began in the early 1900s with Max Weber who set about designing an ideal type of organization (bureaucracy) that would be the most rational and effective means for achieving complex objectives. Weber and other rationalists believed that there was a "one best way" to organize.

7.4 Subsequent organizational theorists and researchers questioned the rationalist premise of one ideal type of organization. As a result of their research, which employed a variety of perspectives, they revealed how variable organizations in fact are. While they introduced much uncertainty into how various types of organizations actually function, they did put to rest the notion that there is a one best way which works under any circumstance (see Table 7.1).

7.5 Contemporary open systems theories focus on those factors both internal and external to organizations that contribute to task uncertainty and cause modifications in organizational structure. Among those contingencies most studied are organizational size, technology, and the (external and internal) organizational environment.

7.6 As organizations grow in size, they become more horizontally and vertically differentiated, have proportionately smaller administrative components, and are more formalized.

7.7 We may summarize the relationship between technology and organization structure in the following manner: (1) technical complexity varies directly with organizational complexity; (2) technical uncertainty is inversely related to formalization and centralization; and (3) technical interdependence results in more resources being allocated to coordination.

7.8 Recent research on the effects of environment on organizations has concentrated on what part culture plays in producing differences between organizations. Studies have found that organizations in Japan generally have taller hierarachies, are less horizontally differentiated, and are more decentralized with respect to decision making than organizations in either Great Britain or the United States. Japanese organizations are more involved with group collaboration and are more task oriented than Western organizations.

7.9 Various avenues of research on organizations have identified what may be described as emergent organizational forms. A composite model of these prototypes has the following features: task organization; loose, flexible structure (low emphasis on vertical and horizontal differentiation, and rules and regulations); lateral collaborative communication; decentralized decision making; and high responsiveness to the environment. It was noted how similar this composite model is to the so-called "Japanese model" of organization.

7.10 Explanations offered for the appearance of this new organizational form include the highly complex, volatile, and changing environment in which organizations now operate, and the upgrading of the organizational workforce such that now many organizations are comprised of highly educated, trained experts who are relied upon as much for their judgment as for their actual performance. While it was suggested that the "Japanese model" of organization may be culturally compatible, it is not culturally specific.

NOTES

1. This section of the chapter is based on Hedley, 1986b.
2. Note that the areas of responsibility of both the vice president for administration and the vice president for finance are not represented in this organization chart.

3. For example, in the United States, Aldrich and Marsden (1988, p. 365) report that "more than 50% of the civilian labor force is employed by only 2% of employing units, . . . the top 200 [manufacturing] firms control about 50% of all assets," and 30 out of 14,000 banks and 8 out of 1,800 insurance companies control 50% of all assets in their respective industries.

4. Lammers and Hickson acknowledge that there may also be a fourth socialist or communist type, but there are insufficient data to document it.

5. Lammers and Hickson did not explicitly address the issue of what type of organization is characteristic of Japan.

6. Remember that Hofstede was measuring *subordinates'* perceptions. Thus, according to unskilled and semiskilled workers, not only were they treated in an autocratic manner, but they also considered this to be correct and proper.

7. Only Israel, with a score of 13, did not fit into this group of nations.

Chapter

8

Transnational Corporations

We are now heading towards a world of rapidly increasing international production, dominated by a few hundred private enterprises from the developed countries, with investment, trade and technology all coming under their aegis. "It is beyond dispute," in the view of the U.S. Tariff Commission, "that the spread of multinational business ranks with the development of the steam engine, electric power, and the automobile as one of the major events of modern economic history.

Lall and Streeton, 1977, p. 15

A transnational corporation (TNC) is "any enterprise that undertakes foreign direct investment, owns or controls income-gathering assets in more than one country, produces goods or services outside its country of origin, or engages in international production" (Biersteker, 1978, p. xii).[1] A transnational corporation is a formal business organization that has spatially dispersed operations in at least two countries. In this chapter, we examine the TNC as an emergent organizational form, as one particular empirical manifestation of how organizations adapt to their environment. If one part of this environment is the material culture (i.e., "the applications of scientific discovery and the material products of technology") to which Ogburn (1956, p. 79) referred (see Chapter 2), and the other part is the non-material adaptive culture that includes the political, legal, and social institutions of all countries in the world, then the transnational corporation may be characterized as an organizational form that benefits from cultural lag. Through a series of techno-organizational innovations, the TNC has rendered former space-time constraints as relatively inconsequential, and is thus in the position of working to its advantage the many differences it faces in how business is conducted and regulated throughout the world. For example, differences in tax laws, exchange rates, trade conventions, and other cultural practices all may be applied to ultimate advantage as transnational corporations selectively establish various facets of their operations in those countries which offer the best conditions.

TNCs may be seen as a logical and rational extension on the part of formal organizations to adapt to their environment. Alternatively, employing the population-ecology model described in Chapter 7, TNCs may be seen as especially suited to the particular conditions that comprise the world today, and consequently are being "selected out" as a newly emergent organizational form. Whatever the theoretical rationale, the proliferation of TNCs does constitute "one of the major events of modern economic history" in that they have significantly altered the traditional balance of world power. By moving beyond the legal restraints and other customs imposed by their home countries, TNCs are thus freed from the "normal" conventions to which the rest of us (individuals and groups alike) are still bound. As we shall see, some TNCs have amassed resources and power on a scale never before even imagined.

We will begin first with a descriptive profile that places TNCs in historical and national context: demonstrates their increasing concentration in all aspects of world trade; indicates where in the world they are primarily engaged; and shows how they have established an integrated global economy. We then will consider some of the problems and dilemmas that this emergent organizational form poses for other already established organizational entities, most notably the nation state. Finally, the chapter will conclude with a comparative analysis of the various investment and organizational strategies employed by TNCs headquartered in Great Britain, the United States, and Japan. This permits us to evaluate once more the impact that culture plays in organizational design and development, and what factors are important in determining organizational structure.

DESCRIPTIVE PROFILE

Although TNCs were in existence prior to the twentieth century (e.g., the far-flung enterprises of the European colonial powers were the precursors to the modern TNC), it is only since the 1960s that they have become a major force on the world scene (World Bank, 1987, p. 45). As illustrated in Table 8.1, in 1900, foreign investment was concentrated within three European nations, the majority of this stock being held in British transnationals. Total foreign investment represented $23.8 billion. Through the twentieth century, American TNCs have replaced British enterprises in world dominance, and total investment has grown, particularly since 1960, such that by 1977 it stood at $311.5 billion.[2]

Table 8.1   FOREIGN INVESTMENT STOCK BY COUNTRY, 1900–1977

	Year				
	1900	1930	1960	1971	1977
United States	2.0%	35.3%	59.1%	52.0%	48.1%
United Kingdom	50.8	43.8	24.5	14.5	13.7
Germany (West)	20.2	2.6	1.1	4.4	6.2
France	21.8	8.4	4.1	5.8	4.8
Switzerland	neg	neg	neg	4.1	4.7
Japan	neg	neg	neg	2.7	4.5
Netherlands	4.6	5.5	3.1	2.2	3.5
Canada	neg	3.1	5.5	3.6	3.1
Sweden	neg	1.3	0.9	2.1	1.6
Others[1]	neg	neg	1.0	8.5	9.8
Total	100%	100%	100%	99.9%	100%
Total Billions of U.S. Dollars	$23.8	$41.6	$53.8	$159.2	$311.5

[1]The centrally planned Comecon countries have been excluded from this listing. In l978, it was estimated that the stock of foreign direct investment held by Comecon countries was valued at 0.72 billion dollars.

Source: Adapted from Buckley, 1985, p. 200.

Corporate Concentration

Although foreign investment by TNCs located in countries other than the nine developed countries listed in Table 8.1 has been increasing, it is still very much concentrated nationally, and within countries it is further concentrated by company. Table 8.2, which presents annual sales figures of the top 200 industrial corporations from 1960 to 1980, reveals the increasing percentage share of the world gross domestic product that these leading transnationals have assumed. For example, in 1960 the 200 sales leaders accounted for a remarkable 18 percent of world GDP; however, just 20 years later the top 200 were responsible for almost 30 percent of total world output!

From 1960 to 1980, the national composition of the top 200 has undergone considerable change. American transnationals have declined in proportional representation, both numerically and in terms of sales; however, they still constitute approximately half of this leading group of corporations. British firms, while dropping in numerical representation, nevertheless have remained relatively constant in their percentage contribution to total sales (just under 10%). On the other hand, as transnational corporate investment has mushroomed, TNCs from Japan, France, and the less-developed countries (including South Korea) have substantially increased their presence in the top 200, although it should be noted that TNCs from nondeveloped countries still make up less than five percent of total sales of this industrial elite. Further evidence of corporate concentration is gained by examining world commodity trade statistics. For example, the 15 largest TNCs in their respec-

Table 8.2   NATIONALITY AND SALES OF THE TOP 200 INDUSTRIAL CORPORATIONS, 1960, 1970, 1980

	Number			Sales (billions of U.S. dollars)			Percent of sales		
	1960	1970	1980	1960	1970	1980	1960	1970	1980
United States	127	123	91	144.6	313.5	1,080.4	72.7	66.0	50.1
Germany, Fed. Rep. of	20	15	21	13.4	34.6	209.0	6.8	7.3	9.7
United Kingdom	24	17	$16\frac{1}{2}$[a]	19.6	39.2	199.5	9.9	8.2	9.2
France	7	13	15	3.5	19.8	161.0	1.8	4.2	7.5
Japan	5	13	20	2.9	28.1	155.2	1.5	5.9	7.2
Netherlands	3	3	5	6.4	15.0	89.6	3.2	3.2	4.2
Italy	3	5	$4\frac{1}{2}$[a]	1.9	9.6	69.5	0.9	2.0	3.2
Canada	5	2	5	2.6	2.4	32.5	1.3	0.5	1.5
Switzerland	2	4	4	2.0	6.4	31.9	1.0	1.3	1.5
Belgium	1	1	2	0.5	1.3	14.5	0.2	0.3	0.7
Sweden	1	1	2	0.4	1.0	11.0	0.2	0.2	0.5
Rep. of Korea	—	—	2	—	—	10.0	—	—	0.5
Others	2	3	12	1.1	4.4	91.1	0.5	0.9	4.2
Total (excl. United States)	73	77	109	54.4	161.7	1,074.8	27.3	34.0	49.9
Total	200	200	200	199.0	475.2	2,155.2	100.0	100.0	100.0
World GDP[b]				1,126.2	2,489.0	7,548.0			
Top 200 as percent of GDP				17.7	19.1	28.6			

[a]Corporations owned by interests in two countries are counted as one-half.

[b]Excluding socialist countries.

Source: Clairmonte and Cavanagh, 1984, p. 52.

tive industries are responsible for marketing at least 75% of all world production in certain foods (e.g., bananas, corn, pineapples, wheat, cocoa, coffee, and tea), agricultural raw materials (cotton, forest products, jute, natural rubber, and tobacco), and ores and minerals (bauxite, copper, iron ore, tin, and crude petroleum). In most cases, just three to six transnationals control these markets (Clairmonte and Cavanagh, 1984, p. 58).

The increased concentration of transnational corporate power and control is accounted for in large part by mergers and acquisitions. Basically, these are of three types: horizontal, vertical, and conglomerate. Horizontal mergers, the earliest strategy employed, involve organizations taking over other organizations in the same industry, thus increasing their share of earnings in that industry. The world's major brewing companies have been very successful in applying this strategy. Vertical mergers, the next form of consolidation to be adopted extensively, involve organizations acquiring other organizations that either supply their raw materials (backward integration) or handle their output (forward integration). The giant food chains are an example of vertical consolidation as they have largely bought up their suppliers and are now termed agribusinesses. Conglomerate mergers, an increasingly popular form of organizational consolidation and concentration, are acquisitions by organizations of other organizations that may have little or no relevance to the acquiring organizations' operations. They simply represent sound business investments. Most major companies listed in *Fortune's* "world biggest industrial corporations" are now conglomerates, as well as being horizontally and vertically integrated (see *Fortune*, 1989b). These conglomerations in turn are almost impervious to the effects of the environment, which they are increasingly able to manipulate to their advantage.

> The worldwide drive to conglomeration, in combination with oligopoly, has been a source of prodigious economic power for TNCs. While different markets expand and contract, the conglomerate which straddles several oligopolies can ride with the tide, shifting its resources into whatever happens to be the most profitable business at a given moment. By means of cross-subsidization, the conglomerate operating in many fields deploys its earnings from various profit centers to subsidize losses in temporarily depressed lines of business. (Clairmonte and Cavanagh, 1984, p. 50)

Both the ascendancy of the TNC as an emergent organizational form and the growing concentration of transnational corporate power can be explained in large part by technological innovation. While transnational organizations (private and governmental) have been around for some time, until recent decades they have been unwieldy and extremely cumbersome to manage. Spatially separated organizational units were perforce decentralized, and it was impossible to produce current information in sufficient detail upon which to base important decisions crucial to the organization as a whole. However, with advances in information and communications technology, the deleterious effects of space and time have been virtually eliminated. It is now as possible to manage an organization with branches and subsidiaries located throughout the world, and have as much up-to-the-minute information, as it is to run an equally sized organization located at just one site.

Naisbitt (1982) discusses how various innovations in information and communications technology have collapsed what he calls " the information float," that is, the time it takes for a sender of information first of all to collect and digest the information at his or her disposal, and then to transmit it through some communication channel to a receiver. Whereas 100 or even 50 years ago the information float was a factor that could not be ignored, today it is or can be a nonentity.

> One way to think about the foreshortening of the information float is to think about when the world changed from trading goods and services to standardized currencies. Just imagine how that speeded up transactions. Now, with the use of electrons to send money around the world at the speed of light, we have almost completely collapsed the money information float. The shift from money to electronics is as basic as when we went from barter to money. . . .
>
> To the benefit of both sender and receiver, the new technology has opened up new information channels with wider range and greater sophistication. It has shor-

tened the distance between sender and receiver and increased the velocity of the information flow. But most importantly, it has collapsed the information float. (Naisbitt, 1982, p. 23)

The Nature of Foreign Direct Investment

With the technological elimination of the information float, the modern corporation has broadened its scope to take advantage of the multifaceted environment in all parts of the world. Table 8.3 presents a listing of the reasons why it may be profitable for an organization to become transnational. First, direct cost factors as they pertain to raw materials, labor, and transportation, as well as indirect cost considerations such as tariff barriers and trade restrictions, local tax structures, and various government inducements obviously loom large in the decision to establish operations overseas. Second, market factors may be equally important in deciding to become transnational. Direct and easy access to local markets unfettered by foreign trade quotas and other legislative restraints can give TNCs an edge over their nontransnational competitors. Finally, the decision to become transnational may hinge on factors related to organizational control. Control over raw materials (backward integration) and markets (forward integration) as well as achieving sufficient (regional and product) diversification to withstand temporary downturns of the economy are other reasons that prompt transnational relocation.[3]

Although much has been written about transnational corporate investment in less-developed countries, in fact the overwhelming majority of foreign direct investment occurs within the developed countries. Through the 1970s, only between one-fifth and one-quarter of all foreign direct investment was in the developing countries, with Latin America and south and east Asia being the major investment locales (Buckley, 1985, pp. 204–205). The United States was by far the most preferred country in which to invest foreign funds, having attracted between one-fifth and two-fifths of all foreign investments made in developed countries during the same time period. Great Britain was the second most favored foreign investment site (Buckley, 1985, pp. 204–205).[4] Consequently, as revealed in Table 8.1, not only are American and British companies responsible for making more than 60% of all foreign investments, but also these two countries between them serve as the locations in which close to half (44.8% in 1980) of all foreign capital is invested.

Analysis of TNC ventures indicates that the two major prerequisites to foreign investment are a relatively secure and stable national environment and a reasonably well-developed infrastructure. For these reasons, investments in developed economies make rational sense, and they also help to explain why TNCs invest as they do in the developing countries of the world. Foreign investment in the LDCs is very selective, being restricted by and large to the most advanced of the developing countries.

These advanced developing nations, also called newly industrializing countries (NICs), for the most part have reliable political regimes, little social unrest, and fairly extensive infrastructures that provide among other things constant energy supplies, developed transportation and communication networks (internal and external), and a literate labor force. Consequently, they serve as prime invest-

Table 8.3   REASONS FOR ORGANIZATIONS BECOMING TRANSNATIONAL

1. Cost-related Reasons
   a. To take advantage of differences in technological development, labor potential, productivity, and mentality, capital market; and local taxes
   b. Reduction of transport costs
   c. Avoidance of high tariff barriers
   d. To take advantage of local talents when establishing R & D overseas

2. Sales Volume Reasons
   a. Foreign middlemen unable to meet financial demands of expanded marketing
   b. For quicker adaptation to local market changes and better adaptation to local conditions
   c. Following important customers abroad
   d. Keeping up with competitors
   e. Persuasion and coercion of foreign host governments
   f. To obtain a better international division of labor, larger production runs, and better utilization of available economies of scale
   g. To avoid home country regulations, for example, fiscal and antitrust legislation

3. Reasons Related to Risk Factors
   a. To avoid exclusion from customers' and suppliers' markets promoting forward and backward integration
   b. To counter inflexibility and avoid country-specific recessions
   c. To reduce risks of social and political disruption by establishing operations in a number of host countries

Source: Taylor and Thrift, 1982, p. 21.

ment sites. These nations are also responsible for producing much of the industrial output that originates from the Third World. In 1980, just seven countries produced 70% of all LDC industrial exports, and TNCs through their subsidiaries or subcontracts, or by way of joint ventures, were instrumental in much of this production (Clairmonte and Cavanagh, 1984, p. 64).[5]

Transnational corporate activities in both developing and developed countries have changed dramatically since the 1960s as a result of both technological innovations and the rationalization of the production of goods and the distribution of services. Originally motivated in large part by the desire to achieve vertical integration and consolidation with regard to both raw materials and markets, TNCs invested heavily in agricultural holdings and mineral resources, primarily in the Third World, and expanded their distribution and sales outlets mainly in the First World. However, as a result of a variety of factors, including declining birth rates in the developed countries, saturation of existing markets, rising labor costs, political shifts toward independence among the LDCs, and enhanced technological capabilities in transportation, communication, and information processing, transnationals now have shifted their emphasis from primary commodities to manufacturing, distribution, marketing, finance, and the provision of other essential services throughout the world. For example, in 1960 direct investment in primary commodities by United States transnationals accounted for 43% of all investments, but by 1980 this had declined to 25%, with manufacturing, finance, and trade becoming the major sources for investment (Berberoglu, 1983).[6]

With regard to manufacturing, not only is it taking place on a transnational basis (see Figure 1.1), but also there is occurring a change in product mix. While the production of the automobile and related industries (e.g., petroleum refining, metals, industrial and farm equipment, and rubber products) still represents the mainstay of the manufacturing sector in the developed nations of the world, other industries are beginning to challenge these traditional leaders. As indicated in the discussion on the four technological revolutions in Chapter 1 (see Table 1.3), industries associated with the automobile were spawned by the third technological revolution in transportation and communication, which began at the turn of the century. However, the fourth "information" revolution, which came into being shortly after World War II, was also responsible for producing new industries, notably in computers, electronics, and aerospace. These and other industries have grown such that now many of the largest corporations in the world are manufacturing these products. For example, IBM is currently the fifth largest publicly held corporation in the world in terms of sales ($59.681 billion in 1988), and electronic giants such as General Electric, Hitachi, Siemens, and Matsushita all are in the top 20 (*Fortune*, 1989b, p. 282).

Table 8.4 divides the world's largest 100 industrial corporations into two rough industry types—traditional and modern. All those corporations manufacturing automobiles (as well as the related industries previously mentioned), forest products, building materials, food, beverages, tobacco, soaps and cosmetics are classified as "traditional" in that these products (although not in their present form) date back to at least the beginning of the century. "Modern" industries include computers, electronics, aerospace, chemicals, and scientific and photographic equipment. With the exception of some chemicals and basic electric goods, all products manufactured by the corporations in these "modern" industries did not exist prior to World War II. Although the classification is crude, it does highlight an important distinction. Currently, almost two-thirds of the top 100 corporations, in terms of both numbers and sales, are manufacturing "traditional" products while one-third are producing so-called "modern" goods.

Table 8.4 also lists these corporations by national origin so that it is possible to discern the traditional–modern ratio by country. While obviously a nation cannot produce " modern" goods to the total exclusion of "traditional" products (including food), nevertheless, to the extent that we are experiencing a new technological revolution and these industries represent the wave of the future, it becomes important in terms of national policy to evaluate the traditional–modern mix. While only 100 corporations are listed in this table, they are nonetheless indicative of broad trends because of their dominant status.

Table 8.4 THE WORLD'S LARGEST 100 INDUSTRIAL CORPORATIONS BY NATIONALITY AND TYPE OF INDUSTRY, 1988

Country	Type of industry		Total
	Traditional[1]	Modern[2]	
United States	23	16	39
Japan	8	7	15
West Germany	8	4	12
France	6	3	9
United Kingdom	4	2	6
Italy	3	1	4
Switzerland	2	1	3
Netherlands	1	1	2
South Korea	0	2	2
Sweden	1	1	2
Spain	1	0	1
Brazil	1	0	1
Mexico	1	0	1
Kuwait	1	0	1
Belgium	1	0	1
India	1	0	1
Total corporations	62	38	100
Total sales ($ millions)	$1,529,817.8	778,993.0	2,308,810.8
Percent of sales	66.3%	33.7%	100%

[1]Traditional industries include motor vehicles, petroleum refining, metals, industrial and farm equipment, rubber products, forest products, building materials, food, beverages, tobacco, soaps and cosmetics.

[2]Modern industries include computers, electronics, chemicals, aerospace, scientific and photographic equipment.

Source: Adapted from *Fortune*, 1989b, pp. 282–283.

For example, with regard to British, American, and Japanese corporations, note that Great Britain has the most traditional ratio, the United States is second, and Japan exhibits the most modern industry mix. While these ratios by themselves are not compelling, they do fit with other evidence presented so far. Because Great Britain and the United States industrialized considerably before Japan, it is reasonable that many of their leading corporations are in "traditional" industries. However, to the extent that the industry mix is indeed changing, Japan is most advantageously placed with respect to manufacturing in the future.

The Integrated Global Economy

Clairmonte and Cavanagh (1984) explain how the entire manufacturing process, from the acquiring of raw materials to the marketing of finished manufactured goods, has become so rationalized and so specialized that even though TNCs do not now exercise much direct control through ownership of primary commodity outlets, nevertheless they have retained effective control of this end of the production chain. Through a variety of innovative practices, which include licensing and subcontracting agreements, control over marketing and distribution networks, and the setting up of free trade zones within countries, TNCs not only maintain control but also have carved out a more profitable niche for themselves into the bargain. In establishing these revised terms of manufacture and trade, TNCs have entered a new phase that some have named the "global economy" (see Taylor and Thrift, 1982; Stein and Das, 1988).

A significant feature of the integrated global economy is the internationalization of finance and the growing role of transnational banks (TNBs). Increasingly, they have become active participants in transnational mergers and takeovers. By encouraging their already huge organizational clients to acquire additional corporations, they have made vast profits through the immense loans extended, as well as ending up with even larger clients to service financially. In this way TNBs have played a direct part in the growing concentration and power of TNCs (see Clairmonte and Cavanagh, 1984).

Table 8.5 lists the 50 largest banks in terms of assets and national origin. "Their total assets are $8.2 trillion—more than the combined gross national products of the U.S., Britain, Brazil, France, and West Germany. Put another way, that's enough to buy a Porsche 944 for every man, women and child in America" (*Fortune*, 1989a, p. 286). Almost half these banks are Japanese, including the nine largest. Together they account for nearly 60 percent of the assets listed. Consequently, although Japan has not (yet) achieved the industrial preeminence of the United States (see Tables 8.2 and 8.4), in the area of finance it has clearly eclipsed the older and more established financial institutions. Japanese banks have been and continue to be active partners in Japan's meteoric rise to the status of world superpower.

In summary, transnational corporations and banks represent an increasingly important segment of the world economy. Since the 1960s, their share of the world gross domestic product has grown to the point where just a handful of these corporate giants from the developed nations virtually control the bulk of world trade in primary commodities, manufacturing and marketing, and the provision of services including the important area of financial services. The result is that these emergent organizations have gained power that in many respects equals or even surpasses the power of the nation state.

TNC AND NATION STATE

The quotation that opens this chapter equates multinational business with the invention of the steam engine, electric power, and the automobile in terms of its impact on contemporary life. While the latter three developments represent technological innovations, transnational corporations are an emergent organiza-

Table 8.5   NATIONALITY AND ASSETS OF THE WORLD'S 50 BIGGEST COMMERCIAL BANKS, 1988

Country	Number of banks	Assets ($ millions)	Percent of total assets
Japan	23	4,779,897.1	58.4
France	5	863,391.4	10.5
West Germany	5	588,800.2	7.2
United Kingdom	4	562,172.3	6.9
United States	4	483,691.1	5.9
Switzerland	2	213,509.8	2.6
Italy	2	172,616.8	2.1
Netherlands	2	169,036.9	2.1
China	1	149,997.5	1.8
Hong Kong	1	113,165.7	1.4
Canada	1	90,230.7	1.1
Total	50	8,186,509.5	100.0

Source: Adapted from *Fortune*, 1989a, p. 286.

tional form—an adaptive response by capitalist enterprise to the complex changes in the environment, including technological changes, that have taken place through the last half of the twentieth century. Although the impact of the steam engine, electric power, and the automobile on society can be traced more directly in cause–effect sequences than can the impact of the transnational corporation, nevertheless TNCs are no less imposing in their repercussions. In fact, it has even been asserted that the transnational corporation as an emergent organizational form represents a distinct threat to the nation state, and consequently to the very basis upon which the peoples of the world are presently organized (see, for example, Evans, 1981, p. 199).

It is certainly clear that the emergence of the TNC into the global economy has resulted in a redistribution of the balance of world power. By almost any indicator—gross sales, assets, numbers employed, control over leading-edge technology, ability to influence the world economy—the TNCs represent a viable challenge to many nation states, particularly in the Third World. For example, as indicated in Chapter 1 (see Table 1.1), annual sales of the largest TNCs far surpass the gross domestic products of many (both more and less developed) countries. Comparisons such as this, plus the fact that TNCs have been seen to interfere in the previously sacrosanct affairs of the nation state, have resulted in a voluminous literature and debate dealing with the costs and benefits of TNCs in world development.[7] Because most of the concern has been expressed over the relatively less powerful Third World nations, we will attempt to detail and make sense of the argument as to whether TNCs are an aid or a hindrance to development in the LDCs.

Jacques Ellul (1981) reminds us that our political and legal institutions, that is, those institutions that legislate, govern, and administer the actions of modern corporations (transnational and otherwise), were created between the seventeenth and eighteenth centuries and consequently "are adapted to situations that have nothing to do with what we now know. . . . No political action in the normal, strict sense of the term is adequate today" (1981, p. 71). As indicated earlier, William Ogburn (1956) would have identified the rational, technologically enhanced transnational corporation as part of the cumulative material culture which changes at a faster rate than does the noncumulative, nonmaterial, adaptive culture that consists of values, norm, and social institutions, including political and legal institutions. Thus, there occurs maladjustment and strain within society owing to the inability of these institutions to keep pace with changed material circumstances.

Examples of currently unmanageable or difficult techno-organizational problems either initiated or exacerbated by TNCs range across many fronts. One particularly sensitive area is the control of capital flow among subsidiaries of the same TNC located in different countries. Because of the collapse of the money information float, detection and regulation of this flow is often impossible. Therefore, problems can arise in maintaining exchange rate stability and in having TNCs declare profits (and thus pay taxes) in the countries in which they were actually earned. Closely related problems occur in the transfer of goods and services within internal corporate networks. Prices can be artifically adjusted in some parts (i.e., countries) of the organization in order to benefit the corporation overall.

The problems just cited illustrate how difficult it is for nation states to exercise sovereignty over TNCs located within their borders. However, other problems arise when TNCs operate in the nonnationally controlled interstices of the world (i.e., the oceans, seabed, airwaves, sky, and space). Because there are no universally acknowledged regulatory bodies capable of enforcement, TNCs are virtually free to set their own agenda. Sometimes the consequences for the world community are difficult to bear (e.g., pollution, resource depletion, and toxic waste disposal).

Transnational corporations, aided by information and communications technology, conduct their business in an innovative and novel fashion. In large part, they can avoid or circumvent nationally imposed laws and regulations. Through various technological and organizational strategies, they have been able to establish themselves in a twilight zone between national boundaries, and thus beyond the law. As Gill and Law (1988, pp. 364–365) conclude, there is a "growing lack of congruence between the 'world economy,' with its tendencies to promote ever-greater levels of economic integration, and an 'international political system' composed of many rival states."

Never before have we confronted the situation in which foreign organizations have been granted license almost as a matter of course to operate freely within the legally defined boundaries of a sovereign state.[8] This, together with the fact that transnational corporations and nation states are different organizational forms, established for different purposes, administered by different principles, and loyal to different constituencies, means that structural problems are virtually bound to arise. And to the extent that the executive home offices of TNCs are located in powerful nation states while subsidiary branches are situated in less developed countries, there develops a parallelism the symbolism of which cannot be ignored.

While the present statements are descriptive of global enterprises operating within and between the confines of individual nation states, it is also true that transnational corporate investment is a matter of choice, both for the TNC and for the nation state in which the TNC chooses to invest. Table 8.3 lists the reasons why corporations might want to become transnational. Let us now concentrate on why nation states, particularly less-developed nation states, opt to have foreign TNCs invest in their countries.

Table 8.6 presents the results of a cross-national questionnaire survey of 84 leaders and policy makers from 35 less-developed countries (Jain and Puri, 1984). These policy makers were asked to rate the importance of 26 possible contributions that TNCs might make to developing countries. Table 8.6 rank orders the twelve factors that were seen to be most important. A scanning of this list reveals that not only is the infusion of foreign capital the most important single attraction, but also it comprises a major component in many of the other desirable features that were cited. Particularly in these times, given the huge debt load of many developing countries plus recent import restrictions imposed by the developed countries (see World Bank, 1987), most Third World nations are unable to finance adequately their own industrial development.

A second set of factors considered important by LDCs concerns the employment and training of local workers, particularly managers, in new industrial techniques and processes. The majority of policy makers in the countries surveyed were of the opinion that foreign nationals should be restricted to fewer than 25 percent of the managerial positions in the host country, and that at least half the technical positions in a foreign subsidiary should be reserved for indigenous personnel (Jain and Puri, 1984, pp. 126–127). Directly related to these employment and training attractions was the possibility of technology transfer, both materially in the form of plant and equipment, and symbolically in terms of vocational and technical training.

Problems and Dilemmas

As Tables 8.3 and 8.6 indicate, there are potential benefits that can accrue from foreign direct investment for both TNCs and host countries. However, at times problems and conflicts do arise in that the goals of transnational capitalist enterprise and indigenous national government are for the most part vastly different. This constitutes the foundation of the debate as to whether TNCs are an aid or a hindrance to national development in the Third World. According to Biersteker (1978), the major points of contention in this debate are the degree to which TNCs (1) are responsible for a net outflow of capital from the LDCs; (2) displace indigenous production; (3) engage in technology transfer; (4) introduce "inappropriate" (capital-intensive, labor-displacing) technologies; (5) encourage "inappropriate" (elite-oriented) patterns of consumption; (6) produce divisiveness

Table 8.6   ATTRACTIONS OF FOREIGN DIRECT INVESTMENT ACCORDING TO POLICY MAKERS IN LESS DEVELOPED COUNTRIES

	Importance of attraction		
	Very important	Important	Not important
1. Bring in foreign capital	71%	26%	3%
2. Make more capital-intensive investments than local investors	68	32	0
3. Create favorable climate for other foreign direct investment	58	40	2
4. Create favorable climate for loans from international organizations	58	37	5
5. Materially add to industrial infrastructure	55	40	5
6. Introduce new managerial techniques to national managers	50	45	5
7. Set example for national corporations to become more efficient and productive	48	52	0
8. Help increase exports	48	50	2
9. More efficient use of capital than local investors	48	47	5
10. Help develop natural resources	48	37	15
11. Increase labor productivity compared to domestic companies	45	55	0
12. Train local people in new industrial processes	45	48	7

Source: Adapted from Jain and Puri, 1984, pp. 122–123.

within the local social structure owing to competing loyalties to TNC and nation state; and (7) exacerbate the existing unequal distribution of income.

Critical theorists, employing dependency, colonialist, nationalist, and/or Marxist perspectives, basically argue that transnational corporate investment works to the detriment of LDCs on each of the above seven points. "Although not always explicitly stated, critical writers assume that there are feasible alternatives to the multinational corporation, in the form of state corporations, an indigenous private sector, or some combination of both" (Biersteker, 1978, p. 2). On the other hand, conventional and neoconventional theorists assert that foreign direct investment introduces essential but missing ingredients of Third World development in the form of capital, technology, managerial skills, and organizational expertise. The net effect of TNCs on host countries is positive.

Whereas critical and conventional theorists agree on most of the strategies that TNCs use and on many of the first-order consequences of these strategies (see Biersteker, 1978: Chapter 3), they violently disagree in their interpretations of what the repercussions and ramifications of foreign direct investment will mean for the development chances of Third World countries. A large part of the discrepancy in interpretation arises from the alternatives that critical and conventional writers pose to foreign investment (see Biersteker, 1978). Put simply, for critical theorists, the alternative to transnational enterprise is local indigenous enterprise and self-sustaining development; for conventional theorists, the most likely alternative to foreign investment is stagnation and ever-increasing disparity between the developed and the underdeveloped nations. Both arguments are stated in the extreme.

Aside from the fact that both sides of the debate often focus on different aspects and effects of foreign investment, and thereby end up talking past each other, it is virtually impossible to set up a comparative research design that would permit an adequate test of these competing alternative propositions. This would entail a series of matched comparisons of specific outcomes in pairs of less-developed countries that are comparable in every important respect except that half of these countries have permitted foreign investment while the other half have not. Given that these countries represent different cultural traditions, exhibit a variety of political and social structures, and have different natural and human resources, it is unlikely that many matched comparisons would be possible. Furthermore, the process of foreign investment itself is not uniform. TNCs also have different national origins and varying organizational philosophies, structures, and resources. In addition, the nature of foreign investment is affected by its scope, the type of industry, and a multitude of other situational factors.[9] Therefore, although illustrative examples can be used to defend either the critical or conventional alternatives, it is impossible at this stage to offer valid generalizations or make definitive statements on such a complex issue as the effects of transnational corporate investment on Third World development. However, it is safe to say that any transnational investment will produce both costs *and* benefits for the host country involved.

Both TNCs and nation states face a succession of dilemmas as they negotiate individual investment opportunities that will work to their advantage and at the same time be sufficiently attractive to the other side. While recent evidence suggests that TNCs have become more attuned to the specific needs and expectations of various Third World countries, and that LDCs are now more sophisticated in the bargaining process (see Frank, 1980; Gill and Law, 1988, pp. 211–217), nevertheless the bargain finally achieved is often reached through a maze of seemingly impossible Catch-22 situations. Consider the following:

> Third World governments face a series of frustrating dilemmas as they seek to shape a national policy toward foreign direct investment. If multinationals repatriate the bulk of their profit, they are depriving the nation of the newly created wealth; if, on the other hand, the firms reinvest the bulk of their profits locally, they are further increasing their ownership and control of the economy of the host country. If multinationals pay local workers the standard wage, they are exploiting cheap labor and garnering excess profits; if, on the other hand, they pay more than the prevailing wage, they are siphoning off the best of the labor supply and rendering local firms noncompetitive. If multinationals bring in the latest and best machinery and equipment, they are introducing inappropriate technology and diminishing job opportunities in the host country; if, on the other hand, earlier and simpler technologies are introduced, they are shortchanging the local economy. Resolving

these dilemmas has entailed policy shifts and adaptations on the part of developing countries in response to their changing perceptions of how to maximize their gains from the foreign investment process (Frank, 1980, p. 29).

Although less than one-quarter of all transnational corporate investment occurs in the Third World, nevertheless it may be seen as crucial in terms of world development. Whether one adopts a critical or a conventional perspective, it is certain that the introduction of immensely powerful transnational organizations into less-developed countries with their already established systems of social stratification do cause great social upheavals. Furthermore, the impact of these corporate giants is not only great in its initial magnitude, it is also prolonged in terms of its many effects. As in the case of the steam engine, electric power, and the automobile, the world, particularly the Third World, will not be the same as a result of the transnational corporation.

BRITISH, AMERICAN, AND JAPANESE TRANSNATIONALS

As indicated above, the transnational corporation is not a monolithic entity; it is remarkably variable in terms of purpose, structure, and activity as it interacts with an equally variable environment. In this section, we examine the extent to which transnational corporate variation is a function of national origins as we look at some of the characteristics and features of British, American, and Japanese TNCs.

One important source of variation arises out of the political and economic histories of Great Britain, the United States, and Japan, as well as their respective geographic catchment areas. For example, British transnationals have relied heavily upon the trading networks that were established in former colonial times; in fact some of these corporations date back to the previous century. Just over half of all British overseas direct investment is in either the developed (37%) or developing (15%) Commonwealth countries, that is, previous colonies. In addition, a further one-fifth is in the United States, also a former colony but, more important, the current most attractive transnational investment site. The final major share of British investment capital (24%) is located in the countries that form the European Free Trade Association (see La Palombara and Blank, 1984, p. 11). Not only do British TNCs invest preponderantly in countries with previous colonial ties but also as one study has shown Britain along with other postimperial countries has a higher propensity to invest abroad than do countries without a history of colonial enterprise (see Buckley, 1985).

American foreign direct investment follows a quite different pattern. While the largest portion of its transnational corporate activity occurs in the Western European nations, the single most important investment locale, accounting for one-quarter of all American foreign investment, is in Canada immediately to the north (Crow and Thomas, 1983, pp. 60–61). This together with the fact that almost half of all American investment in the Third World occurs in Latin America (principally in Brazil and Mexico) reveals a New World orientation to American business investment. Within the past two decades, United States enterprise has also increased in southeast and east Asian countries, including Japan, such that now it is developing a Pacific rim focus along with its concentration in North and South America (see Berberoglu, 1983; Abegglen and Stalk, 1985, pp. 242–268).

Japanese transnational business represents yet another configuration. In contrast to Great Britain and the United States, Japan is a relatively late starter in direct foreign investment, having relied instead on exports to achieve a favorable trade balance. However, with the increase in the value of the yen, together with rising labor costs and a growing protectionist stance in the developed nations with whom Japan trades, it has also become highly visible as a major source of transnational corporate investment. The main portion of Japanese foreign investment is divided equally between Asia (27%) and the United States (26%). Eight countries within Asia serve both as sources of raw materials as well as labor-intensive manufacturing,[10] while the United States represents a prime investment site for Japanese commerce and finance and, recently, capital-intensive manufacturing. In addition, Japan has foreign direct investments in Central and South America (17%), Western Europe (12%),[11] and Oceania, primarily Australia (6%) (See Abegglen and Stalk, 1985, pp. 242–268.)

Consequently, although there is a broad general pattern of transnational investment, there are also differences when these investments are analyzed according to national origin. Even though British, American, and Japanese TNCs prefer to invest primarily in the developed market economies, nevertheless each country represents a unique investment configuration largely based on both its history and geographical prominence. The foreign investment portfolio of Japan is particularly revealing in this respect. Up until the early 1970s, it both actively discouraged foreign investment within its boundaries (see Safarian, 1983, pp. 24–29) at the same time that it shunned outward investment by its own corporations. However, now, not only is it attracting moderate internal investment, but also, because of the reasons stated, it has become a major player in the transnational corporate scene. By the turn of the century, it is estimated that it will be second only to the United States in the magnitude of its foreign investment. (Abegglen and Stark, 1985, p. 247).

Third World Investment

We now turn to a study of *Foreign Enterprise in Developing Countries* (Frank, 1980) in which senior executives of 90 TNCs in Britain, the United States, and Japan as well as five other developed nations were the subject of in-depth interviews on "private foreign direct investment and the role of multinational corporations in the developing countries" (Frank, 1980, p. 2). In addition to the interviews, factual information was gathered on 402 subsidiaries of these TNCs, all of which were situated in Third World countries located throughout the world.[12] Effort was made to stratify the sample according to industry type (i.e., primary, secondary, and tertiary), company size, geographic location of subsidiaries, and the developmental stage of host countries. Thus, firms representative of transnational British,

American, and Japanese enterprise are included in this research (see Frank, 1980, pp. 163–165).

Table 8.7 provides some of the data collected on the affiliates of these TNCs. While it is possible to make direct comparisons between American and Japanese affiliates, unfortunately, due to sample size, the British subsidiaries are grouped together with those of other developed countries.[13] Consequently, specific reference to British transnationals must be gleaned entirely from the interview material. However, this data set does provide an excellent opportunity to determine both the similarities and differences in British, American, and Japanese TNCs in their dealings with Third World countries.

Concerning the number of years that transnationals affiliates have been established, Table 8.7 confirms the earlier observation about Japanese corporations being relatively late starters in foreign direct investment. On average, the 84 Japanese affiliates have been in operation for less than half the time of affiliates of other countries. According to Frank (1980, pp. 182, 184), the majority of Japanese subsidiaries were established or acquired in 1969–1970, fully 10 years later than the American branches, which in turn were established slightly after those from the other countries surveyed. In other words, except for the Japanese, foreign investment on a large scale is a phenomenon that began in the late 1950s and early 1960s.

Investment Decisions   The ownership pattern of these affiliates also varies significantly by national origin. American transnationals have traditionally opted for wholly owned subsidiaries, while Japanese TNCs have preferred joint ventures and minority ownership. European transnationals fall in between these two extremes (Frank, 1980, p. 21). Although American companies are now recognizing the advantages of partial ownership, thus allowing host governments some say in their own determination, Japanese corporations are increasingly adopting the minority ownership option. Given that much of Japan's Third World investment is in east and southeast Asia, it is sensitive to its postwar image as a superpower, and therefore appears to have taken a relatively low profile in these formerly occupied areas (Frank, 1980, p. 22). This may also explain, at least in part, why the size of Japanese affiliates is considerably smaller than those of either the United States or Europe (see "Number of employees" in Table 8.7).

Japanese TNCs also have adopted the policy that they will not establish operations in less-developed countries that entail direct competition with local firms unless the market served is of sufficient size for two or more manufacturers. Because Japanese affiliates tend to produce more for their home market and for export in general (see below), they thereby avoid setting up in direct competition. British TNCs also refer to explicit corporate policy that discourages competition with indigenous firms. "The British tend to invest only in sizable markets that are not already being served by efficient local producers" (Frank, 1980, p. 45). While American TNCs have no formal policy with regard to local competition, nevertheless they are sensitive to this issue and attempt to avoid it.

Part of the decision on whether or not to invest in a particular LDC rests on financing. Most transnationals surveyed have attempted to raise capital from local sources within the host country. "Indeed, it would appear that only about one-

Table 8.7   MEAN CHARACTERISTICS OF TNC AFFILIATES LOCATED IN DEVELOPING
COUNTRIES BY NATIONAL ORIGIN OF TNC

Selected characteristics	Affiliates of TNCs headquartered in:		
	United States	Japan	Other developed countries[1]
Age of affiliate (number of years since first established)	18.1 yrs	8.5 yrs*[3]	20.2 yrs
Ownership (% equity owned by parent)	85.8%	50.5%*	73.0%*
Number of employees	876	525	1114
Employment of local nationals (%)			
Production workers	97.9%	95.8%	97.5%
Foremen	98.2	86.2*	94.0
Engineering	97.1	72.1*	87.8*
Management	83.9	59.5*	50.2*
Purchases of raw materials and supplies (%)			
Within host country	45.9%	37.6%	34.7%
Intra-firm	35.6	51.9*	46.2*
Other foreign supplier	18.5	10.5	19.1
Sale of manufactured goods (%)			
Within host country	81.8%	74.7%	90.1%
To home market	3.4	12.3	0.5
Other export	14.8	13.0	9.4
(Total numbers of affiliates[2])	(≥77)	(≥50)	(≥66)

[1]Other countries represented include Britain, Australia, Sweden, France, Belgium, and Italy.

[2]Reports the lowest number of affiliates upon which statistics were computed. The number of cases varied according to the availability of data.

[3]Using the American affiliate means as the base, Frank computed the statistical significance of the differences between United States and Japanese means and between United States and other developed countries' means. The significance level reported is at the .01 level (see Frank, 1980, p. 186).

Source: Adapted from Frank, 1980, pp. 182—186.

quarter of foreign investment in manufacturing is financed directly by parent companies" (Frank, 1980, pp. 60–61). However, here again there is variation by national origin. By virtue of their minority or equal shareholder status, Japanese TNCs invariably raise part of their equity capital through local partners. The British also attempt to raise capital locally, but more through borrowing than through the extension of shares. By committing indigenous agencies financially, the intent of both the Japanese and the British TNCs is "to create a sense of identification with the host country" and "to avoid foreign exchange risks" (Frank, 1980, p. 62). Also, there is less financial risk to the parent companies in the case of nationalization. On the other hand, American TNCs are least likely to borrow money in local markets, preferring instead to use sources outside the country. While senior executives from the United States stated that capital was often not available to them locally, their reluctance to borrow within the host country does coincide with their desire to retain complete affiliate ownership.

Another aspect related to transnational investment decisions is the type of policy adopted by home governments toward foreign investment. For example, the Japanese government actively encourages foreign direct investment through low-interest loans, equity financing, and tax deferrals, while the official policy of both the British and American governments is one of neutrality, although TNCs headquartered in these countries are permitted to defer taxes on subsidiary earnings until profits are repatriated (Frank, 1980, pp. 157–158). British and American corporate executives were of the opinion that neutrality is the most appropriate policy of their home countries even though they also recognized that this puts them at considerable disadvantage in relation to their Japanese (and German) competitors.

American executives suggested further that their government has at times placed them in a most unfavorable position vis-à-vis their corporate competitors. Because of the American government's sometimes overzealous efforts to extend its jurisdiction to subsidiaries operating in foreign countries, American TNCs have been constrained by two, occasionally conflicting, sets of laws and policies. "For example, an American company observed that it is only reasonable for the Mexican government, in line with its general policy of stimulating exports, to encourage a U.S.-owned subsidiary to trade with Cuba, even though such trade is prohibited under the U.S. Trading with the Enemy Act" (Frank, 1980, p. 124). None of the non-American TNCs reported problems of this type, except for issues related to apartheid in South Africa.

Of particular concern to the development prospects of LDCs is the type and amount of technology transfer that occurs as a result of transnational investment. Third World countries seek modern technological processes and equipment that can at the same time be adapted to their particular requirements. Among the most important of these requirements is the enhancement of employment prospects of the local labor force. TNCs, while they have become increasingly aware of these concerns, nevertheless do have a different agenda. "Most transnationals stated that their choice of process is based mainly on technical considerations, the anticipated scale of output, the availability of skilled labor, and the need to ensure high standards of quality" (Frank, 1980, p. 77). For these reasons, TNCs, particularly the Japanese, set up capital-intensive plant and processes which are essentially similar to their home operations. "The British, for example, normally install the most modern plant possible because they are not experienced in the efficient use of labor-intensive plants" (Frank, 1980, p. 77). Consequently, while TNCs do engage in significant technology transfer, at times it is of only limited advantage to less developed host countries.

Managing the Enterprise Concerning the actual management of transnational corporate subsidiaries in developing countries, Table 8.7 reveals that here also there are differences by national origin. For example, there is considerable variation in the employment of local nationals. While the data show an inverse relation between hierarchical level and the employment of indigenous personnel for all TNCs, this relationship is much stronger for non-American transnationals than it is for American TNCs. Although local personnel constitute the majority of each organizational rank, their proportions at the managerial level are severely diminished in Japanese and other TNCs when compared to American employment practices. Except for production workers, Japanese TNCs employ significantly fewer local nationals than do American firms, a practice that extends as well to their investments in developed countries (see Rapaport, 1989, pp. 52,56).

There is also variation by national origin in the amount and type of autonomy granted to managers of affiliates by their home offices. While Frank (1980, p. 53) notes that autonomy varies "primarily on the product and technology involved and on the degree of parent ownership of subsidiaries," he does discern national differences. Generally, Japanese firms have the most formalized guidelines stating the issues that should be referred to the head office. "These include such decisions as investing large amounts of capital, hiring top managers, and making changes in technology or product mixes" (Frank, 1980, p. 54). Other subsidiaries, particularly British, appear to exercise more local autonomy. However, regardless of nationality, all firms are granted discretion in direct proportion to the percentage of shares owned locally.

Finally, Table 8.7 presents data on national differences in the acquisition of raw materials and the sale of finished manufactured goods. American firms are considerably more likely to purchase their supplies locally than the Japanese or other TNCs. Whereas American transnationals buy almost half of all their raw materials in local markets, Japanese TNCs acquire most of their input from the parent firm or other affiliates within the transnational network.

With regard to purchases by foreign subsidiaries, LDCs have two major concerns: (1) that affiliates rely on local sources as much as possible; and (2) that purchases be acquired at "fair market value." The latter point raises the issue of transfer pricing, which has been hotly debated within the research literature. Because a considerable amount of transnational trade, including costs of research and development, technology transfer, royalties, patents, trademarks, and licensing fees occurs within affiliates of the same firm, there arises the possibility that the prices charged in internal trading are artificially set and therefore do not reflect what would be charged in the open market.

In theory, the foreign subsidiaries are subject to control by the parent company. Hence, theoretically, the multinational has the power to fix the level of prices applying to international trade between subsidiaries, and to deviate artificially from "normal" or "true" prices, if, against the interests of individual subsidiaries, the overall profits of the multinationals can be increased, or, more accurately, some "costs," such as overall corporate tax liabilities, reduced. Internal trade, theoretically, allows a degree of freedom, which is not available in uncontrolled trade between unaffiliated companies. Thus internal prices—an essentially neutral concept—can be manipulated and converted into transfer prices which, in our terminology, carries the connotation of such manipulative powers or, more precisely, of the *a priori* possibility of such manipulations. The term is then no longer a neutral one. It suggests that internal prices may be fixed at the discretion of the multinationals to the detriment of other economic agents, more particularly of governments. (Plasschaert, 1979, p. 4)

While there are documented cases of exorbitant transfer pricing contained in the literature (see, for example, Vaitsos, 1974), there are no clear indications of how extensive this practice is nor what constitutes "normal" behavior. Obviously, the greater the amount of internal trading there is, the greater is the opportunity to fix prices. However, to date we have no evidence of the relationship between available opportunity and actual behavior; and given the unethical and in some cases illegal nature of the practice under consideration, it is unlikely that we will ever be able to arrive at firm generalizations.

In the transnationals that Frank studied, although many executives acknowledged that transfer pricing does indeed take place and is "probably widespread" though not extreme, at the same time as might be expected most stated that their firms did not use these tactics (Frank, 1980, pp. 96–101). British, American, and Japanese managers all stated that their home governments have tough tax legislation in effect that provides both a monitoring and a regulatory function, and therefore handles any irregularities that may arise. Parenthetically, they added that this legislation is designed to serve the interests of home governments, and consequently may not work to the simultaneous advantage of host governments. One executive in considering what is "an optimal amount of profit" revealed that here also TNCs are involved in a Catch-22 situation. "If the subsidiary's profits are too high, it is accused of exploitation; if its profits are too low, it is charged with 'ripping off' the host country's revenues through transfer pricing" (Frank, 1980; p. 100). As long as there is internal trading within firms, particularly at the levels revealed in Table 8.7, there will be questions raised as to whether the internal prices charged are "fair" or "manipulative."

With regard to the sale of manufactured goods, there are fewer national differences between TNCs than occurs in the purchase of raw materials and supplies. However, as Table 8.7 indicates, Japanese affiliates are more export-oriented, particularly as this involves servicing home markets. Other transnationals (especially non-American) appear to be established almost exclusively to take advantage of indigenous markets. Overall, these data suggest that the rationale for transnational affiliates is that they form a global network of individual profit centers, each operating within its own local protected market.

Summarizing the Differences   Of the strategies employed with respect to investment in and management of affiliates located in Third World countries, the greatest differences generally occur between American and Japanese TNCs. British transnationals more closely resemble American corporations in their tactics than they do the Japanese who, similar to the findings presented in Chapter 7, have a distinct, although not culturally unique, approach.

One way of summarizing the differences in national corporate practices is to examine how each of the strategies noted earlier contributes to organizational control or the ability of transnational organizations to deal effectively with their environment in the achievement of their goals. Another way involves assessing how well TNCs from different countries accommodate themselves to the aims and purposes of the less-developed countries in which they invest. As can be imagined, because the objectives of TNCs and LDCs are vastly different, these two approaches will in the majority of circumstances yield opposite conclusions. However, they are not logically opposite, and therefore the possibility does exist for TNCs both to attend to the needs of LDCs *and* to attain their organizational objectives. To the extent that TNCs lengthen their investment time frames, the apparently divergent goals of transnational corporation and nation state become more compatible.

In their initial investment decisions, it would appear that American TNCs achieve more control than do Japanese transnationals. By establishing relatively large, wholly or majority-owned affiliates, not relying on host governments for financing, and not being formally bound by indigenous competition, American TNCs are able to exercise more direct control than Japanese firms that have adopted a more collaborative stance in their Third World investments. Only with respect to the support that Japanese transnationals receive from their home government do they exercise more control in their initial investment decisions.

On the other hand, Japanese investment strategy seems to be more in accord with Third World goals. By entering into minority partnership and joint ventures, and by not investing in areas that entail direct competition, Japanese TNCs appear more supportive of local concerns than their American counterparts. However, to the extent that the Japanese raise capital internally rather than bringing it from outside the country, they are tying up funds that local nationals could otherwise use. Also, the fact that Japanese transnationals are backed formally by their own government may not work to the ultimate advantage of less developed host governments.

At the operations or management level, the picture is reversed. Japanese TNCs assume decidedly more control than do American transnationals. In hiring proportionately fewer local nationals, particularly at the managerial and professional levels, granting less autonomy to affiliates, and engaging in more internal trading, Japanese TNCs exercise relatively strict control over ongoing operations in contrast to American firms. The latter, at this level, have adopted management strategies that are considerable more attentive to host country needs. American policies regarding employment, autonomy, and purchasing all work to the benefit of their Third World hosts. Only with respect to export sales are Japanese TNCs more aligned with host country purposes.

Thus, American and Japanese TNCs appear to operate from quite different organizational principles regarding foreign direct investment in less-developed countries. Whereas both are concerned with corporate goals, including the maintaining of sufficient control to achieve these goals, they set about acquiring control in distinctly different ways. On the one hand, American transnationals in general attempt to establish an investment climate that is structured according to their dictates; they then yield a good deal of operating control to indigenous personnel. On the other hand, Japanese TNCs strike an initial investment deal that is mutually agreeable to both transnational and nation state. Subsequently, they assume operating control through a variety of managerial strategies including authority over the selection of top management and technological processes, centralized decision making, and internal trading.

The fact that neither American nor Japanese TNCs attempt to gain maximum control at both these levels indicates that they are sensitive to host country needs as these bear on the overall agreement that is made. In other words, there is a trade-off between TNC and LDC. In order to reach agreement, it is necessary for the TNC to yield some control, either initially as part of the deal that is struck, or subsequently in terms of the ongoing management of the enterprise (see Box 8-1, **O.E.C.D. Guidelines for TNCs**). This becomes one of the constant costs of foreign direct investment in less-developed countries. Only the manner in which it is yielded varies by national origin.

FUSION OF RATIONAL ORGANIZATION AND TECHNOLOGICAL MASTERY

The transnational corporation is an emergent organizational form that has evolved in response to the environment of which it is a part. Not only is it flexible and adaptable similar to the composite model of organization described in the preceding chapter, but also it is technologically enhanced such that it can deal effectively with the total global environment. In so doing, it achieves advantages that are not available to nontransnational organizations that are bound by the physical, economic, and social constraints of just one country. Because resources and markets are geographically dispersed, and because all countries have different laws and customs, TNCs can systematically select where in the world it is most profitable to conduct particular types of business. Because of technological advances in transportation, communication, and information processing, spatial dispersion on a global basis is an asset that carries few if any of the liabilities previously associated with it. The electronically integrated transnational corporation is the ultimate empirical manifestation of the fusion between rational organization and technological mastery.

What this rather awesome-sounding assertion means is that modern complex organizations because of their enhanced technological capabilities are not bound as much by their previous physical constraints. Recent evidence suggests that several of the hitherto "firm" generalizations about organizations are beginning to break down. For example, in the above section on Third World investment, American and Japanese TNCs exhibited quite different organizational styles even though they might very well have been managing similar enterprises in terms of

Box 8-1   O.E.C.D. Guidelines for TNCs

In 1976, the Organization for Economic Co-operation and Development (O.E.C.D.), which is comprised of 24 industrially developed member countries, published guidelines "for the voluntary regulation of the activities of enterprises engaged in international investment" (Rojot, 1985, p. 379). The guidelines cover seven areas of activity: general policies, disclosure of information, competition, financing, taxation, science and technology, and employment and industrial relations (see Blanpain, 1982). "The observance of the guidelines was voluntary, but member countries were recommended to apply the guidelines to multinational enterprises operating on their territory" (Rojot, 1985, p. 379).

Adherence to these voluntary guidelines is achieved by making them generally available to all TNCs, having member countries apply the same standards uniformly, setting up consultative bodies within all O.E.C.D. countries in order to clarify and interpret the guidelines, and appealing cases that appear to be in violation. In addition, the main committee responsible for the guidelines indicated that it would "accept short summaries by enterprises of their experiences under the guidelines, biannual follow-up reports by governments and biannual reports by the Committee itself" (Rojot, 1985, p. 381).

Although formal evaluation of the impact of these guidelines has yet to be undertaken, it is hoped that they will produce the following results: (1) more effective control and monitoring of the activities of TNCs across national borders; (2) greater concern by TNCs as to the multiple effects of centralized decision making on subsidiaries in other countries; (3) less conflict between TNCs and host countries; (4) more attention paid by TNCs to the adverse effects of technology and organization on host countries; and (5) a better fit between economic reality and national and international law (see Rojot, 1985, pp. 386–391).

size, technology, and product mix. In contrast to the Japanese, American firms adopted a more laissez-faire stance in management. In other words, the chief executive officers of these organizations were at liberty to institute a set of controls more or less independently of such previously important considerations as organization size and production technology. Other factors such as organizational climate and composition, as well as various environmental considerations can impinge more strongly on the particular style adopted.

Consider also the findings presented at the beginning of the chapter regarding increasing transnational corporate concentration, most of this being accomplished by mergers and acquisitions of conglomerates by conglomerates. When Du Pont, the nineteenth largest industrial corporation in the world, acquired Conoco (the ninth largest American oil company), what was the production technology that "determined" the resulting organization structure? Conglomerates, of which there are an increasing number, are by definition "large corporations formed by the merger of a number of companies in unrelated, widely diversified industries." Clearly, there are no overarching production technologies that can characterize companies such as these. Other factors must influence how they tailor their organization structures and institute systems of control.

In Chapter 7, while some studies were found to support the traditional inverse relationship between organization size and centralization of authority, others found that centralization varies independently of organization size. In other words, increases in organizational size do not necessarily entail a loss of centralized control. In a recent comparative study of organizations in Iran, Jordan, Sweden, and the United States, Miller (1989), contrary to previous research results, found no support for the inverse relationship between formalization and centralization nor between differentiation and centralization. This means that despite increasing organizational complexity (i.e., vertical and horizontal differentiation and spatial dispersion) and the expansion of formalized procedures, centralized control can be maintained.

All these results suggest that increasingly organizations may establish structures and introduce control systems independently of factors previously deemed to be crucial to their very survival. In the days of physical "hands-on" management, changes in organizational size, complexity, or technology necessitated other adaptive changes in organization structure. However, with developments in integrated, on-line computer control, increases in size and complexity or changes in production technology become in large part merely technical problems to be solved. Organizations may instead focus on other issues.

In Chapter 7, I described what some of these issues are: (1) adapting quickly to novel and changing circumstances; (2) dealing effectively with other organizations, including nation states; (3) establishing motivation in an increasingly specialized work force; and (4) creating a climate or culture that promotes dominant organizational values. The introduction of communications and information processing technology into a purposive and responsive framework permits modern organizations to change their focus. Thus, one of the most important consequences of the information revolution that we are currently experiencing may well be the revolutionary changes that are occurring in organizations. In that most of our activities, work and nonwork alike, take place in organizational contexts, the changes that we are witnessing in organizations have significant impact upon us as individuals. In the following chapters, we will explore this changing relationship between individual and organization.

SUMMARY

8.1   A transnational corporation (TNC), also called a multinational corporation, is "any enterprise that undertakes foreign direct investment, owns or controls income-gathering assets in more than one country, produces goods or services outside its country of origin, or engages in international production." As an emergent organization form, TNCs are the epitome of environmental adaptation.

8.2 TNCs have become a major force in the world economy only within the past 30 years largely as a result of technological innovations in transportation, communication, and information processing. By 1980, the top 200 industrial corporations in the world, of which approximately half were American, accounted for almost 30 percent of total world output. Transnational corporate concentration is increasing, being limited primarily to firms in industrially developed nations.

8.3 Transnational corporate investment takes place mainly in the developed countries, the United States being the most preferred locale. Whereas primary commodities used to constitute the bulk of foreign direct investment, activity is now concentrated in manufacturing and the tertiary sector. Transnational banks (TNBs), which are dominated by the Japanese, have contributed to what has been termed the integrated global economy.

8.4 The emergence of TNCs into the global economy has caused a redistribution in the balance of world power. By almost any indicator, TNCs as an emergent organizational form rival the nation state, particularly governments in less-developed countries. There is a growing lack of congruence between economic and political systems of organization on the international level.

8.5 With regard to foreign direct investment in the Third World, critical theorists charge that TNCs (1) produce a net outflow of capital; (2) displace local entrepreneurs; (3) introduce inappropriate capital-intensive technology; (4) encourage elite-oriented patterns of consumption; and (5) contribute to dissension and unequal patterns of growth within developing societies. On the other hand, conventional theorists argue that were it not for foreign direct investment, the less developed nations would be in worse circumstances than they presently are.

8.6 Because of the complexities of foreign investment and the measurement problems involved, it is impossible to make truly causal statements about the effects of transnational corporate investment on Third World development. While it does introduce much needed capital, foreign investment is not without its attendant problems.

8.7 Comparing British, American, and Japanese transnationals, all prefer to locate the bulk of their foreign operations in developed market economies. Yet there are also preferred regional areas of investment, which vary by national origin of TNC. Up until the early 1970s, Japanese TNCs were relatively rare, and Japan as a host country actively discouraged foreign investment.

8.8 In a study of British, American, and Japanese transnational investment in Third World countries, it was found that American and British TNCs differed in significant respects from Japanese transnationals. With regard to the initial investment decision, American (and British) firms sought more control than did Japanese TNCs who tended to strike a mutually beneficial partnership with Third World states. However, at the ongoing management or operations level, Japanese transnationals maintained more strict control by hiring fewer local managers and technical staff, granting less autonomy to affiliates, and relying extensively on their own corporate trading networks. At this level, American (and British) companies were considerably more attentive to host country needs. It was concluded that the yielding of transnational control at some stage of the investment process is a necessary condition in TNC–LDC negotiations.

8.9 The chapter closes with an examination of the transnational corporation as an emergent organizational form. Not only has it proved to be extremely responsive to the global environment, but as a result of technological advances in transportation, communication, and information processing, it has eliminated virtually all of the disadvantages previously associated with spatial dispersion on a worldwide basis.

8.10 Because of the enhanced technological capabilities of emergent organizations such as the TNC, it was suggested that organization structure and management control systems can be designed almost independently of what hitherto have been limiting factors (e.g., organization size and production technology). Partial evidence provided support for this hypothesis. It was concluded that modern organizations may instead focus on other issues relating to the environment and to their own organizational climates.

NOTES

1. A transnational corporation (TNC) is also called a multinational corporation (MNC) or a multinational enterprise (MNE). However, most current researchers prefer the term "transnational corporation" in that it implies an enterprise which is owned and controlled in one country, but which extends across its own national borders. On the other hand, "multinational corporation" could imply an enterprise in which controlling interest is held in more than one country.

2. This figure represents only foreign *direct* investment. If fixed assets are taken into consideration, the total is considerably higher.

3. For a discussion of integration and diversification as organizational strategies and how they were used throughout American industry during the first half of the twentieth century, see Chandler, 1969.

4. Of all the developed countries, Japan notably is a country in which there is not much foreign investment. Between 1970 and 1980, generally less than two percent of all foreign investments made in developed countries were in Japanese enterprises (see Buckley, 1985, pp. 204–205).

5. These seven countries in order of 1980 export contributions are as follows: Taiwan (18%); South Korea (15%); Hong Kong (14%); Singapore (9%); Brazil (7%); India (5%); and Mexico (2%). (See Clairmonte and Cavanagh, 1984, pp. 84, fn. 34.)

6. If investments by American transnationals are limited only to their holdings in the Third World, then primary commodities equaled 61% of the total 1960 investment but only 23% in 1980 (Berberoglu, 1983).

7. Murdoch (1980, pp. 253–260) provides examples of how TNCs have interfered in the internal affairs of host countries. Perhaps the most notorious example is the collusion of International Telephone and Telegraph (ITT) with the United States Central Intelligence Agency in overthrowing the socialist government of Salvador Allende in Chile.

8. One possible exception to this statement might be the Roman Catholic Church, which has its official headquarters in Vatican City.

9. Also, it would be necessary to control for all other significant but extraneous factors that could affect the relationship between foreign investment and national development.

10. These countries are South Korea, Taiwan, Hong Kong, Singapore, Indonesia, Malaysia, the Philippines, and Thailand.

11. In anticipation of 1992 when the 12 nations of the European Community (EC) will form one integrated free-trading bloc, Japan has substantially increased its direct foreign investment in Europe so that it will be *inside* this affluent market of 320 million people rather than exporting from outside, and therefore subject to growing protectionist

policies. "Direct Japanese investment in EC countries more than doubled between 1986 and 1988, and this year may reach a record 8.6 billion" (*Newsweek*, 1989, p. 29). According to another article (Rapaport, 1989), it is very difficult to get a precise fix on where in the world the Japanese are investing, except to say that this investment is increasing dramatically, particularly in the developed countries.

12. Of the 90 TNCs surveyed, 13 were British, 27 American, and 17 Japanese. Of the 402 subsidiaries on which information was gathered, 7 were British, 188 American, and 84 Japanese.

13. The other countries represented include Sweden, France, Belgium, Italy, and Australia. Because of the preponderance of European nations, they are sometimes referred to as "European" in the text for ease in expression.

Chapter
9

Workers and Work

Being a tradesman is viewed with such disdain these days that most young people I know treat the trades like a temporary summer job. I've seen young guys take minimum-wage jobs just so they can wear suits. It is as if any job without a dress code is a dead-end job. This is partly our own fault. We even tell our own sons, "Don't be like me, get a job people respect." Blue-collar guys ought to brag more, even swagger a little. We should drive our families past the latest job site and say, "That house was a piece of junk, and now it's the best one on the block. I did that." Nobody will respect us if we don't respect ourselves.

Our work is hard, hot, wet, cold and always dirty. It is also often very satisfying. Entailing the use of both brain and body there is a product—a physical result of which to be proud. We have fallen from your roofs, died under heavy equipment and been entombed in your dams. We have done honest, dangerous work. Our skills and energy and strength have transformed lines on paper into physical reality.

Steve Olson, construction worker, 1989

*U*p to this point, we have focused on the structural aspects of work. We have seen first how industrialization and then later postindustrialism changed the type of work that people do and how they make their living. We have also noted how the trend toward increasing bureaucratization transformed the context of work. As a result of these complex processes, the overwhelming majority of workers in modern postindustrial societies such as Great Britain, the United States, and Japan are now organizational employees engaged in producing either manufactured goods or a growing variety of services.

In the present chapter, we switch the focus of analysis and examine work from the perspective of individual workers. First, we pose two general questions: (1) What motivates people to work? and (2) What are important attachments to work? Answers to these questions allow us to sketch out a model of individual–work linkages involving the necessary and voluntary components of work. This analysis is supplemented by examining the characteristics associated with "a good job" and ascertaining how satisfied workers are with their own particular jobs. The chapter concludes by addressing the question of how the changing composition of work is affecting workers' jobs and their individual–work linkages.

In examining the perceptions and attitudes of workers employed under a variety of circumstances and working in different countries, we can identify some of the factors underlying the relationship that people form between themselves and their work. In other words, we will be able to assess the impact of the many changes that have occurred from the point of view of those who have been affected.

MOTIVATION TO WORK

> What brings the worker to the work-place? The same motivator that brings the manager to work: pay. How many managers would continue on their jobs without it? Pay is the common denominator that brings all people to work. It seems useless to debate whether money is first or fourth on value scales for workers or executives. No one works without it (Fein, 1976, p. 517).

Work is a necessary activity. Most of us do not have the choice of deciding whether or not to work. Work is essential for our survival. Therefore, a universal, core motivation for work is the pay that we earn from doing it. Notwithstanding any other reasons that might bring us to work, we are instrumentally motivated to work for the livelihood that it provides.

Because pay is both a vital and ongoing link between worker and work, anything that jeopardizes it is a source of great concern. The need for employment security has generated many strategies over the years to ensure not only continuity of income but also worker control over the conditions of its disbursement. Labor legislation determines the outside limits within which employers may operate and the minimum wages they may pay. Union and other employment contracts clearly stipulate the terms of employment and the grounds for dismissal and layoff. Seniority clauses invoke assurances of job tenure. Day laborers and free-lance professionals alike attempt to become organizational employees, or at least seek organizational affiliation in order to regularize their incomes. Employees and employers both contribute to various funds to ease the financial burden should the employment link be broken for any reason (e.g., unemployment insurance, severance pay, sickness and disability, worker compensation, and old age pensions).

According to the late James F. Lincoln, president of the highly successful Lincoln Electric, not only is it in the interests of workers to establish an adequate and secure employment relationship, it is also crucial to the interests of management.

> It is management's duty to make the worker secure in his job. Only so can the worker feel that he can develop the skill and apply the imagination that will do his job more efficiently, without fear of unemployment from the progress he makes. If a man is threatened with loss of his job by a better way of producing, which eliminates the need for his service, he cannot do his best. . . .
>
> No man will willingly work to throw himself out of his job, nor should he. (Lincoln, cited in Fein, 1976, p. 512)

Because worker and managers are both motivated by pay, "the common denominator," it is in the interest of management to provide job security to workers so that they are in a position to do their best. In turn, the increased productivity of workers contributes to the job security of managers, not to mention the profitability of the firm. While workers and managers do not have the same goals, both are motivated by the prospect of secure and adequate incomes.

As noted previously, Lincoln states that it is management's responsibility to provide job security for workers. However, as we observed in Chapter 7, management does not exercise complete control. Various factors in the organizational environment can produce structural unemployment and therefore threaten job security. These include "international competition, technological change, deregulation, and demand shifts" (Bednarzik and Shiells, 1989, p. 34). How then can management protect workers (and themselves) from these structural factors?

There appear to be two institutionalized responses to this question—the Western way and the Japanese way. When faced with an economic downturn, the typical strategy of Western firms is retrenchment. Depending upon the business cycle, workers find themselves either on one side or the other of the revolving factory gate. Job security is the exception rather than the rule. On the other hand, in Japanese organizations there is a norm of lifetime employment. Although only about one-third of the labor force are actually covered by these lifetime agreements, nevertheless "job turnover is lower and job tenure is higher in Japan" compared with other industrialized nations (Bednarzik and Shiells, 1989, p. 38). For example, "Japan's unemployment rate is less than half the United States' rate" (Bednarzik and Shiells, 1989, p. 35), whereas the median years of employment of Japanese workers with their current employer is over twice that of American workers (Hashimoto and Raisian, 1989, p. 33). "A typical U.S. male worker is projected to hold approximately 11 jobs over his working life, whereas a typical Japanese worker will hold only 5 jobs" (Hashimoto and Raisian, 1989, p. 34).

The principle of lifetime employment in Japan, that is, employment security, is achieved through a variety of mechanisms, the most important of which is the creation of internal labor markets within firms (see, for example, Dore, 1973; Lincoln and McBride, 1987). Typically, young employees are recruited at relatively low organizational levels and then proceed to advance within the highly calibrated hierarchical system (see Chapter 7) over the course of their working careers. Thus, most high-level Japanese managers today were once junior employees in the organizations they are presently managing. Internal recruitment and promotion are facilitated by job rotation and flexible work assignments (see Chapter 7) which enable the organization more easily to match the supply of labor with positional demand.[1] In order for employees to be sufficiently competent to perform their shifting bundle of work responsibilities, Japanese organizations rely extensively on in-house educational programs and on-the-job training.

Consequently, in general, the Japanese system of employment is more attuned to the basic motivations of workers for secure employment than are either the British or American approaches. However, a definite cost of employment tenure is that employees are obliged to accept virtually any job they are assigned. In order for the norm of lifetime employment to work, managers must have the freedom to allocate workers according to the work that needs to be done. Thus, as will be explained more fully in Chapter 10, while Japanese workers have a stronger guarantee of employment than do workers in the West, they are also more limited in their ability to exercise choice in the actual work they perform.

In Great Britain and the United States, the employment contract is based on different premises. While it is acknowledged that the institution of work is necessary as a means for survival, choices are also available. In the West, workers most often gain employment through the external labor market in which all employing organizations advertise most positions they have available. Because there is a great variety of jobs from which to choose in order to secure one's livelihood, and to the extent that workers avail themselves of these choices, the Western system of employment provides more job opportunities than the Japanese. However, because the open labor market is in essence a competition among employers for the best workers and among workers for the best jobs, there is consequently less structural attention paid to employment security.

Dore (1973, p. 264) summarizes the differences between the Japanese and Western employment systems:

> Lifetime employment, a seniority-plus-merit wage system, an intra-enterprise career system, enterprise training, enterprise unions, a high level of enterprise welfare, and the careful nurturing of enterprise consciousness, are all of one piece; they fit together—as do the contrasting features of the British firms: considerable mobility of employment, a market-based wage and salary system, self-designed mobile rather than regulated careers, publicly provided training, industrial or craft unions, more state welfare and a greater strength of professional, craft, regional or class consciousness.

We are thus offered two structural solutions to the problem of employment and worker motivation. On the one hand, the Japanese system concentrates on the underlying core factor that motivates all people to work—secure employment over a lifetime. In that this employment usually occurs within the context of a single firm, the firm stands to benefit from the increased commitment workers bring to their jobs in the knowledge that they will enjoy tenure throughout their working careers. On the other hand, the Western system, although it does not provide a similar degree of initial job security, it does offer the prospect that workers, because of their increased work mobility (and thus greater opportunity to select from a variety of jobs with several employers) will ultimately end up in jobs that are individually tailored to their own particular needs. Consequently, they will be highly committed to these jobs. As Lincoln and McBride (1987, p. 297) state, "A common characterization is that Americans pursue careers within occupations that cut across firms, while the opposite pattern holds in Japan."

In general, Japanese firms stand to gain more commitment from workers than Western firms in that it is these same firms that undertake responsibility for the workers (see Lincoln and McBride, 1987). In the Western case, whereas the possibility exists that workers will end up in careers more suited to their individual choice, there is more risk involved and they are not as secure in their employment. Thus, there is a trade-off. To the extent that work security is most important, the Japanese system with its more limited job opportunities is to be preferred; however, if an "ideal" person–job match is the prime motivator, the Western system is superior. In the following section, we will explore some of the individual–work linkages that serve as additional motivators to work.

ATTACHMENTS TO WORK

In 1976, Dubin and his colleagues conducted a comprehensive search of the empirical research literature to locate those "objective features of the work environment to which workers become attached" (Dubin et al., 1976, p. 288) and which thus serve as potential work motivators. Based on their survey of over 300 research reports spanning many different areas of investigation, Table 9.1 presents their typology of workplace systems, objects, conditions, and payoffs that have been identified as sources of work attachment.

Systems of the Work Environment

Among the systems of the work environment, the "self" is a necessary condition and may in fact constitute the only work system for the self-employed. Attachment to work through self provides a sense of identity (e.g., "What do you do?") and can contribute toward a positive self-image and self-respect (see Hughes, 1958). A whole body of research has investigated the relation of self to work (see, for example, Argyris, 1964; McGregor, 1960), asserting that while work can and should provide opportunities for self-actualization (i.e., the realization of one's full potential), this source of work attachment is blocked for most lower-level employees.

Other systems of work, and therefore potential sources of attachment, are the work group and employing organization. As we have noted, both these systems are particularly important to Japanese workers. Because of the norm of lifetime employment and the structure and climate of Japanese organizations, workers establish close bonds and develop an esprit de corps throughout their working careers with colleagues in their immediate work group as well as the larger organization (see Dore, 1973; Lincoln and McBride, 1987). The work group as an im-

Table 9.1 ATTACHMENTS TO WORK
Sources of Work Attachment

1. *Systems of the Work Environment*
    Self
    Work group
    Company/organization
    Union/professional association
    Craft/profession
    Industry

2. *Workplace Objects and Human Conditions*
    Technology
    Product
    Routine
    Autonomy
    Personal space/things

3. *Payoffs*
    Money
    Perquisites
    Power
    Authority
    Status
    Career

Source: Adapted from Dubin et al., 1976, p. 290.

portant source of solidarity and attachment to work was first identified by researchers in the Human Relations school in the 1930s (see Chapter 7).

As we will note in Chapter 10, attachment to a union is a diminishing source of work attachment for American workers, and also is not very important for Japanese workers who have organized into "company unions." However, for British workers, half of whom are union members (Goldfield, 1987, p. 16), attachment to a union provides a vehicle for them to express their working class solidarity and to achieve control over their working lives. With the significant growth of white-collar professional and managerial unions and associations during the past two decades, this source of attachment to work has opened up for a much broader spectrum of workers than has been the case traditionally.

Attachments to craft, profession, and industry stress the intrinsic performance characteristics of work and occupations, as well as the social relations that are formed with people who are similarly employed and therefore who share similar problems and prospects. The sociology of occupations is replete with studies of miners, steelworkers, railroaders, fishermen, engineers, clerics, doctors, and craftworkers of all types who identify with the work they and their coworkers do that sets them apart and thus distinguishes them from the ordinary.

Workplace Objects and Human Conditions

In addition to systems of the work environment, workplace objects and the human conditions arising out of work are also sources of attachment. Workplace objects include technology and product. Attachment to technology is an effective linkage to the means (i.e., the equipment, processes and/or ideas) by which goods and services are produced, while attachment to product is the forming of a bond to the end result or outcome of one's work. Particularly among craftworkers, artists, and professionals, there are attachments to both technology (the knowledgeable utilization of hard-won skills) and product (the ultimate expression of the creative process) as clearly both are integral to the work that is performed. Pride in craft is expressed in the hallmark or signature which signifies a unique and personal contribution.

The structure and routine of work are aspects which many researchers have evaluated negatively (see, for example, Kornhauser, 1965; Walker and Guest, 1952). Yet there is also evidence that workers value the security of knowing to the last detail what their job demands are (see Box 4-3 on **The Unintended Consequences of Bureaucracy** in Chapter 4). Loscocco (1989, p. 17) reports that workers "value what is most available from their jobs." Thus, workers who have spent many years with the same employer value the routines which have been established over time and being familiar with their jobs, coworkers, and surroundings (see Dubin et al., 1976, pp. 316–318).[2] In a study of what older workers in five occupational groups would miss upon retirement, one of the most frequently mentioned responses was simply "having something to do." As the researchers themselves conclude:

> Our studies of the significance of work in the lives of people underline for us the importance of an activity that fills the day, gives people something to do, and makes time pass. Sheer passing of time seems to be an important value of work. Work is admirably designed to provide this value, since it usually requires orderly routines. Even people who dislike their work as dangerous, unpleasant, or monotonous often recognize the value of the work routine to them and cannot imagine how they would fill the day if they were to retire. Friedmann and Havighurst, 1954, p. 190)

Like routine, autonomy is a human condition that may be experienced as a result of the manner in which work is organized. The research literature is filled with examples of how autonomy constitutes an important work attachment (see, for example, Hall, 1987, pp. 79–87). As will be noted later in the chapter, great concern has been expressed by some writers that individual autonomy at work has been continually eroded due to industrialization, bureaucratization, and now, computerization (see Braverman, 1974). However, as Katz (1967) has pointed out, whereas the work roles of many blue collar workers may be tightly circumscribed, there are opportunities for these workers to exercise considerable autonomy in their informal behavior and interaction on the job.

> It must be noted that [blue-collar] worker autonomy, although enacted *in* the work organization is essentially *external* to his work role. This contrasts with the autonomy pattern for white-collar workers . . . . They have greater autonomy *within* their work role, but their role is more broadly defined than that of the [blue-collar] worker. In a

sense the white-collar worker takes his work role *outside* the organization; the blue-collar worker brings his nonwork role *into* the organization. (Katz, 1967, p. 292)

Autonomy, like routine, can vary from one extreme to the other. While a job in which there is maximal autonomy and no established routine might seem appealing at first glance, it can also be very anxiety producing and disorienting. With autonomy there is responsibility, and without routine there is uncertainty. Many workers have expressed preference for jobs in which they assume little responsibility and know exactly what to expect. In this way, they are able to separate their work activities from their lives away from the job (see Hedley, 1982). While it has been demonstrated that both routine and autonomy are important sources of work attachment, the data indicate that not all people prefer the same mix of these features in their work:

> . . . the evidence is unclear in regard to exactly what people are like in their interactions with organizations. Some writers . . . believe that people move toward "adulthood," in which they seek autonomy, independence, control over their world, and the development of their abilities to the utmost. Others are not so sure . . . . Some people simply may not have the desire for autonomy or self-actualization of any sort . . . . Thus, while some people are highly frustrated in a highly formalized setting, others would not be. By the same token, a low degree of formalization would be a satisfying condition to some but not to others. (Hall, 1987, p. 86)

The final work attachment listed under workplace objects and conditions in Table 9.1 is personal space and things. Whether it be the president's office or the secretary's desk (and equipment) or the operator's machine, most workers indicate attachment to *their* workspace and *their* things by first defining and then personalizing them. While Dubin and his colleagues did not find any research studies to document this type of attachment, it is easy enough to corroborate on a casual basis. For example, note what goes on when bus drivers change shifts, or compare two apparently identical taxicabs. Observe the mechanic's workbench or your professor's office. Attempt to sit in "someone else's place" during your next lecture.

> The importance that individuals assign to place and things in their work environment may be simply interpreted as signifying that the person does literally have a place in the organization. There is nothing more obvious to signal this than the assigned work station to which the individual repeatedly returns and which is given a personal touch of decor and possessions to confirm this unique place. (Dubin et al., 1976, p. 303)

Payoffs

Among the strongest attachments to work are the payoffs received, and money is the most universally acknowledged of these. As we noted in the previous section, money is the basic core motivator to work. In addition, varying amounts of pay for work are used to reward differential contributions and to reinforce the prevailing stratification system, both within work organizations and the larger society. Money is also used to motivate people to perform extraordinary work (e.g., shiftwork differentials, isolation pay, danger pay, and so on) as well as to meet and exceed production targets (e.g., incentive systems and bonuses). Money is an inducement to work and to work well under a variety of conditions at all levels of work. Indeed, devising attractive systems of executive compensation has become an important specialty of management consulting firms as various compensation packages consisting of money and other perquisites are put together in an effort both to attract and to keep senior executives. (See Box 9-1, **Executive Compensation**.)

Perquisites represent another set of payoffs from work which also serve as attachments. They may be formalized as "fringe benefits," which are computed as part of the total compensation package, or they may be informal privileges and benefits accruing from work. Standard fringe benefits include medical and dental services, life and disability insurance, paid vacations, sick leave, pension plans, and, more recently, employee stock ownership plans (ESOPs). Other "perks" depend in large part on the type of work organization and the goods and services it produces. Some organizations make the following amenities available to their employees as part of the employment relationship: discounts; company cars; expense accounts; free or subsidized meals, housing, education, and travel; club memberships; and sports and recreational facilities.

Perquisites that are not formally written into the employment contract are by definition privileges rather than rights that employees (or certain categories thereof) are eligible to receive by virtue of their membership in the organization. Although they may come to be perceived as rights, they are extended to employees as organizational largesse in the expectation that this largesse will be repaid in terms of increased commitment and loyalty to the organization. This form of organizational benevolence, or, as some have termed it, paternalism, is more characteristic of Japanese firms, which have made heavy use of perquisites in their attempts to build attachment to company (see Dore, 1973, pp. 269–275).

Power, authority, and status are all payoffs from work that mainly serve as attachments for higher level organizational participants, although not exclusively so. For example, Mechanic (1962) found that employees in lower organizational ranks can exercise considerable power through their access to and control of information vital to the functioning of the organization. Also, as we will see in "Worker–Management Relations" (Chapter 10), when many organizational members combine together into a union they can gain power and control that none of them could attain individually. Power, or the ability to exert one's will despite resistance (Weber, in Gerth and Mills, 1958, p. 180), is a great motivator of human behavior both at work and elsewhere. Although there is a striking direct relationship between organizational rank and power, at the same time senior executives do not hold absolute dominion over their subordinates. They are limited in their authority.

Authority as defined by Weber is legitimate power (see Chapter 4) and thus can serve as a work attachment only for those who manage or supervise others. The fact that employees at all organizational ranks compete with one another to attain ever higher levels of command is testament that authority is a strong attachment to work.

Attachment to status is an attachment to one's standing on some dimension along which people are ranked. Consequently, there are many ways to achieve a

Box 9-1   Executive Compensation

How are senior executives paid? Thomas Taveggia, an organizational sociologist and managment consultant specializing in executive compensation, outlines briefly the highly complex process by which organizations attempt to ensure that they are managed by the best executive talent available. At all organizational levels, money is a powerful motivator.

"I remember reading several years ago about a senior executive of a large, well-known company in the area where I lived who made over $100,000 a year! Since I only made about $1.75 an hour at the time, I was offended—in fact outraged. No one is worth that kind of money! What a rip-off!

"I wasn't alone in my reaction—then or now. In fact, you probably have had similar reactions when you've read in the newspaper or *Time* magazine that many of today's executives make over $1,000,000 per year and that some make considerably more than that. According to *BusinessWeek* (May 7, 1990), for example, Craig O. McCaw, Chief Executive Officer of McCaw Cellular Communications, made $53.9 million in salary, bonuses, and stock options in 1989. (See table for the runners-up.)"

AMERICA'S HIGHEST PAID CORPORATE EXECUTIVES

Executive	Company	1989 salary and bonus	Long-term compensation	Total pay in 1989
		Thousands of dollars		
1. Craig O. McCaw	McCaw Cellular	$ 289	$53,655	$53,944
2. Frank G. Wells	Walt Disney	4,820	46,126	50,946
3. Gary Wilson	Walt Disney	2,500	47,488	49,988
4. Steven J. Ross	Time Warner	4,800	29,400	34,200
5. Wayne M. Perry	McCaw Cellular	274	23,787	24,061
6. Donald A. Pels	Lin Broadcasting	1,363	21,428	22,791
7. Jim P. Manzi	Lotus Development	991	15,372	16,363
8. Rufus W. Lumry	McCaw Cellular	272	14,472	14,744
9. Paul Fireman	Reebok International	14,606	—	14,606
10. Ronald K. Ruchey	Torchmark	1,078	11,588	12,666

Source: Business Week, May 7, 1990, p. 57.

How do executives come to make so much money? The answer is relatively straightforward—executives, like McCaw, make whatever a willing employer will pay them for their services. But, you ask (perhaps with more than a little self-interest), why are employers willing to pay so much?

To answer this question, it is important to understand both (1) the typical makeup of executive compensation packages; and (2) the process by which executive compensation packages and levels are established.

1. Executive compensation packages are *typically* comprised of the following elements:

(a) *Fixed salary payments and welfare benefits*—executives, like all other employees, are normally paid a regular salary (wage, in the case of hourly employees) and are covered under various welfare benefit plans (e.g., medical, dental, vision, disability, and life insurance, as well as defined benefit and/or defined contribution retirement plans).

(b) *Short-term, typically annual incentives*—like some employee groups and most middle-managers, executives are usually eligible to receive cash bonuses *contingent* upon a judgmental or formularized assessment of how well they meet their company's short-term, typically annual, performance objectives.

(c) *Long-term incentives*—*unlike* most other employee groups, executives can have a dramatic effect on their company's long-term performance; thus they also are eligible to receive *contingent* awards in company stock or stock options, and in many cases large cash awards based on how well they meet their company's long-term, strategic performance objectives.

(d) *Special fringe benefits or "perquisites"*—finally, many companies provide their executives with special fringe benefits or perquisites, such as company cars, personal financial planning advice, supplementary welfare benefits, first-class or business air travel, and so forth.

Needless to say, these various elements are not present to the same degree in all companies. Smaller, cash-conscious, start-up companies, for example, typically emphasize contingent forms of compensation (especially stock compensation), and deemphasize fixed salary and benefit forms of compensation.

2. The process of establishing an executive compensation package generally involves four overlapping steps:

(a) *Strategic review*—consideration of the company's short- and long-term objectives, that is, what the company hopes to achieve now and in the future, and the fit of various possible executive compensation policies and strategies with these objectives.

(b) *Market scan*—an informal or formal assessment of what other, usually competitor, organizations are offering and/or paying executives with similar responsibilities and objectives, as well as how they are paying them (e.g., cash or stock).

(c) *Pay structure design*—development of a business appropriate, competitive, and equitable executive compensation package that defines the relative emphasis to be placed on each of the compensation elements described above: how large each element will be, the form and timing of payment, and so forth.

(d) *Negotiation*—once all the above has been accomplished, companies engage in a delicate negotiation process with their current or prospective executives to ensure the "fit" of their compensation packages with these executives' individual needs and circumstances and, thereby, help ensure the ultimate motivational value of the dollars that will be spent on executive compensation.

In some companies these steps are only loosely adhered to. However, in many companies the process of establishing an appropriate executive compensation package has become a very sophisticated undertaking, involving not only the company's board of directors and senior management, but also external compensation consultants, accountants, and attorneys. This is because a great deal of money can be (and usually is) involved.

Interestingly, organizational research has raised a question regarding whether or not this money is being wisely spent; several correlational studies have suggested that executive pay is only marginally related to executive performance. This should not be surprising, however, since this research has failed to take into account the complexities of the process of establishing executive compensation. For example, many companies appropriately tie executive incentives to desired levels of company performance, but desired (and rewarded) performance varies depending on the nature of each company's strategic and operational objectives. Whereas one company might emphasize sales growth, another might emphasize profitability, and still another persistence. Correlational research cannot begin to do justice to complexities like this.

Although it is relatively easy to conclude, based on the reported compensation levels of executives like McCaw or on the basis of some organizational research studies, that executive pay has gotten out of hand, this brief box item has attempted to show that there is method, however imprecise, to the seeming madness. The ultimate test of this method, of course, is how good a job companies do in attracting, motivating, and retaining the caliber of executives who can provide effective leadership. In the end, high compensation levels may be a relatively small price to pay for performance (however defined), persistence, and, perhaps most important of all, stakeholder value."

Source: Prepared especially for this text by Thomas C. Taveggia.

high status or ranking. Within work organizations, those dimensions deemed important to the organization and its members constitute the bases of formal status ranking: authority, pay, performance, qualifications, and seniority are among those most often used.[3] (See Box 9-2, **The $1.00 Rebound Shot**.) Because authority is so crucial to the functioning of an organization, people's positions within the organization are formally defined in a hierarchy according to authority status. Depending upon one's rank along this and the other dimensions mentioned, recognition, prestige, and deference accrue to the position holder. Obviously, these dimensions covary, and to the extent that a person achieves a similar status ranking (at any level) along all these dimensions, he or she has status consistency (see Lenski, 1966).[4] Those who rank consistently high on all relevant dimensions (e.g., senior executives) have the most status overall.

Box 9-2 The $1.00 Rebound Shot

Bill Russell, former player-coach of the Boston Celtics and five times the Most Valuable Player of the National Basketball Association, always had a running feud with his close friend and archrival Wilt Chamberlain, most recently the 7 ft. 1 in. center with the L.A. Lakers and also voted the NBA's Most Valuable Player.

Who was really "the best"?

When Chamberlain was with the Philadelphia 76ers in the mid-1960s, he was the first player in the history of the game to be paid the then unheard of salary of $100,000 a year. Certainly by this measure he was basketball's "most valuable player."

But Russell was not to be outdone by this historic event. When his contract came up for renewal, he asked for and received an annual salary of $100,001!

Factual information taken from *Time*, 1 April 1966, pp. 36–37; 29 April 1966, pp. 36–37; *Newsweek*, 2 May 1966, pp. 72–73.

Career is the final source of work attachments listed in Table 9.1. Defined as "a series of connected stages of an occupation or profession" (Dubin et al., 1976, p. 310), a career implies an orderly work-related progression throughout one's participation in the labor force. It has been estimated that only about one-third of American workers have careers as such (Wilensky, 1960), and consequently this source of attachment motivates workers primarily at the higher occupational levels (see Miller and Form, 1980, pp. 196–259).

Of the career paths available, Gouldner (1957) has identified two dominant types that are also generally descriptive of the Japanese and Western employment patterns presented earlier in the chapter. Based on his research of professors, Gouldner discovered that career progression followed two relatively pronounced career tracks. On the one hand were what he termed "locals" who were "high on loyalty to the employing organization, low on commitment to specialized role skills, and likely to use an inner reference group orientation." Professors with a "local" orientation were attached more to their university than to the discipline in which they were trained. They sought to advance themselves through the academic administrative ranks of their university, marking their progress against the efforts of other "locals." On the other hand, there were the "cosmopolitans" who were "low on loyalty to the employing organization, high on commitment to specialized role skills, and likely to use an outer reference group orientation." These professors were highly involved in their discipline, doing research, publishing articles, and interacting with colleagues in the field. For them, their university was quite simply a convenient place to work, which they would give up should a more attractive offer be made that would give them a better environment in which to work. "Cosmopolitans" advanced themselves through achieving recognition, awards, and honorific titles in the discipline (see Hedley, 1987).

The career pattern of "locals" is analogous to the Japanese employment system, which stresses internal labor markets and lifetime employment within a single firm. In the same way, "locals" attach themselves to one employing organization, and thereby virtually limit their career prospects to what this one organization has to offer. This includes jobs for which the incumbent is not directly trained but which are learned on the job.[5] The career orientation of "cosmopolitans" reflects the external labor market system operating in Western countries. "Cosmopolitans" attach themselves to the profession or occupation in which they were trained. They advance in their careers through a series of strategic moves that permit them to expand their professional horizons with each subsequent employer.

Although it is possible to draw parallels between employment systems and career orientations, it is important to keep in mind that no one employment system nor career orientation is found exclusively in any one culture. Not all Japanese firms offer lifetime employment, and not all American organizations reject this concept. Similarly, as Gouldner found both "local" and "cosmopolitan" orientations present in American society, one no doubt would also find evidence of both in Japan. However, given the contrasting systems of employment in Japan and the West, it is reasonable to expect that proportionately more Japanese than Western workers will be "locals," and conversely that more Western than Japanese workers will be "cosmopolitans."

INDIVIDUAL–WORK LINKAGES

From the above discussion, we can draw a number of general conclusions about individual–work linkages. First, work is a necessary activity for most of those who do it. There are two consequences that flow from this empirical generalization. (1) Because work is necessary for the livelihood it provides, money is a basic attachment to work. As Dubin (1968, p. 568) states it, "Workers in modern industrial society do not make a living; they make money and buy a living." (2) Because work is necessary, attachments are made to "the most obvious characteristics of the work situation" (Dubin, 1956, p. 133). Given the mandatory nature of employment and the instrumental orientation toward work, workers have little recourse but to accept and therefore to become attached to just those features that comprise their jobs (see Hedley, 1984). In other words, workers "value what is most available from their jobs" (Loscocco, 1989, p. 17), regardless of what this might be (see, for example, Lieberman, 1956).

The second general conclusion that we can draw is that the work world also involves choices. While it is true that most people do not have choice over whether or not to work, many do have discretion with respect to the type of job and where and for whom they work (Taveggia and Hedley, 1976). Because choice involves selecting what is preferred among the options available, workers can become effectively involved in those work features over which they exercise choice. The more choices workers have, either objectively determined or as perceived by them, the greater is their attachment to work (Hedley, 1984).

Consequently, attachments to work may be summarized in three analytically distinct but empirically overlapping stages. First, money (i.e., the need to survive) forms the initial and universal linkage. Second, acceptance of this fact leads individuals to accept also the basic contractual agreements and working conditions under which they are employed. Third, because all jobs are not the same, and workers have varying interests, qualifications, and opportunities, there is individual choice as to which set of employment conditions is preferable. The more choice that workers can exercise over the type and terms of employment, the greater is the likelihood that they will achieve an optimal person–job match, and therefore the greater will be their attachment to work. Thus, this analysis reveals that there are both common and variable attachments to work. The common attachments stem from the fact that work is necessary, whereas the variable attachments spring from the additional fact that within the necessary individual–work bond there is also some freedom of choice.

Table 9.2, which presents the views of representative samples of British, American, and Japanese workers, corroborates both the necessary and voluntary aspects of work. On the one hand, the majority in each country feel that the principal reason why people work is to earn money: Work is necessary. On the other hand, if workers had sufficient incomes whereby it was unnecessary to work, overwhelmingly they would choose to work anyway, either in their present jobs or in some other work.[6] Note also the internal consistency of the responses to these two questions. Whereas more British than American or Japanese workers replied that people work primarily to earn money (i.e., the "necessary" response), correspondingly fewer British than American or Japanese stated that they would continue working ("voluntary" response).[7] Thus, while most workers view work as necessary, if they are given choice, they will continue to work.

JOB DESIRABILITY

A recent approach to identifying the linkages between workers and their work was conducted by Jencks and his colleagues (1988). Beginning with the question, "What is a good job?," these researchers engaged in an extensive literature search to identify those objective features of the work environment that form the answer to this question. Armed with 48 such characteristics that measured aspects of pay, fringe benefits, hours of work, occupational status, training and promotion opportunities, job hazards, educational requirements, technical job features, autonomy, authority, and the organizational setting of work, they interviewed a nationally representative sample of the American labor force. As well as asking all these workers to describe their jobs in terms of the above characteristics, the investigators asked them to evaluate their jobs compared to "an average job."[8]

Table 9.3 lists the 14 attributes that are significantly related to workers' evaluations of their jobs. "While earnings are the most important single deter-

Table 9.2   WORK MOTIVATION OF BRITISH, AMERICAN, AND JAPANESE WORKERS

Measure of motivation	United Kingdom	United States	Japan
Why do people work?[1]			
Earn money	80%	59%	55%
Self-fulfillment	14	30	34
Duty to society	4	11	11
No answer/opinion	2	0	0
Total	100%	100%	100%
Percent who would continue to work if they won or inherited enough money to live comfortably for the rest of their lives[2]	69%	88%	93%

[1]Gallup International representative samples of young people aged 18 to 24. See de Boer, 1978, p. 416.

[2]Random samples of the labor force in each country. See Harpaz, 1989, p. 149.

minant of a job's desirability, the 13 nonmonetary job characteristics together are twice as important as earnings" (Jencks et al., 1988, p. 1322). Altogether these 14 characteristics explain 41% of the variance in workers' job ratings, and consequently go a long way to providing the essential ingredients of "a good job." Provided that the values for all 14 characteristics can be attained, it is possible to score any job on these criteria, and therefore determine its overall desirability from the perspective of a potential jobholder, or in relation to all other jobs.

It is interesting to note that of the workers surveyed, on average they evaluated their jobs considerably higher than the "average job" against which they were asked to compare. While they were told that "an average job [has] a rating of 100," the median rating they gave their jobs was 149. "Two-thirds of all ratings were above 100, 11% were exactly 100, and only 21% were below 100" (Jencks et al., 1988, p. 1334). Given that these workers constituted a nationally representative sample, theoretically one would expect their median rating to be relatively close to 100. However, similar to other research that has noted how workers consistently rate themselves better than average with respect to job satisfaction and ability (see Hedley, 1986a), these data indicate that workers, like people in general, portray themselves and their circumstances in a somewhat idealized form. Thus, a considerable portion of self-perceptions about work and other matters involves presenting the self in a light consonant with prevailing values and norms. For this reason, Jencks and his colleagues (1988, p. 1342) suggest that their research "should be replicated by asking workers how favorably they think *others* would rate jobs like theirs."[9]

An important contribution of the job desirability research is its ability to disentangle in quantifiable terms the separate effects of monetary and nonmonetary rewards. For example, according to the sample data, the jobs that men typically hold pay 2.0 times as much as women's jobs. However, this is not the whole story. Men's jobs also have "nonmonetary advantages equivalent to their being paid . . . 2.1 times more than women. Thus, if jobs' nonmonetary characteristics were to remain as they now are, women's jobs would have to pay (2.0)(2.1) = 4.2 times more than they now do in order to be rated as favorably as men's" (Jencks et al., 1988, p.

Table 9.3   RANK ORDER OF CHARACTERISTICS CONTRIBUTING TO JOB DESIRABILITY

Rank characteristic	Measurement	Sign[1]
1. Earnings	Total annual job earnings	+
2. Educational requirements	Years of education most people require to perform job	+
3. Hours of work	Total number of hours worked per week	+
4. On-the-job training	Whether jobholder learns new things on the job that could lead to promotion	+
5. Dirty work	Whether jobholder gets dirty at work	−
6. Vacations	Number of paid vacation days per year	+
7. Decides own hours	Whether jobholder can decide when to come to work and when to leave	+
8. Supervision frequency	How many times per hour, day, week, month, or year work is checked	−
9. Union	Whether job is covered by a union contract	+
10. Repetitiveness	Percentage of time jobholder does same things over and over	−
11. Federal employment	Whether jobholder is employed by a federal government agency	+
12. Hierarchy	Whether jobholder's boss has a boss	−
13. Job loss	Probability of losing job within next two years	−
14. State/local employment	Whether jobholder is employed by a state or local government agency	−

[1]A positive sign indicates that the characteristic contributes to job desirability; a negative sign indicates that it detracts from job desirability.

Source: Adapted from Jencks et al., 1988, pp. 1326–1327, 1336.

1350). The separate and identifiable weights of the job desirability index make it possible to calculate both the independent and combined effects of monetary and nonmonetary characteristics. Similar calculations can determine the differential money and nonmoney rewards by race.

Like the attachments to work project, the job desirability study has specified those attributes of work that workers consider important and that together in the appropriate amounts constitute "a good job." We now turn to a line of research which was first formally addressed over 50 years ago (see Hoppock, 1935), but which has provoked interest among all working people ever since work first came to be defined as a separate activity: "How do you like your work?"

JOB SATISFACTION

In a massive review of the job satisfaction literature in the United States, Hamilton and Wright (1986, p. 66) report that "very small proportions of the working population indicate even 'a little dissatisfaction' with their work. In all surveys, the most

Table 9.4   JOB SATISFACTION IN THE AMERICAN LABOR FORCE, 1969, 1973, 1977

Measure of job satisfaction	1969 (N ≥ 1498)	1973 (N ≥ 2042)	1977 (N ≥ 2242)
1. All in all how satisfied would you say you are with your job?			
Very satisfied	46.4%	52.0%	46.7%
Somewhat satisfied	39.1	38.0	41.7
Not too satisfied	11.3	7.6	8.9
Not at all satisfied	3.2	2.4	2.7
2. In general, how well would you say that your job measures up to the sort of job you wanted when you took it?			
Very much like what wanted	63.0%	57.6%	52.5%
Somewhat like what wanted	23.6	33.7	35.9
Not very much like what wanted	13.4	8.7	11.6
3. If a good friend of yours told you he/she was interested in working in a job like yours, what would you tell him/her?			
Would strongly recommend it	63.2%	64.4%	61.8%
Would have doubts about recommending it	24.7	26.4	29.7
Would advise friend against it	12.1	9.2	8.6
4. Knowing what you know now, if you had to decide all over again whether to take the job you now have, what would you decide?			
Decide without hesitation to take same job	64.0%	70.5%	63.9%
Have some second thoughts	26.9	23.7	28.3
Decide definitely *not* to take the job	9.1	5.8	7.8

Source: Quinn and Staines, 1979, pp. 210–211.

common response is 'very satisfied,' the most positive answer provided in the response categories." Table 9.4 presents four commonly used measures of job satisfaction that have been replicated on representative samples of the American labor force over a 10-year period. On each of these four indicators for each of the three time periods in which the survey was conducted, the "most satisfied" response is the one most frequently chosen, usually by the majority of the workers surveyed. According to Blauner (1969, p. 247), "the vast majority of workers, in virtually all occupations and industries, are moderately or highly satisfied, rather than dissatisfied, with their jobs." This is one of the most consistently produced findings in all of industrial research.

The first two questions in Table 9.4 ask workers to evaluate their jobs as they are; the latter two are more hypothetically constructed and therefore call upon different frames of evaluation in which workers are given more latitude to express any dissatisfaction they may have. Particularly in the last question, in which workers are asked to decide all over again, *knowing what they know now*, one would expect there to be more negative assessments of jobs in relation to all other hypothetically available jobs. Yet even in this case, almost two-thirds of those American men and women surveyed would "decide without hesitation to take the same job" they now have; less than 10% would "decide definitely *not* to take the same job." The highest overt dissatisfaction expressed is in response to Question 1, in which, depending upon the survey year, only between 10 to 15 percent of workers are "not too satisfied" or "not at all satisfied." Incidentally, these figures mirror almost exactly the job change rates of American workers during the past 20 years. From 1965 to 1987, the overall annual occupational mobility rate varied between 9 and 12 percent (see Markey and Parks, 1989, p. 4).

Table 9.5 expands the analysis by including data from available comparative studies of British, American, and Japanese workers on these same four measures of job satisfaction. Although the samples in most cases are not nationally representative·as they are in Table 9.4, nevertheless, except for Japanese workers, the results are similar. Overwhelmingly, British workers, like their American counterparts, express satisfaction with the work they do. Only in the two studies that compare American and Japanese workers is the universality of the satisfied worker called into question (see Cole, 1979; Lincoln and Kalleberg, 1985).

Virtually all studies of Japanese work attitudes have noted the relatively low levels of job satisfaction in comparison to workers from other countries (see Lincoln and McBride, 1987, pp. 304–306). Given the greater supposed reciprocal commitment of Japanese employees to their firms, the norm of lifetime employment, and the sense of collective collaboration and common destiny discussed earlier, how is it that these workers score lower on job satisfaction than other workers who do not have these features as part of their employment contract? Cole (1979, p. 238) suggests the following explanation:

> Because Japanese workers are so highly committed to finding fulfillment in their work, they expect a good deal more from work and are therefore likely to display greater dissatisfaction when their expectations are not met. In short, high expectations vis-à-vis work may coexist with low job satisfaction. Indeed this may be the most likely outcome.

Support for Cole's reasoning may be seen in item 7 in Table 9.5. Of all the indicators of job satisfaction presented in this table, Japanese workers score lowest in response to whether or not the job measures up to their expectations. In contrast, a comparable sample of American workers responded approximately three times more favorably, stating that their present jobs are more or less what they initially wanted.

Cole argues that work is more of a central life interest for Japanese than American workers. He cites a comparative study of rank-and-file production workers in which two-thirds of the Japanese employees surveyed thought of their company either as "the central concern" in their lives (9%) or "at least equal in importance" to their personal lives (57%). On the other hand, over three-quarters of the American workers interviewed stated that their company was simply a place for them "to work with management, during work hours, to accomplish mutual

Table 9.5   JOB SATISFACTION OF BRITISH, AMERICAN, AND JAPANESE WORKERS

Measure of job satisfaction	United Kingdom	United States	Japan
1. Percent satisfied with job and working conditions[1]	86%	83%	60%
2. Percent satisfied with job[2]	76	68	—
3. Percent satisfied with job[3]	81	—	—
4. Percent who would advise qualified friend to take same job[4]	—	71	44
5. Percent who would choose same kind of work again[4]	—	54	33
Mean Average Satisfaction[5]			
6. How satisfied? (0 = not at all; 4 = very)	—	2.95	2.12
7. Job measure up to expectations? (0 = not what I wanted; 2 = what I wanted)	—	1.20	.43
8. Recommend job to a friend? (0 = advise against; 1 = second thoughts; 2 = would)	—	1.52	.91
9. Take same job again? (0 = not take; 1 = second thoughts; 2 = would)	—	1.61	.84

[1]Gallup International representative samples of young people aged 18 to 24. See de Boer, 1978, p. 420.

[2]Purposive samples of industrial shop floor workers in several factories. See Hedley, 1981, p. 12.

[3]Nationally representative sample of employed workers. See de Boer, 1978, p. 421.

[4]Representative samples of working males in Detroit and Yokohama. See Cole, 1979, p. 233.

[5]Representative samples of workers in manufacturing plants in central Indiana and a similar manufacturing region in Japan. See Lincoln and Kalleberg, 1985, p. 744.

goals" (54%), or "strictly a place to work and entirely separate" from their personal lives (23%) (see Cole, 1979, p. 237). Because work occupies such a central part of Japanese workers' lives, they therefore have high levels of expectation of their jobs and their employers. Consequently, they are less satisfied with both job and firm than are Western workers (for a British–Japanese comparison, see Dore, 1973, pp. 215–219).

While Cole's argument is reasonable, it is not compelling. Lincoln and his colleagues (1981) suggest alternative explanations. Based on their study of 522 Japanese, Japanese-American, and American workers in 28 Japanese-owned establishments in southern California, they found that work satisfaction varied inversely with "Japaneseness." In other words, native Japanese citizens were less satisfied than Japanese-Americans who in turn were less satisfied than other Americans with no Japanese ancestry. These workers were all employed in the same 28 organizations, and therefore were exposed to the same objective conditions; only their subjective reactions were different.

Lincoln and his research associates explain their findings in two ways. First, they note that organizational structure (i.e., vertical and horizontal differentiation) has a differential impact on Japanese and American workers' attitudes toward work. For example, whereas vertical differentiation is directly related to work satisfaction for Japanese workers, the reverse is true for American workers. It would appear that for Japanese if an organization is not sufficiently hierarchically graded, thus providing a viable career path, they are less satisfied with their work. For American workers, less vertical differentiation is associated with higher work satisfaction, although not significantly so.

The second explanation for differences in work satisfaction by cultural origin offered by Lincoln and his colleagues is that these differences in large part are a measurement artifact produced by different cultural responses to questionnaire surveys. In other words, the substantive differences in work attitudes are more apparent than real.[10] On this point, Dore (1973, p. 218) offers additional comment:

> There is . . . involved, perhaps, a difference in culture or average personality, a difference on a dimension which has cheerfulness and good-humored complacency at one pole and a worried earnestness and anxious questing for self-improvement at the other. That such national differences do exist seems clear from a comparison of the results of various surveys of professed "job satisfaction" carried out in a number of countries.

Whatever may be the "true" cause(s) of the difference in work satisfaction between Japanese and Western workers, whether it be differing work expectations or different structural needs or even measurement artifact, it is certain that its basis is cultural. Lincoln et al. (1981) through their particular research design have demonstrated that it is subjective (cultural) perceptions rather than objective (structural) conditions which produce these differences. Whether Japanese workers express less satisfaction with their work because they have greater expectations, or because they perceive their career paths are potentially blocked, or simply because they have a different way of responding to questions, the fact remains that different cultural orientations and backgrounds do produce different world views.

Antecedents and Consequences of Job Satisfaction

The most important predictor of job satisfaction is occupational level. In general, studies have found that job satisfaction is higher among professionals and managers than it is among lower white collar and blue collar workers (see review by Kahn, 1972, pp. 181–184), and that skilled blue collar workers are more satisfied than lower white-collar workers (see Hedley and Taveggia, 1977). Thus, there are two overlapping direct relationships between occupational level and job satisfaction, one for white-collar workers and one for blue collar workers.[11] Given that occupational level covaries with other important attributes of both the worker (e.g., education, skill, and training) and the job (e.g., pay, benefits, autonomy, power, authority, and career) which are also related to work satisfaction (see Kahn, 1972), it is not surprising that high occupational status results in comparatively greater job satisfaction.

Concerning the consequences of job satisfaction for worker behavior, one long-standing myth in the organizational literature is that a happy worker is a productive worker, or that there is a direct relationship between satisfaction and productivity (i.e., work performance). In fact, it may be stated that one of the underlying reasons for the voluminous research on worker satisfaction has been to increase productivity.[12] However, from all the systematic reviews of the satisfaction–productivity relationship (see, for example, Brayfield and Crockett, 1955; Kahn, 1972; Locke, 1976), the evidence indicates that it is negligible. Locke (1976, pp. 1332–1333) suggests that productivity might be more causally related to satisfaction than the other way around, in that with higher productivity often comes a sense of accomplishment in the work completed and recognition in the form of commendation, merit pay, bonuses, or even promotion.

Interest in job satisfaction has also been stimulated by its purported effects on absenteeism and job turnover. Although Locke (1976, p. 1331) notes that the reported relationships are consistently in the expected direction, the correlations "have not been especially high (usually less than .40)." Concerning absenteeism, it should be noted that the effects of job satisfaction are stronger if absence is measured by frequency (i.e., number of times absent) rather than duration (i.e., length of total absence). These two measures distinguish between absentees who, for example, typically take "long" weekends as opposed to those who are genuinely ill or otherwise unable to work. Concerning job turnover, the stage of the business cycle and the general availability of alternative employment are better predictors than job satisfaction.

In examining the dependent variables that have traditionally been studied in relation to work satisfaction, it is apparent that they are heavily management oriented. In that this research field was initiated by managers and business professionals interested in solving practical industrial relations problems, it is not surprising. As Krupp (1961, pp. 131–132) notes, "the practical needs of the administrator [whose ultimate approval had to be attained in order for the research to take place] dictated the direction that measurement and theorizing should take." Because of this, it can be charged that much of the research on human relations in industry has focused on management goals rather than on the more objective problem of determining individual–work linkages.

> Basically, the goals of management, including reducing turnover and absenteeism, increasing productivity and work-involvement, and overcoming "resistance to change," are among the dependent variables we have studied most frequently. (Nord, 1977, p. 1028)

In an important respect, the research on job satisfaction may be seen as determining the degree of acceptance of prevailing work organizations with their systems of constraints and controls (see Krupp, 1961). In this regard, it would appear that Japanese workers are less accepting than Western workers, but only because of their greater personal involvement in these systems. However, regardless of cultural background and orientation, it is clear that those responsible for devising, instituting, and maintaining these systems are more accepting (i.e., satisfied) than those who are subject to them.

THE CHANGING COMPOSITION OF WORK

As noted throughout this book, the type of work we do has changed over time and is still undergoing profound transformation. Therefore, an important research question is whether the changing composition of work has an impact on individual–work linkages. If it has, then what are its specific effects? In order to address these questions, it is necessary first to identify and then to measure the actual changes that have occurred so that we may determine precisely how they affect the relationship between workers and their work.

One change, long identified as resulting directly from the combined processes of specialization, mechanization, and standardization, is the diminution of work skills.

> For over two centuries social scientists believed that the mechanization of labor and the factory system speeded up the division of labor, diluted workers' skills, and increased their unhappiness. In 1776 Adam Smith described the stultifying effects of specialization in terms quite like those that Marx used in 1850 to condemn capitalism's mechanization of labor. And in 1893 Durkheim condemned as immoral the process whereby mechanization was turning workers into appendages of machines. (Form, 1987, pp. 29–30).

Subsequent technological and organizational developments, including the introduction of the assembly line and mass production methods designed according to "principles of scientific management," appeared to erode work skills even further. According to the Report of a Special Task Force to the Secretary of Health, Education, and Welfare (O'Toole et al., 1973, p. 19), while the rationalization of work may produce organizational efficiency, "it rigidifies tasks, reduces the range of skills utilized by most of the occupations, increases routinization, and opens the door to job dissatisfaction for a new generation of highly educated workers."

Currently, some researchers contend that "deskilling" arises not so much out of technical considerations involving productive efficiency but out of management's desire to gain total control over the enterprise (see, for example, Shaiken, 1984). Thus, the decision to degrade skills is primarily social, not technical. Given the tremendously enhanced capability that computers can offer, the prospects could be ominous (see Box 10-3, **Computers as Strikebreakers**, in Chapter 10).

> . . . management's development of new machines and systems reflects the desire to increase control over production, over the activities of workers as well as over the movement of materials. This propels the design of automation in a direction that seeks to minimize the disruptive potential of workers. There are two ways to do this. One is to automate the job entirely; this is not always technically possible or economically feasible. The other is to reduce the input of the worker on the job. This calls for designs that reduce skill requirements, transfer decision-making off the shop floor, and exert tighter control over the workers who remain. The result can be more boring and stressful work in a more tightly controlled work environment. (Shaiken, 1984, p. 5)

This is a strong indictment of the industrialization process and of management's role in it. It is charged that the systematic stripping of workers' skills results in unhappiness, job dissatisfaction, boredom, and stress. Workers become alienated both from the products of their labor as well as the means by which these products (including services) are produced. Consequently, they lose the possibility of attachment to work normally associated with craftworkers and professionals. Furthermore, it is charged that deskilling is a cumulative process that will result in the proletarianization of an increasingly larger group of blue- and white-collar workers, including professionals and middle managers. In this regard, Braverman (1974, p. 139) declares that "the transformation of working humanity into a 'labor force', a 'factor of production', an instrument of capital, is an incessant and unending process."

Another important implication of deskilling is that earnings are affected. To the extent that a work force is deskilled, there is justification for paying lower wages and salaries. Although this would be less true in Japan where earnings are tied more to extra-job characteristics (e.g., age and seniority) than they are in either the United States or Great Britain (Amaya, 1988, p. 108), nevertheless a systematic deskilling of the labor force has serious potential repercussions for society as a whole.

What is the evidential base of these charges? How does one determine the extent to which the contemporary postindustrial labor force is less skilled than it was 10 or 50 or 100 years earlier? Presumably, if deskilling is a function of industrialization, then the labor force prior to the industrial revolution would have been more skilled on average than at any time since. On this point, Blauner (1969, pp. 245–246) offers the following observation:

> When we read modern accounts of what work and workers were like before the industrial revolution, we continually find that the dominant image of the worker of that period is the craftsman. Viewed as an independent producer in his home or small shop with complete control over the pace and scheduling of his work, making the whole product rather than a part of it, and taking pride in the creativity of his skilled tasks, his traits are typically contrasted with those of the alienated factory worker—the allegedly characteristic producer of modern society.
>
> It is remarkable what an enormous impact this *contrast* of the craftsman with the factory hand has had on intellectual discussions of work and workers in modern society, *notwithstanding its lack of correspondence to present and historical realities*. For indeed, craftsmen, far from being typical workers of the past era, accounted for less than 10 percent of the medieval labor force, and the peasant, who was actually the representative laborer, was, in the words of the Belgian socialist Henri DeMan, "practically nothing more than a working beast." Furthermore, the real character of the craftsman's work has been romanticized by the prevalent tendency to idealize the past, whereas much evidence suggests that modern work does not fit the black portrait of meaningless alienation. In fact, it has been asserted "that in modern society there is far greater scope for skill and craftsmanship than in any previous society, and that far more people are in a position to use such skills." (Emphasis in the original.)

In order to assess accurately the contention that the labor force is being deskilled, it is necessary to have reliable data that are comparable over time. Unfortunately, this means that we are primarily limited to those years following World War II, although one systematic study did span the entire twentieth century (see Spenner, 1983). Basically, there are five strategies that may be adopted: (1) comparison of the occupational shift of jobs over time by skill level (i.e., occupational composition); (2) examination of the average skill content of those occupations that represent a net addition to the economy (occupational growth); (3) examination of the average skill content of those occupations projected to grow most rapidly (projected occupational demand); (4) comparison of the average skill levels in the regulated and informal economies over time (informal economy); and (5) comparison of the skill content of the same jobs over time (job content).

Occupational Composition

As noted in Chapter 6, the largest occupational shift in this century has been the movement out of the primary (mainly agricultural) sector and the corresponding increase in the tertiary sector. This along with a substantial increase in female labor force participation has occurred in all postindustrial societies. Thus, in order to address the deskilling hypothesis, it is necessary to apply some standard measure of skill against all occupations over discrete time periods to determine whether there has been a net skill loss or gain.

A reliable operational definition of skill that can be applied to all occupations is difficult to construct. One easily computed measure, level of education, reveals that the average formal education received by all labor force participants has increased dramatically over the century. In the United States, almost two-fifths of the labor force had at least some college training in 1986 compared with just over one-quarter in 1972 (Bureau of Labor Statistics, 1988, p. 9). Furthermore, workers in the service sector are more highly educated than those in the other sectors (Bednarzik and Shiells, 1989, p. 37). However, this indirect measure of skill is rejected by advocates of deskilling on the grounds that whereas the capitalist system demands various credentials of employability, these credentials are largely irrelevant to the work that people actually do (see Braverman, 1974). The skills that workers have are underutilized.

According to Spenner (1983), skill can be conceived as residing in the job rather than the person. It is comprised of two dimensions: substantive complexity and autonomy-control. Based on eight studies that systematically measured occupational skill change using indicators of either or both of these dimensions, Spenner notes that five found evidence to substantiate the claim of a modest skill upgrading, two found essentially no change, and one reported a decline in skill as measured by the percent of the labor force classified as supervisors. From the evidence, Spenner (1983, p. 834) concludes that "the dominant impression from these studies is one of approximate aggregate stability. Yet virtually all of the aggregate studies show upgrading and downgrading occurring within sectors or subgroups of the population." In other words, there is no empirical foundation for overall skill decline measured at this level. Any loss of skill observed in some sectors of the labor force is matched by an increase in skill requirements in other sectors.

Occupational Growth

In a 1988 article, Loveman and Tilly reviewed studies of employment growth in the United States, and attempted to answer whether the jobs created are on the whole "good jobs or bad jobs." Compared with other countries, job growth in the United States has been substantial: "from 1973 to 1986 total civilian employment grew by 28 percent in the United States compared with 11 per cent in Japan and 0 percent in the European Community" (Loveman and Tilly, 1988, p. 593). Virtually all these jobs were in the tertiary sector, which traditionally pays lower wages than those paid in manufacturing. Furthermore, this wage gap increased between 1973 and 1986, as did earnings inequality within and between occupations generally.

This has prompted some analysts to conclude that structural occupational recomposition (i.e, changes in the occupational mix of jobs) is responsible for the increase in low-paid service sector jobs (see Bluestone and Harrison, 1982). On the other hand, Loveman and Tilly cite studies that suggest the rise in low-paid service jobs is cyclical (i.e., due to the recession of 1981-82) and, therefore, neither long-term nor structural.

While the evidence points to a disproportional increase in "bad jobs" in the United States during the past 15 years, this fact should be evaluated in comparative context. As indicated above, there was little or no job growth in either the European or Japanese economies. In part, then, these "bad jobs" may be attributed to government policy that has encouraged labor force expansion by more than one-quarter during a recessionary period with lower than average productivity growth. Consequently, the alternative to "bad jobs" may well be no jobs at all. As Loveman and Tilly (1988, p. 593) state, "Over the long run, real wage growth and, more generally, increases in a society's standard of living are limited by the rate of productivity growth." Thus, the fact that the proportion of low-paid jobs has increased is moderated partly by the additional fact that on average between 1972 and 1987 *all* American workers experienced losses in their real earnings.

Projected Occupational Demand

As noted in Chapter 6, by far the largest projected job demand will occur in the tertiary sector, such that by the year 2000, nearly 80 percent of an expanded American labor force will provide services in some capacity (see Figure 6.2).[13] Thus, the trend noted from 1973 to 1986 will continue. However, it is by no means apparent that so called "bad jobs" will increase at the expense of "good jobs."

Table 9.6 lists the 40 occupations that are expected to contribute most to overall employment growth. In 1986, these 40 occupations accounted for 38 percent of all those employed in the civilian labor force. By the turn of the century, because of the fact that these occupations are growing most rapidly, it is expected that they will comprise 42 percent of all workers. The table lists occupations according to whether they are less or more skilled. Following Spenner (1983), the skill classification is based on both substantive complexity and autonomy-control.

Note at the bottom of the table that while the less-skilled occupations are expected to increase by almost 29%, the more-skilled jobs will increase at a slightly higher rate. The consequence of this differential rate of increase is that by the year 2000, the more-skilled occupations will constitute a marginally larger proportion of the top 40 than they did in 1986. While not all occupations are represented in this table, nevertheless there is no indication that less-skilled jobs are replacing the more skilled. Overall, these data suggest that the skill composition of the labor force will remain relatively stable in the forseeable future.

Informal Economy

Another way to address the deskilling hypothesis is to examine the size and nature of the informal economy over time. The informal or underground economy consists of those income-generating activities that occur "outside the arena of the normal, regulated economy" (Portes and Sassen-Koob, 1987, p. 30). Although this definition includes criminal occupations, we will consider only those work activities that are illegal simply because they are not reported. Examples include exchanging goods or services (bartering) without reporting the value received, off-the-books employment, and other unreported entrepreneurial activity. Obviously, if the value of goods and services and wages and profits are not formally reported, then no record exists by which these benefits may be taxed. Thus, the informal economy coexists with the regulated economy by operating in the margin between the value of goods and services in the open market minus any taxes owed.

Another important feature of the informal economy is that it is not subject to the laws and regulatory agencies that guide practices and behavior in the legitimate economy. Consequently, various cost-cutting measures can be employed that are not permissible in the open economy. For example, "by toiling off the books, workers give up minimum wage and overtime regulations, health insurance, pensions, occupational safety standards—in other words, social security in the broadest sense" (Mattera, 1985, p. 122).

The informal economy is of relevance to the deskilling hypothesis if it can be demonstrated that (1) this economy has expanded over time, and (2) its average skill level is significantly lower than the regulated economy. If both these conditions prevail, this would lend credence to deskilling in that it has not been ascertained in the regulated economy (see *Occupational Composition*). However, given the fact that the informal economy operates "underground," good reliable data are difficult to obtain.

In a comprehensive analysis of research studies that have attempted to estimate the size of the informal economy in Great Britain and the United States, Mattera (1985) draws similar conclusions for each country. He states that in terms of both the proportion of the gross national product contributed by informal economic activity and the relative size of the labor force, the informal sector accounts for approximately 10 percent.[14] It is important to note that all business is not conducted exclusively in either one economy or the other; crossovers do occur. Thus, although 10 percent represents the best estimate available, the boundary between the two economies is extremely fluid and permeable.

With regard to the size of the informal economy over time, Castells and Portes (1989) argue that although there has been an historic movement away from infor-

Table 9.6   OCCUPATIONS WITH LARGEST PROJECTED JOB GROWTH BY SKILL LEVEL,[1] 1986 to 2000

Less-skilled occupations	Number employed	
	1986 (000s)	2000 (000s)[2]
1. Salespersons, retail	3579	4780
2. Waiters and waitresses	1702	2454
3. Janitors and cleaners	2676	3280
4. Cashiers	2165	2740
5. Truck drivers, light and heavy	2211	2736
6. General office clerks	2361	2824
7. Food counter, fountain, and related	1500	1949
8. Nursing aides, orderlies	1224	1658
9. Secretaries	3234	3658
10. Guards	794	1177
11. Food preparation workers	949	1273
12. Receptionists and information clerks	682	964
13. Gardeners and groundskeepers	767	1005
14. Stock clerks, sales floor	1087	1312
15. Dining room, cafeteria attendants, barroom helpers	433	631
16. Cooks, short order and fast food	591	775
17. Bartenders	396	553
18. Medical assistants	132	251
19. Legal assistants, technicians	170	272
Total employed	26,653	34,292
Percent of total	62.5%	62.0%
Percent increase		28.7%

More-skilled occupations		
1. Registered nurses	1406	2018
2. General managers and top executives	2383	2965
3. Accountants and auditors	945	1322
4. Computer programmers	479	813
5. Teachers, kindergarten and elementary	1527	1826
6. Computer systems analysts, EDP	331	582
7. Cooks, restaurant	520	759
8. Licensed practical nurses	631	869
9. Maintenance repairers, general utility	1039	1270
10. First-line supervisors and managers	956	1161
11. Electrical and electronics engineers	401	592
12. Lawyers	527	718

Table 9.6 **OCCUPATIONS WITH LARGEST PROJECTED JOB GROWTH BY SKILL LEVEL,**[1] 1986 to 2000 (continued)

More skilled occupations (continued)	Number employed	
	1986 (000s)	2000 (000s)[2]
13. Carpenters	1010	1192
14. Financial managers	638	792
15. Food service and lodging managers	509	663
16. Teachers, secondary	1128	1280
17. Electrical and electronics technicians	313	459
18. Real estate sales agents	313	451
19. Computer operators	263	387
20. Social workers	365	485
21. Marketing, advertising, public relations managers	323	427
Total employed	16,007	21,031
Percent of total	37.5%	38.0%
Percent increase		31.4%

[1]Occupations are classified as "more skilled" if they score 2 or less on any of the functional ratings of job complexity in relation to Data, People, or Things computed in the *Dictionary of Occupational Titles*. Furthermore, all supervisory and managerial occupations are also here defined as "more skilled." See Robinson et al., 1969, pp. 433–453.

[2]Of the three employment projections calculated by the Bureau of Labor Statistics, the middle or "moderate" one is presented in this table.

Source: Adapted from *Statistical Abstracts of the United States*, 1989, p. 387.

mal activity with increasing industrialization and bureaucratization, nevertheless since the mid-1970s this trend has been reversed in all developed countries. Reasons advanced include union avoidance, contracting out, deregulation, international competition, and global recession. While some of these causes may be seen as ephemeral, others are of a more long-lasting nature. Thus, it is likely that "the level of informal economic activity, if not actually on the increase, is at least staying the same" (Harding and Jenkins, 1989, p. 72).

In attempting to identify the skills employed in the informal economy and whether these have changed over time, the data are even less amenable to direct analysis. As Castells and Portes (1989, pp. 25–26) state, "The informal economy encompasses such a diversity of situations and activities that it represents a heterogeneous universe, irreducible to any subset of specific rules of economic calculation." However, Portes and Sasson-Koob (1987) argue that by examining the economic activity of very small firms (i.e., employing fewer than 10 workers), which have increased in number in both Great Britain and the United States in recent years (see Standing, 1989 for British data), inferences can be made as to what transpires in the informal economy.

Very small establishments (VSEs) are relevant to the question of informality for two reasons. First, by reason of their low visibility, ease of displacement, and other factors

VSEs provide the most appropriate setting for casual hiring, nonreporting of income, and other informal practices. Direct observational studies . . . indicate that, because of extensive regulation, many small concerns are forced to obtain licenses (and thus appear in the aggregate statistics), although their labor practices are mostly informal. Second, VSEs are easier to convert into totally underground enterprises. While it is generally difficult to informalize a plant employing hundreds of workers, this is not the case for one with a few employees. Such a firm can close down "officially" one day and reopen the next as an underground concern. (Portes and Sasson-Koob, 1987, pp. 42–43)

What do VSEs do? Recent data (1983) for the United States indicate that 85% of all contracting and building firms employ fewer than 10 employees, and consequently according to Portes and Sasson-Koob (1987, p. 45) are prime candidates for informal activity.[15] Other industries previously identified as major contributors to the informal sector include apparel and textile products (i.e., the garment trade), footwear, electronics, household furniture, and various consumer services.

Concerning the skill of the workers involved in these industries, Sasson-Koob (1989, p. 74), reporting on a detailed study of informalization trends in New York City, found that while many jobs in these industries were "unskilled, with no training or advancement opportunities, and involving repetitive tasks," the growing concentration of the construction and furniture industries which for the most part employ highly skilled workers counteracts this trend. Data from the Miami metropolitan area corroborate these findings (see Portes and Sasson-Koob, 1987).

Thus, although it can be stated that the informal sector has been increasing both in terms of its contribution to the national economy and numbers employed, contrary to popular opinion not all workers in this sector are unskilled and exploited. The growth of particular industries has brought about "a certain reskilling of the labor force" (Sasson-Koob, 1989, p. 74). While these data are less than ideal to address the deskilling hypothesis, they are virtually the only data available given the nature of the activities involved. We may conclude that given the estimates of the size of the informal economy plus that fact that both unskilled and skilled workers occupy it in significant proportions, the claim of widespread deskilling cannot be sustained by what goes on in this sector of the labor force.

Job Content

The *Dictionary of Occupational Titles* (DOT) is a systematic and comprehensive source from which it is possible to assess the degree of change in the average skill of the same jobs over time. Whereas several studies have examined particular clusters of jobs from one era to another, or have engaged in organizational case studies over time, it is impossible to generalize these results to the labor force at large. The DOT, on the other hand, can be used to make generalizations. It is the most inclusive and detailed compendium of all occupations in the United States at three separate times (1949, 1965, and 1977) such that one can compare the same job types over three decades.[16] The Dictionary consists of specific analyses of over 12,000 individual jobs. Of the many variables examined, skill is prominent among them.

The indicators include: levels of involvement with data, people and things; general educational development (GED; mathematical, language, and reasoning development required); specific vocational preparation (SVP; total training time for an average performance at the job); 11 aptitudes (including verbal, numerical, spatial, motor coordination, and manual dexterity); and 12 work conditions (including variation, repetitiveness, discretion, direction, precision, and working under stress). (Spenner, 1983:830).

Of the eight systematic studies of skill change in jobs reviewed by Spenner (1983), five used the *Dictionary of Occupational Titles* to obtain their sample of jobs. Four of these studies found a small upgrading in the skill content required over time, while the other concluded that while there was evidence of both upgrading and downgrading of skills, in total there was virtually no net change. Of the remaining three studies, two compared the results of successive national surveys, while the third employed a retrospective question on the job skills required of respondents five years earlier. One of these studies found a small upgrading of skills, one reported no net change, and the remaining study concluded that there was a small decline in skill over time. Consequently, in examining the broad spectrum of jobs that comprise the work performed in the American labor force, there is scant evidence to support the deskilling hypothesis. In fact, the data support the reverse claim of upgrading more than they indicate a lessening of skills.

The deskilling hypothesis arose from various studies of work and industry in which the combined processes of specialization, mechanization, and standardization mentioned above were clearly and specifically employed by management to break down complex jobs into relatively simple task components each of which could then be performed by unskilled and semiskilled workers (see the box items on "Time is Money" and "Taking the Work to the Men" in Chapter 3). Under the guiding principles of scientific management and the division of labor, it appeared to some that the entire work process was becoming deskilled and therefore dehumanized (see, for example, Braverman, 1974). Early studies of factory workers, particularly in the automobile industry, chronicled the rudimentary skills required of workers engaged in highly repetitive tasks paced by assembly lines over which they had no control (see, for example, Walker and Guest, 1952; Chinoy, 1955; Kornhauser, 1965).

While it is true that assembly line work is designed to be accomplished mainly by semiskilled machine operatives, Blauner (1969) marshaled data that indicated that this type of work is not nearly so pervasive and therefore characteristic of work in modern industrial society as has commonly been believed by researchers and laypersons alike. For example, in the automobile industry, "the conveyor belt industry par excellence," Blauner (1969, pp. 248–249) determined that assembly line workers comprise less than five percent of all workers employed in the manufacture, sales, repair, and servicing of automobiles. They are far outnumbered by skilled workers in all branches of the industry.

Subsequent advocates of the deskilling hypothesis pointed to automation as producing a society of "robots" (Sheppard and Herrick, 1972); and, most recently, the advent of computer-aided design and manufacture (CAD/CAM), numerical control (NC), and flexible manufacturing systems (FMS) has prompted other critics to decry "transferring the control of a machine from a skilled worker to a preprogrammed set of instructions" (Shaiken, 1984, p. 47). (See Box 1-1 on "Flexible Manufacturing Systems" in Chapter 1.)

While undoubtedly deskilling has occurred in some jobs and even in whole occupations, the data on the entire labor force indicate that this is not a general phenomenon. There is no evidence to suggest that as a result of the industrialization process all of us are being constantly and systematically stripped of our work skills. Rather, it is more reasonable to state that work skills, like job descriptions and the organizations we work in, are in a constant state of change.

Changing skills are just a small part of the complex formula that makes up the individual–work relationship. The ultimate value that we place on work is dependent not only upon our own training, talent, and personal circumstances, but also upon the values and structure of society, the characteristics of the workplace, the particular job we do, and the rewards we receive. Out of all of this come our reactions to that activity which is both a necessary curse and an important link to the larger society.

SUMMARY

9.1   Money is a universal core motivation to work. Money provides the means for survival. Without secure employment, workers cannot perform to their utmost capabilities.

9.2   Under the Japanese system of employment, job security is accorded high priority. Operating from the norm of lifetime employment, many firms set up internal labor markets to regulate the flow of employees through various organizational ranks and positions during the course of their working careers. On the other hand, the British and American systems of employment emphasize greater occupational mobility. Ideally, external labor markets operate to match person to job such that workers find positions individually tailored to their particular needs and circumstances.

9.3   In addition to money, motivations to work are many and varied. Potential sources of attachment to work include systems of the work environment, workplace objects and conditions, and payoffs such as perquisites, power, authority, status, and career (see Table 9.1). Work attachments vary according to personal circumstance, training, culture, the employing organization, type of job performed, and the rewards received.

9.4   Individual–work linkages may be summarized as follows: (1) money or the need for survival forms the initial and universal linkage to work; (2) acceptance of this fact promotes acceptance of and attachment to the basic conditions that constitute the employment contract; and (3) because all jobs are not the same and because individuals can exercise varying degrees of choice as to their employment, attachments are formed to those work features over which workers have choice. The more choice workers have, the greater is their attachment to work.

9.5.   According to recent research on American workers, earnings as well as 13 nonmonetary job characteristics are most important in determining what is a "good job." The nonmonetary aspects include features related to educational requirements, hours of work, training and promotion opportunities, technical job characteristics, fringe benefits, autonomy, the organizational setting, and job security (see Table 9.3).

9.6   Overwhelmingly, British and American workers at all organizational ranks report that they are satisfied with their jobs. Only between 10 to 15 percent state that they are dissatisfied. On the other hand, Japanese workers register significantly lower levels of job satisfaction. Of the reasons advanced for this discrepancy, all of them are culturally based. Either they stem from the nature of the employment relationship and the perceived centrality of work in Japanese workers' lives, or from different interpretations of organization structure, or from a different cultural response set.

9.7   The independent variable most strongly related to job satisfaction is occupational level. Greater job satisfaction among professionals and managers is explained by the fact that other variables such as pay, fringe benefits, authority, and prestige covary with occupational level. The dependent variables most researched in relation to job satisfaction are productivity, absenteeism, and job turnover. Of these, productivity is negligibly related to job satisfaction, while there are moderate inverse relationships between satisfaction and absenteeism and turnover.

9.8   Researchers have attempted to discover what effects the changing compositon of work has on individual–work linkages. One prominent hypothesis states that various processes inherent in industrializtion have diminished work skills, which in turn results in job dissatisfaction, boredom, stress, and alienation from work. Furthermore, management in seeking greater control over the total work environment has played an active role in the cumulative deskilling of work.

9.9   To test the deskilling hypothesis, the following procedures were employed: (1) examining the skill composition of pre- and postindustrial labor forces; (2) determining the effects on skill of major occupational shifts in the labor force; (3) assessing the skill content of those occupations that represent a net growth to the economy and those occupations that are projected to grow most rapidly in the future; (4) measuring the growth of the informal economy over time and comparing the average skill level of this economy with the regulated economy; and (5) evaluating the skill content in the same jobs over time.

9.10 The conclusion drawn from all these tests of the deskilling hypothesis is that while some jobs and occupations have experienced deskilling, others have been upgraded. There is no evidence of a cumulative job deskilling; in fact, most of the evidence points to a modest upgrading in skill. Consequently, while the changing composition of work does produce changes in individual–work relationships, there is no systematic decline in skill with the implications that this entails.

NOTES

1. Obviously, the larger the organization, the greater is the possibility that the system of internal recruitment and promotion will work to the mutual advantage of both the employees and the organization. In fact, Dore (1973, pp. 301–337) notes that the concept of lifetime employment is restricted mainly to large firms.
2. Given the Japanese norm of lifetime employment, one could surmise that Japanese workers value routine more than do their Western counterparts.
3. Within different organizations and within organizations in different cultures, the dimensions upon which status is conferred vary somewhat. For example, in Japanese organizations seniority is a more important status dimension than it is in Western firms (see Lincoln and McBride, 1987).
4. For example, socioeconomic status (SES) is a composite measure of status based on three dimensions: income, education, and occupational standing. All people with high SES

have high rankings on each of these dimensions; similarly, all people with low SES rank toward the bottom on all three scales. See Haug, 1977, for further elaboration.

5. For example, in his research Gouldner noted that professors became department heads, faculty deans, and even university presidents as part of their career progression. Other professionals such as engineers and accountants also seek career advancement in managerial positions for which they have received no formal training. See, for example, Dalton, 1950; Goldner and Ritti, 1967.

6. The fixed responses offered for this question were: (1) "I would stop working"; (2) "I would continue to work in the same job"; (3) "I would continue to work, but under different conditions." Unfortunately, responses 2 and 3 were combined in the presentation of results so that it is impossible to disaggregate them (see Harpaz, 1989).

7. In other research also (see Hedley, 1986c, pp. 510–511; Taveggia and Hedley, 1976) it has been found that British workers are considerably more instrumentally oriented toward work than are American workers. As indicated in Chapter 10, perhaps the major reason explaining this difference is the class-based hostilities that characterize British industrial relations. This "permanent state of latent beligerency," as Dore (1973, p. 144) describes it, may induce many workers to state that they would stop working if they could afford to live independently.

8. This question, posed at the beginning and the end of the interview, asked workers, "Compared to all the jobs in the country, if an average job is 100, what number would you give your job?" (Jencks et al., 1988, p. 1334).

9. Discrepancies in result depending upon whether "self" or "other" is being evaluated could explain at least in part the somewhat paradoxical findings reported in Table 9.2. On the one hand, respondents are stating that the principal motivating factor of *others* to work is money, while on the other hand they *themselves* would work regardless of financial necessity. Because work is a value in industrial society, workers portray themselves as subscribing to this value more than they do when assessing others.

10. It is also important to note that Lincoln et al. (1981) did not achieve differences in work satisfaction between Americans and Japanese of the same magnitude as those reported in Table 9.5. On a five-point satisfaction scale, the results are as follows: Americans, 3.88; Japanese-Americans, 3.68; Japanese, 3.54. See Lincoln et al., 1981, p. 102.

11. While the relationship between occupational level and job satisfaction has been firmly established for men, there is some question as to just how strong this relationship is for women (see Hedley and Taveggia, 1977).

12. Locke (1976, p. 1297) states that up to 1972, 3350 articles or dissertations were produced on the subject of job satisfaction.

13. Overall, between 1986 and 2000, employment growth is projected to be 19 percent. See *Statistical Abstracts of the United States*, 1989, p. 387.

14. In another research review, Harding and Jenkins (1989, p. 73) state that similar to the United States, Japan has a "very small" unofficial or underground economy. However, no quantitative estimates are provided.

15. The increase of small contractors and builders in the United States has been associated with the movement toward gentrification in major urban areas.

16. Although the DOT represents the best source to compare jobs over time, there are problems concerning how inclusive the Dictionary is, and how independent job evaluations are from one edition to the next. See Spenner, 1983, pp. 830–831.

Chapter

10

Worker-Management Relations

Power relations always involve mutual dependence and mutual antagonism. In the context of the employment relationship, employers are dependent on employees to perform work tasks to make a profit or, as with public employees, to provide a service. In parallel, employees are dependent on employers to pay wages or salaries so they can live the good life. In simple terms, they come together because each wants something the other possesses: in this respect they are mutually dependent.

Logically, it is in the self-interest of each employer to buy labour as cheaply as possible and, in parallel, it is in the self-interest of employees to sell their services at as high a price as they can. This conflict of interests is not something which only exists during the process of establishing the terms and conditions of the exchange but, like the relationship itself, is a continuing and permanent feature. . . . It is always there because it is in the nature of the employment relationship—and this feature accounts for the mutual antagonism alongside the mutual dependence.

Keenoy, 1985, pp. 218–224

*I*n the preceding four chapters, I have charted both similarities and differences in the effects of industrialization in Great Britain, the United States, and Japan. While industrialization produces structural problems that are similar wherever it is introduced, we have noted that the "solutions" chosen can and do vary according to cultural predilections. Nowhere is this more apparent than in the formalized relationships established between workers and managers.

Worker–management relations, also known as industrial relations, are the institutionalized framework within which the value premises underlying work as well as the more mundane specification of its performance (e.g., rights and responsibilities, type and amount of payment, hours and conditions of employment, and so on) are negotiated and set out in terms of contractual and reciprocal obligations. In determining the ground rules of the management and performance of work, the actors involved generally adopt the values and social conventions of the larger culture in order to make their cases. In a very real sense, worker–management relations are a microcosm of the social interactional patterns which are prevalent in the larger society (see Hofstede, 1979).

During the industrial revolution, conditions of work were not negotiated by those responsible for its performance; they were dictated by employers who according to the prevailing values and norms of the time were justified in the unilateral conditions they imposed. As described in Chapter 3, some workers, many of them children, did not even exercise choice with respect to who they worked for, let alone the conditions under which they labored or the wages they received. They were bound into a life of perpetual servitude. However, with changes in values and the normative structure also came changes in the terms by which employment and its surrounding conditions were determined. In fact, early workers actively fought to achieve many of the changes that now form the institutionalized patterns of worker–management relations that are presently operating in the three countries under examination.

The nature of work in complex, highly differentiated organizations is such that all employees (workers and managers alike) perform many different functions in order to produce integrated organizational goods and services. With a complex division of labor, problems arise in defining and coordinating activities, establishing appropriate rules of operating procedure, and determining individual contribution and worth. As mentioned above, during the early stages of industrialization, these problems were deemed to be the sole prerogative of owners or their designates (managers), and the "solutions" they arrived at were the ones that were universally instituted. However, over time, workers by combining into labor unions were able to challenge management's exclusive "right" to determine the conditions of employment and compensation received. The pages of labor history, filled with cases of protracted confrontation, acrimonious debate, and tremendous loss of life, livelihood, and property, are testament to the fact that this was a battle of the first magnitude. It was, and still is, a struggle in which all parties concerned—owners, shareholders, chief executives, managers, and various categories of workers and their representative unions and professional associations—each propose "just solutions" that will satisfactorily resolve the problems arising out of their division of labor.

Thus, work organizations may be perceived as comprising various different subgroups all vying to achieve and protect their particular interests. Whereas many issues form the subject of their scrutiny, a central focus concerns the decision of who gets how much, and whether the allocation of organizational proceeds is "just" and "fair" both in terms of other organizational members and in relation to outside reference groups. The history of industrial relations has made one fact abundantly clear: The goals of management are not the goals of all.

We begin this chapter by highlighting features that are common to the industrial relations experience of workers and managers in all three of the countries under examination. This is followed by a more detailed presentation of those characteristics that make each system of worker–management relations culturally unique. However, despite these differences in approach and experience, the data reveal that the organized labor movements in Great Britain, the United States, and Japan are all currently in decline. The latter part of the chapter will discuss the points of conflict that have precipitated this decline and will conclude by offering a likely scenario of worker–management relations in the twenty-first century.

LABOR UNIONS IN GREAT BRITAIN, THE UNITED STATES, AND JAPAN

Table 10.1 reveals the percentage of nonmanagerial employees in the labor forces of the United Kingdom, United States, and Japan who are members of labor unions or employee associations. The most recent figures for 1987–1988 indicate substantially more variation between country than those 30 years earlier. Whereas approximately half of all British employees have been union members until very recently, union membership in the United States has been in constant decline since 1945 such that currently fewer than one in five workers is a union member.[1] The figures for Japan show that up until 1980, more than a third of all workers were union members. However, similar to the figures for Great Britain and the United States, union membership among the Japanese also declined during the 1980s.

Before focusing on the peculiarities of the industrial relations scene in each of these countries, it is instructive to note the overall similarities. First, the labor movement in each country was born of protest—protest over changing job skills, protest against rigidly enforced workplace rules and schedules, and protest against bare subsistence wages that offered no hope for improvement. While it must be noted that workers had traditionally been treated in inhumane and dictatorial ways in the past, it was the factory system, which necessitated that large number of workers be gathered in one place, that served as the vehicle by which this protest was mounted. Except for armies, never before had large groups of people in similarly miserable circumstances been assembled together.

Another similarity is that generally the government in each of the three countries sided with the employer in putting down these protests and uprisings. Worker combines or unions were outlawed at various stages in all three countries, although they still continued to form. Pelling (1963, p. 13) notes that in England it was not surprising that government generally favored the employer in that "until the later nineteenth century working men could hardly ever vote in Parliamentary elections,[2] still less stand for Parliament themselves. . . . At any time before then, the claims of labour could be put before Parliament and the Government only by

Table 10.1   UNION MEMBER DENSITY IN THE UNITED KINGDOM, UNITED STATES, AND JAPAN, 1955–1988

| Year | Union members as a percentage of nonagricultural employees in: | | |
	United Kingdom	United States	Japan
1955	46%	34%[1]	38%
1960	45	32[1]	34
1965	45	29[1]	36
1970	52	31	35
1975	54	29	35
1980	57	25	31
1984	53	19	29
1987–1988	42[2]	17	27

[1]Figures exclude members of employee associations.

[2]Union members as a percent of civilian labor force. Hence, the 1987–1988 figure is deflated in relation to the preceding figures for Great Britain, which are computed on the base of nonagricultural workers.

Sources: For 1955–1984, Goldfield, 1987, p. 16; for United Kingdom in 1987, Towers, 1989, pp. 174–175; for the United States and Japan in 1988, Freeman and Rebick, 1989, pp. 579–580.

petitioning or lobbying, by public demonstrations and pamphleteering, or more crudely, by disturbance of the peace."

The first unions to mount a successful challenge to the exclusive rights of managers were comprised of skilled craftworkers. Because their unique skills were scarce and at the same time much in demand, they were in a far more powerful position vis-à-vis employers to negotiate favorable conditions of employment than were less-skilled workers. The first of these craft unions, consisting of workers in the building and printing trades, actually predated the industrial revolution (Reynolds, 1959).

The second, much larger, wave of unionism was represented by factory workers and other semiskilled laborers (e.g., miners) who organized on an industry-wide basis. Because these workers had no unique specialized skills, only by banding together in large numbers could they offer a sufficiently powerful voice. This period in the labor union movement was its most contentious as violent struggles ensued between labor and management. In Japan, the government went so far as to ban all unions in 1940 (Karsh, 1976, p. 892). While craft unions had organized first, it was industrial unions that posed the greater threat to management. Craftworkers, numerically a small proportion of the labor force, did not threaten the status quo; rather they wished to ensure their place within it. On the other hand, industrial unions, potentially representing the vast majority of the working masses, could abolish irrevocably management's sole right to dictate the terms and conditions of work—hence the conflict.

The third wave of unionism, occurring largely over the past three decades, took place among white-collar workers primarily in the public sector. Until this time, the labor movement was basically comprised of male blue-collar workers in manufacturing or construction jobs working in private industry. However, as the traditional recruiting ground became saturated, and as both employment in the tertiary sector and female labor force participation increased, white-collar public sector employees (female and male) at all occupational levels became prime union targets.

In Britain, fully 82% of the public sector were union members in 1979 (Bain and Price, 1983, p. 10).[3] Compared to the overall union rate of 57% in 1980 (see Table 10.1), the public sector is the most highly unionized of all branches of industry in Great Britain. In the United States, although the public sector in 1980 was unionized in approximately the same degree as the labor force as a whole, in 1960 only 13% of public employees were union members (Troyer, 1987, p. 247). Consequently, while private sector unionism was declining over these two decades, the growth rate in the public sector was the highest in the country. In Japan, whereas the overall union rate in 1980 was 31% (see Table 10.1), in the public sector it was 67%, a slight decline from its peak of 69% in 1976 (Koshiro, 1987, p. 149). Thus, also in Japan the public sector is the most highly unionized of all branches.

Another feature common to the labor movements in Great Britain, the United States, and Japan is that eventually each became legally recognized (although in different forms), and thus worker–management relations became institutionalized and, not incidentally, more predictable. Although unions in Japan have less direct input into the determination of issues surrounding work, including pay, nevertheless all workers now are legally acknowledged as having rights that impinge upon the employment relationship.

This raises a final related aspect. Not only have governments recognized that workers and their associations have legal rights, but also over time they have expanded these rights as part of the more general process of extending individual civil liberties and safeguards to all citizens. In addition, they have introduced specific legislation relating to occupational health and safety, income protection, and unjust treatment of workers, not to mention greater provision of social welfare benefits including work injury compensation, unemployment insurance, and old age pensions (see Table 1.2). As Lipset (1986) and others have remarked, the intervention of government into these areas does raise the question of whether it is usurping the labor movement's function. While the most recent figures on union membership do indicate that they are in decline in all three countries (see Table 10.1), this is a point we will return to later in the chapter.

Worker–Management Relations in Great Britain

Unlike the United States and Japan, the labor movement in Great Britain is class based. British labor unions are aligned with the left-wing Labour Party in order to achieve their ideal of a socialist society wherein egalitarian principles, including a more equal distribution of income, will replace a society based on ascriptive privilege in which the upper class dominates and exploits those below it. While this belief or ideology does not drive the average rank and file union member who

is more concerned with the material advantages that accompany union membership (see Goldthorpe et al., 1968, pp. 93–115), it does establish the underlying adversarial relationship that is characteristic of British industrial relations.

> . . . in Britain many among both unionists and managers, while accepting the
> inevitability of the other's existence, refuse fully to accept its legitimacy—or at least
> to accept the legitimacy of the power which the other enjoys. Both sides are apt to
> consider an ideal society as one in which the other does not exist, and to believe, or at
> least sometimes to act as if they believed, that such a society is possible. (Dore, 1973,
> p. 140)

"The permanent state of latent belligerency" that Dore (1973, p. 144) says
characterizes the industrial relations scene in Britain is founded on more than 200
years of mutual distrust reinforced by a combination of both genuine and
apocryphal facts. Despite the many and varied changes that have occurred over
time to improve the lot of the ordinary worker, the battle lines drawn so long ago
are today still very much in evidence, particularly when both sides meet to
renegotiate their collective agreements. (See Box 10-1, **When Auntie Came to Dinner.**)

In order to achieve their broadly based sociopolitical and economic goals,
especially given their extensive representation of workers throughout the labor
force, trade unions in Great Britain are relatively centralized, certainly compared
to the United States and Japan. Collective agreements between employee and
employer are usually negotiated at the national level, and then tailored to fit local
conditions of individual operating sites by committees of plant or office-based
managers and union officials. However, because of this centralization that has increasingly engendered feelings of remoteness among rank and file workers, there
has developed, particularly within the last 30 years, a complementary system of
shop stewards who handle daily problems as they arise on the shop floor or in the
office. Shop stewards form an important countervailing force to centralized unions
in that they are intimately familiar with local conditions, surprisingly independent
from the official union structure, able to secure informal agreement among lower-
level managers and supervisors, and can interpret collective agreements most advantageously for the workers they represent (Terry, 1983, pp. 71–73).

Contributing to the independent strength of front-line shop stewards is the
fact that not only are British unions centralized, they have also become increasingly
concentrated. Whereas in 1960, the average membership of a British union was
15,000, by 1980 it had doubled. Mergers and amalgamations during this period
have resulted in fewer unions of larger size. In 1980, 25 unions out of a total of 438
had memberships in excess of 100,000; together these unions accounted for four-
fifths of all trade union members in Britain (Hyman, 1983).

While British unions have become more concentrated and centralized, Table
10.1 indicates that they have also been in decline during the 1980s. From 1979 to
1987, there was a loss of more than one-fifth of all union members, that is, close to
3 million workers. In a 1989 article, Towers attempts to determine how much of
this decline in trade union membership may be attributed to specific policies and
legislation of the Conservative (i.e., industry-backed) government of Margaret

Box 10-1 # When Auntie Came to Dinner

In the following anecdote, Charles Handy, a British author of several books on management and work, brings to life "the permanent state of latent belligerency" that characterizes "them and us."

———————

My aunt by marriage is a splendid character, but from a bygone age. Her father never
worked, nor his father before him nor, of course, had she ever earned a penny in her life.
Their capital worked for them, and they managed their capital. Work was done by
workers. She sees all governments today as insanely prejudiced against capital, all
workers as inherently greedy and lazy, and most managements as incompetent. No
wonder the world is in a mess and she getting poorer every day.

Tony is a friend from work. His father was a postman. He started life as a draftsman
in a large engineering firm. He grew up believing that inherited capital was socially wrong.
He had never met any man who did not or had not worked for his living.

They met, by chance, at my house over a meal. It started quietly, politely. Then she
inquired what he did. It transpired that he had recently joined his staff union. Auntie had
never met a union member.

"Good heavens, how could you?" she said.

"It makes very good sense," said Tony, "to protect your rights."

"What rights? What poppycock is this? If people like you spent more time at their
work and less looking after their own interests, this country wouldn't be in its present
mess."

"Don't you," said Tony, "spend your time looking after your rights?"

"Of course," she said, "but then, I've got rights. I provide the money that makes it
possible for people like you to live."

"I provide the labor that keeps your money alive, although why I should work to
preserve the capital of rich people whom I've never met is something that puzzles me."

"You talk like a Communist, young man, although you dress quite respectably. Do
you know what you're saying?"

"You don't have to be a Communist to question the legitimacy of inherited wealth."
My aunt turned to me.

"You see why I'm worrried about this country?" she said.

Each regarded the other as an example of an unnatural species. Given their opposed "core beliefs," no proper argument or dialogue was possible, only an exchange of
slogans or abuse. It is a score which is replicated at negotiating tables as well as dinner
tables.

Source: Handy, 1978, pp. 161–162.

Thatcher, which came to power in 1979, the year in which union membership peaked. While it is impossible to isolate the independent effects of government from other factors (e.g., rising unemployment rates, the trade deficit, a recession, and the changing composition of the labor force) that also may have contributed to the decline in membership, nevertheless Towers does identify significant instances in which the government intervened to suppress labor and specific legislation that reduced the power of organized trade unions.

For example, in 1980 as a result of the abolishing of certain statutory procedures, "British employers are not legally required to recognize or bargain with trade unions and can withdraw recognition previously granted" (Towers, 1989, pp. 168–169). Subsequent legislation abolished closed-shop agreements, placed limitations on the conditions and types of industrial action possible, overturned legislation ensuring comparable pay in similar jobs, and placed the onus of responsibility for unfair dismissal more upon employees.[4] Thus, regardless of the particular impact of these legislative acts upon the membership decline, they do indicate that polarized labor–management relations are not restricted to the workplace.

Industrial relations in Britain are a product of and mirror the larger cultural setting in which class-based antagonisms have been an inherent aspect for centuries. Indeed, the manner in which industrial relations are conducted reinforces a stratification system with social institutions which evaluate individual worth as much by one's origins as by one's contribution. Consequently, "them" and "us" symbolize considerably more than just managers and workers who all must perform certain functions in order to gain their livelihoods.

Worker–Management Relations in the United States

In American labor history, 1935 was a watershed year. With the passage of the National Labor Relations Act, also known as the Wagner Act, the trade union movement in the United States gained recognition, legitimacy, and even encouragement. In that year, union members numbered 3.6 million and represented 13% of the non-agricultural labor force, this result being achieved over many years and under the most adverse circumstances. By 1938, just three short years later, both their numbers and their percentage representation had more than doubled (Goldfield, 1987, p. 10). According to Adams (1989, p. 49), the Wagner Act produced a "Labor Accord" with the following conditions as its basis:

> . . . unions would accept the right of management to manage within the bounds set by law and collective agreements; management would accept the right of unions to exist and to negotiate agreements providing their members with security, dignity, and economic benefits consistent with the market position of the firm, but reserved the right peacefully and legally to resist unionization where collective bargaining had not yet been established. The State undertook to ensure that individual employees could choose collective bargaining free from threats or coercion and also to guarantee that unions and companies would negotiate in good faith with a view to signing collective agreements covering wages and conditions of employment.

Although some factions of the early trade union movement in the United States were left-wing, in the main organized labor both accepted and endorsed the principle of free enterprise. In the words of Samuel Gompers (1898, p. 667), the first president of the American Federation of Labor, the mission of American trade unions was to secure for workers "the right to be full sharers in the abundance which is the result of their brain and brawn, and the civilization of which they are the founders and the mainstay." In other words, and in contrast to some of the more radical union movements in Britain and the rest of Europe, American workers by and large did not want to change the prevailing system; they sought only an equitable share within it. Generally, American unions have espoused the principle of "business unionism," which meant that they organized and negotiated on bread and butter issues—the securing of adequate wages and decent working conditions.

This pragmatic philosophy together with the value of individualism that permeates American life (see Lipset, 1986) has resulted in a collective bargaining structure considerably less centralized than its European counterpart. Predominantly, bargaining occurs either at the company or even plant level rather than nationally as in the British case, and there are indications that the structure is becoming even more decentralized (see Katz, 1985).[5]

Centralized and decentralized bargaining structures both have their advantages (see Anderson, 1982). On the one hand, centralized bargaining is more efficient because of economies of scale; it allows for greater professional expertise because of larger bargaining units; it achieves greater parity throughout industry; and potentially it results in fewer work stoppages because fewer negotiating units are involved. On the other hand, decentralized bargaining is more responsive to local conditions; permits more rank and file participation; provides greater prestige for local union and management officials; and also can result in fewer work stoppages in that greater attention is given to local conditions.[6] As may be inferred, the advantages of one type of structure often become disadvantages in the other. Because there is no optimum solution, the particular structure chosen depends in large part on the prevailing values and norms in the larger society.[7]

While the bargaining structure of American industrial relations may be relatively decentralized, a countervailing tendency is that bargaining units have grown larger. In other words, similar to the British experience, the American labor movement has become more and more concentrated. Table 10.2, which lists the ten largest unions in the past three decades, reveals that the share of total union membership accounted for by these unions has steadily increased. In 1985, the top 10 unions, led by the almost two-million-strong Teamsters, claimed as members almost three-fifths of all American trade unionists (see Gifford, 1986, p. 4). Like Britain, this concentration has come about through merger and amalgamation.

Table 10.2 also identifies these unions by type. For example, in 1964 the list contained three traditional craft unions comprising the skilled trades and seven newer industrial unions whose membership was composed mainly of the semi-skilled. Of these 10, nine represented workers employed primarily in the blue-collar manufacturing and construction sector. In 1974, while there was some jockeying for position, the top six unions remained intact. However, three unions representing employees in the tertiary sector, one of these being a public sector union,

Table 10.2　TEN LARGEST AMERICAN LABOR UNIONS BY TYPE OF UNION, 1964–1985

	1964		1974		1985	
	Union	Type	Union	Type	Union	Type
1.	Teamsters[1]	Industrial	Teamsters[1]	Industrial	Teamsters[1]	Industrial
2.	Steelworkers	Industrial	Auto workers	Industrial	National Education Assoc.	Public
3.	Auto workers	Industrial	Steelworkers	Industrial	Food & commercial workers[2]	Industrial
4.	Machinists	Craft	Electrical workers	Craft	State, county	Public
5.	Electrical workers	Craft	Machinists	Craft	Auto workers	Industrial
6.	Carpenters	Craft	Carpenters	Craft	Steelworkers	Industrial
7.	Meat cutters	Industrial	Retail clerks[2]	Industrial	Service employees[2]	Industrial
8.	Hotel & restaurant[2]	Industrial	Laborers	Industrial	Electrical workers	Craft
9.	Ladies' garment workers	Industrial	State, county	Public	Machinists	Craft
10.	Laborers Industrial	Industrial	Service employees[2]		Carpenters	Craft
Total craft unions	3		3		3	
Total industrial unions						
secondary sector	6		4		3	
tertiary sector	1		2		2	
Total public sector unions	0		1		2	
Top 10 unions as a % of total union membership	48.1%		49.9%		56.7%	

[1]The membership of the Teamsters union spans the secondary and tertiary sectors, particularly in successive decades.

[2]While these unions are termed "industrial" in that they are organized on an industry-wide basis, the membership work primarily in the tertiary sector.

Sources: Gifford, 1986, p. 4; Goldfield, 1987, p. 10; Miller and Form, 1980, p. 435.

became among the largest in the country. By 1985, the changing structure of American unionism was most apparent. The three older craft unions fell in prominence and were replaced by four tertiary sector unions, two representing public employees. Together, these "new" unions comprised almost half of the top 10 membership (see Gifford, 1986, p. 4). Thus, as noted above, the American trade union movement itself is being reconstituted as it attempts to represent a changing occupational and labor force structure.[8]

Most recent attention on American trade unionism has focused on its falling representation of the labor force (see Table 10.1). Not only has organized labor in the United States been in decline for more years than any other industrialized country (Cornfield, 1986, p. 1113), since 1980 it has also suffered a serious drop-off in absolute numbers (see Goldfield, 1987, pp. 10–11). In an attempt to explain this decline, Farber (1985) examined the impact of the following structural factors: (1) the industrial shift of the labor force out of the traditionally heavily unionized manufacturing sector; (2) the regional shift of the employment base to the less unionized South; (3) the occupational shift toward less unionized white-collar occupations; and (4) the increase in female labor force participation. Employing a regression analysis that plotted the movement of the labor force on these four factors from 1953 to 1978, at the same time noting the specific corresponding unionization rates, Farber (1985, p. 22) reached the following general conclusion:

> Overall, these results suggest that industrial, regional, occupational, and sexual shifts in the composition of the labor force can account for at most 40% of the decline in the extent of unionization over the past 25 years. In addition, it is likely that at least some of the shifts in composition are the result of unionization rather than a cause of its decline. Therefore, a complete explanation of the decline must lie elsewhere.

In a comparable analysis, Lipset (1986) argues that while structural features such as those examined by Farber may explain part of the decline of organized labor in the United States, they cannot represent the major cause. Because all industrially developed countries have experienced similar structural shifts in their labor forces and yet not all these same countries are undergoing union decline, there must be something unique about the United States that is causing the decline. The unique factor that Lipset comes up with is national values as expressed through public opinion polls. It is his contention that "the falloff in union strength is associated with the decline in public support for trade unions" (Lipset, 1986, p. 436).

Figure 10.1 graphs the percentage of nationally representative samples from 1947 to 1981 that approved of unions in response to the question: "In general, do you approve or disapprove of labor unions?" Net approval, also graphed, is the percentage difference between those approving and disapproving. In addition, union density figures for the various poll years are also plotted. As Lipset reports, there are high correlations (see Figure 10.1) between the level of public approval (both measures) and union density, which leads him to conclude that " a major, if not the major, factor affecting union growth or decline . . . is variation in the public estimation of unions" (p. 438).

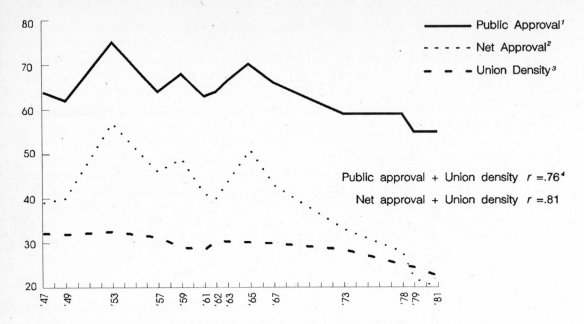

[1]Percent of representative national poll (Gallup) who "approve" in response to the question, "In general, do you approve or disapprove of labor unions?"

[2]Net approval refers to the percentage difference between "approve" and "disapprove."

[3]Union density refers to the percent of the nonagricultural labor force that are union members, as reported by Lipset, 1986, p. 437.

[4]Correlation coefficients were computed by Lipset, 1986, p. 437.

Sources: Public approval data from Goldfield, 1987, p. 35; union density and correlation coefficients from Lipset, 1986, p. 437.

Figure 10.1   Public Aproval and Net Approval of Unions and Union Density, U.S. 1947–1981

Given this conclusion, Lipset then ponders why public support of unions in the United States has been so low in comparison to other industrially developed countries. Similar to many of his other writings, Lipset argues that significantly different value structures characterize nations as a result of their social and political origins. Accordingly, "contemporary America is the outcome of processes which began with an egalitarian, individualistic revolution" (p. 441). It is the "classic or extreme example of a 'born modern' bourgeois or classically liberal society, stressing antistatism, individualism, and competitive meritocracy" (pp. 441–442).

The initial surge in trade unionism and public support of it during the 1930s and 1940s came in response to the debilitating effects of the Depression. "That unprecedented event undermined traditional American beliefs among large sectors of the population, led to the acceptance by a majority of the need for state action to reduce unemployment and to assist those adversely affected by the economic collapse and to support trade unionism" (p. 443). However, with the upsurge of the business cycle following World War II and the guarantee of basic individual rights by the state, there was a "restoration of faith in traditional American values" (p.445) as indicated by opinion polls of the time, and a consequent decline in support for trade unionism as a way of life.

Other researchers have suggested that while Americans may value individualism and thus reject unionism, this is not the whole story. Historically, opposition to unionism by American management has been strong, and recently, "pro-business" government actions, particularly rulings by the National Labor Relations Board, have been most injurious to organized labor (see Fantasia, 1988, pp. 25–72; Moody, 1988, pp. 127–146). Although the hostilities between management and labor are not class based as they are in Britain, nevertheless parallels may be drawn. In both countries, the tenor of collective bargaining can only be characterized as adversarial. While the conflict is institutionalized, this does not detract in any way from its intensity.

Worker–Management Relations in Japan

Japan represents yet another contrast in that its industrial relations are markedly different from either the United States or Great Britain. Although the early trade union movement in Japan was similar to and in fact modeled on American industrial relations, it was largely unsuccessful due to aggressive assaults on it by both employers and the government (Karsh, 1976, p. 892). In the 1920s, union officials, at the height of their drive to establish independent trade unionism in Japan, were able to organize only 8% of the industrial labor force. Through the 1930s, events both inside and external to the labor movement curtailed further growth, and in 1940 the military government declared all unions illegal, thus bringing to a close Western-style industrial relations in Japan (see Karsh, 1976).

Following World War II, during the American occupation of Japan, enterprise unionism, or the organization of all workers within a single enterprise, came into being. Enterprise unionism has been called one of the "three pillars" of Japanese-style management, the other two being lifetime employment and career progression based on seniority and age (Abegglen and Stalk, 1985). Together, these features produce a loyal work force collaboratively committed to the goals of the enterprise, certainly an anomaly in American and British industrial relations.

The characteristics of an enterprise union are as follows:

1. Within a given private or public enterprise that is unionized, all *regular* employees (both blue- and white-collar) below a designated managerial level are members of the same enterprise union. Excluded from membership are temporary workers (i.e., those hired without employment tenure) and workers employed on subcontracts.
2. By dint of regular employment status as described above, an employee also necessarily becomes a member of the enterprise union. The union collects dues from every regular employee through a "checkoff" system.[9]

3. In most cases, the enterprise provides the union with offices and other administrative facilities. These offices may be on the actual work site.
4. The structure of the union organization parallels the enterprise structure.
5. Union officials do not forego career progression through the enterprise. In many cases, being a union officer may actually enhance one's career. (See Karsh, 1976, pp. 891–892, for a more detailed elaboration of these characteristics.)

Virtually all unions in Japan are of the enterprise type. Thus, for every private corporation or public agency that is unionized, there is a separate enterprise union. (Company branches have branch unions.) There are some nationally federated union bodies, but they do not exercise direct power; their major function is "the exchange of information and the coordination of bargaining strategy" (Dore, 1973, p. 124). Real power lies at the central enterprise level.

Enterprise unions are formed mainly in large organizations in that only these enterprises (private and public) offer the possibility of employment tenure, an essential ingredient of this type of unionism (see above). This is confirmed by the fact that about one-third of all Japanese workers are assured of lifetime employment (see Chapter 6), and approximately one-third of the labor force is unionized (see Table 10.1). Additional confirmation is provided by Karsh (1976, p. 894) who documents the enterprise size—enterprise unionism relationships. For example, while only 11% of enterprises employing less than 50 workers are unionized, 77% of firms with 500 or more are unionized, and in firms employing more than 1000 workers, fully 96% are unionized.

Consequently, the Japanese industrial relations system offers yet another approach to solving the problems incurred by the complex division of labor necessary to achieve organizational objectives. Because of the internal labor market that encompasses the first two pillars of Japanese-style management (i.e., lifetime employment and advancement based on age and seniority), the employing organization is the pivotal focus of worker's careers (see Chapter 9). As a result, there has developed a system of industrial relations that is centered around the firm, is supportive of firm-based careers, and reflects the Japanese characteristics of diligence, persistence, and politeness.[10]

Because all employees—workers and managers—are tied to a single firm throughout their working lives, they have established a system that will permit them to work out their problems in as harmonious and collaborative a way as possible. While Japanese unions are proportionately strong in those companies that are unionized, they are nevertheless "relatively weak as collective bargaining organizations" (Karsh, 1976, p. 891). Because the fate of both company and union are so inextricably tied, the union acts more as a symbolic "counterweight to potential abuses of management authority" (Abegglen and Stalk, 1985, p. 205). Box 10-2, **Union Song of the Hitachi Company Enterprise Union**, is indicative of how large the firm and the spirit of cooperation, diligence, and persistence figure in Japanese workers' lives.

Box 10-2 **Union Song of the Hitachi Company Enterprise Union**

The storm still blows, the mountain pass is long
But we will never give up.
Though still the sun gives no glimpse of light
Dawn approaches for the working man.
Our Hitachi! Hitachi where the muscles tense!
Never slacken. Shoulder to shoulder we move ahead.
Soon you shall see! Soon you shall see!

The path is dark, precipitous. Cold penetrates the bone
But no one walks alone.
Though still the sun gives no glimpse of light
Somewhere, faintly, the first cock crows.
Our Hitachi! Hitachi where the muscles tense!
In amity and unison, with laughter and song we move ahead.
Soon you shall see! Soon you shall see!

Now to be born anew: the history of Japan.
Wave the union flag on high.
The sun thrusts up over the horizon
The century of the working man arrives!
Our Hitachi! Hitachi where the muscles tense!
Grit teeth, tighten belts, just one more short haul
Soon you shall see! Soon you shall see!

Source: Dore, 1973, p. 164.

Because industrial relations in Japan are centered at the enterprise level, this makes them the most decentralized of all those being discussed. However, like American and British unions, Japanese unions also have become increasingly concentrated. Because of the structural parallels between enterprise and union, as Japanese industry has become increasingly concentrated, so also have enterprise unions consolidated their members. Another similarity to the American and British experiences is the recent decline in union membership in Japan (see Table 10.1). In analyzing this phenomenon, Freeman and Rebick (1989, p. 578) offer the following explanation:

Much of the decline in density is associated with the inability of Japanese unions to organize new establishments. We attribute this in part to lowered worker interest and stiffened management opposition to unionism following the oil shock, buttressed by unfavorable changes in the political and legal environment for collective bargaining and for union organization, and to other management actions, such as creating additional pseudo-managerial posts for older workers.

Union Decline

It would appear there are a number of common factors underlying declining union membership in all three countries. First, whereas each country has experienced structural changes in its economy (e.g., the shift toward tertiary sector employment, an increased proportion of white collar workers, greater female labor force participation, and more part-time and temporary employment), so also have West Germany, Canada, and Australia. However, these latter countries have not experienced a decline in union membership (Freeman and Rebick,1989, p. 580), and therefore structural factors *per se* cannot be the cause.

Second, declining union representation is associated with falling public support of unionism in each of these three countries.[11] In that "the public" is comprised of "workers," this fact by itself is not all that illuminating. It is in the reasons underlying this disaffection that we can attribute cause. In the United States, where the decline in membership and support has been long running (see Figure 10.1), the reason inferred is that collective defense organizations are inimical to the individualistic, competitive spirit of most Americans. In Great Britain and Japan, where the declines are recent and the level of unionism is higher than in the United States, no doubt the underlying reasons are more transitory and not so deeply embedded in national character. Unfortunately, no direct reasons for falling public support are provided in the poll data.

Third, whether simply mirroring public opinion or forming it, the governments in each country have also recently acted in ways opposed to organized labor. In Great Britain, the Conservative Thatcher government has adopted policies antithetical to the interests of unions (Towers, 1989); in the United States, the Reagan administration has been charged with being antilabor (see Goldfield, 1987); and in Japan, the long-standing conservative government has become increasingly nonsupportive of enterprise unionism (Freeman and Rebick, 1989). While these governments have also enacted legislation protecting and extending the rights of *individual* workers (as have governments in other industrially developed countries), it appears that *organized associations* of workers receive different treatment. The combination of these two policies—individual worker protection and union restraint—may well have contributed to the growing public opinion against unions.

Fourth, management, never totally accepting worker "interference" in the workplace whether it be in Great Britain, the United States, or Japan, have assessed the prevailing mood and openly challenged organized labor (see, for example, Klein and Wanger, 1985). Especially given the worldwide business recession during the early 1980s, British, American, and Japanese managers have demanded greater operating and strategic flexibility than traditional union-management collective bargaining allows. Backed by public opinion and favorable legislation, professionally trained "human resources" managers have proposed options that could result in a transformation of industrial relations (see Kochan et al., 1986).

All these factors point to basic changes in worker–management relations in each of the countries being analyzed. Given the recomposition of national labor forces and work organizations, plus the radically transformed technological performance of work within an interdependent, integrated global economy, it is little wonder that traditional industrial relations systems established 50 to 150 years ago are experiencing problems. In the remainder of this chapter, we examine the major issues of conflict as well as some of the structural adaptations that have been proposed.

ISSUES OF CONFLICT

As indicated in Chapter 9, work is a necessary activity. Because all of us must work to survive, the amount we earn and the probability of a continuing livelihood (i.e., job security) are extremely important, no matter where in the world we live. There are, however, different institutional arrangements for handling this problem. As we have seen, the Japanese internal labor market system places more emphasis on security of employment than does the Western external labor market which affords more individual choice and therefore potentially greater reward. As Abegglen and Stalk (1985, pp. 209–210) put it: "Viewed in terms of individual motivation, the Japanese system of employment is a trade-off of opportunity for security. It provides security above all, at the loss of opportunity for unusually high reward."

Because of these two systems of employment, there are significant differences in worker–management relations between East and West. In Japan, the three pillars of Japanese-style management form an integrated structure within which all are protected. The enterprise provides the context and the frame of reference in which workers' life chances unfold. Levels of pay are determined by how well the organization as a whole performs, and thus it is in the interest of all to give their utmost. The system is designed to produce "close identification of corporate and individual interests" (Abegglen and Stalk, 1985, p. 207), and therefore "the union does not exist as an entity separate from, or with an adversarial relationship to, the company. The union includes all company members, and only company members. Its future and the [Company's] are identical" (Abegglen and Stalk, 1985, p. 205).

Contrast this with the Western system of employment in which the external labor market constitutes the relevant arena in which both workers and managers evaluate their prospects. Levels of pay and other conditions are determined more by the outside marketplace than by the internal workings of the organization. Because of this, there is relatively low commitment or loyalty to the organization; mobility is high and security is low as individual and organization seek to maximize their respective interests. In this context, the union, comprised of similarly talented workers employed in a variety of firms, attempts to play the market to the best advantage of its individual members. Collective bargaining occurs as an endless series of rounds in which those members most highly compensated at any one time serve as the reference group for those who are seeking "parity."

Japan

In one system, conflict is apparently absent; in the other, it is overt and institutionalized. However, if conflict is negligible in the Japanese system, then why should employers and government officials resist unionization as they have during the 1980s? Freeman and Rebick (1989, p. 592) report that managers have resorted to attacks on organizing leaders and discrimination against prounion employees in their attempts to break up union organizing drives. Abegglen and Stalk (1985) note that while enterprise unionism has served both corporations and the country well in the past, there are signs of strain on the "three pillars" that support the system.

At the center of the problem of Japanese-style management is the issue of flexibility (see above). According to Abegglen and Stalk (1985, pp. 181–213), the system that was developed almost 50 years ago was extremely well suited to the conditions at that time. Japan, in economic and social disarray following World War II, needed a committed and integrated workforce in order to capitalize on the postwar economic boom and to become a fully fledged industrial nation. By providing secure employment at nominal wages together with essential welfare benefits (e.g., housing support, family allowance, pension plans, and so) and in offering seniority-based raises and promotions, Japanese corporations gained a highly productive and motivated labor force. However, this was achieved at a price; there was a tradeoff of "flexibility in personnel management for maximizing employee involvement and commitment to the company" (Abegglen and Stalk, 1985, p. 203).

Largely as a result of its phenomenal success, Japan now finds itself in somewhat of a quandary. Japanese workers are among the highest paid in the world; they have extremely generous perquisites relative to workers from other countries; and they have the longest life expectancy. As a result of slower economic growth, particularly during the 1980s, the "three pillars" that were largely responsible for "the miracle" are now forcing Japanese corporations into increasingly noncompetitive positions in the international marketplace.[12]

Abegglen and Stalk note particular problems with each of the pillars. First, with regard to lifetime employment, Japanese employers are responsible for maintaining a workforce they may not always need. For example, in 1974 when Japan experienced a real decline in its economy together with high inflation, Japanese corporations, which on average suffered losses during that year, were extremely hard pressed not only to keep their regular employees but to pay them wage increases of close to 30%. Consequently, Japanese companies, in comparison to their Western counterparts, find it more difficult to accommodate contractions in the market.[13]

Also related to maintaining "unnecessary" employees, particularly in times of expanding technological change, is the fact that invariably companies end up with older, technologically obsolescent workers who are not fully competent to perform their duties, and yet who must be kept on the payroll until they retire. This problem is compounded by increased life expectancy in Japan, which has resulted in the extension of the average retirement age.[14]

Finally, Abegglen and Stalk point to problems that Japanese companies have with respect to mergers and acquisitions. Much of the purpose in these moves is to consolidate operations such that the "new" companies have greater resources that they can more efficiently put to use. However, given the fact that the merging companies are comprised of lifetime workers, the end result is more often duplication of resources rather than economies of scale.

Concerning the second pillar, seniority-based raises and promotions, Abegglen and Stalk conclude that it is most under siege. With the now initially high base wage rate together with the fact that Japan, similar to other industrially developed countries, is an aging society, the cost of uniformly rewarding workers on the basis of their length of service with the firm is becoming prohibitive. As Abegglen and Stalk explain, during times of rapid economic growth, there is heavy employment of young recruits, with the consequence that the overall wage cost is kept to a minimum as the company expands. "As average age declines, so then does average wage level" (p. 203). However, during periods of relatively slow growth (e.g., the 1980s), employment slackens, and employees age through the system, all the time consuming a proportionately greater share of total operating costs. With guaranteed employment and longer work careers due to increased life expectancy and the extension of the retirement age, "the seniority-based pay system has come under considerable pressure in recent years" (p. 204).

The third pillar, enterprise unionism, supports the other two. Because enterprise unions consist of all regular employees who are guaranteed employment tenure and seniority-based raises and promotions, together these employees represent a strong voice in support of a system which has largely contributed to Japan's current economic prominence. Thus, in this instance, enterprise unionism is a conservative force attempting to preserve those features that not only have made Japan an economic superpower, but have improved substantially the quality of these Japanese workers' lives.

Examining the system as a whole, its integrated, mutually reinforcing elements are designed to eliminate conflict and discord between workers and managers. There is "close identification of corporate and individual interests" (p. 207). However, also of paramount importance is the fact that it is a "high-growth" system. In other words, given a prolonged period of little or no economic growth, corporations cannot expand to accommodate seniority-based pay increases over a lifetime, and consequently they become bloated. Thus, although little conflict occurs *within* the system, the system itself is now being questioned. In order that managers may have the flexibility to manage, "the general view is that seniority-based pay and promotion systems will need to give way to a job and output-based system, but that security of employment will continue" (p. 212).

Consequently, in Japan, managerial resistance to unionization may be seen as an attempt to renegotiate the bases upon which Japanese industrial relations have stood during the postwar era. To the extent that there are proportionately fewer union members, that is, regular employees entitled to lifetime employment with seniority-based wage increases, management has greater flexibility to adapt to upturns and downturns in a highly complex, competitive global economy. While there is little overt conflict apparent, nevertheless if the three pillars upon which this system has rested are redesigned to any appreciable degree, we may expect open resistance. What constitutes flexibility for management is job security and a way of life for workers.

The West

In the United States and Great Britain, conflict is occurring at two levels. On one level, there is the regularized conflict over entitlement that takes place within the institutionalized collective bargaining structure as unions and management wrestle to achieve an "equitable" division of the proceeds that result from their joint labors. On another, broader level, a more complex agenda is being played out as differently constituted groups of workers and managers attempt to place themselves strategically and advantageously within a constantly changing system in which the end result cannot be known. The first level may be contrasted with Japan where collective bargaining occurs collectively in the interests of the enterprise; the second level finds a parallel in Japan where there also a power struggle is beginning to take shape that will no doubt change worker–management relations in the years to come.

With regard to conflict at the collective bargaining level, Table 10.3 reveals that the issues have not changed substantially since unions first represented workers' interests. Based on a representative sample of union and professional association members in the United States, the table indicates that overwhelmingly wages, benefits, and job security constitute the most important issues on which members think their union should focus. Only one-quarter to one-third stated that intrinsic features of their jobs or gaining more control of their companies should be issues of top priority for their union. Table 10.3 also presents union members' evaluations of how well their unions are performing. On those issues of highest importance, approximately three-quarters of the members rated their union as doing a very or somewhat good job. Issues of lesser importance received considerably lower evaluations.

Concerning conflict on the broader level, we are witnessing, particularly in the United States, a challenge to the entire system of industrial relations as it has been practiced for more than 50 years. In a recent book, which examines just this issue, Kochan, Katz, and McKersie (1986, p. 231) conclude that "the New Deal collective bargaining system that was given stability by the passage of the National Labor Relations Act and its subsequent administration and enforcement is no longer well-matched to contemporary industrial relations." As evidence for this assertion, Kochan et al. cite declining union representation, the increasing inability of unions to win union certification elections, passage of "antilabor" legislation, active union avoidance by management, and the implementation by management of innovative personnel policies to thwart union objectives.

Table 10.3 RANK ORDER OF WHAT UNION MEMBERS WANT THEIR UNION TO DO, AND HOW WELL THE UNION DELIVERS (U.S. 1977)[1]

	Union members'	
	Priorities[2]	Evaluations[3]
Activity	Percent saying union should spend a lot of effort	Percent rating union very or somewhat good
Extrinsic Benefits		
1. Getting better fringe benefits		
White collar	61%	69%
Blue collar	65	71
2. Getting better wages		
White collar	62	76
Blue collar	54	75
3. Improving job security		
White collar	53	76
Blue collar	55	74
4. Improving safety and health on job		
White collar	40	74
Blue collar	51	71
Intrinsic Benefits		
5. Getting workers a say in how they do their jobs		
White collar	27	57
Blue collar	32	48
6. Helping to make jobs more interesting		
White collar	24	39
Blue collar	33	32
7. Getting workers a say in how their employer runs the business		
White collar	24	42
Blue collar	26	34

[1]Based on a representative sample of 1515 employed adults in the coterminous United States. In the above table, white-collar union members, 148; blue-collar union members, 327. The possible response categories were: (a) very good; (b) somewhat good; (c) not too good; (d) not at all good.

[2]The question asked regarding priorities was: "How much effort do you think *your* (union/employees' association) *should* be putting into . . . ?" The possible response categories were: (a) a lot of effort; (b) some effort; (c) a little effort; (d) no effort at all.

[3]The question asked regarding evaluations was: "Now think about what *your* (union/employees' association) is *actually* doing. How good a job does it do in . . . ?"

Source: Adapted from Quinn and Staines, 1979, pp. I86–I89.

At the crux of the impasse between unions and management is job definition. As noted in Chapter 9, workers in the West are identified by the jobs that they do, whereas workers in Japan are identified according to their place of employment. The history of industrial relations in the West has revolved around unions providing employers with properly qualified workers for specifically defined jobs. Compensation and other fringe benefits are determined by the formally specified positions that individual workers occupy. However, due to technological innovation and organizational restructuring, management has put pressure on unions to relax their job classification system so that workers may be more flexibly positioned within the organization. Unions for the most part have resisted these proposals on the grounds that by giving up job control, they also necessarily yield job security for their members.

Kochan and his colleagues argue that organized labor has been too restrictive in its focus on job protection, and thus has not given sufficient attention to broader issues of work and organization that also are crucial to worker–management relations. To the extent that unions do not take cognizance of these issues, their diminishing influence will erode even further.

> American unions will continue to be under intense pressure to move away from many of the job-control traditions associated with the New Deal model of collective bargaining. The highly detailed [union-management] contract with uniform rules governing individual job rights fit a stable, high-volume, and mass-oriented production system. But the job control model is at a severe competitive disadvantage in a world of just-in-time inventories, short production runs, technologies that require greater analytical reasoning, and a workforce with greater interest in how work is conducted. (Kochan et al., 1986, p. 239)

On the other hand, management for its part has been riding a patriotic wave of trying to save jobs and help the country prosper. Managers insist that if they are to do their job, they must be granted greater flexibility to maneuver in this new, highly competitive, international environment. If they are hamstrung in their efforts by recalcitrant trade unions, then everyone will suffer. Judging by recent labor legislation, management has made a more persuasive case than labor.

In Britain also, management's demand for greater flexibility is framed in terms of broader issues in the economy:

> Markets have declined; there has been an intensification of competition both at home and overseas; and there is great uncertainty. In such circumstances industrial relations which emphasize long-term stability achieved through cooperation can come to be challenged as corporations are compelled to adopt short-term actions to meet immediate product-market and financial demands. (Purcell and Sisson, 1983, p. 117)

A more Machiavellian interpretation of management's appeal for greater flexibility (i.e., control) is made by Shaiken (1984). He contends that management is motivated more by its desire to retrieve total operating control than by any real need to maintain organizational viability. Armed with the computer and all its many possible applications, management is now able to change the balance of power that has been established over the latter half of this century. Thus, while management may claim that its actions are dictated by the exigencies of the situation, in fact other options are available. For example, in Box 10-3, **Computers as Strikebreakers**, Shaiken argues that although management claimed that it had no other choice but to act as it did and assume total operating control, other choices of action were at hand and would have more satisfactorily achieved the stated goals of the organization.

Notwithstanding the particular motivations of management, indications are that a new relationship is being formed between workers and their employing organizations. In both East and West, the guiding principles of a new labor–management contract are being negotiated that it is hoped will accommodate the changed conditions under which all work. In the next section, we identify the major elements of this emerging system of worker–management relations.

AN EMERGING CONVERGENCE IN WORKER–MANAGEMENT RELATIONS

Despite the differing goals of managers and workers, a new general understanding is being reached in light of changed circumstances. While hardly an "accord" as was proclaimed when unions first gained the right to represent workers, nevertheless this "accommodation" forms the foundation upon which future worker-management relations are likely to be based. Furthermore, the essential elements of this accommodation are now apparent in the industrial relations systems of all three of the countries we have been examining.

Job Flexibility Similar to the Japanese system in which workers in task groups learn a variety of skills and perform a number of different jobs, Kochan et al. (1986, p. 96) note an increase in American firms in which "flexibility is designed into the new systems by having a small number of broad job classifications, few rules governing specific job assignments, less restriction on the work supervisors can perform, and more limited weight given to seniority in promotion and transfer decisions." Workers are assigned to task groups rather than specific positions, and their rank within the organization is based on the overall skill level they have achieved.

Job Security/Career Orientation Again like the Japanese model, greater security of employment is being offered to select groups of workers within various American and British firms. In exchange, management seeks greater employee commitment rather than simple compliance (Purcell and Sisson, 1983, pp. 118–120). In order for the career system of employment to be effective, management must devote considerable attention to personnel recruitment, selection, and training, and involve employees at all levels in the strategic and workplace issues that the organization is confronting (see Kochan et al., 1986).

Box 10-3 Computers as Strikebreakers

On August 3, 1981, members of the Professional Air Traffic Controllers (PATCO) walked off the job, the culmination of a decade of bitter and often turbulent labor relations in the nation's air traffic control system. The Reagan Administration, determined to thwart a walkout of public employees, gave the strikers 48 hours to return to work or face permanent dismissal. The resources and muscle of the federal government were arrayed against a tiny union that threatened to cripple air transport throughout the United States. . . . For PATCO, the battle ended almost before it was joined in a rout that included the firing of 12,000 air traffic controllers and the decertification of their union.

PATCO was weakened by a lack of public support, lukewarm aid or even hostility from other unions, its own inexperience, and a tough adversary. But what ultimately doomed the union was the government's skillful use of computer technology to keep air traffic moving, gutting the strikers' leverage. Soon after the walkout occurred, 75% of commercial flights were operating in spite of the fact that some 75% of the air traffic controllers were on the picket line. The centerpiece of the Federal Aviation Administration's strategy was "flow control," a computerized procedure to regulate departures and to space aircraft uniformly along air traffic routes, thus maximizing the use of airspace, facilities, and controllers. . . .

Computers reduce but do not eliminate the need for air traffic controllers, an occupation that remains labor intensive and skill based. According to a Rand Corporation report:

> Much, if not most, of a controller's time is spent on tasks that require distinctly human skills: negotiating flight-plan changes with pilots, vectoring aircraft around rapidly changing severe weather, deciding upon general operational configurations with other controllers, and the like. These tasks also require experience, maturity, and flexibility—the blips on those screens are, after all, real people who change their minds and make mistakes. . . .

As a result, supervisors were requalified as controllers during the planning period so that they could become the core of a group to replace any strikers. But one early study indicated that a work force largely limited to supervisors could maintain only about one-third of normal operation, so clearly success depended on the number of controllers who remained on the job. As it happened, the 3000 supervisors were supplemented by 5700 nonstriking controllers and 1000 military personnel when PATCO walked out, bringing the total to over half of the prestrike work force.

This turned out to be enough. With the new flow-control strategies in use and with nearly 10,000 controllers on the job, air traffic was disrupted within politically tolerable limits and the striking controllers were left essentially powerless. In pursuing this strategy, however, the government may have taken a major gamble on safety. In a complex system such as air traffic control where human life is at stake, built-in redundancy assures that if one aspect of the operation fails, the system itself will not. An important element of that redundancy is the skill and experience of the human operators.

• • •

With the strike over, the administration turned its attention to rebuilding the air traffic system, criticized by many as being overburdened and outmoded even in the prewalkout days. On January 28, 1982, J. Lynn Helms (the FAA chief) announced a 20-year program, costing between $15 and $20 billion, to replace the system's aging computers and significantly automate air traffic control. An important question is to what extent the design of this program has been influenced by the government's strike experience and its turbulent record of labor relations. Whoever controls technological decision making has the power to shape technology to conform with their desired goals.

Technically, there are a number of very different options available: These range from seeking total automation to giving controllers and pilots new tools that enhance human judgment. The FAA's proposal leans heavily in the former direction. Writing in the April 1982 issue of *Technology Review*, Hoomin D. Toong, a faculty member of the Sloan School of Management at MIT, and Amar Gupta, a postdoctoral research associate, describe an important aspect of the FAA's new program:

> Between 1989 and 1995, an automated en-route air traffic control (AERA) facility will be implemented to carry out normal routing and conflict-avoidance without controllers' intervention . . . . Such a system implies that the entire task of routing air traffic will be done with minimal human intervention, changing the controller's role from that of an active participant to that of a monitor. Only if the computer system shut down or judgments beyond the programmed instructions were required would direct human intervention be expected. . . .

The pressures to minimize the role of the controllers conflict with the development of the optimal technical alternatives. The Rand Corporation raises some probing questions about the role of the controller in any new system:

> The critical question in designing the ATC (Air Traffic Control) system of the future is not really what can be done but what *should* be done. Exactly how much and what kind of automation should assist or replace the human controller? Should we strive for a system in which the machine has the primary responsibility of control and human expertise is used in a secondary, backup fashion? Or should men, in spite of their intrinsic limitations, retain primary control responsibility and utilize machine aids to extend their abilities?

Rand then blasts the direction of FAA research and development for heading in the first direction:

> The AERA scenario presents serious problems for each of the three major goals of ATC—safety, efficiency, and increased productivity. By depending on an autonomous, complex, fail-safe system to compensate for keeping the human controller out of the route decision-making loop, the AERA scenario jeopardizes the

goal of safety. Ironically, the better AERA works, the more complacent its human managers may become, the less often they may question its actions, and the more likely their system is to fail without their knowledge. We have argued that not only is AERA's complex, costly, fail-safe system questionable from a technical perspective, it is also unnecessary in other, more moderate ATC system designs.

Rand proposed an alternative called Shared Control in which the primary decision-making responsibilities remain with the controller but in which the operator has an increasing "suite of automated tools." The role of the controller would be expanded so that "he is routinely involved in the minute-to minute operation of the system." The system itself would consist of a "series of independently operable, serially deployable aiding modules." Whatever its technical merits, Shared Control would add to the responsibilities of an occupational category in which over two-thirds of the existing members had just been dismissed.

The story of the confrontation between PATCO and the FAA underscores the potential importance of computers in labor–management relations in general and the strike situation in particular. On the one hand, computer technology and telecommunications make possible central direction of far-reaching activities, concentrating enormous power into relatively few hands. On the other hand, complex computer systems often lend themselves to operation by a reduced and less skilled work force in an emergency situation. The leverage of the air controllers evaporated because less-experienced workers could successfully take over the job."

Source: Abridged from Shaiken, 1984, pp. 248–255.[15]

Preferred Employment Status/Contracting Out   It is not possible for all workers to have job security *and* for management to exercise employment flexibility. In anticipation of variability in demand and economic downturns, a two-tier employment system is also part of the new industrial relations model. This is handled in two ways: (1) the permanent work force is supplemented by temporary workers as demand for products or services requires; and (2) work is contracted outside the firm during periods of high demand and performed internally by regular employees during other times. Again, these features parallel the Japanese system.

Contingency-based Compensation The new system of industrial relations rewards employees (both workers and managers) more on the basis of how well the organization is doing rather than a fixed sum which may bear little relationship to performance. Already in Japan there is a bonus payment system in effect which on average accounts for about one-third of total compensation, and which is paid "contingent on the continuing adequate financial performance of the company"

(Abegglen and Stalk, 1985, p. 197). In the United States, Kochan et al. (1986, p. 240) point to comparable developments:

> At the level of collective bargaining, pressures to moderate the growth in compensation and to adopt contingent compensation are likely to continue. Profit sharing, gain sharing, employee stock ownership plans, and bonus incentive and performance-based pay systems will take on added importance as managers search for ways to become more competitive while rewarding employees for helping them to do so.

In Great Britain, Purcell and Sisson (1983, p. 119) likewise report that "the number of plantwide incentive and cost reduction schemes is likely to increase, the logic being not simply to relate some element in the pay packet to performance but also to encourage employees to identify more with the corporate objectives."

Performance-based Raises and Promotions As discussed earlier, Japan is likely to move more toward a system of raises and promotions based on output rather than seniority. In the United States and Great Britain also, the tendency is to give less emphasis to seniority and more to merit in the career progression of employees.

These five interrelated elements are likely to become increasingly predominant in the industrial relations systems of the United States, Great Britain, and Japan. Indeed, in Japan they have been established in modified form for some time. Each element is designed to be compatible with a highly competitive economy in which there is little or no growth (e.g., the 1980s). Thus, in every organization in which this system is established, there is a core of highly committed career employees who are trained in a variety of tasks, and who perform to their utmost in that their earnings and chances for promotion are tied to how well the organization performs overall. In a "high-growth" economy, these features are not so important because the chances of success are greater; however, in a "low-growth" economy they may be absolutely crucial for success.

It is important to note that each of these elements has been vigorously opposed by the organized trade union movements in both the United States and Great Britain. For example, job flexibility as a system can destroy hard-won, integral craft skills and cause a blurring of occupational distinctions. In that workers traditionally have gained their identity and earned their livelihood in a system of clearly demarcated occupations in which the skills associated with each occupation command their own price in the open labor market, there is strong resistance to the alternate system in which workers learn organizationally based skills that are neither easily transferable nor immediately identifiable.

With regard to job security, unions obviously are not opposed. However, to the extent that security is offered only to a small core of "elite" workers leaving the large mass unprotected, there is vehement opposition. A two-tier employment system essentially creates two classes of workers—advantaged and disadvantaged. Whereas temporary workers have always been laid off during periods of low demand, trade unions are opposed to the institutionalization of this process.

Regarding contingency-based compensation, the history of British and American industrial relations has taught labor unions to be extremely wary of incentive systems (see, for example, Miller and Form, 1980, pp. 167–169). First, the amount of extra work achieved has not always been commensurately rewarded, and second, greater productivity has often resulted in layoffs and greater unemployment. Concerning performance-based raises and promotions, unionists state that because it is managers who evaluate "performance," advancement may be based on nonrelevant, particularistic criteria (e.g., favoritism). On the other hand, with seniority as the basis of raises and promotions, all employees are treated equitably according to one universal and observable standard.

Although none of these elements is endorsed by unions in the United States and Great Britain, nevertheless they are being introduced, either in nonunion work settings as complete packages or in unionized workplaces as piecemeal concessions gained through collective bargaining (Kochan et al., 1986). Notwithstanding union opposition, it is the perception of both management and government in these countries that industrial relations must become more cooperative in order that British and American business may become more competitive internationally. Particularly in the United States, if unions do not continue to make concessions, they will be left out of the bargain.[16] When it is considered that 83 percent of all employees in the United States are *not* union members (in all probability a growing percentage), this is not an idle threat. (See Box 10-4, **Union Avoidance**.) As mentioned earlier in the chapter, the governments in all three countries have recently legislated against unions and yet at the same time have extended individual worker rights. If unions do not cooperate in this new "accommodation," then government could very well end up as the sole protector of the worker.

Finally, it is interesting to observe that despite the differing historical origins and cultural practices of industrial relations in these three countries, there is definite convergence now taking place. From the discussion above, it is clear that the model being adopted is more Japanese than it is either American or British. How may this be explained?

In Chapter 7 on Formal Organizations, we noted the emergence of a new organic, flexible, consultative form of organization. In response to a host of novel environmental contingencies and a more sophisticated variable work force, organizations have become less structured, not as rule bound, more task oriented, and more collaborative rather than hierarchical. While we found that these features were characteristic of Japanese organizations, we noted also that several researchers had independently observed these same properties becoming more apparent in Western organizations. In other words, this emergent type of organization represents a viable adaptation to the current environment of rapid change.

Given this emergent organization, what kind of worker–management relationship is most compatible or concordant? In the industrial relations models described above, the Western versions may be characterized as polarized, adversarial, legalistic, and rigid, in contrast to the Japanese model, which is collaborative, integrative, and responsive. Notwithstanding the fact that there is empirical foundation for these contrasting styles, the Japanese form of industrial relations is more compatible with an organization that must be sufficiently flexible to adapt to variable external pressures as well as to a complex individualized work force. Hence, the shift toward Japanese-style industrial relations on the part of Western business

Box 10–4 Union Avoidance

Among the increasing proliferation of management consulting firms in the United States are a variety that specialize in keeping organizations "union free." These firms are comprised of various labor, legal, and psychological experts whose sole function it is to advise companies on how they may resist union organizing drives and combat strikes and other labor action. Reproduced below is part of an advertising brochure distributed by one of these firms that indicates the services it offers.

Introducing the most authoritative and comprehensive action plan ever developed for keeping your company union free.

Maintaining Union-Free Status, a new three-part video training program, unveils for the first time, inside secrets on how unions operate, what areas of your company they're likely to target . . . and how you can take advantage of this information to keep your company union-free.

After viewing this training program, every participant will be armed with a proven, step-by-step defense against the union organizer . . . and specific instructions on how to boost employee morale and loyalty . . . encourage greater teamwork, cooperation, and communication between management and staff . . . and virtually guarantee that your company's employees would never vote in favor of a union.

Act today. Tomorrow may be too late.

You can stop the union organizer from ever getting into your company by taking the right preventive measures today.

In Part 1 of this program, *The Pre-Organizing Drive*, you learn a proven 9-step plan for keeping every employee satisfied. So when the union organizer knocks, they don't open the door.

Plus, you learn why supervisors play such a critical role in your union defense . . . and how to train them to work for you . . . not against you.

Learn what to expect . . . and what to do when the union strikes.

What do you do when the union targets your company? When union organizers knock at your doors . . . and membership and authorization cards begin to appear?

Part 2, *When the Union has Targeted Your Company*, answers these questions and more. You'll hear never before revealed union organizing strategies and how to combat them. And you'll learn exactly how to sell non-unionization to employees and how to conduct an anti-union campaign . . . and win!

Discover the perfect defense against the union organizer . . . and the perfect offense.

When union organizers succeed in filing a petition for election, every member of your management team must be prepared to act . . . or you may find yourself faced with a unionized workplace.

In Part 3, *The Union Has Filed a Petition for Election,* you learn your legal obligations and how to avoid unfair labor practices. Then, you'll watch one successful tactic after another for increasing your odds of winning the election. All from an attorney who has won more than 95% of the elections he has been involved in.

The power of video makes learning quick and easy.

Combine the proven training powers of audio, video, workbooks, and hands-on participation, and you get results.

Like high retention. And information and skills that can be applied immediately.

Plus, you'll find every step explained and demonstrated in easy to understand language. With no legalese. Or pie-in-the-sky theory.

Just every essential element—from A to Z—you need to uncover potential problem areas and to keep unions out of your company.

Table 10.4   RANK ORDER OF STRIKE ACTIVITY IN INDUSTRIALIZED COUNTRIES[1]

	Measures of strike activity				
Rank	Frequency (no. of strikes)	Size (no. of strikers)	Duration (average days on strike)	Extent (strikers per 100,000 workers)	Cost (person days lost per 100,000 workers)
	(few)	(small)	(short)	(narrow)	(low)
1.	Switzerland	Switzerland	France	Switzerland	Switzerland
2.	Norway	Finland	Denmark	Sweden	Sweden
3.	Sweden	Sweden	Finland	Norway	Denmark
4.	UNITED STATES	New Zealand	Italy	Belgium	Norway
5.	Belgium	Belgium	Israel	UNITED STATES	JAPAN
6.	Denmark	UNITED STATES	Australia	Denmark	Belgium
7.	JAPAN	UNITED KINGDOM	New Zealand	UNITED KINGDOM	Israel
8.	UNITED KINGDOM	Denmark	JAPAN	JAPAN	France
9.	Israel	France	UNITED KINGDOM	Israel	New Zealand
10.	Canada	JAPAN	Switzerland	Canada	Finland
11.	France	Norway	Belgium	New Zealand	UNITED KINGDOM
12.	Italy	Australia	Sweden	France	UNITED STATES
13.	New Zealand	Canada	Norway	Finland	Australia
14.	Australia	Israel	Canada	Australia	Canada
15.	Finland	Italy	UNITED STATES	Italy	Italy
	(many)	(large)	(long)	(broad)	(high)

[1]Averages for 1974 to 1976.

Source: Adapted from Chermesh, 1985, p. 289.

organizations may be seen not as emulation but more as the evolving of a set of relationships that match the properties of this new type of organization.

Independent behavioral data indicating that Japanese industrial relations are more harmonious than either British or American come from international comparisons of strikes. Table 10.4 rank orders 15 industrialized countries according to five commonly accepted measures of strike activity: frequency, size, duration, extent, and cost. The far-right column, cost, or the person-days lost per 100,000 workers due to strikes, is a composite measure of the other four columns. For example, note that while there are relatively few strikes in the United States (column 1), when they occur they are likely to last a relatively long time (column 3). On the other hand, Great Britain ranks close to the middle on all four columns. However, column 5 reveals that both the United States and Great Britain rank among the highest in terms of person-days lost due to strikes. By contrast, Japan is among the lowest one-third with regard to lost time arising out of labor–management disputes.

As we have noted previously, there are critics of the new system of industrial relations (see, for example, Moody, 1988; Shaiken, 1984). They charge that it is a management-dominated rather than a collaborative approach to industrial relations. The history of the trade union movement provides a running record of the fact that managers do not act in the interests of workers; only workers themselves, organized into strong groups, can present and have heard their concerns to already too powerful managers. A paternalistic company union does not provide such a forum, and therefore workers will lose many of the hard-won gains they have achieved over the years. The result will be a greater material and symbolic gulf between "them" and "us."

Although these concerns are historically valid, they may be overstated under current circumstances. The new role of the state as watchdog does place outside formal limits on what either management or unions may do. Also, the media act to provide strong informal pressure. While no doubt there will be abuses of the new system as there have been of the old, given current safeguards it is likely that these will be fewer and less serious than in the past. In any system in which there are competing interests, there will be problems. However, from some of the successes to date, both in Japan and in the West, it is possible that the present "accommodation" could become an "accord."

SUMMARY

10.1 Worker–management relations, or industrial relations, are the institutionalized framework within which the rights, responsibilities, and conditions of work, as well as compensation, are negotiated and set out in contractual form. Because of the division of labor, there must be some mechanism to determine who does what and how much each is worth. Formerly, this was the exclusive prerogative of management.

10.2 In Great Britain, the United States, and Japan, workers originally organized into unions to protest against the harsh conditions dictated by management. Unprotected and even outlawed by government, they sought a voice in establishing the conditions of work and the earnings they received. The first to organize were craftworkers who banded together on the basis of their specialized skills. They were followed by semiskilled workers who organized on an industry-wide level. In the last half of this century, white-collar public sector employees have also formed unions. Today, trade unions are recognized legally and have the right to bargain with management for the workers they represent. In addition, workers enjoy substantial protection under the law.

10.3 In Britain, until very recently, more than half of all workers were trade union members. British unions are politically affiliated with the socialist Labour Party, and are highly centralized and concentrated. Industrial relations mirror class-based antagonisms that have been an inherent aspect of British society for centuries. At least part of the reason for the recent decline in union membership can be attributed to the antilabor legislation of the present Conservative government.

10.4 In the United States, fewer than one in five workers are union members. At their peak in 1945, unions represented only slightly more than one-third of all workers. Consequently, trade unionism has not been a particularly strong force in American society. American unions espouse the principle of "business unionism," which means that they are primarily concerned with securing adequate wages and decent working conditions for their members. One explanation for the relatively small presence of unions in the United States is that the concept of unionism is antithetical to the basic American values of "individualism and competitive meritocracy." However, unionism in America has also faced serious challenge from organized business and, more recently, antiunion legislation.

10.5 In Japan, until the 1980s, approximately one-third of all workers were members of enterprise unions that are organizations of all regular employees (blue collar and white collar) within a single firm. Thus, enterprise unionism is very decentralized. Because of the fact that most Japanese workers and managers are employed in just one firm throughout their careers and therefore their joint fate is determined by how well their organization performs, enterprise unions tend to be very collaborative and generally supportive of managerial initiatives. Similar to Great Britain and the United States, there has been a decline in Japan in the percentage of workers who are represented by unions. Explanations for this include falling public support of unions, antiunion legislation, and managerial opposition.

10.6 Japanese industrial relations are based on the "three pillars" of Japanese-style management: lifetime employment, seniority-based career progression, and enterprise unionism. Together, these features have produced a highly involved and committed work force that is largely responsible for Japan's phenomenal economic success. However, now the system is coming under strain in that Japanese managers, operating under conditions of little or no economic growth, do not have sufficient flexibility to maneuver in a highly competitive, international environment.

10.7 In the United States and Great Britain, conflict between workers and management is institutionalized in the collective bargaining procedure. The most important concerns of workers are getting better wages and fringe benefits and improving their job security (see Table 10.3).

10.8 At the broader level, there is also conflict over the entire system of industrial relations in the United States and Great Britain. While unions are concerned with job protection and providing management with qualified workers for specifically defined jobs, managers are demanding greater flexibility in the assignment of workers in order to run their organizations efficiently and profitably in a limited growth economy. Unions charge that management is simply attempting to gain greater control at the workers' expense.

10.9 Despite union resistance, the industrial relations systems in all three countries are undergoing transformation. The new "accommodation" that is being established contains the following common elements: (1) job flexibility; (2) limited job security; (3) a two-tier employment system; (4) contingency-based compensation; and (5) performance-based raises and promotions. If unions do not cooperate in this new system of industrial relations, they are in peril of having their ranks diminished even further than they are now.

10.10 Thus, there is occurring a convergence in the industrial relations systems of all three countries. It is argued that this convergence arises in response to the changes that have occurred in organizations. Compared to work organizations in a more stable, predictable environment, contemporary organizations are less structured, not as rule bound, more task oriented, and more collaborative rather than hierarchical. The new form of industrial relations, which emphasizes consultation over conflict, is more compatible with this emergent organizational structure.

NOTES

1. The statistics on labor union membership over time are not completely reliable (see Goldfield, 1987, p. 9, fn. 9), and are often computed on different bases. For example, the figures in Table 10.1 are calculated as percentages of *nonagricultural* employees which reveal that American union membership peaked at 35.5% in 1945. However, if percentages are computed on the base of *all* employees, membership peaked in 1954 at 25.4%. A further problem is introduced by the addition in 1968 of employee association members (e.g., the National Education Association and the American Nurses Association) to the labor union membership rolls, which explains the apparent increase in union membership in 1970. Excluding this group, the percentage of union members in the nonagricultural labor force in 1970 was 27. Finally, it is important to note that while the *percentage* of union members has declined over time, their *numbers* have been steadily increasing, at least until the 1980s. During the late 1970s, more than 22 million American workers were union and employee association members. See Goldfield, 1987, pp. 10–14.
2. Women, working and otherwise, did not receive the franchise until 1918. See Table 3.5.
3. The public sector comprises "national government; local government and education; health services; post and telecommunications; air transport; port and inland water transport; railways; gas, electricity and water; and coal mining" (Bain and Price, 1983, p. 10).
4. A closed shop is "a provision in a collective agreement whereby all employees in a bargaining unit must be union members in good standing before being hired, and new employees must be hired through the union" (*Glossary of Industrial Relations Terms*, 1984, p. 7).
5. While collective bargaining is less centralized in the United States than in Great Britain, nevertheless a number of large unions have until recently engaged in industry-wide "pattern bargaining" in which a "master contract" is negotiated for all workers in a given industry. See Moody, 1988, pp. 2–3.
6. Anderson (1982) states that while centralized bargaining results in fewer work stoppages resulting from breakdown in contract negotiations, decentralized bargaining leads to fewer stoppages arising out of wildcat strikes. A wildcat strike is "a spontaneous and short-lived work stoppage, not authorized by the union. It is usually a reaction to a specific problem in the workplace, rather than a planned strike action" (*Glossary of Industrial Relations Terms*, 1984, p. 24).
7. Anderson (1982) does point out that collective bargaining often occurs at several different levels or stages. For example, a centralized master agreement may be reached, which is then individually fine-tuned by local union–management committees at various operating sites.
8. In Britain in 1987, the ten largest unions were comprised of four craft unions, one industrial union similar to the teamsters, two industrial unions representing workers in the tertiary sector, and three public employee unions. See Towers, 1989, p. 176.

9. Checkoff is "a clause in a collective agreement authorizing an employer to deduct union dues and, sometimes, other assessments, and transmit these funds to the union" (*Glossary of Industrial Relations Terms*, 1984, p. 7).

10. In a Japanese "national character" survey, the sample "was asked to pick from lists the adjectives which they thought generally characterize the Japanese people" (Dore, 1973, p. 296). The three most frequently chosen items were "diligent" (selected by 61%), "persistent" (58%), and "polite" (47%). See Dore, 1973, pp. 295–298.

11. Falling public support of unionism in the United States is documented in Figure 10.1. In Great Britain, Towers (1989, p. 185) notes that in 1983 and 1987, for the first time ever, fewer than half of the trade unionists who voted in the national elections cast their ballots for the Labour Party. In Japan, Freeman and Rebick (1989, p. 603), reporting on two separate national surveys of workers in 1973 and again in the mid-1980s, observed a falling percentage in those who said "they would try to form a union if they were dissatisfied with working conditions in their company."

12. This state of affairs serves as a major reason for Japanese transnational investment (see Chapter 8).

13. This is one important reason why lifetime employment does not extend to *all* employees within a firm.

14. In Japan, the mandatory retirement age for most workers is 55. However, in recent years this has been extended to 60 or even 65 in some companies. See Maeda, 1980.

15. In the 29 January, 1990 issue of *Newsweek* ("Can we trust our software?" pp. 70–73), it was reported that on 22 January AT&T's nationwide telephone system malfunctioned for nine hours due to a probable programming error, still not located at the time of press release. The error delayed or aborted more than half of all calls placed.

    According to Gregory Simon, coauthor of a congressional report entitled "Bugs in the System," "We're just lucky the first major software accident happened in the telephone system, rather than in the air-traffic-control system" (p.71). The article details how programming errors can remain undetected, and the consequences this could have for air traffic control:

    > A large software program can be tested only by actually trying every conceivable combination of challenges to see whether it fails. But when programs get very large, says John Shen, a computer researcher at Carnegie-Mellon University, "it would take tens, if not hundreds of years, to go through the combinations." The national air-traffic-control system, which ensures the safety of all commercial aircraft, will be massively retooled this decade, and the Federal Aviation Administration is still determining just how to certify that the system works under all conditions. It may not be able to: "The sky," says FAA resource specialist Mike De Walt, "is home to an infinite number of aircraft velocities and positions" (pp. 71, 73).

16. For a systematic documentation of the concessions already allowed by American unions, see Moody, 1988, pp. 165–191.

Chapter

11

Work, Workers, and Society

. . . the structural imperatives of jobs affect workers' values, orientations to self and society, and cognitive functioning through a direct process of learning from the job and selected "generalization" of what has been learned.

Spenner, 1988, p. 75

*C*onsider that for approximately 40 or even 50 years of our lives the greater part of our waking existence is taken up with work—not only doing it, but thinking and talking about it, scheduling our lives around it, living according to what it provides, and being identified by it. In important ways, the work we do shapes who we become. By knowing a person's occupation, we feel that we know a lot about that individual. Complex and composite images surround occupational titles such as trial lawyer, heavy duty equipment operator, chief executive officer, accountant, machinist, brain surgeon, high school teacher, janitor, and real estate agent. Occupation is the single most important indicator that we use to identify who we are dealing with. Depending upon a person's occupation, we vary our behavior "to match."

In this chapter, we will focus on the impact that work has on people's lives. First, we will examine how the work that people do influences not only what they value as human beings, but also how their work affects the values they impart to their children. Consequently, work roles and behavior are important ingredients in the socialization process. Next, we will determine how work is related to stress and how it affects overall evaluations of happiness and well-being. This is followed by an examination of the relationship between work and nonwork, including research reports that document how much time workers actually apportion to the various necessary and discretionary activities that make up their daily lives. The chapter will continue by noting the universal importance of occupation in the determination of social standing and will conclude by observing what happens to workers when they sever their relationship to work through retirement.

WORK STRUCTURE AND PSYCHOLOGICAL FUNCTIONING

The most systematic, comprehensive, and long-standing research on the effects of work on workers' lives has been conducted by Melvin Kohn and his colleagues associated with the project (see Kohn, 1969; Kohn and Schooler, 1983). Almost 30 years ago, Kohn engaged in a cross-national study of the values that middle and working class parents in the United States and Italy held to be most important for their children. Of the 17 values listed, he found that middle class parents (regardless of gender or nationality) consistently ranked "self-control" more highly for their children than did working class parents (again regardless of gender or nationality), while working class parents rated "obedience" as being important for their children significantly more than did middle class parents.

Kohn noted that self-control and obedience are opposite ends of the same continuum—control by self and control by others, and asked why social class should produce such differences in parental values. He reasoned that because middle and working class people have different jobs and job demands, there must be something about the nature of the work that produces these differences. For example, jobs held by the middle class are usually more loosely supervised than are working class jobs. Similarly, middle class jobs are more involved with ideas and people than they are with things; the opposite is true for working class jobs. Finally, there is a greater degree of self-reliance required in jobs held by middle than by working class employees.

When Kohn controlled on each of these three features of work, the original relationship between social class and parental values disappeared. In other words, class by itself does not produce a difference in values. Instead, class is related to the type of work performed, and the type of work one does influences values. Kohn found that if workers had jobs in which they were loosely supervised, involved primarily with ideas and/or people, and required to be self-reliant, then, regardless of their social class, they valued self-control over obedience for their children. Conversely, if workers were closely supervised, worked primarily with things, and were not required to be self-reliant, they valued obedience more highly than self-control. Consequently, Kohn determined that it is the nature of work, not social class, that influences parental values. If workers exercise autonomy at work, self-control is valued both for self and children; however, if they are subject to direction by others, conformity and obedience are more highly valued.

In their most recent research report, Kohn and his colleagues (1990) describe a new cross-national investigation. Among the countries surveyed, the United States and Japan are most relevant for our comparative purposes. Continuing with their interest in the relationship between social class and self-direction (both for the respondents themselves as well as their children), once again they find moderate positive correlations. However, among Japanese workers the relationships are not as strong as among Americans. Furthermore, when Kohn and his fellow researchers introduce a composite indicator (occupational self-direction) that measures "the use of initiative, thought, and independent judgement in work" (p. 988) into the analysis, it explains or accounts for less of the original class/self-direction relationship among Japanese than among Americans (see Table 11.1).[1] In other words, whereas the most recent survey yields essentially the same results for American workers as the initial American-Italian research, the results for Japanese workers are less compelling.

What is it about Japanese workers that diminishes the relations between class and self-direction and between work structure and self-direction? As we have noted in previous chapters, Japan is a country in which the general value of self-direction is shunned. As Dore (1973, p. 297) puts it, "The Japanese are lesser individualists, are more inclined to submerge their identity in some large group to which they belong, and more likely to be obsessed by a sense of duty". In the place of self-direction, the Japanese value consensual collaboration, and this in turn affects the relationships in question.

Compared to American work settings, occupational self-direction in Japan is minimized, regardless of class or occupational level. For example, with regard to one aspect of occupational self-direction, two members of the Kohn research team (Naoi and Schooler, 1985) report that Japanese supervision is tighter than it is in the United States. Japanese workers more than Americans responded that "the boss decides what to do and how" and that they are "not at all free to disagree with the boss." However, they did state that their boss "discusses" more with them rather than "telling" them what to do.

Similarly, concerning another aspect of occupational self-direction, Japanese employees stated that their jobs were more routine and predictable than did Americans. Presumably, because of the norm of collaboration, everyone knows

Table 11.1   CORRELATIONS OF SOCIAL CLASS AND SELF-DIRECTION AMONG AMERICAN AND JAPANESE WORKERS, AND THE PERCENTAGE OF THESE CORRELATIONS EXPLAINED BY OCCUPATIONAL SELF-DIRECTION

Correlation of social class with	Americans	Japanese
1. Parental valuation of self-direction	.47	.28
Percent of correlation explained by occupational self-direction	78%	70%
2. Self-directedness of orientation	.43	.27
Percent of correlation explained by occupational self-direction	70%	59%

Source: Adapted from Kohn et al., 1990, pp. 996–997.

more what others are doing; there are fewer surprises from workers striking out on their own initiative. Only with respect to overall job complexity, the final component of occupational self-direction, did Japanese workers indicate more than Americans that their jobs require "thought and independent judgment" (Kohn et al., 1990, p. 988). Consequently, even though Japanese managers empirically exercise more occupational self-direction than do manual workers (see Kohn et al., 1990, pp. 992–993), because self-direction is not culturally valued, the connection between class and self-direction is depressed, as is the effect of occupational self-direction on this relationship.

Given that Americans value individual free will while Japanese elevate group consensus, it is amazing that social class has anything approaching a consistent effect on psychological variables concerned with self-direction. In two radically different sociocultural systems in which self-direction is as prized in one as it is scorned in the other, how can social class produce such apparently similar outcomes?

Kohn et al. (1990, p. 1006) argue that the answer lies not in class *per se*—"not because of ownership or control over resources, nor because of control over other people, nor because of the employment situation, but primarily because class position affects opportunities for occupational self-direction." In other words, because self-direction is an integral and important aspect of managers' and employers' jobs, regardless of prevailing value structures, they "value what is most available from their jobs" (Loscocco, 1987, p. 17). Thus, although dominant cultural values do reduce the magnitude of the relationship between class and self-direction in the case of Japan, nevertheless the structure of the work itself influences individual values *whether we like it or not*. This is a very strong conclusion that follows directly from the Kohn line of research and provides striking support for the theoretical position he has advanced over the years.

> The Kohn-Schooler program of research helped to refocus the study of social structure and personality; it also generated new knowledge on the relationships among social stratification, work, and personality. The program established as a truism the finding that much of the effect of social stratification position (education, occupational status, and income) and organizational position on personality flows through the objective conditions of day-to-day work experiences. Because of this program we have a more comprehensive understanding of which objective conditions of work generate socialization changes in particular dimensions of personality. Similarly, we know more about the dimensions of personality that select workers into jobs of given type or that lead to alterations of jobs by workers. We know that occupational self-direction, in particular the substantive complexity of work, plays a central role in this larger web of socialization and selection processes (Spenner, 1988, p. 79).

Work and Stress

A more specific aspect of Kohn's interest in the effects of work structure on psychological functioning is the relationship between work and stress. As indicated in Chapter 1, stress may be conceived as emanating out of an inadequate person–environment fit, with the degree of fit being a product both of objective circumstances and individual perception (mediation) of these circumstances. It may arise as a result of significant social events which cause disruption in people's lives (e.g., being laid off from work) or "the presence of relatively continuous problems" (Pearlin et al., 1981, p. 338) that indicate a persistent mismatch between individual and environment. For example, in that socioeconomic status (SES), gender, and marital status are all related to stress (Mirowsky and Ross, 1986), it would appear that people of lower SES, women, and the unmarried more often find themselves inappropriately placed in the social system than do higher status people, men, and those who are married.

Figure 11.1, a skills utilization model, presents the major objective determinants of stress at work which are mediated by individual workers. To the extent that workers do not perceive an adequate fit between their capabilities and the opportunities present in the work environment, either as a consequence of a discrete event (or events) or because of continuing problems, job dissatisfaction and strain occur that can lead to a sense of impotency and possibly loss of self-esteem. The principal forms of stress—malaise, anxiety, and depression (Mirowsky and Ross, 1986)—are manifested in lowered work performance and/or a deterioration in

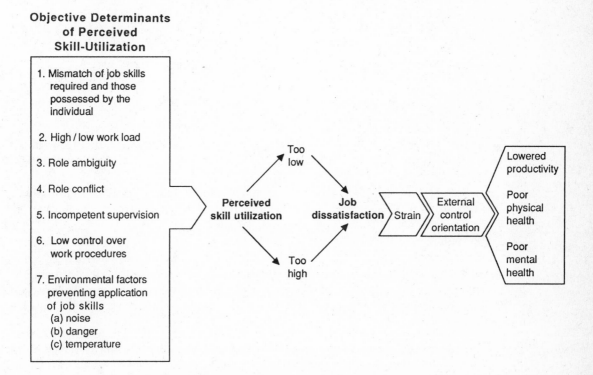

Figure 11.1 A Model of the Relationship Between Perceived Skill Utilization, Job Strain, and Stress
Source: O'Brien, 1986, p. 89.

physical and mental health, the latter two conditions not being restricted to the workplace. As O'Brien (1986, pp. 89–90) describes the model:

> If an employee is pressured by time or people, if he lacks control over work procedures, if there is ambiguity in the specification of what it is that should be done, if the job is too easy or too hard, then the employee cannot use his skills properly. When this occurs, things are perceived as being out of control and various systems and consequences of strain appear.

In a slightly different vein, Mirowsky and Ross (1986) state that the sources of stress are either lack of control (alienation), authoritarianism, or inequity. Of these, Kohn et al. (1990) focus on the notion of control as a principal determinant. In their study of American and Japanese workers, consistent with other research on this topic, they found that managers and employers from both countries suffered less distress (i.e., "anxiety, self-deprecation, lack of self-confidence, nonconformity in one's ideas, and distrust") than did either lower nonmanual or manual workers. Although the correlations of social class to distress are lower than those revealed for class and self-direction, they are statistically significant (see pp. 984–985). Kohn and his colleagues conclude that employees in lower organizational ranks experience higher levels of distress because they lack sufficient opportunity to exercise occupational self-direction. In other words, referring to Figure 11.1, they have low control over work procedures and consequently are not in a position to change their circumstances to match more closely their capabilities. Thus, workers who perceive an inadequate person–environment fit *and* who believe they are unable to do anything about it are prime candidates for job stress.

Subjective Well-Being

As there is a relationship between the structure of work and individual feelings of stress or strain, so also is work related to subjective perceptions of well-being. Table 11.2 presents various measures of well-being for nationally representative samples of British, American, and Japanese adults, and Table 11.3, employing a 10-nation European data set (including Great Britain), reveals the effect of occupational status on perceptions of life satisfaction and happiness.

Similar to the results on job satisfaction (see Table 9.5), Table 11.2 indicates that Japanese perceive themselves to be significantly less content with their present circumstances and less optimistic about the future than either the British or Americans.[2] In explaining these results, Inglehart and Rabier (1986, pp. 44–45) note that the Japanese more than other nationalities tend to coalesce around the mean:

> . . . on a 10-point scale, the Japanese were twice as likely to place themselves near the middle as were any Western publics. . . . This may reflect a distinctively Japanese cultural norm: a desire not to stand out from the group, linked with a pervasive emphasis on being part of a collective. . . .
>
> Discussing the low levels of both satisfaction and happiness reported by his countrymen, a Japanese analyst commented that "in Japanese society, people are expected to restrain themselves and express modesty."

Table 11.2 WELL-BEING IN THE UNITED KINGDOM, UNITED STATES, AND JAPAN

Measures of subjective well-being	Country		
	United Kingdom	United States	Japan
Life Satisfaction[1]			
1983	7.56	—	—
1981	7.67	7.72	6.39
1974–1976	7.33	7.41	—
Mean across surveys	7.52	7.57	6.39
Happiness[2]			
1981	3.33	3.26	2.96
Optimism[3]			
1987	40%	53%	18%
1983	43	50	20
1981	31	49	19
1976	31	—	20
Mean (1976–1987)	34%	50%	20%

[1]Mean score on 11-point scale: 0 = very dissatisfied, 10 = very satisfied. Respondents were asked the following question: "On the whole, are you very satisfied, fairly satisfied, not very satisfied, or not at all satisfied with the life you lead?"

[2]Mean score on 4-point scale: 1 = not at all happy, 4 = very happy. Respondents were asked the following question: "Taking all things together how would you say things are these days—would you say you're very happy, fairly happy or not too happy these days?"

[3]Percent responding "better" to question: "So far as you are concerned, do you think that [next year] will be better or worse than [this year]?"

Sources: For life satisfaction and happiness, Inglehart and Rabier, 1986, pp. 40–41; for optimism, Michalos, 1988, p. 178.

According to research conducted by Andrews and Withey (1976) and Campbell (1981), overall life satisfaction is comprised of a number of components or domains, one of which is work. Other domains include family, neighborhood, friends, leisure time, and so on. Michalos (1986, p. 62) notes that in 23 studies of job satisfaction and life satisfaction, over 90% of the 350 relationships examined were positive; satisfaction with work contributes to overall life satisfaction. Campbell (1981, pp. 48–49), commenting on the relative strength of 12 domains on life satisfaction, offers the following conclusion:

> . . . we find that satisfaction with self has the strongest relationship with general life satisfaction; satisfaction with standard of living is second and satisfaction with family life is third. Satisfaction with marriage is also high on the list, as are satisfaction with friends and work.
>
> Satisfaction in these domains—*self, standard of living, family life, marriage, friends, and work*—has the greatest influence in accounting for the level of satisfaction people feel with their life in general. The other domains are of diminished importance.

Table 11.3 reveals that similar to job satisfaction, overall life satisfaction and happiness are related to occupational level. While the overwhelming majority of

Table 11.3   LIFE SATISFACTION AND HAPPINESS AMONG EUROPEAN HEADS OF HOUSEHOLD BY OCCUPATION, 1982–1983[1]

Occupation	Percent "satisfied" or "very satisfied"	Percent "very happy"
In Labor Force		
Executive, top manager	93%	29%
Professional	86	29
White-collar employee	86	18
Shopkeeper, craftsman	80	17
Manual worker	80	19
Farmer, fisherman	75	11
Not in Labor Force		
Retired	80	19
Housewife	78	21
Unemployed	68	13
Total (N = approx. 19,000)	80%	21%

[1]Countries represented include Great Britain, Belgium, Denmark, France, Greece, Ireland, Italy, Luxembourg, Netherlands, and West Germany. The samples, approximately 1500 to 2000 respondents in each country, were nationally representative.

Source: Adapted from Inglehart and Rabier, 1986, p. 21.

respondents indicate that they are satisfied with their lives, managers and professionals apparently have more to be happy about. Not only does occupational level converge with other important variables such as education, income, and authority (see Chapter 9), but also, as Kohn and his colleagues (1990) have noted, higher occupational levels are associated with greater opportunities for occupational self-direction. Thus, occupational level, like nationality, is related to life satisfaction.

Within countries, Inglehart and Rabier (1986) explain that life satisfaction covaries most with those variables over which individuals have some degree of control. Consequently, while there is little difference in life satisfaction and happiness between men and women or among age groups, occupation and income are variable over a lifetime and are at least partially dependent upon people's own efforts. Thus, to the extent that they achieve high occupational levels and earn much money, they are generally more satisfied with their lives than are people who have not done so well. While work is only one domain in which individuals can exert control, nevertheless it is substantial in its impact on overall individual happiness and well-being.

WORK AND NONWORK

The relationship between work and other activities has received increased attention since Wilensky (1960, 1961) formalized some of the problems in this area of research. One such formalization is his restatement of the classic debate on the interaction of work with the rest of life. On the one hand, he proposed the compensatory hypothesis that states that workers denied opportunities to express themselves at work will make up for these deprivations by engaging in more creative activities in their leisure. On the other hand, he advanced the spillover hypothesis that states that these same deprived workers will carry over these deprivations into their nonwork lives, exhibiting a withdrawal and alienation from life similar to that which they manifest at work.

While Wilensky was specifically concerned with the effects of work on nonwork, and restricted himself primarily to manual workers whose employment he viewed as alienating, recent formulations have been proposed in more general terms. For example, not only does work spill over to nonwork activities, but spillover in the opposite direction also occurs (see Hedley, 1982; Crouter, 1984). Champoux (1978) has suggested that there are four logical possibilities concerning the work–nonwork relationship depending upon whether workers identify more closely with their work or nonwork experiences. Similar to the notion of "central life interests" (Dubin, 1956), Champoux argues that workers may locate their primary interests and identity in either the work or nonwork sphere. Furthermore, regardless of which sphere they identify with more strongly, they may either maintain a separation or make no essential distinction between their work and nonwork lives.

Champoux's research reveals that nearly two-thirds of his occupationally diverse American sample identified most strongly with nonwork interests, being relatively evenly split between whether they attempted to keep their nonwork life separate or carried it over into their work. Examining the results by occupational level, more than four-fifths of the blue-collar production workers identified with nonwork compared to only three-fifths of the managers surveyed. Thus, while most of these employees were attached more strongly to their interests away from work, those at the higher occupational levels were considerably more evenly divided in their loyalties.

The largest single group of managers, slightly more than one-third of them, identified with their work to such an extent that it spilled over into the rest of their waking lives. This is the classic image of the workaholic manager. In 1956, William H. Whyte wrote a bestseller entitled *The Organization Man*, in which he documented not only how the lives of these individuals were governed by their jobs and careers, but also how their families were affected. Whyte described the strict protocol established by firms that dictated who managers of various levels should socialize with, where they should live, and what kind of automobiles they should drive. While this group of highly dedicated managers does not constitute the majority of its ranks, it has nevertheless attracted the lion's share of interest.

As we have noted in previous chapters, more Japanese identify strongly with their work than do Western workers. "The [work] organization provides the framework through which individuals crystallize their personal identities" (Cole, 1979, p. 243). This extends through all occupational levels, although it is more pronounced among managers and professionals. In explaining this phenomenon, Cole (1979) gives as an underlying reason the fact that Japanese companies figure more prominently in the total lives of their workers than is true in Western industrial countries. For example, Japanese firms own approximately 7% of all private dwellings in Japan, more even than publicly owned rental accommodation

(Cole, 1979, p. 245). Furthermore, corporations are responsible for providing educational subsidies to employees and their families, recreational facilities, and company-sponsored vacations (see Dore, 1973, pp. 209–215). "These structured dependency relationships are a primary factor in the Japanese employee's high level of commitment to organizational goals and need to find fulfillment in work" (Cole, 1979, p. 246). Paraphrasing a Japanese expression, Cole states that "the enterprise and its employees share a common destiny—a community of fate" (p. 243).

Consequently, in Japan the spillover effect from work to nonwork is substantial in that most workers identify strongly with their work lives. In contrast, work is simply one of several important domains in the lives of most American and British workers. In a review of 29 studies of "central life interest" conducted mainly in the United States and Great Britain, Dubin and his colleagues (1976, pp. 282–283) found that work was not the focal interest for the vast majority of workers, particularly those at lower organizational levels (see also Dore, 1973, pp. 209–215). Nonwork locales were preferred. However, in one study of Japanese middle managers (Endo, 1978), fully 82% responded that work was the preferred context for social participation.

Table 11.4 presents the results of another study (Marsh and Mannari, 1976) in which Japanese male workers of varying organizational rank were asked to select from among three statements the value that most closely resembled their own (see note 1, Table 11.4). Overall, the most frequently chosen statement was, "Work is my whole life, more important than anything else." Almost half the men in the large electrical company surveyed selected work over either a "happy family" or the "pleasures of life," and this response was increasingly preferred the higher the organizational level. It is interesting to note also that family was the least chosen of the three options available.

From this brief analysis of the research evidence, we may conclude that both nationality (culture) and occupational level exert significant effects on the relationship between work and nonwork. For Japanese, because of the complex structural interrelations between these two spheres of activity and because of the high level of individual commitment, work assumes a centrality that it does not in the United States and Great Britain. For these reasons, there is greater spillover of work into nonwork attitudes and behavior. In the Western countries, work is viewed more segmentally. While it is crucial to individual survival, nevertheless it must compete with other important aspects of life (e.g., development of self, family, and lifestyle) in commanding the attention of workers. The predominant patterns established involve either maintaining a separation between work and nonwork activities or allowing the interests and pursuits of one's nonwork existence to spill over into work (Champoux, 1978; Hedley, 1982).

Concerning occupational level, there is a greater tendency for those at the higher ranks to manifest spillover from work to nonwork, while at the lower levels nonwork activities assume more importance and there is greater separation between the two domains (Katz, 1967). Because lower organizational participants are more constrained at work than those in the higher echelons, they do not have the same opportunities to become involved. For them, work is comprised of mainly necessary activities in which they consequently make less affective investment of

Table 11.4 VALUE ORIENTATIONS OF MALE JAPANESE WORKERS BY ORGANIZATIONAL RANK[1]

Organizational rank	(N)	Value orientations		
		Work	Pleasure	Family
Section and subsection chiefs	(41)	85.4%	7.3%	7.3%
General foremen and first-line foremen	(53)	56.6	39.6	3.8
Rank and file workers	(329)	43.2	37.7	19.1
Total	(423)	48.9%	35.0%	16.1%

[1]Organizational personnel 21 years of age and older in a large electrical factory were asked to choose one of the following three statements that best describes their own view of their work: (a) Work is my whole life, more important than anything else. (b) Work is only a means to get pay to spend on the pleasures of life. (c) Happy family life is more important than a company job.

Source: Recomputed from Marsh and Mannari, 1976, p. 116.

themselves than do those who have the discretion to organize work more as they see fit. Thus, the higher the occupational level, the greater is the probability that work will assume increased individual meaning and therefore pervade all aspects of life.

Paid Employment, Housework, and Leisure

In examining the relationship between work and nonwork, several researchers have attempted to determine how people actually fill their time—the various activities such as eating, sleeping, working, caring for children, cleaning the house, and relaxing that constitute the daily round of existence (see, for example, Szalai et al., 1972). Most of this research involves the use of diaries or logs that selected people are asked to fill in during the course of a day or week (see Figure 11.2). Researchers subsequently analyze these time budgets, classifying major and minor activities according to the amounts of time each of them consumed (see Figure 11.3). By this laborious method, it is possible to obtain a reasonable approximation of how people proportionally allocate their time to the necessary and voluntary activities of life.

Table 11.5 presents the results of two nationally representative time–activity studies of American adults in 1965 and again in 1985. The table indicates the number of hours in a week that employed men and women, as well as women not employed in the labor force, devote to major categories of activity. The largest single category is that given to personal needs (sleeping, eating, and personal care). Approximately 40 to 45% of the entire week is taken up in this fashion. Of the remaining time, paid employment and work-related activities (mainly commuting) consume the next greatest proportion of the week for those who are in the labor force (about 30% for men and 25% for women). The third essential group of activities involves housework and childcare, and here the variation is greatest, both over time and between gender and employment status.

Time	What Did You Do?	Time Began	Time Ended	Where?	List Other People With You	Doing Anything Else?
Midn ↓						
1 AM ↓						
2 AM ↓						
3 AM ↓						
4 AM ↓						
5 AM ↓						
6 AM ↓						
7 AM ↓						
8 AM ↓						

What You Did from Midnight Until 9 in the Morning

Figure 11.2   Sample Page from a Time–Activity Log Book
Source: Robinson et al., 1989, p. 10.

From 1965 to 1985, American men increased the number of hours they devoted to housework, although it will be noted that this increase did not equal the reduction they experienced in the average number of hours they were employed. In terms of daily duties, their increased housework can be visualized in the following manner. In 1965, men on average spent an hour a day during the work week on household chores (including childcare) and an hour and a half on each of their two days off; in 1985, their work week load remained the same but they contributed an extra hour and ten minutes on both of their nonwork days. While employed women in 1985 experienced a decline in household and childcare duties compared to 1965, nevertheless on average they spent *two* hours per day on these chores during the work week and four and a half hours on each of their "days off." In other words, while the division of household labor between men and women has become more equal over this 20-year period, nevertheless women still spend almost twice as much time as men engaged in these tasks. This may explain, at least in part, why women are employed fewer hours in the labor force then men.

With regard to women not employed in the labor force, the reduction in housework and childcare from 1965 to 1985 has been substantial (15.3 hours per week, or a one-third reduction in this category). Several factors account for this. First, the number of children per family unit has declined radically over this 20-year interval. The peak of the baby boom occurred in 1960 (see Gee, 1983, p. 426),

Working and related time (00-09)
00	Regular work
01	Work at home
02	Overtime
03	Travel for job
04	Waiting, delays
05	Second job
06	Meals at work
07	At work, other
08	Work breaks
09	Travel to job

Domestic work (10-19)
10	Prepare food
11	Meal cleanup
12	Clean house
13	Outdoor chores
14	Laundrey, ironing
15	Clothes upkeep
16	Other upkeep
17	Gardening, animal care
18	Heat, water
19	Other duties

Care to children (20-29)
20	Baby care
21	Childcare
22	Help on homework
23	Talk to children
24	Outdoor planning
25	Child health
26	Other, babysit
27	Other, child, relative
28	Blank
29	Travel with child

Purchasing of goods (30-39)
30	Marketing
31	Shopping
32	Personal care
33	Medical care
34	Administrative service
35	Repair service
36	Waiting in line
37	Other service
38	Blank
39	Travel, service

Private needs: meals, sleep (40-49)
40	Personal hygiene
41	Personal medical
42	Care to adults
43	Meals, snacks
44	Reataurant meals
45	Night sleep
46	Daytime sleep
47	Resting
48	Private, other
49	Travel, personal

Adult education and training (50-59)
50	Attend school
51	Other claasses
52	Special lecture
53	Political courses
54	Homework
55	Read to learn
56	Other study
57	Blank
58	Blank
59	Travel, study

Organizational activities (60-69)
60	Union, poli6tics
61	Work as officer
62	Other participation
63	Civic activities
64	Religious organization
65	Religious practice
66	Factory council
67	Misc. organization
68	Other organization
69	Travel, organization

Spectacles, entertainment, social life (70)
70	Sports event
71	Mass culture
72	Movies
73	Theatre
74	Museums
75	Visiting with friends
76	Party, meals
77	Cafe, pubs
78	Other social
79	Travel, entertainment

Recreation (80-89)
80	Active sports
81	Fishing, hiking
82	Taking a walk
83	Hobbies
84	Ladies hobbies
85	Art work
86	Making music
87	Parlor games
88	Other pastime
89	Travel, pastime

Communication (90-99)
90	Radio
91	TV
92	Play records
93	Read book
94	Read magazine
95	Read paper
96	Conversation
97	Letters, private
98	Relax, think
99	Travel, leisure

Figure 11.3 Major and Minor Activity Codes of Daily Life
Source: Robinson et al., 1989, p. 40.

Table 11.5   WEEKLY ACTIVITIES IN HOURS OF AMERICAN MEN AND WOMEN BY
EMPLOYMENT STATUS, 1965 AND 1985

	Men		Women			
	Employed		Employed		Not Employed	
Weekly activities[1]	1965	1985	1965	1985	1965	1985
Paid employment	44.8	41.5	35.3	33.3	.9	3.1
Work related	9.0	7.3	7.2	5.8	.3	.9
Housework	7.4	9.7	21.1	17.1	39.1	27.3
Childcare	.6	.6	2.1	2.0	7.4	3.9
Nonwork trips	5.7	6.9	5.0	7.1	7.2	8.1
Personal needs	67.8	68.4	68.9	70.8	71.7	75.2
Free time	32.8	33.8	28.4	31.8	41.4	49.4
Number of cases	(506)	(437)	(305)	(403)	(386)	(239)

[1]See Figure 11.3 for a more detailed listing of activities.

Source: Adapted from Robinson et al., 1989, p. 100.

which means that not only were there many preschool children requiring childcare
at the time of the 1965 survey, but also there was a corresponding increase in
general housework. Second, the sampling frames of the 1965 and 1985 surveys
were slightly different. While the early study sampled only from among those between 18 and 64 years of age, the more recent investigation did not make an upper-
level restriction on age (see Robinson et al., 1989, p. 6). Consequently, the 1985
sample was comprised of older retired women as well as full-time homemakers.
Finally, other changes, including more meals being consumed outside of the home,
permanent-press fabrics, and labor-saving devices, have contributed to the general
ease of housework over the past two decades. Parenthetically, values regarding
housework and "cleanliness" may also have changed as the domestic role of
women is perceived to be less important to their overall identity (see Berk, 1985).

The final category of major activity in Table 11.5—free time—is residual; that
is, it is the time left in a week after all the necessary duties and needs have been
met. Approximately 20% (for employed women) to 30% (for nonemployed
women) of a typical week remains for the average person to engage in discretionary activity.[3] Both men and women have made gains over the past 20 years in this
valuable commodity, although it will be noted that employed women are still two
hours less rich per week in this respect than employed men.

Table 11.6 specifies in detail the particular activities in which men and women
participate during their free time. In an attempt to approximate the effect of occupational level which was not included in the data analysis presented by Robinson and his colleagues (1989), I have instead controlled on educational level in that
these two variables are strongly related. Attained occupational level is in part a
function of educational achievement (see Haug, 1977). Also, the data in this table
are not nationally representative as in Table 11.5, but are based on a random sample
of the residents of Jackson, Michigan, in 1986 (see note 1, Table 11.6). However,

Table 11.6   WEEKLY LEISURE ACTIVITIES IN HOURS OF AMERICAN MEN AND WOMEN BY EDUCATION, 1986[1]

MEN

Leisure activities	Years of education				Total men (301)
	0–11 N = (48)	12 (89)	13–15 (101)	16+ (63)	
Passive					
Television	23.6	21.3	15.4	15.3	18.2
Reading	2.3	2.4	3.5	4.0	3.0
Radio	1.0	1.0	0.1	0.2	0.6
Resting	3.5	2.4	1.4	2.0	2.2
Total passive	30.4	27.1	20.4	21.5	24.0
Active/interactive					
Sports	0.6	3.4	1.6	2.2	2.1
Walking	0.5	1.0	0.9	0.3	0.8
Education	4.1	1.4	1.9	0.8	1.9
Organizations	0.7	2.3	1.7	1.6	1.7
Spectacles	0.0	0.2	0.7	0.3	0.3
Social life	9.3	5.4	8.2	6.6	7.2
Conversation	2.3	1.3	1.5	3.0	1.9
Various leisure	0.7	1.0	0.9	2.0	1.2
Total active/interactive	18.2	16.0	17.4	16.8	17.1
Total leisure hours	48.6	43.1	37.8	38.3	41.1
Percent passive	62.6%	62.9%	54.0%	56.1%	58.4%
Percent active/interactive	37.4	37.1	46.0	43.9	41.6

WOMEN

Leisure activities	Years of education				Total women (329)
	0–11 N = (43)	12 (130)	13–15 (115)	16+ (41)	
Passive					
Television	21.7	19.9	13.3	9.4	16.4
Reading	2.9	2.4	3.4	5.5	3.3
Radio	0.2	0.1	0.2	0.0	0.1
Resting	2.2	2.4	2.0	1.3	2.1
Total passive	27.0	24.8	18.9	16.2	21.9
Active/Interactive					
Sports	0.9	1.3	1.7	1.4	1.4
Walking	0.5	0.1	0.1	0.2	0.1
Education	5.1	1.4	3.7	0.6	2.6
Organizations	1.5	1.6	2.1	5.0	2.1
Spectacles	1.3	0.7	0.5	0.2	0.7
Social life	7.6	10.1	6.1	7.2	8.0
Conversation	3.1	2.7	3.3	2.7	2.9
Various leisure	2.0	1.2	1.6	2.1	2.0
Total active/interactive	22.0	19.1	19.1	19.4	19.8
Total leisure hours	49.0	43.9	38.0	35.6	41.7
Percent passive	55.1%	56.5%	49.7%	45.5%	52.5%
Percent active/interactive	44.9	43.5	50.3	54.5	47.5

[1]Based on a 24-hour time–activity diary completed by a representative sample of the adult residents (18 to 65) of Jackson, Michigan, between January and April 1986.

Source: Adapted from Robinson et al., 1989, pp. 82–83.

Robinson and his fellow researchers (1989, p. 9) do state that the Jackson study is highly correlated with the results of earlier national time–activity studies. With these caveats in mind, let us now turn to the substantive results.

With regard to total leisure time, both men and women with less education have more free time at their disposal than more highly educated people. Those who have not completed high school have between ten to fifteen more hours of discretionary time per week than those who have college degrees. However, it may well be that this extra free time is not entirely appreciated in that less educated men and women also put in considerably less than a 40-hour work week (see Robinson et al., 1989, p. 82). Thus, the relationship between education and leisure time revealed in this table may in fact be part of the better-known and well-documented inverse relation between education and unemployment or underemployment (see Miller and Form, 1980, p. 87).[4]

Table 11.6 is divided into two main types of leisure activity: passive and active/interactive. Of these, passive activities account for a greater proportion of total leisure time for both men and women (more so for men). Furthermore, there is a pronounced tendency for those with less education to be more passively involved in their discretionary time than those with college training (see Wilson, 1980, p. 27). This relationship is particularly strong for women. By far the major passive activity is watching television. It consumes 44% of all men's free time and 39% of women's. Like passive activities in general, the amount of television watched is inversely related to years of education. Also, it will be noted that as television watching increases, the time spent reading declines.

Among active/interactive leisure pursuits, social life and conversation constitute the major activities, taking up more than half of the 17 to 20 hours per week devoted to this classification of free time. Getting together with family, friends, and neighbors is a time-honored traditional way of spending one's leisure time. As might be expected, the overwhelming majority of these hours are spent with the immediate family (fewer for men than for women), the remainder being divided more or less evenly among parents, other relatives, friends, and neighbors (Robinson et al., 1989, p. 126). The next largest portions of active/interactive time are spent on sports and walking (more for men), education (more for women), and organizational activities (including church).

With regard to all of the active/interactive activities, there appear to be no clear relationships between educational level and the kind of activity chosen, although highly educated women are more heavily involved in organizations while those less educated are more frequent viewers of spectacles (e.g., movies). However, Robinson and his colleagues (1989, p. 81) do state that "a major factor differentiating the lifestyles of college-educated people . . . is the greater diversity of activities both in terms of work and of free-time activities."

While there are relationships between educational level and the ways in which people spend their free time, there is no discernible pattern between education and housework (including childcare). The same general male–female ratio in the division of household labor discussed above pertains at all levels of education. Male college graduates spend no more time at household chores (11.2 hours/week) than do high school graduates (11.4). Both groups of men put in about half the time that correspondingly educated women devote to these tasks.

The results of these and other time–activity studies indicate that most of the variation in behavior in nonwork time is explained by gender, employment status, and stage in the life cycle. However, the type of work that people do or, in other words, the activity that consumes the second greatest proportion of their time (after personal needs) also makes an impact. There are both universal and particular effects. Because work is comprised of mainly nondiscretionary activities, leisure affords the opportunity for all to engage in more individually tailored behavior. According to one study (O'Brien, 1986, p. 262), most individuals "rate autonomy, relaxation and family activities as the most important functions of their leisure." However, depending upon the particular characteristics of their job and the opportunities it provides, they may well choose different ways to achieve autonomy, to relax, and to be with their families. "Although work activities may have a small direct effect on leisure needs, the attributes of work that determine satisfaction are similar to the attributes of leisure that determine leisure satisfaction" (O'Brien, 1986, p. 262).

Cross-national Comparisons

There are no directly comparable time–activity studies that have been conducted in Great Britain, Japan, and the United States. However, Koseki (1989) does report on one Japanese study. In this 1985 survey, the results reveal similar time required for personal needs by both men and women in the United States and Japan; however, Japanese men worked considerably longer at their jobs than did American men. Unfortunately, no data are provided for female labor force participants. With regard to housework and childcare, Japanese men spent less than half as much time in household duties as American men. Consequently, Japanese women worked more at these tasks than did their American counterparts. Finally, both American men and women enjoyed slightly more free time than did the Japanese; however, Japanese of both sexes watched more television than Americans. Thus, their total leisure time was considerably more passive than it was for Americans.

This brief analysis reinforces the earlier conclusions drawn above regarding the relationship between work and nonwork. Because Japanese men perceive work to be more centrally important in their lives than do American men, they are only tangentially involved in their home lives. Instead, home is a place where they can recharge their batteries so that they may once more face the challenges offered by another working day. While these data cannot speak of the values and motivations of these workers, they do reveal behavior, and these behavioral date provide strong support for the above mentioned attitudinal survey in which a plurality of Japanese men agreed with the statement, "Work is my whole life, more important than anything else" (see Table 11.4).

According to the most recent statistics (United Nations, 1988, p. 89), there is little difference in the length of the work week in Japan, the United States, and Great Britain. The average number of hours worked per week in manufacturing

(1985) in Japan (41.5) was only one hour more than in the United States (40.5), but almost identical to the United Kingdom (41.8). Furthermore, there has been little change in these figures during all of the postwar years. However, these data do not tell the whole story. In line with the relative centrality of work discussed above, Cole (1979) notes that Japanese men put in more overtime and take fewer vacations than do Americans and most Europeans (see also Dore, 1973, p. 97; Koseki, 1989, pp. 122–124). Concerning holidays, not only are Japanese officially granted approximately half the vacation allotment that American employees receive, but many of them do not take the full leave to which they are entitled.

> A 1970 national survey reports that only one-fifth of the people surveyed took all of the paid leave available to them and 40% of them utilized only a half or less. . . . The underutilization of paid leave is particularly notable among older age groups, who have few alternatives to their current employment and stronger commitments to work by virtue of higher wages and benefits. Some 70% of male workers from age 40 to 49 took less than half of the paid leave to which they were entitled. (Cole, 1979, p. 231).

Cole offers two reasons why Japanese men do not take their full share of holidays even though "they could receive [the same] compensation simply by staying home" (p. 232). First, as indicated above, they have a stronger commitment to work than their Western counterparts. When they do take holidays, very often the reasons they give imply that they have no other choice (e.g., illness, fatigue, and family obligations).[5] "In short the whole notion of a fixed vacation time taken for personal enjoyment free from the work situation is relatively unestablished in Japan" (p. 231).

The second reason hinges on the notion of the employing organization as a "community of fate." Because all employees—workers and bosses alike—"share a common destiny," Cole (pp. 240–241) argues that Japanese managers take advantage of their workers' commitment and sense of purpose:

> . . . the provision of the Labor Standards Law referring to paid vacations specifies that they must be taken so as not to disrupt the normal operation of the business. This is a critical clause, for it allows the company to mobilize enormous formal and informal pressures to discourage workers from taking their full vacations. For large numbers of employees to take their full vacations would conflict with the company goal of raising productivity. If we assume high identification of individual employees with organizational goals, this would be unwise. It would conflict with individual self-interest in improving one's own situation, in particular promotion, since maximizing organizational interests tends to maximize individual interests. Evidence for this interpretation comes from a 1971 Ministry of Labor survey in which employees who used less than half of their allotted vacation time were asked to give the reason . . . Only 4.4% chose to respond "because I am happy when I am working." Rather, the majority stressed the "pressure of work" (38%), "the atmosphere of work is such that it is hard to take off" (23%), and "intend to add them up and use them later" (11%).

Not only do Japanese male workers take less time off from work, but Cole reports that when they do it is more likely to be spent with fellow workers than is the case in the United States. Furthermore, many of these leisure activities, including vacations, are organized by the company. In his British–Japanese comparison, Dore (1973, p. 205) describes the extensive facilities maintained by the Hitachi factory he studied. They include a 1200-seat auditorium, "an athletics stadium, one large and one smaller baseball stadium, a gymnasium, a swimming pool, and various tennis and volleyball courts." In Dore's sample of Hitachi workers, "83% belonged to some sports or social club or hobby group organized exclusively for members of the firm or union; only 14% belonged to any outside social or political or religious organization" (p. 214). By contrast, substantially fewer British workers belonged to company-sponsored organizations. "Only 21% of the Hitachi workers had not been to any social function organized by the firm in the previous year; 73% of the British sample" (p. 214). As Cole (1979, p. 231) remarks, "Japanese employees are not well accustomed to utilizing their discretionary time on an individual basis." In this regard, note Box 11-1, **They Come in Groups.**

While all the evidence presented makes it difficult to dispute the Japanese work ethic, there are recent indications that it is moderating somewhat (see Koseki, 1989). For example, the sale of sporting gear and lessons has increased 68% in the last five years; the number of health clubs have doubled since 1984; and outward bound air travel from Japan has increased more than 100% during the 1980s (Impoco, 1988; Polunin, 1989, p. 5). In part, the new emphasis on leisure is being promoted by the government in order to increase consumption and thereby reduce the growing trade imbalance between Japan and the other industrial nations. As well, it reflects a desire of Japanese workers to enjoy more the results of their labor.

Impressive as these figures might be, Impoco (1988) points out that even now, according to a recent government survey, the majority of Japanese workers still take only half their allotted holidays. Similarly, Polunin (1989, p. 8) states that although the increase in air travel has been dramatic, nevertheless the number of passengers in 1987 represented only 5.6% of the Japanese population. Comparable figures for West Germany and Great Britain are 36.1% and 48.2%, respectively. Thus, while changes in attitude are occurring, particularly among the younger generation, comparatively speaking Japanese workers experience considerably more work spillover than do Americans and British. Both the attitudes and the behavior of the Japanese, especially men, indicate that the impact of work upon nonwork is substantial.

WORK AND SOCIAL POSITION

Not only does the work we do influence our own attitudes and behavior, it also has a profound impact upon those around us. The jobs we hold in large part establish our social standing in society. Other people, including organizations, evaluate and treat us according to occupational title. Occupation forms a fundamental basis of social ranking:

> In all complex societies, industrialized or not, a characteristic division of labor arises that creates intrinsic differences between occupational roles with respect to power; these in turn promote differences in privilege; and power and privilege create prestige. Since the same process operates in all complex societies, the resulting prestige hierarchy is relatively invariant in all such societies, past and present. (Treiman, 1977, p. 128)

Box 11-1 They Come in Groups

Go to any major airport in the world, visit any principal tourist attraction, and there you will see them—groups of Japanese tourists intently absorbing the sights and scenery in minute detail. According to Fields (1983, p. 135), "The Japanese may have been the first to invent the group tour as a way of traveling for pleasure." And as the table below indicates, you are likely to see more of them in the years to come. By 1991, the Japanese government predicts that ten million travelers will be outward bound from Japan (Polunin, 1989, p. 5), and the vast majority of them will make their trip as part of an all-inclusive package or guided tour.

NUMBER OF JAPANESE OVERSEAS TRAVELERS, 1967–1987

Year	Number	Percent Increase in five years
1967	267,538	
1972	1,392,045	420%
1977	3,151,431	126
1982	4,086,138	30
1987	6,829,338	67

Source: Japan National Tourist Organization, 1988, p. 6.

Prior to 1964, foreign travel was restricted by the government, which was sensitive to anti-Japanese attitudes emanating from World War II (Fields, 1983, pp. 136–137). However, this did not discourage domestic travel, particularly in groups. From feudal times to the present, groups of fellow villagers and work mates have traveled together. Group travel is also encouraged among the young. In 1986, 95% of all junior high schools in Japan organized school excursions lasting at least three days (Japan National Tourist Organization, 1988, p. 5).

Among overseas Japanese travelers, approximately three-quarters go as part of organized tours. Aside from language difficulties and dealing with strange customs which are alleviated by all-inclusive package tours, there are other reasons for the propensity of Japanese to travel in groups. Even though many of the tour groups are comprised of individuals who do not know each other prior to the trip, nevertheless for the purposes of the trip they form a tightly knit and self-contained primary group.

According to Fields (1983, pp. 146–149), this particular sense of group goes back to feudal times. "The *hatagos*, the inns in the old days, brought together a hodgepodge of travelers, sometimes in groups but most often individually. Once under the roof of the *hatago*, the idea was that you entered a temporary family. The sliding paper doors did not have locks and that night's guests shared a common fate" (p. 147). Thus, given the orientation of Japanese to groups discussed throughout this book, there is security in group formation, particularly when individuals are experiencing unfamiliar customs and situations.

As part of its campaign to promote overseas travel by Japanese people, the government is also encouraging group travel. Travel agencies, particularly those focusing on package tours, are being expanded; overseas school tours are being promoted; and tax incentives to encourage company recreational travel to foreign countries have been introduced (Japan National Tourist Organization, 1988, pp. 17–23). While there have been recent increases in the number of *individual* Japanese tourists, these efforts will also more than likely result in substantial increases in group travel among the Japanese.

According to Treiman, not only does the work that we do determine our social ranking, but also because of the similarity in the division of labor from one society to another and the fact that comparable increments of power and privilege accrue to the same positions cross-culturally, people holding the same job in different societies experience approximately the same relative prestige. Prestige Treiman equates with moral worth, esteem, respect, and regard (p. 20). In other words, much of the respect that we merit in society flows directly from the work we do.

As mentioned in Chapter 6, Treiman set out systematically to determine how similar occupational prestige is across societies. Altogether he found prestige surveys from 60 different countries representing a total of 509 separate occupations. He then created a correlation matrix in which he computed the degree of fit of one country's prestige ranking with all other countries that had at least ten occupational titles in common. Out of a total of 1386 rank order correlations, the overall mean correlation was .79.[6] In other words, he found that in spite of cross-cultural variation and differences in the degree of industrialization, most countries had reasonably similar occupational prestige hierarchies.

Further analysis revealed that for each pair of countries, "the greater the similarity in level of industrialization [measured by proportion of the labor force in agriculture, level of education, and per capita GNP] the greater the similarity in prestige rankings" (p. 139). Thus, because Great Britain, the United States, and Japan are all similarly industrialized, we would expect their intercorrelations to be higher than the overall average correlation of .79. In fact this is true: Great Britain – United States = .94; Great Britain – Japan = .87; and United States – Japan = .90 (see pp. 81-92). This means that British and American occupational prestige rankings are virtually interchangeable, and that there is a very good match of the Japanese prestige hierarchy to both the United States and Great Britain.

From the national prestige rankings of all 60 countries, Treiman constructed standard prestige scores for each of the 509 occupations that were originally evaluated. This resulted in the Standard International Occupational Prestige Scale, which ranges from "chief of state" (90 points on the scale) to "gatherer" (–2). The mean average score of the scale (43.3) is represented by "office clerk" (standard deviation = 16.9). Table 11.7 presents the standard prestige scores of 50 common occupations that Treiman evaluated. Immediately it can be seen that not only do power and privilege vary along Treiman's prestige scale, but also it is highly correlated with income, education/training, authority, autonomy/control, and substantive complexity. Thus, it may be concluded that the prestige attached to particular occupations is a function of all these dimensions that together define what an occupation is.

The mean correlation of the Standard International Occupational Prestige Scale with each of the national rankings from which it is derived is .91 (pp. 176–177). In other words, Treiman's scale is an excellent approximation of how the citizens of all these countries apportion relative worth associated with one's employment. Only seven correlations are less than .87. With regard to Great Britain, the United States, and Japan, the correlations of their prestige scales with Treiman's standard version are each .96. Consequently, it is safe to say, for example, that in each of these countries on average a physician is more highly evaluated in terms of prestige than is a lawyer (see Table 11.7). Similarly, non-manual occupations are generally regarded with more esteem that are manual occupations. As Treiman himself concludes, "the Standard Scale scores will provide highly accurate estimates of the prestige of specific occupations in any nation in the world" (p. 179).

It is important to note that Treiman's scale measures relative, not absolute prestige. For example, we cannot assert that physicians in Great Britain, the United States, and Japan receive identical amounts of prestige; it is only legitimate to state that they are accorded more prestige on average than heads of large firms, engineers, and high school teachers. The standard prestige scale measures the relative merit of ocupational worth as perceived by all members of society (see p. 80).

According to Treiman, the similarity of occupational prestige rankings throughout the world is explained by the fact that work is similarly organized from one society to another. Regardless of economic development or cultural values, all social systems engage in a division of labor in order that their members can survive. Because all societies, past and present, face essentially the same problems in order to survive, the basic rudimentary structure of the division of labor in each society is similar. This division of labor may be simple or complex, but its fundamental characteristic is that it differentiates people according to function. Some tasks virtually anyone can do, while others only a relatively few are capable of performing. Also, in order to coordinate functions, it is necessary that some people be placed in a position of authority over others.

The horizontal and vertical differentiation arising out of the division of labor creates differences among people with regard to skill and authority, and those with unique skills which are highly prized and those with authority over others have more power than those who do not. With power comes the privileges it commands, and because power and privilege are universally valued, deference is bestowed upon the similarly powerful and privileged few among the world.

In short, occupational groups are able to convert their command of scarce resources—skill and knowledge, economic power, and authority—into material advantage both by virtue of the superior market position command of these resources

Table 11.7   RANK ORDER OF FIFTY COMMON OCCUPATIONS ON THE STANDARD INTERNATIONAL OCCUPATIONAL PRESTIGE SCALE

Occupational title	Score	Occupational title	Score
1 Physician	77.9	26 Garage mechanic	42.9
2 University professor	77.6	27 Mechanic, repairman	42.8
3 Lawyer, trial lawyer	70.6	28 Shopkeeper	42.4
4 Head of large firm	70.4	29 Printer	42.3
5 Engineer, civil engineer	70.3	30 Typist, stenographer	41.6
6 Banker	67.0	31 Police officer	39.8
7 Airline pilot	66.5	32 Tailor	39.5
8 High school teacher	64.2	33 Foreperson	39.3
9 Pharmacist	64.1	34 Soldier	38.7
10 Armed forces officer	63.2	35 Carpenter	37.2
11 Clergyman	59.7	36 Mason	34.1
12 Artist	57.2	37 Plumber	33.9
13 Teacher, primary teacher	57.0	38 Sales clerk	33.6
14 Journalist	54.9	39 Mail carrier	32.8
15 Accountant	54.6	40 Driver, truck driver	32.6
16 Civil servant, minor	53.6	41 Bus, tram driver	32.4
17 Nurse	53.6	42 Miner	31.5
18 Building contractor	53.4	43 Barber	30.4
19 Actor, actress	51.5	44 Shoemaker, repairer	28.1
20 Bookkeeper	49.0	45 Waiter	23.2
21 Traveling salesperson	46.9	46 Farm hand	22.9
22 Farmer	46.8	47 Street vendor, peddler	21.9
23 Electrician	44.5	48 Janitor	21.0
24 Insurance agent	44.5	49 Servant	17.2
25 Office clerk	43.3*	50 Street sweeper	13.4

*This number represents the mean score on the scale.

Source: Treiman, 1977, pp. 155–156.

provides and by virtue of the ability to directly manipulate the system that such power creates. For this reason, there is a general consistency in the skill, economic control, authority, and material reward hierarchies of occupations in all societies, and a similarity in these hierarchies across societies. (Treiman, 1977, p. 19)

Treiman's research demonstrates the powerful and universally constant impact of occupation upon one's social standing in society. The spillover of work into nonwork is enormous in that it influences not only how we think and behave outside of the work role, but also how others act toward us. Given these effects of work, what happens when we withdraw from the roles that are so important in determining who we are and how we function?

Retirement

Retirement is a relatively recent social institution limited in large part to the industrialized nations. Most workers in the world do not have the discretion to cease their employment; they must work until either they die or they are physically unable. Only with the introduction of private and public pension plans that provide income through the retirement years has it been possible for most people even to consider withdrawing from the labor force. For many, retirement is still equated with a life of poverty.

As indicated in Chapter 1, only three of the twenty most industrially developed countries had publicly administered old-age pension programs established by 1900 (see Table 1.2). The first pension program in the United States was instituted by the Baltimore and Ohio Railroad in 1884[7]; a national retirement plan did not come into effect until 1935 (Atchley, 1982). It was not until after the Second World War that the vast majority of industrial countries finally established national pension programs (Mishra, 1973), and "only in the 1960s did retirement come to be viewed as a legitimate part of the life course rather than an unfortunate fact of some working lives" (Atchley, 1982, p. 279).

Even now, there are large differences among national pension plans in the extent and adequacy of coverage. According to Scott and Johnson (1988, pp. 13–16), in 1980 retired couples entitled to state pensions received anywhere from almost half of their previous employment income (in Great Britain) to just under two-thirds (in the U.S.). However, for a variety of reasons, not all older retired people are eligible to receive public pensions (see ILO, 1984, p. 36). For example, in Japan less than one-quarter of the people qualified by age to receive old-age pensions actually obtained the full benefits under the plan (Maeda, 1980, p. 263). Although the amount and extent of coverage is improving (see ILO, 1985), nevertheless publicly administered social security programs in Japan "are much less developed compared with those of the countries of the Western world" (Maeda, 1980, p. 263). In 1980, social security benefits paid out in Japan represented 9.8% of the gross domestic product. The comparable figures for Great Britain and the United States were 16.9 and 12.2 percent respectively (ILO, 1985, pp. 56–59).

Not all retirement income is generated by public pensions. Privately administered plans, interest on savings, assistance from family members, and part-time employment are other sources of funds. For example, in Japan, where the mandatory retirement age is 55 for most workers and men are not eligible to receive public pensions until age 60 (55 for women), virtually all must seek alternative employment (Maeda, 1980). Even between the ages of 60 and 64, 81% of Japanese people are employed. In the United States, nearly one-quarter of men and 10% of women aged 65 and over are employed either part time or full time (see Table 6.4).

Notwithstanding these different sources of funds and assistance, many retired people still find it difficult to cope financially. In Great Britain, almost one-quarter of all pensioners applied to a government-run commission for supplementary benefits in order to survive (Bytheway, 1980, p. 425); in the United States, "over 15% of persons over age 65 had incomes below the official poverty levels in 1975, and another 10% were below the near-poverty level" (Palmore, 1980, p. 434); and in Japan, "the second most important cause of poverty, next to illness and/or disability, is old age" (Maeda, 1980, p. 260). Thus, even in developed industrial economies, for many people the most serious loss that occurs as a result of retirement is the ability to live independently and to enjoy the basic amenities.

Retirement may be mandatory or voluntary. Traditionally, it was forced solely as a result of ill health, disability, or incapacity; but with the growth of large formal work organizations at the beginning of the twentieth century, it also became compulsory on the basis of age. "'Scientific' management provided a rationale—efficiency—and bureaucratic organization provided the means—impersonal procedures . . . " (Atchley, 1982, p. 270). Thus was created the norm of an upward age limit beyond which most people should not or could not work.[8] Currently, in Great Britain and Japan the ages of mandatory retirement are 65 and 55, respectively, although they do not apply universally to all categories of workers. In the United States, while social security benefits normally begin at age 65, retirement can be deferred until age 70 (see Robinson et al., 1985), and it is anticipated that mandatory retirement on the basis of age will soon be eliminated altogether.

Recently, as the figures in Table 6.4 indicate, there has been an increase in voluntary retirement, that is, a withdrawal from the labor force based on individual personal considerations. Particularly in Great Britain and the United States, the labor force participation of men aged 55 to 64 and 65 and older has declined dramatically in the past 20 years. As described in Chapter 6, this has largely been in response to enhanced social security plus various schemes which have made "early" retirement more attractive. However, Robinson and her colleagues (1985, p. 508) caution that all of this reduced labor force participation may not be entirely voluntary: "unemployment may be the first step to early retirement for as many as one in five men." They cite a study in which the authors "estimate that a 1.0 percentage point increase in the overall unemployment rate results in a 1.2 percentage point decline in the labor force participation of workers between the ages of 55 and 64" (p. 514). Other nonvoluntary reasons for lower labor force participation may include limited health and disability. Whereas workers suffering various maladies and afflictions in the past may have had no other recourse but to continue working until retirement age, now they have the choice to retire early on a reduced pension.

The process of when to retire is contingent upon two sets of factors: (1) personal decisions on the part of individual workers; and (2) variable institutional or structural arrangements, including regulations, that set outside limits within which individual decisions are made. Table 11.8 presents a classification of these. Concerning the individual factors, research has demonstrated that workers' financial resources and health status are by far the most important in deciding when to retire (Robinson et al., 1985). As noted above, only when these matters have been settled do attitudes toward work and social support pressures (mainly spouses) come into play. However, to the extent that workers hate their jobs and are encouraged by their spouses, then lower levels of income may be contemplated and/or nagging health problems may be perceived as more severe.

Regarding the institutional factors, both employers and governments attempt to fine-tune their retirement and pension policies to match labor supply to

Table 11.8   FACTORS IN THE DECISION TO RETIRE

Individual	Institutional
Financial resources	Workplace conditions and employer policies
Health status	Public policy regulations
Attitudes toward work and retirement	Economic conditions
Social support pressures	Societal events and values

Source: Robinson et al., 1985, p. 513.

projected demand. In the late 1970s and early 1980s, when the world economy was in a recession, employers offered many of their senior, most costly employees special financial incentives to retire early, and governments modified their pension regulations in order to encourage retirement and thus ease unemployment. Partly as a result of these measures, in the United States in 1980, "56.2% of all male and 69.2% of all female social security beneficiaries were receiving benefits reduced for early retirement before age 65" (Robinson et al., 1985, p. 507). Similarly, in European countries (including Great Britain), governments instituted a number of early retirement and disability options in order to reduce unemployment (see Mirkin, 1987). Concerning future trends, Robinson and her colleagues (1985, p. 521) offer the following analysis:

> Recent changes in the Social Security Act are intended to extend the labor force participation of older workers of the "baby boom" generation by gradually raising the age for full retirement benefits from 65 to 67 between 2000 and 2027 and by reducing early retirement benefits. Other countries (e.g., Japan) are also instituting policies to encourage later retirement. In western Europe, on the other hand, the pressures of high unemployment have resulted in a trend to lower the retirement age even further.

Thus, although retirement is in the final analysis an individual decision, institutional factors influence when precisely this decision is made. As well as general economic conditions and institutional policies and regulations, prevailing social values also impinge upon this decision. As mentioned earlier, when retirement came to be accepted as a legitimate and normal sequence in the life cycle during the 1960s, and social security programs were already established to support this emerging societal value, labor force participation dropped substantially among older workers (see Table 6.4). Judging from the participation rates of the three countries from 1967 to 1986, neither the value of retirement nor the institutional supports are as firmly entrenched in Japanese society as they are in both Great Britain and the United States.

Finally, let us consider the personal effects of retirement upon individual workers. Aside from the loss of income, which has already been discussed and which for many can be severe, researchers have also studied changes in health status and various psychological conditions that can arise following retirement. In a review of the health effects of retirement, Minkler (1981) notes that while there are both American and British studies that find increases in morbidity and mortality three to six years following retirement, other studies indicate that "retirement may in fact result in improved health" (p. 124). Because of the difficulties of isolating the specific effects of retirement from general physiological conditions and the aging process itself, this area of research has not yielded clear unequivocal results.

Research on the psychological consequences of retirement does not appear to have fared much better (see Robinson et al., 1985, p. 516). Given that work is important in providing identity, status, and structure, and that retirement is a "roleless role," obviously there are problems of adjustment. However, because retirement has now come to be an accepted part of the life course, and because work represents just one of several domains of interest and activity, adjustment to retirement does take place. Rather than representing a potential crisis to be overcome, it is eagerly anticipated by many. For example, "in a survey of workers age 40 and older, conducted for the American Association of Retired Persons by the Gallup Organization, 41% of all workers surveyed responded that they would be likely to accept incentive offers for early retirement" (Herz and Rones, 1989, p. 18).

Where difficulty is likely to arise in response to retirement is among workers who identify almost exclusively with their work roles. The stronger the central life interest in work, the more problematic will be the adjustment to retirement. While no studies have investigated this particular relationship, it is interesting to speculate that Japanese workers who are heavily committed both to work and to collective work objectives will experience a more difficult adjustment to retirement than British and American workers who are not as likely to have a central life interest in work. Although the evidence is not compelling, partial support for this assertion lies in the fact that because pension programs are not as well established in Japan as they are in Western countries, retirement as such is not as highly valued. Certainly the comparative data on holidays and vacations presented earlier supports this interpretation. However, regardless of these speculations, the fact remains that because so many older Japanese, particularly men, are still participating in the labor force, most have not actually had the opportunity of adjusting to retirement. For many, it does not even represent a possibility, let alone a normative expectation.

In this chapter, we have noted the important spillover effects of work into virtually all aspects of nonwork life, including retirement. Yet work is only one of several social arenas in which we participate. However, depending upon the perceived centrality of work, it will exert more or less impact upon our values and behavior outside of work. With regard to the three countries under examination, this may be one of the principal factors underlying the cultural differences that have been revealed.

SUMMARY

11.1   Work varies in the degree of autonomy required. Workers with jobs that demand initiative, thought, and independent judgment place greater value on self-control for themselves and their children than do workers who have little discretion in their work. These workers lay greater emphasis on the values of conformity and obedience.

11.2   Stress arises out of an inadequate person–environment fit which may occur as a result of a significant social event or a continuous problem. Stress is manifested by malaise, anxiety, and depression and can result in lowered work performance and deterioration in physical and mental health. Workers with low control over their work situation are more likely to experience stress than workers who are able to adjust their circumstances to match their capabilities.

11.3   Satisfaction with work is related to overall life satisfaction. However, work is only one of several domains (e.g., self, standard of living, family life, marriage, and friends) that contribute to a general sense of well-being. Life satisfaction and happiness are directly related to occupational level. While most people state that they are satisfied and happy with their lives, Americans and the British do so with significantly greater frequency than do the Japanese (see Table 11.2).

11.4   The value placed on work varies directly with occupational level, and therefore there is greater spillover of work into nonwork values and behavior among managers and professionals than among lower white- and blue-collar workers who maintain a greater separation between their work and nonwork lives. Lower organizational employees identify more with their nonwork interests.

11.5   Japanese at all occupational levels have a greater central life interest in work than do American and British workers. This is explained by their greater commitment to work and the fact that the employing organization plays a more crucial, all-pervading role in their lives. Consequently, in Japan the spillover effect from work to nonwork is substantial.

11.6   According to a recent nationally representative time budget study of how Americans allocate their time to the necessary and voluntary activities of life, paid employment consumes the second-largest proportion of time after personal needs (sleeping, eating, and personal care). Housework and childcare, the third-largest category of essential activities, is unequally divided by sex. Employed women spend almost twice as much time on these tasks as employed men, which explains why women have less free time than men (see Table 11.5). Concerning leisure or free time, the greatest single activity is watching television. Because of this, Americans spend more time in passive than active/interactive leisure activities (see Table 11.6). There is an inverse relation between educational level and passive involvement in leisure.

11.7   Japanese men work longer, spend less time on housework, and have fewer hours of leisure than do American men. In addition, Japanese workers are granted fewer official holidays than either American or British workers, and they do not take the full leave to which they are entitled. The picture portrayed of Japanese workers, particularly men, by these time-use data is that they are strongly committed to their work roles. These behavioral data are corroborated by attitudinal studies which find substantial proportions agreeing that work is more important than family life.

11.8   Occupation forms a fundamental basis of social ranking. Because of the similarity in the division of labor cross-culturally, and because power and privilege accrue to the same occupational positions cross-culturally, occupational prestige hierarchies throughout the world are similarly ordered. After first determining this fact, Treiman constructed the Standard International Occupational Prestige Scale that provides "highly accurate estimates of the prestige of specific occupations in any nation in the world" (see Table 11.7).

11.9   Retirement is a relatively recent social institution limited in large part to the industrial nations. Only since 1945 have the large majority of developed countries established pension programs whereby it is financially feasible for the bulk of older workers to withdraw from the labor force and enjoy their retirement years. However, even in industrially developed economies such as Great Britain, the United States, and Japan, significant proportions of elderly workers end up in poverty or near-poverty upon retirement. The extent and adequacy of old-age pension coverge is less developed in Japan than it is in the United States and Great Britain.

11.10 The decision on when to retire is influenced by individual personal circumstances as well as institutional contingencies. For the individual worker, financial resources and health status are the most important factors to consider when retiring. Retirement is also influenced by regulations concerning retirement age, employer and government policies, general economic conditions, and social values. Generally, except for lower income levels, people adjust satisfactorily to retirement. However, the stronger the central life interest in work, the more problematic is the adjustment process.

NOTES

1. Similar to their previous measure of work autonomy, occupational self-direction is comprised of three components: substantive complexity of work; closeness of supervision; and routinization or repetitiveness.
2. With respect to optimism, there are significant differences among all three countries. Of the 30 countries for which Michalos (1988) presents data, the United Kingdom represents the median of the distribution. "On average about 32% of the people in all countries every year expected the next year to be better" (Michalos, 1988, p. 177).
3. Obviously, there is no such thing as a purely "typical" week. Because people are so time bound, and because many of their activities (particularly discretionary ones) are influenced by the time and season of the year, the selection of an appropriate time in which to sample behavior is a very important consideration. The 1965 survey was conducted mainly in the fall, while the 1985 research continued throughout the year in order to even out the effects of particular times and seasons. See Robinson et al., 1989, p. 6.
4. While there are direct relations between education and number of hours worked for both men and women, the data are difficult to interpret for women. Because both employed and not employed women are grouped together, it is impossible to say whether the fewer number of hours by less educated women is a matter of choice or because of lack of employment opportunities.
5. Dore (1973, pp. 187–188) notes that "It is almost universally the practice to ask that days taken off for sickness should be counted as part of one's annual holiday. (That way one gets a perfect attendance record which automatically gets one some way towards a good merit rating.)"
6. As mentioned in Chapter 6, the mean correlation of prestige rankings across 55 countries is .81. Treiman eliminated five countries from his analysis in that the surveys upon which these rankings were based did not measure occupational prestige. In three cases "job desirability" was measured, in another "ideal income," and in the fifth the people holding the jobs rather than the positions themselves were ranked. See Treiman, 1977, p. 94.
7. According to Atchley, 1982, p. 267, "the plan stipulated that at age 65, workers with at least 10 years of service to the company were entitled to a pension. Retirement at 65 was

compulsory. Pensions were paid entirely by the company and the amount was 1% of the worker's final wage, multiplied by years of service."

8. Atchley (1982, p. 270) notes the consequences of mandatory retirement in the United States in a time when there were few private pension plans and no public social security program: "As a result, the numbers of older persons living in poverty swelled dramatically. In 1910, about 23% of older Americans were dependent on welfare; this figure rose to 33% in 1922, and 40% by 1929. Only sizeable government expenditures for veteran's pensions kept the proportion on welfare from being substantially higher."

Chapter

12

Work in the Twenty-first Century: Prospects and Problems

It is a persistent irony of comparative studies that the study of the Other, the foreign, the different, ultimately reveals itself to be a search for the self, the familiar, the same.

Wolfe, 1990, p. 49

We have now come to the point where it is instructive to weave together the facts and ideas presented in the preceding chapters in order both to summarize the paths that we have taken and to project some of the directions we are likely to take as we enter the next century. To put it another way, what have we learned that we may use "to shape the future we want to have" (Simon, 1987, p. 11)?

As a starting point, we return to the debate concerning the relative impacts of industrialism and culture upon individuals in society. On the one hand, we have noted how technology and organization produce common responses to the problems involved in human survival; on the other hand, we have observed that despite these similarities, cultural differences do persist with respect to the particular manner in which industrialism is implemented. In the first part of the chapter, we highlight the differences we have uncovered among the three nations we have been examining, particularly those between Japan and the two Western countries. This allows us to summarize the argument for cultural diversity and to reflect on what future developments might be.

In the next section, we switch focus and concentrate on the similarities that the process of industrialization has produced in these three countries. This analysis will summarize the case for organizational and technological convergence as it points to similar developments that have occurred in Great Britain, the United States, and Japan. Furthermore, given current projections, it is likely that a stronger argument for convergence will be possible in the future.

Finally, we conclude by raising once more the issue of industrialization in the world context. What are the likely patterns of development, and what may we expect with regard to the gap between the industrially developed rich nations and the developing poor ones? This section also will deal with the dilemma of achieving economic development on a global scale *and* preserving a strong and viable world ecosystem.

INDUSTRIALISM AND CULTURE

In order to summarize the debate concerning the relative effects of industrialism and culture, consider once more the cross-national research project conducted by Hofstede that was first introduced in Chapter 7. You will remember that Hofstede engaged in a questionnaire survey of approximately 60,000 employees working in one transnational corporation that was located in forty countries. While the employees were indigenous to the countries in which they worked, the firm itself represented a technological and organizational constant. Thus, to the extent that workers from different countries responded similarly, this demonstrated the dominant universal impact of industrialism; however, any differences revealed were attributed to the unique effects of culture (see Hofstede, 1980).

To determine the extent of variation across culture, Hofstede constructed four indices that reflect major values that individuals hold in society. Thus, for each of the 40 countries he investigated, his purpose was to discern whether or not there was a distinctive modal personality—a national character that sets one country off from another. The four indices that he devised are: uncertainty avoidance (how we cope with uncertainties represented by the future); individualism (the value pattern underlying the relationship of individuals to collectivities); ego strength (the relative strength of assertiveness versus nurturance); and power distance (the degree of tolerable inequality among people). For our comparative purposes, we will concentrate on the first two of these indices—uncertainty avoidance and individualism—as they reveal by far the greatest differences among the three nations we have been examining. Also, concentration on these value patterns will permit us to summarize the major cultural variations we have uncovered throughout the text.

Table 12.1 presents the actual indicators Hofstede used to measure these two value patterns. Uncertainty avoidance taps three dimensions associated with our ability to tolerate the ambiguity which is necessarily part of the unknowable future: rule orientation, employment stability, and stress. Those who have difficulty living with uncertainty and seek to avoid it attempt to build structure into their lives that will resolve any contingency that may arise. Thus, the establishment of absolute rules and permanence of setting represent two strategies to avoid uncertainty. However, for people who do not tolerate ambiguity well, this means that there is a less than ideal person-environment fit, and consequently stress will be the result. Therefore, according to these measures, employees with high uncertainty avoidance will not break rules (even when they appear to be counterproductive); they will seek employment stability; and they will be relatively nervous and tense. On the other hand, employees who have a high tolerance for ambiguity will more likely interpret general rules in light of particular circumstances, base decisions on whether or not to change their employment on criteria other than a need for stability, and will be relatively serene in their surroundings.

The individualism index that Hofstede also entitles "independence from the organization" is based on a factor analysis of 14 personal work goals. According to Hofstede, employees who rank "collectivistic" goals highly have a "greater emotional dependence . . . on their organizations" (p. 217), while those who choose "individualistic" goals manifest an underlying disharmony between individual and organization. In general, this dimension measures the degree to which individuals rely upon the group as a provider of their own personal identities.

Table 12.2 presents the mean scores that employees in Great Britain, the United States, and Japan received on these indices. For comparative purposes, the overall average scores for the 40 countries that Hofstede surveyed are also included.[1] Generally, these scores range between 0 and 100, with a grand mean of approximately 50. In addition, the relative positions of the United Kingdom, United States and Japan within the 40-country rankings are also presented. Finally, in that the scores and ranks of Japanese employees differ significantly from employess in Britain and the United States, these differences are noted at the bottom of the table.

Uncertainty Avoidance

Both absolutely and relative to other countries, Japan scores very high on uncertainty avoidance. It ranks fourth on this index out of the forty nations surveyed. Particularly in relation to Great Britain and the United States, Japanese employees are more rule bound, concerned with employment stability, and anxious. On the other hand, British and American employees tolerate comparatively well the uncertainty with which we all must deal. The Japan–U.K./U.S. differences recorded at the bottom of Table 12.2 indicate that this value pattern produces the greatest dissimilarity.

The bases for the difference on this index between Japan and the two Western industrial nations have been systematically noted throughout the preceding six

Table 12.1   OPERATIONAL DEFINITIONS OF HOFSTEDE'S CULTURAL DIMENSIONS

1. *Uncertainty Avoidance Index.* Workers who responded in the following ways were scored as having high uncertainty avoidance:
   (a) Rule orientation: Agreement with the statement "Company rules should not be broken—even when the employee thinks it is in the company's best interests."
   (b) Employment stability: Employee's intention to continue working for the company "more than five years" or "until I retire."
   (c) Stress: Employee "usually" or "always" feels "nervous or tense at work."

2. *Individualism Index* (also labeled "independence from organization"). Based on a factor analysis of 14 work goals. The following six goals, listed in descending order of importance, distinguish between either an individual or collective orientation:
   (a) Having a job that leaves you sufficient time for your personal or family life (individual orientation).
   (b) Having training opportunities (to improve your skills or to learn new skills) (collective orientation).
   (c) Having good physical working conditions (good ventilation and lighting, adequate work space, etc.) (collective orientation).
   (d) Fully use your skills and abilities on the job (collective orientation).
   (e) Have considerable freedom to adopt your own approach to the job (individual orientation).
   (f) Have challenging work to do—work from which you can get a personal sense of accomplishment (individual orientation).

Source: Hofstede, 1980.

chapters. For example, the entire Japanese system of employment is designed to achieve uncertainty avoidance (i.e., control) from the point of view of both the firm and the individual employee. Through the internal labor market, the firm is assured of a loyal work force over which it extends a paternalistic umbrella of extra-work benefits in order to gain even more commitment. Through the norm of lifetime employment and orderly career progression based on age and seniority, a Japanese firm can demand more from its employees than can an equivalent British or American firm. For their part, Japanese employees are guaranteed employment stability within a clearly delineated system of advancement and promotion. The three pillars of Japanese-style management form an integrated structure designed to achieve stability, predictability, and therefore certainty. On the other hand, the Western system of employment involves more risk (i.e., uncertainty), but at the same time offers greater opportunity for both self-actualization and high financial reward.

In addition to the Japanese system of employment, certain features of Japanese organizations also exhibit characteristics of uncertainty avoidance. For example, in Chapter 7 it was noted that Japanese firms are more formalized (i.e., rule oriented) and that there is less formal delegation of authority than in Western companies. To these features we may add relatively close supervision and high job routine, as reported in Chapter 11. Furthermore, in the comparative analysis of

Table 12.2 BRITISH, AMERICAN, AND JAPANESE SCORES AND RANK ORDER ON TWO CULTURAL DIMENSIONS

Nation	Cultural dimensions[1]	
	Uncertainty avoidance	Individualism
Britain		
Score	35	89
Rank order	35	3
United States		
Score	46	91
Rank order	32	1
Japan		
Score	92	46
Rank order	4	22
Total (40 nations)		
Mean score	64	51
High score	112	91
Low score	8	12
Japan–U.K./U.S. Differences[2]		
Score difference	51.5	44.0
Rank difference	29.5	20.0

[1]See Table 12.1 for operational definitions of these dimensions.

[2]Differences obtained by summing United Kingdom and United States scores and ranks, and dividing by 2. The differences between these average scores and ranks and Japanese scores and ranks are Japan–U.K./U.S. differences.

Source: Adapted from Hofstede, 1980, pp. 165, 222.

transnational corporations (Chapter 8), it was revealed that Japanese TNCs through a variety of techniques maintain tighter operating control over their subsidiaries than do American or British transnationals. According to Hofstede, a large part of this difference in managerial style may be explained by the greater emphasis Japanese attach to uncertainty avoidance.

In the relationship of workers to work, it is also possible to discern differences in the value placed on uncertainty avoidance. In Chapter 9, it was pointed out that Japanese workers trade the possibility to maximize their individual–work fit for security of employment. However, even with this security, they have more stress than British and American workers (see Hofstede, 1980, p. 411). This may in turn explain in part their lower job and life satisfaction in that stress arises out of a perceived inadequate fit between person and environment, and the belief that little can be done about it. Certainly the significantly lower optimism regarding the future on the part of the Japanese (see Table 11.2) attests to this interpretation.

Finally, worker–management relations in Japan also bear the imprint of uncertainty avoidance. The whole concept of enterprise unionism is designed to instill a stable and harmonious relationship between workers and managers such that there is "close identification of corporate and individual interests" (Abegglen and Stalk, 1985, p. 207). The additional feature of decentralization limits the impact of unions to those workers who are actually employees of the organization. Consequently, the firm can exercise maximal control. In that enterprise unionism is reputed to be one of three pillars of Japanese-style management, it may be seen as a vehicle wherein employers mobilize workers to perform in the interests of the organization. In this manner, enterprise unionism is part of the "structured dependency relationships" that Cole (1979, p. 246) says characterize Japanese industry.

Thus, based on the concept of uncertainty avoidance, it is possible to distinguish major differences between the Japanese and Western systems of industrial organization. The greater perceived need of Japanese employees to structure and control their environment is a reflection of an important cultural value configuration that differentiates Japan from Great Britain and the United States. Depending upon how comfortable people are in dealing with ambiguity (including the future), behavioral and normative consequences follow. Based on Hofstede's research and his analysis of other studies that relate to uncertainty avoidance, Table 12.3 provides a rendering of some of these consequences. As much of the text has demonstrated, certainly part of the differences in the structure and process between Japanese and Western work and organization has derived from these larger cultural differences.

Table 12.3 reveals that high uncertainty avoidance is associated with the need for structure, security, and consensus; rules and regulations; intolerance of deviation; resistance to change; and anxiety. While it would be foolhardy to state that this list of characteristics typifies all Japanese, nevertheless their patterned response to the institution of work does indicate that as a nation they manifest greater concern about uncertainty than is displayed in either Great Britain or the United States. In a very significant way, it can be asserted that the three pillars of Japanese-style management—the norm of lifetime employment, career progression based on age and seniority, and enterprise unionism—together represent a systematic and unified formula for uncertainty avoidance. Consequently, as a prominent cultural value configuration, it does provide a partial explanation as to why similar problems of survival are met by different cultural responses.

Individualism

Table 12.2 also reveals considerable dissimilarity between Japan and the two Western nations on the individualism index. Here, though, it is the United States and Great Britain that represent the extreme cases, with the former being the highest on individualism among all 40 countries surveyed and the latter ranking third. Japan is located in the middle of the distribution. However, if only the 19 more developed countries are considered, Japan is the least individualistic. As the Japan–U.K./U.S. differences indicate, this index reveals a large contrast between East and West.

Throughout the comparative chapters, we have noted, particularly with respect to the United States and Japan, how one is individualistically oriented and the other collective. In Chapter 7, the historical and geographical underpinnings of

Table 12.3   THE UNCERTAINTY AVOIDANCE SOCIETAL NORM

Low uncertainty avoidance	High uncertainty avoidance
*The uncertainty inherent in life is more easily accepted and each day is taken as it comes	*The uncertainty inherent in life is felt as a continuous threat that must be fought
*Ease, lower stress	*Higher anxiety and stress
*Hard work is not a virtue per se	*Inner urge to work hard
*Weaker superegos	*Strong superegos
*More acceptance of dissent	*Strong need for consensus
*Deviance is not felt as threatening; greater tolerance	*Deviant persons and ideas are dangerous; intolerance
*More positive toward younger people	*Younger people are suspect
*Less conservatism	*Conservatism; law and order
*More willingness to take risks in life	*Concern with security in life
*Achievement determined in terms of recognition	*Achievement defined in terms of security
*Relativism, empiricism	*Search for ultimate, absolute truths and values
*There should be as few rules as possible	*Need for written rules and regulations
*The authorities are there to serve the citizens	*Ordinary citizens are incompetent versus the authorities

Source: Hofstede, 1980, p. 184.

these contrasting value patterns were laid out: In the United States, the individualistic ethos of self-reliance and independence was the most successful adaptive strategy in the early days of the new republic; in Japan, collective communal strategies proved to be more appropriate in the struggle for survival. These orientations have endured to the present day.

In the United States, the individual represents the basic core upon which organizations are established; in Japan, it is the group that forms this foundation. In Ouchi's contrast of American and Japanese organizations (see Chapter 7), two of the seven differentiating features he identifies involve the individual–collective continuum. In the United States, decision making is mostly an individual endeavour, the consequences of which are the sole responsibility of the particular manager involved. Either the manager receives recognition for a job well done or he/she must accept personal responsibility for an error in judgment. However, in Japan, collaboration represents one of the central identifying characteristics of Japanese organizations. Decision making occurs collectively and can involve several hierarchical levels. Responsibility is also shared collectively.

This collaborative strategy is also related to uncertainty avoidance. To the extent that more people are involved in a decision, the chances are increased that it will be the correct one; and by sharing the responsibility, *individual* risk is minimized. In his analysis of the relationships among the cultural dimensions, Hofstede (1980, p. 316) found a moderately strong inverse relation between individualism and uncertainty avoidance (r = -.51).[2] In other words, in countries in which a high value is placed on uncertainty avoidance, there is a relatively weak individual orientation.

Other organizational characteristics that accentuate individualism in the United States and Great Britain but minimize it in Japan are vertical differentiation and organizational size. With regard to vertical differentiation, it was noted that Japanese organizations have more finely graded hierarchical levels than do Western firms. Not only do these multilevel hierarchies provide career paths for Japanese managers, but also because there are so many gradients of authority, a gulf between "them" and "us" is not perceived by Japanese workers to the same extent that it is in Great Britain and the United States. Instead, there develops a "we" feeling, or as Cole (1979, p. 243) puts it, "a community of fate" in which all "share a common destiny." In American and British firms, the relationship between employee and employer is decidedly more contractual, an association that is reinforced by the fact that Western organizations are significantly larger than in Japan.

Communality in Japanese organizations is further enhanced by the fact that relatively few extra perks and privileges are associated with high office as they are in Western firms (see Dore, 1973, pp. 251–259). The vertical gradients are blurred in that all workers from the chief executive officer down to the ordinary factory hand share the same basic work conditions. There are no special parking places, entrances, or dining facilities, and in many organizations the wearing of the same uniform by all demonstrates visibly that everyone is working toward the same goal. Furthermore, this downplaying of status distinction is reflected in the pay envelope. In Japan, there is less of a pay differential by level of organizational work than in either Great Britain or the United States. Japanese chief executive officers earn on average less than half of what comparable American executives receive.[3]

The different industrial relations systems in Great Britain, the United States, and Japan are also very much related to the notion of individualism. Put simply, in the West, workers' unions are pitted against employers, attempting to wrest from them the best work contract that can be negotiated. In Japan, enterprise unions that are comprised solely of employees who work in the same firm collaborate with employers to achieve ever greater levels of productivity, the proceeds of which they both share. In the former case, there is solidarity among individual workers who have similar occupational skills but different employers; in the latter case, there is solidarity among diverse workers who are all members of the same organization.

In superior–subordinate relationships also, differences may be plotted along the individualism continuum. In the United States and Great Britain, only task-relevant behavior is deemed to be of concern to the superior in evaluating performance. Nonjob characteristics are excluded from the contractual relationship between employee and employer. However, in Japan, because employees are part of a *collective* enterprise, managers take, and are expected to take, a wholistic concern in the welfare of their employees that goes far beyond the confines of the job. Dore (1973) has called this "welfare corporatism."

All of the above features contribute to a different attachment to work on the part of Western and Japanese workers. As mentioned in Chapter 9, British and

Table 12.4   THE INDIVIDUALISM SOCIETAL NORM

Low individualism	High individualism
*In society, people are born into extended families or clans which protect them in exchange for loyalty	*In society, everyone is supposed to take care of himself or herself and his or her immediate family
*"We" consciousness	*"I" consciousness
*Collectivity-orientation	*Self orientation
*Identity is based in the social system	*Identity is based in the individual
*Emotional dependence of individual on organizations and institutions	*Emotional independence of individual from organizations or institutions
*Emphasis on belonging to organization; membership ideal	*Emphasis on individual initiative and achievement; leadership ideal
*Private life is invaded by organizations and clans to which one belongs; opinions are predetermined	*Everyone has a right to a private life and opinion
*Expertise, order, duty, security, provided by organization or clan	*Autonomy, variety, pleasure, individual financial security
*Friendships predetermined by stable social relationships; but need for prestige within these relationships	*Need for specific friendships
*Belief in group decisions	*Belief in individual decisions
*Value standards differ for ingroups and outgroups, particularism	*Value standards should apply to all; universalism

Source: Hofstede, 1980, p. 235.

American workers may be conceived of as "cosmopolitans," attached to their work through the occupational skills that they possess. Their current job simply represents a convenient context in which to practise these skills. Should a more attractive offer of employment arise, they would have little hesitation in accepting it. Cosmopolitans attempt to maximize their individual work goals. On the other hand, Japanese workers more appropriately fit the characterization of "locals." For them, the employing organization is a lifelong commitment. In exchange for loyalty and duty, they receive a sense of membership and community that pervades their entire lives. Locals strive for collective work goals.

Similar to uncertainty avoidance, the concept of individualism affords us the opportunity to distinguish a major value cleavage between the Western and Japanese industrial systems. In turn, the differences produced flow from more broadly based value patterns found in the larger cultures they represent. Table 12.4 indicates some of the attitudinal and behavioral repercussions of societies based on individualistic versus collectivistic sentiments.

The aspects associated with low and high individualism are very similar to the two "consciences" identified by Durkheim as constituting the bases for cohesion within society (see Chapter 4). On the one hand, Durkheim argued that social integration is achieved through mechanical solidarity (i.e., behavior associated with low individualism). The centripetal forces of collectivism emphasize the common features we all possess as human beings. Thus, we are members of similarly constituted groups and owe our allegiance to them. Our lives are centered around groups (e.g., the family, work groups, and so on) as we achieve our identity, sense of purpose, and security from them. On the other hand, cohesion can be achieved through organic solidarity (i.e., high individualism). In this case, the centrifugal forces of individualism accentuate those features that make us unique and set us apart from each other. The basis of integration under these conditions is individual freedom of expression, free will, and self-actualization.

Durkheim's notions of mechanical and organic solidarity are embedded in the Japanese and Western systems of employment. In Japan, both individuality and individual occupational skills are suppressed in the emphasis placed on groups and common task objectives. The organizational climate may be characterized as one in which the values of consensus, collaboration, and collegiality are dominant. By contrast, the Western system emphasizes individuality and difference in status and function. Just as unique occupational skills distinguish workers, so too are they evaluated on the basis of *individual* worth and merit.

Durkheim contended that owing to technological development and urbanization, the division of labor within a society becomes increasingly complex and the bases for social integration consequently change from mechanical to organic solidarity. Because a complex division of labor exphasizes individual differences, so then do the forces of cohesion change from a collectivist to an individualist focus. Strong support for this assertion is contained in Hofstede's 40-nation study. He found (p. 231) an almost perfect linear relationship between national economic development (GNP per capita) and attachment to individualistic values ($r = .82$). With increasing social differentiation, there is a diminishing in the power of the group over the individual. Autonomy, initiative, and self-direction become the norms of conduct.

While there is a strong correlation between economic development and individualism, there is also considerable variation in the degree to which similarly developed nations exhibit norms of individualism. Among the industrially developed countries of the world, the United States and Japan represent polar opposites on the individualism index. As we have noted, the norms associated with this dimension dictate quite different solutions to the universal problems involved in survival. Despite similar organizational and technological developments, the uncertainty avoidance and the individualism indices together point to the diversifying effects of culture on social behavior.

Cultural Value Clusters

On the basis of the cultural dimensions discussed above, Hofstede grouped the forty countries he investigated into value clusters according to the similarity of their scores on each index. Thus, given the close correspondence in scores between Great Britain and the United States, they form one value cluster together with Australia, Canada, Ireland, and New Zealand, which also scored similarly on these dimensions. Hofstede labels this the "Anglo" cluster, which is different on at least one dimension from the seven other value clusters he identified. The Anglo cluster may be characterized as manifesting low to medium uncertainty avoidance and high individualism.

It is interesting to observe how countries that one would expect to form unique value clusters based on language, geographical proximity, or historical association actually do fit together in Hofstede's analysis. For example, there is a "Nordic" cluster (Denmark, Finland, Netherlands, Norway, and Sweden), a "Less Developed Asian" cluster (Pakistan, Taiwan, Thailand, Hong Kong, India, Philippines, and Singapore), and a "Less Developed Latin" cluster (Colombia, Mexico, Venezuela, Chile, Peru, and Portugal). With only one exception, each of the eight clusters that Hofstede identified is comprised of at least four countries which display similar value orientations.

The exceptional case is Japan. It forms a distinct value cluster of its own. It is neither sufficiently similar to other developed countries or to other Asian countries (e.g., Hong Kong, Singapore, and Taiwan) to warrant its inclusion in their clusters. Characterized by high uncertainty avoidance and medium individualism, it is unique among the forty countries Hofstede studied. Japan's level of economic development differentiates it from other Asian countries, and its oriental culture distinguishes it from the developed West.

Throughout the preceding chapters, we have uncovered strong evidence to corroborate Japan's exceptional position. At this moment in history, it is the only nation without a European-based tradition to have achieved postindustrial status, and, as we have seen both in Hofstede's analysis and in the other data presented, it has attained this status based on quite different value premises. Its particular material and historical circumstances have resulted in value orientations and patterns of social organization that represent an alternative strategy to achieving the same goals sought by European-based cultures.

Whether to minimize individual risk (i.e., uncertainty avoidance) or to achieve communal solidarity (collectivism), the emphasis on the group in Japan distinguishes it from other industrially developed countries. While Japan is not unique from preindustrial countries (past and present) in the importance attached to the group, it is distinctive in its use of the group to achieve postindustrial status. The group serves as an impetus for performance, a standard for conduct, and a source of pride and identity. Through the group, individual interests are met.

In Western countries, particularly in work organizations, individual and group interests are not assumed to be congruent. Etzioni (1969) has suggested that compliance on the part of most employees is based on what he terms "calculative involvement," that is, depending upon the type and amount of material rewards an organization offers (i.e., remunerative power), employees perform more or less well. However, in Japan, while material rewards are used, they are not the sole nor even the most important basis for invoking compliance. Japanese employees have "moral involvement" in their firms in that there is a perceived identity of purpose between individual and organization. They comply with organizational directives because they are personally committed to the ultimate objectives of the organization. Thus, the organization can induce them to work "above and beyond the normal call of duty" (i.e., normative power). While Etzioni reports that moral involvement does occur among professionals and in upper management echelons in Western countries, it is diffused throughout the hierarchy in Japanese organizations.

In attempting to explain why personal and organizational goals coincide in Japan but not in the industrially developed countries of the West, Befu (1989), similar to other analysts, argues that the answer lies in the contrasting ideologies held regarding the preeminence of the individual:

> ... a partial answer is found in the nature of interpersonal relations in Japan, which emphasizes and, moreover, values generalized exchange between individuals. In this situation, mutual trust and bonds between individuals in Japan, which may supersede kinship bonds, are the crux of this issue. Hamaguchi has labeled this *kanjin shugi*, which I translate as "interpersonalism." The basic building block of Japanese society, according to Hamaguchi, is not the individual as is the case in Western civilization, but relationship between individuals. Thus mutual trust based on the generalized exchange of both instrumental and expressive resources is the fundamental substance of the society in Japan, rather than the individual's rights and interests. (Befu, 1989, p. 45).

Because of this basic difference in the underlying value structure of Japanese and Western societies, Befu argues that the theory of bureaucratic organization first propounded by Weber, and later elaborated upon by other sociologists, is culture bound, applying only to organizations in societies in which individual and organizational goals are not consonant. In this situation, but only in this situation, the basis of the relationship between individual and organization is the contract wherein rewards, duties, and the limits of authority are all explicitly set down. Ideally, performance on the part of the employee and responsibilty on the part of the organization should meet but not exceed what is specified in the employment contract. By virtue of the contract, individuals within organizational positions are interchangeable to the extent that each performs according to his or her job description.

In Japan, however, because of the cultural expectation that individuals identify with the organization, the relationship between individual and organization is far more diffuse than in the Western case. Individual performance and control are not at issue given the complementarity of goals, and consequently "the contract" is replaced by a generalized relationship in which employees work to their utmost and organizations take a particularistic concern in their employees. The core of the individual–organization relationship is that which pertains between employees and their immediate supervisors.

> In Japanese bureaucracy a superior and his or her subordinates are likely to be bound together in generalized exchange, and a strong commitment develops between them. Given this commitment of a generalized exchange nature between a leader and subordinates in a bureaucratic organization, subordinates are likely to manifest compliance to their leader, whether or not his demands are strictly based on regulations of the organization. As long as the leader is, then, motivated to help the organization achieve its goals, he has ready and willing help in his subordinates. Now, this leader too, is a subordinate in the organization to a higher level supervisor, to whom he is also bound by a trust relationship of a generalized exchange nature. Thus the dynamic obtaining between the lowest level and its immediately higher level is repeated up the hierarchy until the top level is reached. (Befu, 1989, p. 46)

Consequently, while Japan is in a similar position to the United States, Great Britain, and the other industrially developed Western nations with respect to the development of its occupational and labor force structure, its organizational base (including transnational corporate investment), its infrastructure, and the quality of life enjoyed by its citizenry, it has attained this position in a unique and distinctive fashion. As the analysis above indicates, it has operated from quite different value premises which, although resulting in similar achievements , point to underlying structural differences. In the following section, we will attempt to peer into the future to determine the extent to which these differences will persist, as well as the likely directions of change.

Trajectories of Development

Returning to Hofstede's cultural dimensions, what future developments may we reasonably expect to take place? Concerning uncertainty avoidance, the greatest source of difference, while it is understandable from both an individual and organizational point of view to "need" security and control, we are faced with an uncertain environment. In Chapter 1, it was noted that change (and our ability to deal with it) constitutes one of the most serious of contemporary social problems. To repudiate change or to avoid uncertainty through various defense mechanisms is to deny reality and can have very serious repercussions.

Hofstede's uncertainty avoidance index correlates strongly ($r =.73$) with a "neuroticism" or "anxiety" scale constructed by Lynn and Hampson in their comparative study of 18 developed countries (cited in Hofstede, 1980, pp. 168–169,195). Based on national medical and related statistics, Japan had the second highest neuroticism score, Great Britain the second lowest, and the United States was in the middle of the distribution. Similarly in Müller's 128-nation compendium of world data (1988), the suicide rate (for 1980), one of the factors in Lynn and Hampson's scale, is high in Japan (175.9 per million inhabitants), relatively low in the United Kingdom (87.9), and approximates the mean of distribution in the United States at 118.0. While obviously all suicides cannot be attributed to uncertainty avoidance and the anxiety it produces, nevertheless these and other data reported by Hofstede do indicate that there is a significant relationship that cannot be denied.

In that Hofstede conducted his survey at two separate times (1967–1969 and 1971–1973), he is able to report on changes in stress levels. Overall, he found higher stress recorded in the later period, which is consonant with other data we have examined. Given the fact that the rate of change is increasing, it is reasonable to expect that the level of stress will also rise as people attempt to cope with their constantly changing circumstances. Furthermore, Hofstede found that "the countries with the highest stress in 1968 also show the largest increase" (p. 356). In other words, stress breeds more of the same. However, Japan, a country with an initially high level of stress, did not fit this general pattern. Müller's suicide data corroborate this fact (1988, p. 267). Although Japan's suicide rate in 1980 was high, it had improved its *relative* position in comparison to 1970 and 1975. In these years,

Japan's rate placed it in the eighth decile relative to all 128 countries for which Müller could find data; however, by 1980 its rate, although dropping only marginally from 1975, improved dramatically in relation to these other countries (64th percentile).

Consequently, while the Japanese have been characterized as exhibiting "a worried earnestness and anxious questing for self-improvement" (Dore, 1973, p. 218), it would appear, certainly in relation to other countries, that they are not quite as "worried" or as "anxious" as they once were. Whether they have become more relaxed or people in other countries have become more anxious, the indication is that the difference in stress and uncertainty avoidance between Japan and Great Britain and the United States will abate in the future as all people learn to tolerate the ever-changing contingencies that constitute the present reality.

With regard to individualism, it is likely that Japan will become less collectively oriented than it is now. As Hofstede (and Durkheim before him) points out, there is a very strong direct relation between economic development and individualism. All the researchers who have studied Japan in the past 20 years indicate that while the Japanese people are certainly more attached to groups than are their Western counterparts, nevertheless there are signs that this group solidarity is weakening, particularly within the younger generation. Among the most recent commentators, Koseki (1989, p. 120), a native Japanese, offers the following assessment:

> The desire of the young for self-realisation and individualism or privatism has made an undeniable impact on the lifestyle of adults as well. The traditional Japanese sense of belonging has been weakened. There is a marked increase in the number of young employees who escape from after-five socializing, formerly regarded as a virtually compulsory aspect of Japanese contemporary life. The younger people are eager to pursue their private interests or to return home immediately after work. They are cooperative on the job but not so weak as to give up their individual rights.

If it is reasonable to predict that the Japanese will become more individualistic over time, what can we say about the Americans and British who already are among the most individualistic of all people? The dangers of "moral diversity" and "anomie" that Durkheim foresaw almost 100 years ago have not disappeared (see Chapter 4). To the extent that individualism increases, the basis for social cohesion and integration is weakened. As Hofstede states it, we are constantly trying to strike a balance between "the alienation of the 'privatized' individual" and "the tyranny of the collectivity." "They represent the devil and the deep blue sea, between which societies and man within them have to steer their course" (p. 216). Whereas Hofstede maintains that the process toward individualism may be stabilized, it is unlikely that it can be reversed. Consequently, given the problems associated with extreme individualism, we may well see attempts in the United States and Great Britain to curb some of its excesses. Similar to uncertainty avoidance, this would have the effect of diminishing the differences in individualism between the United States, Great Britain, and Japan in the decades to come.

This analysis of the cultural dimensions studied by Hofstede has permitted us to summarize both differences and similarities with regard to Great Britain, the United States, and Japan that we have identified throughout the text. On the one hand, we noted that different cultural legacies, particularly between East and West, have resulted in quite distinctive approaches to the problems involved in economic development. These differences are especially pronounced early in the trajectories of development experienced by these three countries. For example, while we have concentrated upon the dissimilarities between Japan and the two Western countries, there were also marked differences between Great Britain and the United States in their early stages of industrialization (see Chapter 3).

On the other hand, we have pointed to increasing similarities among these three nations as we have attempted to probe future developments. Owing to a mixture of both cultural and techno-organizational diffusion, aided in large part by the very process we have been examining, there is occurring a convergence in values such that the Great Britain, United States, and Japan of today share more commonalities than they did 50 or 100 years ago. Thus, while there are clear and notable differences among countries in the early phases of industrialization that may be directly attributable to differences in cultural values, over time, as a consequence of the process of industrialization itself (including the continual comparing of its achievements in different cultural contexts), the initially large differences become somewhat diminished.[4] Although significant differences still abound, nevertheless the analysis above indicates that it is the similarities that will figure more prominently in the decades to come.

ORGANIZATION, TECHNOLOGY, AND WORKER–MANAGEMENT RELATIONS

The previous section provided a summary of how individual values both affect and are affected by the process of industrialization; in the present section we focus on the structural elements of this same process. The history of organization and technology may be seen as a series of strategic adjustments to fluctuating conditions and attempts to attain ever more control over both animate and inanimate contingencies. While not all these "solutions" have been successful, especially given the different vantage points of the various actors involved, nevertheless a broad pattern is discernible which does indicate likely courses of future development.

Industrial Organization

It was Max Weber who traced the evolution of authority relations from the personally based, unbounded power of the traditional leader to the impersonal, rational-legal control of the bureaucratic official (see Chapter 4). For Weber, the capitalist system was the embodiment of the systematic and rational pursuit of wealth. As such, previous methods of organization and control were too haphazard and unwieldy to accomplish specifically defined complex objectives. Consequently, part of the industrial revolution involved the establishment and refinement of bureaucratic principles of administrative organization (see Chapter 7).

One of the major differences between traditional and rational-legal authority is the degree of control a superordinate has over a subordinate. In a traditional authority relationship, the power of the leader is absolute. Virtually any command may be given in the full expectation that it will be carried out. However, under rational-legal authority, a leader's power is limited to just those areas of behavior that are contractually defined as being relevant to task performance. Because rational-legal organizations (i.e., bureaucracies) are established to accomplish specific objectives, the authority of rational-legal officials is similarly circumscribed. In this manner, a bureaucracy is "capable of attaining the highest degree of efficiency" (Weber, in Parsons, 1964, p. 337).

The change from traditional to rational-legal authority had profound repercussions for the large working mass. No longer were they at the beck and call of all-powerful masters. They could enter into various employment contracts of their own free will, and within these employment relationships, it was necessary to obey their supervisors only to the extent that the orders given were germane to the task at hand. While early bureaucracies could hardly be described as beneficent, they did represent an improvement over the previous traditional system of almost total control and subjugation.

Although Weber's ideal type of bureaucratic organization was suited well enough to stable and predictable situations in which uniform work forces produced large volumes of similar goods or services, subsequent organization researchers found that it was dysfunctional in several respects. Now, organizations are structured more in response to the particular environmental contingencies they face and as a consequence of the specific makeup of their work forces. In Chapter 7, as a result of several independent research investigations, it was noted that there is emerging a new type of flexible, professional organization that is highly responsive to its environment (task oriented) and more collaborative and decentralized in its operation. Given the rapid rate of change (including the speed with which organizational transactions are made), the growing interdependence of both public and private organizations, and the specialized and variable work forces that comprise contemporary organizations, the flexible, professional type of organization may be interpreted as a strategy for survival.

While Weber's bureaucratic model restricted the authority of the manager to relevant job-related functions, it was cumbersome and rigid in its response to novel situations. By contrast, the professional organization is designed to react quickly to changes in the environment, not only adjusting to them, but using them to utmost organizational advantage. A large part of this flexible strategy involves giving responsibility to individual workers for the tasks they perform. Because employees are trained in diversified and specialized skills, only they and their colleagues with similar training have the requisite knowledge upon which to base their actions. Thus, through a process of mutual collaboration and consultation, task authority is more widely diffused throughout the organization, even though the chief executive officer, as before, assumes ultimate responsibility.

From this brief analysis, we can identify two definite trends in the history of organizational development: (1) decentralization of authority; and (2) increased cognizance of the environment. With regard to authority, not only has it been restricted to organizationally relevant functions, it has been more widely delegated. In turn, decentralization leads to greater individual responsibility and more organizational involvement. Concerning the organizational environment, it has become increasingly evident that for organizations to survive they must be attuned to their broader surroundings. Particularly in times of rapid social change and uncertainty, indifference to the environment is a sure and certain recipe for dissolution. While these trends are apparent now in many organizations, particularly in Japan, it is likely that they will become even more prominent in the years to come.

Technology

Similar to organizational development, there is a broad pattern that characterizes the design and growth of technology. As described in Chapter 3, in the early stages of the industrial revolution in Britain, the predominant mode of manufacture was the factory system in which craftworkers trained apprentices in the use of various machine tools to produce specialized products designed for a limited market. Later, with the invention and development of increasingly complex machinery, particularly with the many applications of the steam engine, it became possible to introduce a division of labor such that the work of many craftworkers could be performed by semiskilled machine operatives. However, it was job-shop, small-batch craft production that predominated in this early period.

With the expansion of the industrial revolution to the United States, the "American system" of manufacture, or mass production, came into being and has represented the leading edge of technology through most of this century. Mass production involves the large-scale production of standardized interchangeable components which are subsequently assembled into integral products in a fixed, time-ordered sequence. Because of a complex division of labor, relatively unskilled workers can operate specially designed, single-purpose machines that are strung out along continuously moving assembly and subassembly lines that guide the workpieces through to final completion. Given the large capital costs of the machinery that is designed solely to produce a limited product range, large-production runs are required in order to be cost effective; the greater the number of units produced, the smaller the cost of each unit. Consequently, an essential feature of mass production is a mass market.

In Chapter 7, it was mentioned that a recent strategy developed by many Japanese firms is flexible production. Due to recent developments in applying computers to manufacturing (computer-aided design and computer-aided manufacturing—CAD/CAM), it is now possible to introduce far more variability into manufacturing at a fraction of the cost that would be required using mass production methods. Flexible production, or flexible specialization as it is also known, permits manufacturers to produce a greater variety of products in limited number and still remain cost competitive. Piore and Sabel (1984, p. 260) outline the principles underlying the technical superiority of flexible specialization:

> Efficiency in production results from adapting the equipment to the task at hand: the specialization of the equipment to the operation. With conventional technology, this

adaptation is done by physical adjustments in the equipment; whenever the product is changed, the specialized machine must be rebuilt. In craft production, this means changing tools and the fixtures that position the workpiece during machining. In mass production, it means scrapping and replacing the machinery. With computer technology, the equipment (the hardware) is adapted to the operation by the computer program (the software); therefore, the equipment can be put to new uses without physical adjustments—simply by reprogramming.

A description of computerized flexible production is included in Chapter 1 (see Box 1-1, **Flexible Manufacturing Systems**). In Figure 12.1, cost–volume comparisons of manual assembly (craft production), dedicated-machine assembly (mass production), and programmable assembly (flexible production) methods are provided. Because of low start-up costs, manual craft assembly methods are the most cost effective in low-volume production runs (up to 200,000 units in Figure 12.1). However, because costs remain constant, manual methods do not achieve economies of scale with longer production runs, and so become relatively more costly. By contrast, because of the huge capital outlay for specialized machinery, mass production methods are exorbitantly expensive for short production runs. Only with a substantial volume of production (approximately 5 million units in Figure 12.1) does dedicated-machine assembly justify its huge start-up costs and become the most cost effective of the three methods.

Programmable, flexible production occupies a cost advantage between craft and mass production (between 200,000 and 5 million units in Figure 12.1), being more cost effective than high-volume manual assembly and achieving lower unit

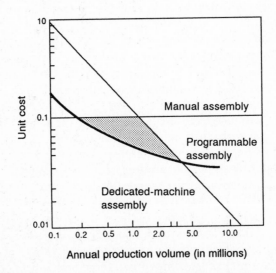

Figure 12.1   Comparison of Assembly Costs as a Function of Annual Volume
Source: Piore and Sabel, 1984, p. 259. Originally from Paul Michael Lynch, "Economic-Technological Modeling and Design Criteria for Programmable Assembly Machines." Ph.D. diss., Massachusetts Institute of Technology, 1976, Figure 6.2, p. 129.

costs than low-volume dedicated-machine assembly. The shaded area in Figure 12.1 represents that portion of the cost–volume ratio usurped by this new technological mode of production in which it enjoys cost advantage over the other two methods.

One important consequence of this redistribution of the cost–volume ratio is that mass production, in order to achieve the economies of scale it has traditionally reaped, must engage in increasingly longer production runs to be economically competitive. However, as Piore and Sabel (1984, pp. 165–193) point out, the state of the world economy is such that shorter rather than longer runs are the more practical option. Throughout the developed nations of the world, there has now occurred a virtual saturation of the market in just those goods traditionally produced via mass production methods—automobiles, television sets, electrical appliances, and so on. Consequently, the market is no longer expanding, being limited instead largely to replacement. Furthermore, within the less-developed nations, the newly industrializing countries (NICs) have established significant manufacturing bases of their own, many of which compete directly with the developed economies. These developments, plus the worldwide recession initially triggered by the oil shocks of the 1970s, point to only modest growth in the foreseeable future. In turn, this means that flexible production methods are more strategically viable than mass production, and will continue to win market share at the expense of this older technological mode of production.

Computer-assisted techniques in the provision of goods and services can achieve economies of scale *and* fulfill individual customer requirements. Consequently, they offer the advantages of both customized craft and mass production methods. While it is not anticipated that the older technological modes will be completely replaced, nevertheless computerized techniques do represent the leading technological edge and will become more widely used in the future.

Worker–Management Relations

Along with developments in organization and technology, the pattern of worker–management relations has also changed dramatically in the past 200 years. As noted in Chapter 10, all conditions of work at the beginning of the industrial revolution, including rates of pay, were unilaterally imposed by owner-managers according to the custom of the time. However, as a result of opposition by an increasingly organized work force and government legislation which reflected a growing recognition of individual citizen rights in all aspects of social life, workers came to have a say in their own self-determination.

The middle part of the present century has been characterized by various forms of collective bargaining in which representatives of management and labor meet at predetermined intervals to negotiate an agreement that both sides must adhere to during the life of the contract. Initially limited to rates of pay and basic conditions and hours of work, these negotiations have expanded over time to include an increasingly broad range of issues dealing with union and management rights and responsibilities, job classification, fringe benefits, promotion and job transfers, technological change, job security, and grievance procedures. Particularly in the Western industrialized countries, the tenor of these industrial relations has been extremely legalistic and adversarial, with each side attempting to gain the utmost advantage over the other.

During the past two decades, and earlier in Japan, worker–management relations have taken a different course. Due to the changing and uncertain circumstances discussed, the traditional system of collective bargaining is considered too rigid and structured by managers who must be able to respond quickly and in sometimes novel ways to a variety of contingencies that can affect the very survival of the organizations they are managing. The new collective bargain that is being struck involves greater flexibility for managers to assign employees on the basis of work demand rather than job classification. In exchange, regular full-time employees are given greater job security and are consulted more on issues that affect them. Also, compensation of all employees, including managers, is tied more closely to actual organizational performance instead of some standard outside criterion (e.g., consumer price index), and raises and promotions are merit driven as opposed to seniority based. Given the current organizational environment, it is likely that these features will become increasingly evident in future collective agreements. It is also anticipated that they will produce a more collaborative relationship between management and workers as the fortunes of all rest upon their combined joint achievement.

An Integrated Pattern of Development

In the preceding analysis, it is possible to discern parallels in the evolution of organization, technology, and worker management relations. Table 12.5 identifies three coherent periods of development: early industrial, mature industrial, and postindustrial. In the early industrial period (roughly from the beginning of the industrial revolution to the latter part of the nineteenth century), organization was rudimentary and extremely dependent upon the capabilities and personalities of individual owner-managers. The history of early industrial organization is in large part a biography of these individuals: Richard Arkwright, Matthew Boulton, Robert Peel, Josiah Wedgwood, and John Wilkinson in Great Britain; and Andrew Carnegie, Samuel Colt, John Deere, Seth Thomas, and Eli Whitney in the United States. Their work was law as they fashioned their organizations around their own idiosyncratic predispositions and sense of purpose. Part inventor, part craftsman, and part entrepreneur, these early manufacturers created the first fledgling industries that led to modern industrialialism.

The mature industrial period exhibits considerably more organization and structure. More dependent upon abstract principles than personal hands-on management, it represents a period of consolidation as well as fantastic growth. Extending through the entire twentieth century, the mature industrial period may be characterized as the time in which mass society was created. Fueled by the mass production of a wide variety of consumer goods and sold by mass-marketing techniques, virtually all American households are now replete with their standard min-

Table 12.5 HISTORICAL DEVELOPMENT OF ORGANIZATION, TECHNOLOGY, AND WORKER–MANAGEMENT RELATIONS

Features of development	Periods of development		
	Early industrial	Mature industrial	Postindustrial
Organization	Traditional and bureaucratic organization	Bureaucratic organization	Professional organization
	Traditional authority	Rational-legal authority	Professional autonomy/rational-legal authority
	Closed system	Closed system	Open system
Technology	Craft production	Mass production	Flexible production
	Machine tools	Integrated assembly line	CAD/CAM
	Manual assembly	Dedicated-machine assembly	Programmable assembly
	Low production volume–low unit cost	High production volume–low unit cost	Medium production volume–low unit cost
Worker–management relations	Unilateral power of management	Collective bargaining	Mutual obligation
	Authoritarian	Adversarial	Collaborative
	Erratic	Structured	Flexible
	Compensation based on managerial whim and market factors	Compensation based on seniority and outside reference groups	Compensation based on individual and organizational performance

imum issue: automobile, television set, telephone, radio, refrigerator, stove, toaster, washer and dryer, vacuum cleaner, and electric iron—all products of this age (Piore and Sabel, 1984, p. 184). In addition, a plethora of other "necessary" products abounds.

The engine of mass society is the mass production factory. As noted in Figure 12.1, high-volume production with special purpose machinery enables manufacturers to sell their goods at a fraction of the cost otherwise possible. However, this requires systematic planning and rational organization in order that all parts of the complex integrated system are geared toward the same objective. (See Box 5-2, **Technology and Capital Costs,** in Chapter 5.) It also requires an abundant source of raw materials and energy, an adequately trained labor force, and a large stable market. All of these elements have been in good supply, particularly during the first half of the century. Consequently, industrial firms conducted their business largely impervious to conditions in which they were not directly involved.

Another feature of the mature industrial period has been the contest between management and labor as to how the proceeds from this industrial abundance should be divided. As was indicated in Chapter 10, this contest has been marked by much confrontation and conflict. However, as a result of the struggle, an elaborately structured set of rules has been established whereby both sides may agree to disagree. In sociological terms, the conflict has been institutionalized. However, in that these rules and procedures were developed in response to conditions different than we face now, some questions have been raised as to their continued viability.

For the purposes of this analysis, the first signs of the postindustrial period began to appear in the 1960s.[5] Thus, as indicated in Chapter 1, we are in the middle of a major transformation, straddling two courses of development. Labeled "the second industrial divide" by Piore and Sabel (1984), they argue that conditions for the continued success of the traditional mass production model are no longer opportune, and therefore we are faced with a series of strategic choices as to how we will proceed. Consequently, the postindustrial period is marked by an awareness that the high-volume, high-growth model that has served us so well in the past cannot guide our actions indefinitely. The set of contingencies that now surround us are decidedly different than when we first set upon this course.

It was in the 1960s when open systems theories of organization were first proposed (see J. D. Thompson, 1967), and when the emergent organizational forms discussed in Chapter 7 initially appeared. Researchers during this period were describing and explaining a new organizational reality, one in which traditional bureaucratic models were no longer appropriate. These investigators observed that organizations were adopting a more outwardly focused orientation at the same time they were becoming increasingly attentive to their own varied work forces. In response to the changing, less predictable external conditions, they became more flexible; with regard to their own organizational climates, they took on a more permissive stance.

One organizational solution to the near-saturation of domestic markets was transnationalization. As we noted in Chapter 8, it was during the 1960s (later in Japan) that foreign direct investment by TNCs became a major force on the world scene as corporations attempted to regain their markets by creating an integrated global economy. Through transnationalization, greatly aided by modern transportation and communication networks, the intended goal was to keep intact the mass production model that had worked so well in previous times.

Another strategy, this one technological, involved applying computers to the design and manufacturing stages of production (i.e., CAD/CAM), thus permitting greater flexibility and yielding a more varied product range than was possible employing mass production techniques. For example, flexible computerized production allows firms to pinpoint particular market niches, providing them with products more tailored to individual tastes than mass production factories can supply. Given the saturation of the market achieved in the previous era, this represents a viable strategy to capture market share.

These and other strategies represent the new reality as highly professionalized organizations, national and transnational, compete with one another in a low-growth world economy. No longer is it possible to operate without a keen awareness of the broader issues in society (e.g., fluctuating exchange rates, international trade agreements, national and international regulations, the stability and intent of various political regimes, social movements, and so on). Any one of these factors can change at a moment's notice prompting immediate reaction by the organizations affected. Those that are not in a position to respond quickly may not survive.

This state of affairs in turn has resulted in the present renegotiation of the management–labor contract. In order to gain the necessary flexibility and to increase organizational commitment in this highly competitive, low-growth economy, employers are offering job tenure and organizational careers to their valued regular employees, and involving them more in the decision-making process. By these means, it is hoped that the corporations will become collaboratively integrated, environmentally adaptive units more able to deal with the many contingencies they face.

It is an interesting exercise to plot the economic growth and development of Great Britain, the United States, and Japan against the three periods of development represented in Table 12.5. Similar to the technological revolutions described in Chapter 1 (see Table 1.3), each period represents a distinctive set of features and trajectory of growth. As noted in Chapter 1, Britain was the first and dominant economic power from the beginning of the industrial revolution to the mid-nineteenth century (i.e., during the early industrial period). The basis of its prominence lay in the ability of British manufacturers to fashion the elements of organization, technology, and worker–management relations depicted in Table 12.5 into a working composite whole. Because it was the first to industrialize, it served as the model for other countries to emulate.

With the industrialization of the United States, not only did American manufacturers borrow from the British experience, they introduced refinements of their own, which were more appropriate to their quite different values and circumstances. Thus was born the "American system" of manufacture. With its emphasis on rational organization and mass production techniques, it was able to capitalize on the burgeoning market in consumer goods. The mature industrial period that spawned a technological revolution in transportation and communication represented the zenith of American capitalism. On the other hand, British industry, being modeled more on the elements of the early industrial period, could not take advantage of this new mass market to the same extent.

Although Japan began its industrialization process in the late nineteenth century, it is the period following World War II that is most relevant to the discussion here. With its infrastructure and industrial establishment in ruins, Japan faced the tremendous challenge of reconstruction. Abegglen and Stalk (1985) describe the various national plans or strategies that were devised as rallying or focal points around which Japanese organizations strove to rebuild (see Chapter 7). These plans had the important effect of making the whole postwar effort a collaborative struggle in which worker, organization, and state came together in a collective entity. Also, starting out very much the underdogs, Japanese manufacturers learned early to pay close attention to the larger national and international environment in order that they might take advantage of any aspect that would help them get ahead.

At first, Japanese industry emulated the American mass production model of industrialization. Relatively low wages coupled with long hours and the national trait of diligence helped to close the gap between Japan and the Western industrial nations.[6] However, during this time, the government also set up state-subsidized local research centers throughout the country (see Piore and Sabel, 1984, pp. 223–226). In turn, these centers established collaborative networks of universities, institutes, and industrial enterprises whose combined responsibility it was to develop new products and techniques. Thus, Japanese industry was innovative as well as imitative as it sought alternate ways to gain competitive advantage.

When the continuing economic viability of the mass production model first came into question during the worldwide recessionary spiral of the 1970s, Japanese industry was much better poised than industry in either the United States or Great Britain to take advantage of alternate modes of production. Not only had it been experimenting extensively with flexible production, but also because of its already established collaborative networks, it could act in a more concerted fashion which is exactly what it did when flexible production became the new national strategy.

As well as the ability to act jointly, other aspects also contribute to Japan's present position of preeminence in flexible production. As indicated in Table 12.5, Japanese organizations resemble closely the features of organizations appropriate to this mode of production, as does the system of Japanese industrial relations mirror what is optimal in this economic and organizational climate. Whether by design or by fortuitous cultural circumstance, organizationally and technologically Japan is presently positioned more advantageously in this postindustrial period than is either the United States or Great Britain. While there are clear and definite signs of change in these two Western countries, their previous attachment to and supremacy, in previous periods, of industrial development make it more difficult for them to remold their present institutional arrangements to fit existing conditions. As it was more difficult for Great Britain to introduce industrialization into an already established economic and social order than it was for the United States to adopt industrialization in a brand-new country (see Chapter 3), so also is it more difficult for Great Britain and the United States to part with their industrial legacies than it is for Japan, which has had no other option but to start anew.

Consequently, while Japan appears to be more firmly ensconced in the postindustrial period than the United States and Great Britain, it is important to point out that within these countries there is a great deal of variability. Both in terms of industrial sector and business firm, the trends indicated here do not always hold. For example, in Japan there are many small firms still employing conventional modes of production and organization. Furthermore, it is likely that there always will be firms of this type. The generalizations proposed here apply more to the modern sector of large firms that are the trend setters. Similarly, in the United States and Great Britain, as suggested by the research evidence in Chapter 7, there are many examples of firms and even industries that appropriately fit into the postindustrial classification.

What this discussion is intended to convey is emerging courses of development. Because of the reasons advanced above, it would appear that Japanese organization, technology, and worker–management relations are more in tune with existing economic and social conditions than is the case in the United States or Britain. However, it is also likely that through the process of cross-fertilization that can occur through transnationalization, joint ventures, cultural exchanges, and a variety of other mechanisms, there will be more similarity in these elements cross-culturally in the century to come.

An Alternative Scenario

While the foregoing analysis is supported by broadly based events and developments that have occurred over the past two hundred years, there are other indications that the period we are entering might not unfold exactly as predicted. Throughout the text we have recorded what may be termed an alternative interpretation of industrial development. From the writings of Marx, Durkheim, and Weber onward, there have been signs of increasing concentration of capital and centralization of power, moral diversity and anomie, and cumulative technological rationalization (see Chapter 4). These problems are still with us.

Whether it be the increasing share by the world's leading industrial corporations of total world output, or the concentrated and, in some cases, unrestrained power of transnational banks, or the global repercussions of electronically connected stock exchanges all engaged in computer-generated program trading, or the fate of 12,000 striking air traffic controllers and their union, or even the reactions of 41,000 Parisians to a "computer error," we must still contend with Weber's bleak prognosis of "cumulative technological rationalization" and all that this entails.

At the very foundation of this "alternative scenario" is the computer and the potential for centralized control it represents. In a matter of years the computer could reverse the long historical process we have taken toward decentralization and democratic participation. In Chapter 7, it was mentioned that the computer is an increasingly powerful "impersonal control mechanism." Not only can it directly monitor and evaluate employee performance, it can also automatically record, process, analyze, and transfer huge amounts of vital information almost instantaneously. With this information, senior executives are in a position to make detailed decisions without relying upon subordinates.

Sophisticated communications and information processing technology operating within modern complex organizations is the epitome of technological rationalization. Because this technology represents such a qualitative change from traditional management techniques, many of the previously "sound" generalizations about organizations are being questioned (see Chapter 8). Also, because this new technology permits managers to alter the historical balance of power, its potential for abuse is being seriously challenged (see Chapter 10).

The computer is a powerful tool that can be put to many uses. It is up to us as human beings—as workers and managers—to decide what these uses should be. As to which scenario will likely occur, perhaps it is instructive to return one final time to Herbert Simon (1987, p. 11):

> Technological revolutions are not something that "happen" to us. We make them, and we make them for better or for worse. Our task is not to peer into the future to see what computers will bring us, but to shape the future that we want to have.

INDUSTRIALIZATION AND DEVELOPMENT

Finally, it is important to make some concluding remarks about industrialization within the broader world community. As indicated in Chapter 5, the more-developed, industrialized countries (MDCs) constitute just under one-quarter of the world's population, yet they consume an overwhelmingly disproportionate share of world resources (see Table 5.4). Furthermore, even though the MDCs represent a diminishing percentage of the world's population, their share of total world income is increasing. Consequently, there is a huge and growing disparity between the industrially developed countries of the world and those that are not industrialized.

This growing imbalance between the rich and the poor cannot be sustained indefinitely, if only because we live in a finite world. Rapid population growth in the LDCs and inexorable resource depletion by the MDCs is a formula for extinction. It is only a matter of time. However, long before this point is reached, the quality of life for all will become intolerable.

Consequently, worldwide development in an environmentally supportable fashion is the responsibility of all. While we ourselves may not be faced with the challenges of daily survival, nevertheless our survival as a species is contingent upon this obligation. From a purely pragmatic point of view, Naisbitt (1982, p. 75) offers the following advice: "In an interdependent world, aid is not charity; it is investment." Or as the president of my own university stated recently: "If the rich are going to stay rich, then the poor will have to get rich, or at least prosperous, and that is going to be the driving force for all matters of public policy in the global village" (Strong, 1990). Thus, on practical as well as humanitarian grounds, reducing the gap between the rich and the poor nations constitutes an item of the highest priority.

At the beginning of this text, I suggested that you read what is contained here from the eyes of "the stranger" or infrequent planetary visitor in order that you might view objectively and evaluate from a distance the complex process of industrialization. This is useful because it permits dispassionate analysis of relationships and consequences. Such analysis fosters understanding of the issues unencumbered by your own values, biases, preferences, allegiances, and ideologies. However, you are also a citizen of the world. Hopefully, the understanding and the knowledge you have gained will afford you the opportunity to see more clearly these same issues as they are embedded in argument and counterargument. Like the century we are leaving behind, the century ahead is full of prospects and problems. Let us hope that we have the intelligence and the understanding to differentiate between the two.

SUMMARY

12.1 The cultural convergence thesis states that because of the common features of organization and technology, similar responses are invoked in people regardless of culture. On the other hand, the cultural diversity thesis proposes that because of the idiosynsyncratic characteristics of culture, people from different cultures react and respond differently despite the fact that they share constant structural elements.

While there are significant cultural differences in values and behavior between the two Western nations (U.K. and U.S.) and Japan, there is also occurring a value and behavioral convergence in that Great Britain, the United States, and Japan now share more commonalities than they did 50 or 100 years ago. Cultural differences are more prominent in the early stages of industrial and economic development.

12.2   Of the two major value dimensions examined, uncertainty avoidance (i.e., how we cope with the uncertainties represented by the future) produces the greatest East–West differences. In general, workers from Britain and the United States have a high tolerance for ambiguity whereas Japanese workers find uncertainty to be anathema. Because of this, they manifest higher stress than do Western workers, and they are more rule bound and concerned with the stability of their surroundings. High uncertainty avoidance is associated with the need for structure, security, and consensus; rules and regulations; intolerance of deviation; resistance to change; and anxiety (see Table 12.3).

12.3   The second value dimension, individualism, also reveals great differences between the two Western nations and Japan. Of all the industrially developed countries, the United States is the most individualistic and Japan the least. American and British workers value autonomy, initiative, and self-direction, while Japanese workers value membership, loyalty, duty, and cohesion (see Table 12.4).

12.4   The values held by British and American workers are similar to those deemed important in Australia, Canada, Ireland, and New Zealand. Together, workers from these countries form a common cultural "Anglo" value cluster. The values held by Japanese workers are unique to them. They are neither similar to other industrially developed nations nor to nearby Asian countries. It is the emphasis Japanese place on the group that distinguishes them most from other developed countries. In turn, this has consequences for individual–organization linkages.

12.5   According to the trajectories of development in Great Britain, the United States, and Japan, it is anticipated that the differences revealed in the cultural values of uncertainty avoidance and individualism will diminish in the future.

12.6   Two major trends in the history of organizational development were identified: (1) decentralization of authority; and (2) increased cognizance of the environment. With regard to authority, not only has it become restricted to organizationally relevant functions, it has been more widely delegated. However, recent developments in computerized control could reverse this trend. Concerning the organizational environment, it has become increasingly evident that for organizations to survive they must be attuned to their broader surroundings.

12.7   Major technological modes of production have evolved from craft production to mass production to computerized flexible production. Manual craft assembly methods are most cost effective in low-volume production runs. Because of high capital costs for specially designed machinery, mass production methods are cost effective only in high-volume production runs; the greater the number of units produced, the smaller the cost of each unit. Computer-assisted flexible production has cost advantage in medium-volume production runs. Because of market saturation and the state of the world economy, it is anticipated that flexible production will become an increasingly prominent technological mode of production.

12.8   The pattern of worker–management relations has evolved from the autocratic system in which owner-managers dictated all conditions of work to the present collective bargaining system in which managers and worker representatives negotiate a collective agreement that specifies all working conditions. Recently, worker–management relations have again begun to change toward a system in which managers have greater flexibility in job assignment and workers have greater employment security. It is anticipated that this will be a more collaborative system of industrial relations that will engender more worker involvement.

12.9 Three periods of industrial development were identified: (1) early industrial; (2) mature industrial; and (3) postindustrial. The early industrial period was characterized by owner-dominated organizations, craft production, and authoritarian industrial relations. The mature industrial period, which has not yet ended, is based on rational bureaucratic organization, mass production, and a collective bargaining system of industrial relations. The postindustrial period, which first began to emerge in the 1960s, is distinguished by professional organization, flexible production, and collaborative worker–management relations (see Table 12.5). Great Britain achieved economic dominance during the early industrial period; the United States assumed dominion in the mature industrial period; and Japan is positioned for leadership in the postindustrial period.

12.10 The gap in per capita income between the more-developed and less-developed countries is increasing. Continued population growth and resource depletion cannot be sustained. Therefore, it is in the interests of the more-developed countries to assist in the environmentally compatible, economic development of the LDCs.

NOTES

1. The 40 countries that Hofstede surveyed were located in all parts of the globe, excluding the socialist-bloc nations. Nineteen countries are classified as "more developed," and 21 are "less developed." See Hofstede, 1980, p. 62, for a listing.

2. This correlation was computed for the 19 more-developed countries. For all 40 countries, $r = -.35$.

3. In a recent survey, it was reported that "the typical chief executive officer of a U.S. company with $250 million in sales this year [1990] has a total compensation package worth $633,000—some 70% more than the typical CEO of a comparable German company and more than twice the pay and perks of his Japanese counterpart" (Koretz, 1990).

4. In addition to differing cultural values, Kerr et al. (1964) cite other sources of diversity: the ideological predispositions of the indigenous elite classes; key resources and central industries; and the actual historical period (e.g., early or late) in which industrialization is introduced, as well as its rate of introduction. See the section on "Cultural Convergence" in Chapter 2.

5. Obviously, it is impossible to pinpoint precisely when a broadly based revolution or transformation occurs, particularly when we are comparing three different countries. Depending in large part upon what specifically we are focusing on, the dates will vary somewhat. However, according to a wide variety of writers representing many disciplines, the period following World War II has represented a time of widespread qualitative social change in the industrially developed market economies. See Table 1.3 for an approximation of other revolutionary changes.

6. Dore (1973, p. 296) reports on a 1968 "national character" survey in Japan in which "the sample was asked to pick out from lists the adjectives which they thought generally characterize the Japanese people." "Diligent" was the most frequently chosen adjective, being selected by 61 percent of the sample.

Bibliography

Abbott, David, ed. *Engineers and Inventors: The Biographical Dictionary of Scientists*. London: Blond Educational, 1985.

Abegglen, James C. *The Japanese Factory: Aspects of Its Social Organization*. Glencoe, Ill. Free Press, 1958.

Abegglen, James C. and George Stalk, Jr. *Kaisha, the Japanese Corporation*. New York: Basic Books, 1985.

Adams, Roy J. "North American Industrial Relations: Divergent Trends in Canada and the United States." *International Labour Review* 128(1) (1989): 47–64.

Aldrich, Howard E. *Organizations and Environments*. Englewood Cliffs, N.J.: Prentice-Hall, 1979.

Aldrich, Howard E. and Peter V. Marsden. "Environments and Organizations," in Neil J. Smelser (ed.), *Handbook of Sociology*. Newbury Park, Cal.: Sage, 1988, 361–392.

Aldrich, Howard E. and Jeffrey Pfeffer. "Environments of Organizations." *Annual Review of Sociology* 2 (1976): 79–105.

Aldrich, Mark and Robert Buchele. *The Economics of Comparable Worth*. Cambridge, Mass.: Ballinger, 1986.

Amaya, Naohiro. "The Japanese Economy in Transition." *Japan and the World Economy* 1(1) (1988): 101–111.

Anderson, John C. "The Structure of Collective Bargaining," in John C. Anderson and Morley Gunderson (eds.), *Union-Management Relations in Canada*. Don Mills, Ontario: Addison-Wesley, 1982, 173–195.

Andrews, Frank M. and Stephen B. Withey. *Social Indicators of Well-Being: Americans' Perceptions of Life Quality*. New York: Plenum, 1976.

Arnold, Horace L. and F. L. Faurote. "Ford Chassis Assembling," in Alfred D. Chandler, Jr. (ed.), *Giant Enterprise: Ford, General Motors, and the Automobile Industry*. New York: Harcourt, Brace and World, 1964, 41–45.

Argyris, Chris. *Integrating the Individual and the Organization.* New York: Wiley, 1964.

Atchley, Robert C. "Retirement as a Social Institution." *Annual Review of Sociology* 8 (1982): 263–287.

Bain, George Sayers and Robert Price. "Union Growth: Dimensions, Determinants, and Destiny," in George S. Bain (ed.), *Industrial Relations in Britain.* Oxford: Basil Blackwell, 1983, 3–33.

Bakker, Isabella. "Women's Employment in Comparative Perspective," in Jane Jenson, E. Hagen, and C. Reddy (eds.), *Feminization of the Labour Force: Paradoxes and Promises.* Cambridge: Polity Press, 1988, 17–44.

Balassa, Bela. *The Newly Industrializing Countries in the World Economy.* New York: Pergamon, 1981.

Banks, Arthur S., ed. *Political Handbook of the World 1986.* Binghamton, N.Y.: CSA Publications, 1986.

Becker, Gary S. *Human Capital.* Chicago: University of Chicago Press, 1964.

Becker, Howard. "Current Sacred-Secular Theory and Its Development," in H. Becker and A. Boskoff (eds.), *Modern Sociological Theory.* New York: Holt, Rinehart and Winston (originally published 1957), 1966, 140–149.

Bednarzik, Robert W. and Clinton R. Shiells. "Labor Market Changes and Adjustments: How Do the U.S. and Japan Compare?" *Monthly Labor Review* 112(2) (1989): 31–42.

Befu, Harumi. "Weberian Bureaucracy in Japanese Civilization: A Revisionist Proposal," in Tadao Umesao et al. (eds.), *Japanese Civilization in the Modern World: III. Administrative Organizations.* Osaka: National Museum of Ethnology, 1989, 37–50.

Bell, Daniel. *The End of Ideology.* New York: Free Press, 1962.

_____. "The Post-Industrial Society: A Speculative View," in Elizabeth Hutchings (ed.), *Scientific Progress and Human Values.* New York: Elsevier, 1967.

Bell, Donald and William Marclay. "Trends in Retirement Eligibility and Pension Benefits, 1974–1983." *Monthly Labor Review* 110(4) (1987): 18–25.

Bendix, Reinhard. *Work and Authority in Industry.* New York: Harper & Row, 1963.

_____. "Weber, Max." *International Encyclopedia of the Social Sciences*, Vol. 16. New York: Macmillan and The Free Press, 1968, 493–502.

Bennis, Warren. "The Decline of Bureaucracy and Organizations of the Future," in Warren Bennis, *Changing Organizations.* New York: McGraw-Hill, 1966, 3–15.

Berberoglu, Berch. "U.S. Transnational Expansion into the Third World, 1950–1980." Paper presented at the American Sociological Association meetings, 1983.

Berg, Ivar. *Industrial Sociology.* Englewood Cliffs, N.J.: Prentice-Hall, 1979.

Berk, Sarah Fenstermaker. *The Gender Factory: The Apportionment of Work in American Households.* New York: Plenum, 1985.

Bidwell, Charles E. and N. E. Friedkin. "The Sociology of Education," in Neil J. Smelser (ed.), *Handbook of Sociology.* Newbury Park, Cal.: Sage, 1988, 449–471.

Biersteker, Thoma J. *Distortion or Development? Contending Perspectives on the Multinational Corporation.* Cambridge, Mass.: MIT Press, 1978.

Blanpain, R. *The O.E.C.D. Guidelines.* Deventer, Neth.: Kluwer, 1982.

Blau, Peter M. *The Dynamics of Bureaucracy.* Chicago: Chicago University Press, 1955.

Blau, Peter M. and W. Richard Scott. *Formal Organizations*. San Francisco: Chandler, 1962.

Blauner, Robert. "Work Satisfaction and Industrial Trends," in Amitai Etzioni (ed.), *A Sociological Reader on Complex Organizations*. New York: Holt, Rinehart and Winston, 1969, 223–249.

Bleviss, Deborah Lynn. "The Role of the Automobile: Future Transportation, Environment and Energy Needs." *Energy Policy* 18(2) (1990): 137–148.

Bluestone, Barry and Bennett Harrison. *The Deindustrialization of America*. New York: Basic Books, 1982.

Bottomore, Tom. *Theories of Modern Capitalism*. London: George Allen and Unwin, 1985.

Brandt Report. *North-South: A Program for Survival. Report of the Independent Commission on International Development Issues*. Cambridge, Mass.: MIT Press, 1980.

Braverman, Harry. *Labor and Monopoly Capital: The Degradation of Work in the Twentieth Century*. New York: Monthly Review Press, 1974.

Brayfield, Arthur H. and W. H. Crockett. "Employee Attitudes and Employee Performance." *Psychological Bulletin* 52 (1955): 396–424.

Brown, Richard D. *Modernization: The Transformation of American Life 1600–1865*. New York: Hill and Wang, 1976.

Buckley, Peter J. "Testing Theories of the Multinational Enterprise," in Peter J. Buckley and Mark Casson, *The Economic Theory of the Multinational Enterprise*. London: Macmillan, 1985, 129–211.

Buckley, Walter. *Sociology and Modern Systems Theory*. Englewood Cliffs, N.J.: Prentice-Hall, 1967.

Bureau of Labor Statistics. *Occupational Outlook Handbook 1988–1989*, Bulletin 2300, Washington, D.C.: U.S. Department of Labor, 1988.

Burns, Tom and G. M. Stalker. *The Management of Innovation*. London: Tavistock, 1961.

Bytheway, W. R. "United Kingdom," in Erdman Palmore (ed.), *International Handbook on Aging: Contemporary Developments and Research*. Westport, Conn.: Greenwood, 1980, 418–433.

Campbell, Angus. *The Sense of Well-Being in America: Recent Patterns and Trends*. New York: McGraw-Hill, 1981.

Campbell, Donald. "Variation and Selective Retention in Socio-Cultural Evolution." *General Systems* 16 (1969): 69–85.

Cantril, Hadley. *The Pattern of Human Concerns*. New Brunswick, N.J.: Rutgers University Press, 1965.

Cardoso, F. H. and E. Faletto. *Dependency and Development in Latin America*. Berkeley, Cal.: University of California Press, 1979.

Carter, E. F., ed. *Dictionary of Inventions and Discoveries*. Herts, U.K.: Robin Clark, 1978.

Castells, Manuel and Alejandro Portes. "World Underneath: The Origins, Dynamics, and Effects of the Informal Economy," in A. Portes et al. (eds.), *The Informal Economy: Studies in Advanced and Less Developed Countries*. Baltimore: Johns Hopkins University Press, 1989, 11–37.

Champoux, Joseph E. "Perceptions of Work and Nonwork: A Reexamination of the Compensatory and Spillover Models." *Work and Occupations* 5(4) (1978): 402–422.

Chandler, Alfred D., Jr., ed. *Giant Enterprise: Ford, General Motors, and the Automobile Industry.* New York: Harcourt, Brace and World, 1964.

Chandler, Alfred, D., Jr. "The Structure of American Industry in the Twentieth Century: A Historical Overview." *Business History Review* 43 (1969): 255–298.

Chapin, F. Stuart. *Cultural Change.* New York: The Century Co., 1928.

Chermesh, Ran. "Strikes as Social Problems: A Social Problem Matrix Approach." *British Journal of Industrial Relations* 23(2) (1985): 281–307.

Child, John. "Predicting and understanding organizational structure," in Derek S. Pugh and C. R. Hinings (eds.), *Organizational Structure: Extensions and Replications.* Farnborough, Hants.: Saxon House, 1976, 45–64.

Chinoy, Eli. *Automobile Workers and the American Dream.* Garden City, N.Y.: Doubleday, 1955.

Clairmonte, Frederick F. and John H. Cavanagh. "Transnational Corporations and Global Markets: Changing Power Relations," in Pradip K. Ghosh (ed.), *Multi-national Corporations and Third World Development.* Westport, Conn.: Greenwood, 1984, 47–91.

Clark, Rodney. *The Japanese Company.* New Haven, Conn.: Yale University Press, 1979.

Coale, Ansley. "The History of Population." *Scientific American* 231 (1974): 41–51.

Cole, Robert E. *Work, Mobility, and Participation: A Comparative Study of American and Japanese Industry.* Berkeley: University of California Press, 1979.

Cordell, Arthur J. *The Uneasy Eighties: The Transition to an Information Society.* Ottawa: Science Council of Canada, 1985.

Cornfield, Daniel B. "Declining Union Membership in the Post-World War II Era: The United Furniture Workers of America, 1939–1982." *American Journal of Sociology* 91(5) (1986): 1112–53.

Coser, Lewis A. *Masters of Sociological Thought: Ideas in Historical and Social Context.* New York: Harcourt Brace Jovanovich, 1971.

Cottrell, W. F. "Of Time and the Railroader." *American Sociological Review* 4 (1939): 190–198.

——. "Death by Dieselization: A Case Study in the Reaction to Technological Change." *American Sociological Review* 16 (1951): 358–365.

Crouter, Ann C. "Spillover From Family to Work: The Neglected Side of the Work–family Interface. " *Human Relations* 37(6) (1984): 425–442.

Crow, Ben and Alan Thomas. *Third World Atlas.* Milton Keynes, U.K.: Open University Press, 1983.

Curtis, James E. and R. D. Lambert. "Culture," in Robert Hagedorn (ed.), *Sociology.* Toronto: Holt, Rinehart and Winston, 1986, 31–61.

Dahrendorf, Ralf. "Out of Utopia: Toward a Reorientation of Sociological Analysis." *American Journal of Sociology* 64 (1958a): 115–127.

——. "Toward a Theory of Social Conflict." *Journal of Conflict Resolution* 2(2) (1958b): 170–183.

——. *Class and Class Conflict in Industrial Society.* Stanford, Cal.: Stanford University Press, 1959.

Dalton, Melville. "Conflicts Between Staff and Line Managerial Officers." *American Sociological Review* 15 (1950): 342–351.

Darmstadter, Joel. *Energy in the World Economy.* Baltimore: Johns Hopkins Press, 1971.

Darmstadter, J., J. Dunkerly, and J. Alterman. *How Industrial Societies Use Energy: A Comparative Analysis.* Baltimore: Johns Hopkins University Press, 1977.

Davis, Kingsley. *Human Society.* New York: Macmillan, 1949.

_____. "The Urbanization of the Human Population." *Scientific American* 213(3) (1965): 40–53.

_____. "The Migration of Human Populations," in *The Human Population.* San Francisco: W. H. Freeman, 1974, 53–65.

Davis, Kingsley, ed. *Contemporary Marriage: Comparative Perspectives on a Changing Institution.* New York: Russell Sage, 1985.

Davis, Kingsley and Wilbert E. Moore. "Some Principles of Stratification." *American Sociological Review* 10 (1945): 242–249.

de Boer, Connie. "The Polls: Attitudes Toward Work." *Public Opinion Quarterly* 42(3) (1978): 414–423.

de Bono, Edward, ed. *Eureka! How and When the Greatest Inventions Were Made.* London: Thames and Hudson, 1974.

Dewey, John. *The School and Society.* Chicago: University of Chicago Press, 1900.

Dohrenwend, Barbara S. and B. P. Dohrenwend. "Life Stress and Illness: Formulation of the Issues," in B. S. Dohrenwend and B. P. Dohrenwend (eds.), *Stressful Life Events and Their Contexts.* New Brunswick, N.J.: Rutgers University Press, 1984, 1–27.

Dore, Ronald. *British Factory—Japanese Factory.* Berkeley, Cal.: University of California Press, 1973.

Drucker, Peter F. *The Practice of Management.* New York: Harper and Brothers, 1954.

_____. *The Concept of the Corporation.* New York: New American Library, 1964.

Dubin, Robert. "Industrial Workers' Worlds: A Study of the 'Central Life Interests' of Industrial Workers." *Social Problems* 3 (1956): 131–142.

_____. "Industrial Research and the Discipline of Sociology." Proceedings of the Eleventh Annual Meeting. Madison, Wisc.: Industrial Relations Research Association, 1959.

_____. "Workers." in *International Encyclopedia of the Social Sciences.* New York: Macmillan and the Free Press, 1968.

_____. *Theory Building.* New York: Free Press, 1969.

Dubin, Robert, R. A. Hedley, and T. C. Taveggia. "Attachment to Work," in Robert Dubin (ed.), *Handbook of Work, Organization, and Society.* Chicago: Rand McNally, 1976, 281–341.

Duncan, Otis Dudley and Beverly Duncan. "A Methodological Analysis of Segregation Indices." *American Sociological Review* 20 (1955): 200–217.

Durkheim, Emile. *The Division of Labor in Society.* New York: The Free Press (originally published 1893), 1964a.

_____. *The Rules of Sociological Method.* New York: The Free Press (originally published in 1895), 1964b.

Ellul, Jacques. *Perspectives on Our Age.* Toronto: Canadian Broadcasting Corporation, 1981.

Endo, Calvin M. "Career Anchorage Points and Central Life Interests of Japanese Middle Managers." Eugene, Ore.: Unpublished Ph.D. dissertation, University of Oregon, 1970.

Estes, Richard J. *The Social Progress of Nations.* New York: Praeger, 1984.

_____. *Trends in World Social Development: The Social Progress of Nations, 1970–1987.* New York: Praeger, 1988.

Etzioni, Amitai. "A Basis for Comparative Analysis of Complex Organizations," in A. Etzioni (ed.), *A Sociological Reader on Complex Organizations.* New York: Holt, Rinehart and Winston, 1969, 59–76.

Evans, Peter B. "Recent Research on Multinational Corporations." *Annual Review of Sociology* 7 (1981): 199–223.

Evans, Peter B. and John D. Stephens. "Development and the World Economy," in Neil J. Smelser (ed.), *Handbook of Sociology.* Newbury Park, Cal.: Sage, 1988, 739–773.

Fantasia, Rick. *Cultures of Solidarity: Consciousness, Action, and Contemporary American Workers.* Berkeley, Cal.: University of California Press, 1988.

Farber, Henry S. "The Extent of Unionization in the United States," in Thomas A. Kochan (ed.), *Challenges and Choices Facing American Labor.* Cambridge, Mass.: MIT Press, 1985, 15–43.

Faunce, William A. and W. H. Form. "The Nature of Industrial Society," in W. A. Faunce and W. H. Form (eds.), *Comparative Perspectives on Industrial Society.* Boston: Little, Brown, 1969, 1–18.

Feagin, Joe R. and Clairece B. Feagin. *Discrimination American Style: Institutional Sexism and Racism.* Englewood Cliffs, N.J.: Prentice-Hall, 1978.

Federal Trade Commission. "Federal Trade Commission Reviews Ford's Experience," in Alfred D. Chandler, Jr. (ed.), *Giant Enterprise: Ford, General Motors, and the Automobile Industry.* New York: Harcourt, Brace and World, 1964, 27–34.

Fein, Mitchell. "Motivation for Work," in Robert Dubin (ed.), *Handbook of Work, Organization, and Society.* Chicago: Rand McNally, 1976, 465–530.

Feldman, Arnold S. and W. E. Moore. "Industrialization and Industrialism: Convergence and Differentiation," in W. A. Faunce and W. H. Form (eds.), *Comparative Perspectives on Industrial Society.* Boston: Little, Brown, 1969, 55–71.

Ferber, Marianne A. and Helen M. Lowry. "The Sex Differential in Earnings: A Reappraisal." *Industrial and Labor Relations Review* 29(3) (1976): 377–387.

Feuer, Lewis, S., ed. *Marx and Engels: Basic Writings on Politics and Philosophy.* Garden City, N.Y.: Doubleday, 1959.

Fields, George. *From Bonzai to Levis. When West Meets East: An Insider's Surprising Account of How the Japanese Live.* New York: Macmillan, 1983.

Foley, Gerald. *The Energy Question.* Harmondsworth, U.K.: Penguin, 1981.

Ford, Henry. *My Life and Work.* London: William Heinemann, 1922.

Ford, Ramona L. *Work, Organization and Power.* Boston: Allyn and Bacon, 1988.

Form, William. "Comparative Industrial Sociology and the Convergence Hypothesis." *Annual Review of Sociology* 5 (1979): 1–25.

_____. "On the Degradation of Skills." *Annual Review of Sociology* 13 (1987): 29–47.

Fortune. "The World's Biggest Commercial Banks." *Fortune* 120(3) (1989a): 286.

_____. "The World's Biggest Industrial Corporations." *Fortune* 120 (3) (1989b): 280–283.

_____. "The Fortune Global 500." *Fortune* 124 (3) (1991): 237–280.

Frank, Isaiah. *Foreign Enterprise in Developing Countries.* Baltimore: Johns Hopkins University Press, 1980.

Franke, R. H. and J. D. Kaul. "The Hawthorne Experiments: First Statistical Interpretation." *American Sociological Review* 43 (1978): 623–643.

Freeman, Christopher, ed. *Long Waves in the World Economy*. London: Butterworths, 1983.

Freeman, Richard B. and Marcus E. Rebick. "Crumbling Pillar? Declining Union Density in Japan." *Journal of the Japanese and International Economies* 3 (1989): 578–605.

Friedmann, Eugene A. and R. J. Havighurst. *The Meaning of Work and Retirement*. Chicago: University of Chicago Press, 1954.

Galbraith, John Kenneth. *The New Industrial State*. Boston: Houghton Mifflin, 1985.

Gallup, George H. "Human Needs and Satisfactions: A Global Survey." *Public Opinion Quarterly* 40 (1976): 459–467.

Gans, Herbert. *The Urban Villagers*. New York: Free Press, 1962.

Gee, Ellen M. "Population," in Robert Hagedorn (ed.), *Sociology*. Dubuque, Iowa: Wm. C. Brown, 1983, 412–439.

_____. "Population," in R. Hagedorn (ed.), *Sociology*. Toronto: Holt, Rinehart and Winston, 1986, 203–233.

Gelderman, Carol. *Henry Ford: The Wayward Capitalist*. New York: Dial Press, 1981.

Gerth, H. H. and C. Wright Mills, eds. *From Max Weber: Essays in Sociology*. New York: Oxford University Press, 1958.

Gibbs, Jack P. and Walter T. Martin. "Urbanization, Technology and the Division of Labor: International Patterns." *American Sociological Review* 27 (1962): 667–677.

Gifford, Courtney D. *Directory of U.S. Labor Organizations 1986–87*. Washington, D.C.: Bureau of National Affairs, 1986.

Gilboy, Elizabeth W. "Demand as a Factor in the Industrial Revolution," in R. M. Hartwell (ed.), *The Causes of the Industrial Revolution*. London: Methuen (originally published in 1932), 1967, 121–138.

Gill, Stephen and David Law. *The Global Political Economy*. Baltimore: Johns Hopkins University Press, 1988.

Glossary of Industrial Relations Terms. Ottawa: Minister of Supply and Services Canada, 1984.

Goldfield, Michael. *The Decline of Organized Labor in the United States*. Chicago: University of Chicago Press, 1987.

Goldner, Fred H. and R. R. Ritti. "Professionalization as Career Mobility." *American Journal of Sociology* 72 (1967): 489–502.

Goldthorpe, John H. et al. *The Affluent Worker: Industrial Attitudes and Behaviour*. Cambridge: Cambridge University Press, 1968.

Gompers, Samuel. "Speech," in John Bartlett (ed.), *Familiar Quotations*. Boston: Little, Brown (originally published 1898), 1980, 666–667.

Gouldner, Alvin W. *Patterns of Industrial Bureaucracy*. Glencoe, Ill.: The Free Press, 1954.

_____. "Cosmopolitans and Locals: Towards an Analysis of Latent Social Roles." *Administrative Science Quarterly* 2 (1957): 281–306.

Granovetter, Mark. "Small Is Bountiful: Labor Markets and Establishment Size." *American Sociological Review* 49(3) (1984): 323–334.

Gusfield, Joseph R. "Tradition and Modernity: Misplaced Polarities in the Study of Social Change." *American Journal of Sociology* 72(4) (1967): 351–362.

Habakkuk, H. J. *American and British Technology in the Nineteenth Century: The Search for Labour-Saving Inventions.* Cambridge: Cambridge University Press, 1962.

Hagedorn, Robert. "Types, Things, and Relationships." *et al.* 2(1) (1969): 23–26.

_____. "What is Sociology?" in R. Hagedorn (ed.), *Sociology.* Toronto: Holt, Rinehart and Winston, 1986, 3–27.

Hagedorn, Robert et al. "Industrialization, Urbanization, and Deviant Behavior: Examination of Some Basic Issues." *Pacific Sociological Review* 14 (1971): 177–195.

Halberstam, David. *The Reckoning.* New York: William Morrow, 1986.

Hall, Richard H. "Professionalization and Bureaucratization." *American Sociological Review* 33 (1968): 92–104.

_____. *Organizations: Structures, Processes, and Outcomes.* Englewood Cliffs, N.J.: Prentice-Hall, 1987.

Hamilton,Richard F. and James D. Wright. *The State of the Masses.* New York: Aldine, 1986.

Handy, Charles. *Gods of Management.* London: Souvenir Books, 1978.

Harding, Philip and Richard Jenkins. *The Myth of the Hidden Economy: Towards a New Understanding of Informal Economic Activity.* Milton Keynes, U.K.: Open University Press, 1989.

Harpaz, Itzhak. "Non-Financial Employment Commitment: A Cross-National Comparison." *Journal of Occupational Psychology* 62(2) (1989): 147–150.

Harvie, Christopher et al., eds. *Industrialization and Culture, 1830–1914.* London: Macmillan, 1970.

Hashimoto, Masanori and John Raisian. "Investments in Employer-Employee Attachments by Japanese and U.S. Workers in Firms of Varying Size." *Journal of the Japanese and International Economies* 3(1) (1989): 31–48.

Haug, Marie R. "Measurement in Social Stratification." *Annual Review of Sociology* 3 (1977): 51–77.

Haupt, Arthur and T. T. Kane. *Population Handbook: International Edition.* Washington, D.C.: Population Reference Bureau, 1980.

Hauser, Philip M. "Observations on the Urban-Folk and Urban-Rural Dichotomies as Forms of Western Ethnocentrism," in P. M. Hauser and L. F. Schnore (eds.), *The Study of Urbanization.* New York: Wiley, 1965, 503–518.

Hedley, R. Alan. "Professional Bureaucracy: Community Mental Health Care Teams." *Organization and Administrative Sciences* 8(4) (1977): 61–76.

_____. "Attachments to Work: A Cross-national Examination." *Comparative Research* 9(1) (1981): 11–13.

_____. "Work, Life and the Pursuit of Happiness: A Study of Australian Industrial Workers." *Journal of Industrial Relations* 23(3) (1982): 397–404.

_____. "Work-Nonwork Contexts and Orientations to Work: A Crucial Test." *Work and Occupations* 11(3) (1984): 353–376.

_____. "Narrowing the Gap Between the Rich and the Poor Nations: A Modest Proposal." *Transnational Perspectives* 11(2–3) (1985): 23–27.

_____. "Everybody But Me: Self-Other Referents in Social Research." *Sociological Inquiry* 56(2) (1986a): 245–257.

_____. "Formal Organizations," in K. Ishwaran (ed.), *Sociology*. Don Mills, Ont.: Addison-Wesley, 1986b, 209–227.

_____. "Industrialization and Work," in Robert Hagedorn (ed.), *Sociology*. Toronto: Holt, Rinehart and Winston, 1986c, 489–515.

_____. "Productivity of Full Professors Before and After Promotion: The Case of the University of Victoria." *BC Studies* 74 (1987): 33–39.

Hedley, R. Alan and S. M. Adams. "Mom in the Labour Force: Verdict—Not Guilty!" *Perception* 6(1) (1982): 28–29.

Hedley, R. Alan and Thomas C. Taveggia. "Textbook Sociology: Some Cautionary Remarks." *The American Sociologist* 12(3) (1977): 108–116.

Herteaux, Michel. "Taking Work Home: A Comeback for Cottage Industry." *World Press Review* 32 (January): 38 (originally published in *Le Monde*), 1985.

Herz, Diane E. and Philip L. Rones. "Institutional Barriers to Employment of Older Workers." *Monthly Labor Review* 112(4) (1989): 14–21.

Historical Statistics of the United States: Colonial Times to 1970, Part 1. Washington, D.C.: U.S. Department of Commerce, 1975.

Hodson, Randy and Robert L. Kaufman. "Economic Dualism: A Critical Review." *American Sociological Review* 47 (1982): 727–739.

Hofstede, Geert. "Hierarchical Power Distance in Forty Countries," in Cornelius J. Lammers and David J. Hickson (eds.), *Organizations Alike and Unlike: International and Inter-institutional Studies in the Sociology of Organizations*. London: Routledge and Kegan Paul, 1979, 97–119.

_____. *Culture's Consequences: International Differences in Work-Related Values*. Beverly Hills, Cal.: Sage, 1980.

Holmes, T. H. and R. H. Rahe. "The Social Readjustment Rating Scale." *Journal of Psychosomatic Research* 11 (1967): 213–218.

Hoppock, Robert. *Job Satisfaction*. New York: Harper, 1935.

Hughes, Everett C. *Men and Their Work*. Glencoe, Ill.: Free Press, 1958.

Hyman, Richard. "Trade Unions: Structure, Policies, and Politics," in George Sayers Bain (ed.), *Industrial Relations in Britain*. Oxford: Basil Blackwell, 1983, 35–65.

I.L.O. *International Standard Classification of Occupations*. Geneva: International Labour Office, 1968.

_____. *Into the Twenty-First Century: The Development of Social Security*. Geneva: International Labour Office, 1984.

_____. *The Cost of Social Security: Eleventh International Inquiry, 1978–1980*. Geneva: International Labour Office, 1985.

_____. *Year Book of Labour Statistics 1988*. Geneva: International Labour Office, 1988.

Impoco, Jim. "Come On, Tanaka, Let the Good Times Roll." *U.S. News & World Report*, (1988) Sept. 12, p. 53.

Inglehart, Ronald and Jacques-Rene Rabier. "Aspirations Adapt to Situations—But Why Are the Belgians so Much Happier than the French?" in Frank M. Andrews (ed.), *Research on the Quality of Life*. Ann Arbor, Mich.: Survey Research Center, University of Michigan, 1986, 1–56.

Inkeles, Alex and D. H. Smith. *Becoming Modern: Individual Change in Six Developing Countries*. Cambridge, Mass.: Harvard University Press, 1974.

International Energy Agency. *Energy Policies and Programmes of IEA Countries: 1988 Review*. Paris: OECD, 1989.

Jacobs, Jerry A. "Long-Term Trends in Occupational Segregation by Sex." *American Journal of Sociology* 95(1) (1989): 160–173.

Jaikumar, Ramchandran. "Japanese Flexible Manufacturing Systems: Impact on the United States." *Japan and the World Economy* 1(2) (1989): 113–143.

Jain, S. C. and Y. Puri. "Role of Multinational Corporations in Developing Countries: Policy Makers' Views," in Pradip K. Ghosh (ed.), *Multi-National Corporations and Third World Development*. Westport, Conn.: Greenwood, 1984, 114–130.

Jalée, P. *The Pillage of the Third World*. New York: Monthly Review Press, 1968.

Japan National Tourist Organization. *Tourism in Japan 1988*. Tokyo: Ministry of Transport, 1988.

Jencks, Christopher, L. Perman, and L. Rainwater. "What Is a Good Job? A New Measure of Labor-Market Success." *American Journal of Sociology* 93(6) (1988): 1322–1357.

Jones, L. J. "The Early History of Mechanical Harvesting," in A. Rupert Hall and Norman Smith (eds.), *History of Technology: Fourth Annual Volume*. London: Mansell, 1979.

Kahl, Joseph A. *The Measurement of Modernization: A Study of Values in Brazil and Mexico*. Austin, Texas: University of Texas Press, 1968.

Kahn, Robert L. "The Meaning of Work: Interpretation and Proposals for Measurement," in Angus Campbell and Philip E. Converse (eds.), *The Human Meaning of Social Change*. New York: Russell Sage Foundation, 1972, 159–203.

Kalleberg, Arne L. and Aage B. Sorensen. "The Sociology of Labor Markets." *Annual Review of Sociology* 5 (1979): 351–379.

Karsh, Bernard. "Industrial Relations in Japan," in Robert Dubin (ed.), *Handbook of Work, Organization, and Society*. Chicago: Rand McNally, 1976, 877–900.

Kasl, Stanislav V. "Epidemiological Contributions to the Study of Work Stress," in Cary L. Cooper and Roy Payne (eds.), *Stress at Work*. Chichester: John Wiley and Sons, 1978, 3–48.

Katz, Fred E. "Explaining Informal Work Groups in Complex Organizations: The Case for Autonomy in Structure," in William A. Faunce (ed.), *Readings in Industrial Sociology*. New York: Appleton-Century-Crofts, 1967, 290–304.

Katz, Harry C. "Collective Bargaining in the 1982 Bargaining Round," in Thomas A. Kochan (ed.), *Challenges and Choices Facing American Labor*. Cambridge, Mass.: MIT Press, 1985, 213–226.

Keenoy, Tom. *Invitation to Industrial Relations*. Oxford: Basil Blackwell, 1985.

Kerr, Clark et al. *Industrialism and Industrial Man*. New York: Oxford University Press (first edition published in 1960), 1964.

Klein, Janice A. and E. David Wanger. "The Legal Setting for the Emergence of the Union Avoidance Strategy," in Thomas A. Kochan (ed.), *Challenges and Choices Facing American Labor*. Cambridge, Mass.: MIT Press, 1985, 75–88.

Kochan, Thomas A., H. C. Katz, and R. B. McKersie. *The Transformation of American Industrial Relations*. New York: Basic Books, 1986.

Kohn, Melvin L. *Class and Conformity: A Study in Values*. Homewood, Ill.: Dorsey, 1969.

Kohn, Melvin L. and Carmi Schooler. *Work and Personality: An Inquiry into the Impact of Social Stratification*. Norwood, N.J.: Ablex, 1983.

Kohn, Melvin L. et al. "Position in the Class Structure and Psychological Functioning in the United States, Japan, and Poland." *American Journal of Sociology* 95(4) (1990): 964–1008.

Koretz, Gene. "American CEOs Rake in the Cash—and Worries to Match." *Business Week*, No. 3187 (1990), 12 November; 22.

Kornhauser, Arthur. *Mental Health of the Industrial Worker: A Detroit Study*. New York: Wiley, 1965.

Koseki, Sampei. "Japan: Homo Ludens Japanicus," in Anna Olszewska and K. Roberts (eds.), *Leisure and Lifestyle: A Comparative Analysis of Free Time*. London: Sage, 1989, 115–142.

Koshiro, Kazutoshi. "Labor Relations in the Public Service in Japan," in Tiziano Treu et al. (eds.), *Public Service Labour Relations*. Geneva: International Labour Office, 1987, 145–176.

Krupp, Sherman. *Pattern in Organization Analysis: A Critical Examination*. New York: Holt, Rinehart and Winston, 1961.

Kurian, George T. *The New Book of World Rankings*. New York: Facts on File, 1984.

Kusaka, Kimindo. "The Power of Japanese Women." *Economic Eye* 10(1) (1989): 29.

Lall, Sanjaya and P. Streeten. *Foreign Investment, Transnationals, and Developing Countries*. London: MacMillan, 1977.

Lammers, Cornelis J. and David J. Hickson, eds. *Organizations Alike and Unlike: International and Inter-Institutional Studies in the Sociology of Organizations*. London: Routledge and Kegan Paul, 1979.

La Palombara, Joseph and Stephen Blank. "Multinational Corporations and Developing Countries," in Pradip K. Ghosh (ed.), *Multi-National Corporations and Third World Development*. Westport, Conn.: Greenwood, 1984, 7–29.

Lawrence, Paul R. and J. W. Lorsch. *Organization and Environment: Managing Differentiation and Integration*. Boston: Harvard University Press, 1967.

Lenski, Gerhard E. *Power and Privilege: A Theory of Social Stratification*. New York: McGraw-Hill, 1966.

Lenski, Gerhard and Jean Lenski. *Human Societies: An Introduction to Macrosociology*. New York: McGraw-Hill, 1982.

Lerner, David. *The Passing of Traditional Society*. Glencoe, Ill.: Free Press, 1958.

Levi, L. *Stress in Industry*. Geneva: International Labour Office, 1984.

Lieberman, S. "The Effects of Changes in Roles on the Attitudes of Role Occupants." *Human Relations* 9 (1956): 385–402.

Lincoln, James R., M. Hanada, and K. McBride. "Organizational Structures in Japanese and U.S. Manufacturing." *Administrative Science Quarterly* 31 (1986): 338–364.

Lincoln, James R., M. Hanada, and J. Olson. "Cultural Orientations and Individual Reactions to Organizations: A Study of Employees of Japanese-Owned Plants." *Administrative Science Quarterly* 26 (1981): 93–115.

Lincoln, James R. and Arne L. Kalleberg. "Work Organization and Workforce Commitment: A Study of Plants and Employees in the U.S. and Japan." *American Sociological Review* 50(6) (1985): 738–760.

Lincoln, James R. and Kerry McBride. "Japanese Industrial Organization in Comparative Perspective." *Annual Review of Sociology* 13 (1987): 289–312.

Lipset, Seymour Martin. "North American Labor Movements: A Comparative Perspective," in S. M. Lipset (ed.), *Unions in Transition: Entering the Second Century*. San Francisco: Institute for Contemporary Studies, 1986, 419–456.

Litwak, Eugene. "Models of Bureaucracy Which Permit Conflict." *American Journal of Sociology* 67 (1961): 177–184.

Locke, Edwin A. "The Nature and Causes of Job Satisfaction," in Marvin D. Dunnette (ed.), *Handbook of Industrial and Organizational Behavior*. Chicago: Rand McNally, 1976, 1297–1349.

Loscocco, Karyn A. "The Instrumentally Oriented Factory Worker: Myth or Reality?" *Work and Occupations* 16(1) (1989): 3–25.

Loveman, Gary W. and Chris Tilly. "Good Jobs or Bad Jobs? Evaluating the American Job Creation Experience." *International Labour Review* 127(5) (1988): 593–611.

MacIver, Robert. *Society: Its Structure and Changes*. New York: Holt, Rinehart and Winston, 1937.

Maeda, Daisaku. "Japan," in Erdman Palmore (ed.), *International Handbook on Aging: Contemporary Developments and Research*. Westport, Conn.: Greenwood, 1980, 253–270.

Maine, Sir Henry James Sumner. *Ancient Law: Its Connection with the Early History of Society and its Relation to Modern Ideas*. New York: Dutton (originally published 1861), 1960.

Malthus, Thomas R. *Essay on the Principle of Population as it Affects the Future Improvement of Society*. London: Johnson, 1798.

Mantoux, Paul. *The Industrial Revolution in the Eighteenth Century: An Outline of the Beginnings of the Modern Factory System in England*. New York: Harper and Row (originally published in 1928), 1961.

March, James G. and H. A. Simon. *Organizations*. New York: John Wiley and Sons, 1958.

Markey, James P. and William Parks II. "Occupational Change: Pursuing a Different Kind of Work." *Monthly Labor Review* 112(9) (1989): 3–12.

Marsh, Robert M. and Hiroshi Mannari. *Modernization and the Japanese Factory*. Princeton, N.J.: Princeton University Press, 1976.

Marsh, Robert M. and Hiroshi Mannari. "Technology and Size as Determinants of the Organizational Structure of Japanese Factories." *Administrative Science Quarterly* 26 (1981): 33–57.

Martindale, Don. *The Nature and Types of Sociological Theory*. Boston: Houghton Mifflin, 1960.

Mattera, Philip. *Off the Books: The Rise of the Underground Economy*. London: Pluto Press, 1985.

Mayo, Elton. *The Human Problems of an Industrial Civilization*. New York: Viking Press (originally published in 1933), 1960.

McGregor, Douglas M. *The Human Side of Enterprise*. New York: McGraw-Hill, 1960.

McMillan, Charles J. *The Japanese Industrial System*. Berlin: Walter de Gruyter, 1984.

Mechanic, David. "Sources of Power of Lower Participants in Complex Organizations." *Administrative Science Quarterly* 7 (1962): 349–364.

Mellor, Earl F. "Weekly Earnings in 1986: A Look at More than 200 Occupations." *Monthly Labor Review* 110 (6) (1987): 41–46.

Meredith, Dennis. "Scientists Demonstrate Use of 'High Temperature' Superconductor in Electronics and Communications." *Computers and People* 36 (11–12) (1987): 25–27.

Merton, Robert K. "Bureaucratic Structure and Personality," in Amitai Etzioni (ed.), *A Sociological Reader on Complex Organizations*. New York: Holt, Rinehart and Winston (originally published in 1940), 1969.

Meyer, Alfred G. "Marxism," in *International Encyclopedia of the Social Sciences*, Vol. 10. New York: Macmillan and The Free Press, 1968, 40–46.

Michalos, Alex C. "Job Satisfaction, Marital Satisfaction, and the Quality of Life: A Review and a Preview," in Frank M. Andrews (ed.), *Research on the Quality of Life*. Ann Arbor, Mich.: Survey Research Center, University of Michigan, 1986.

Michalos, Alex C. "Optimism in Thirty Countries Over a Decade." *Social Indicators Research* 20 (1988): 177–180.

Miller, Delbert C. and W. H. Form. *Industrial Sociology: Work in Organizational Life*. New York: Harper and Row, 1980.

Miller, George A. "The Comparative Analysis of Organizational Structure: A Four Nation Study." Paper presented at the 29th International Congress of the International Institute of Sociology, Rome, 1989.

Minkler, Meredith. "Research on the Health Effects of Retirement: An Uncertain Legacy." *Journal of Health and Social Behavior* 22 (1981): 117–130.

Mirkin, Barry Alan. "Early Retirement as a Labor Force Policy: An International Overview." *Monthly Labor Review* 110(3) (1987): 19–33.

Mirowsky, John and Catherine E. Ross. "Social Patterns of Distress." *Annual Review of Sociology* 12 (1986): 23–45.

Mishra, Ramesh. "Welfare and Industrial Man: A Study of Welfare in Western Industrial Societies in Relation to a Hypothesis of Convergence." *Sociological Review* 21 (1973): 535–66.

Mitchell, B. R. *Abstract of British Historical Statistics*. Cambridge: Cambridge University Press, 1962.

Monthly Labor Review. "Annual Indexes of Manufacturing Productivity and Related Measures, 12 Countries." *Monthly Labor Review* 112(2) (1989): 102.

Moody, Kim. *An Injury to All: The Decline of American Unionism*. London: Verso Press, 1988.

Moore, Wilbert E. *Social Change*. Englewood Cliffs, N.J.: Prentice-Hall, 1963.

——. "Changes in Occupational Structures," in William A. Faunce and W. H. Form (eds.), *Comparative Perspectives on Industrial Society*. Boston: Little, Brown, 1969, 107–125.

Morgan, Gareth. *Images of Organization*. Beverly Hills, Cal.: Sage, 1986.

Mulhall, Michael G. *Dictionary of Statistics*. London: George Routledge and Sons, 1899.

Müller, Georg P. *Comparative World Data: A Statistical Handbook for Social Science*. Baltimore: Johns Hopkins University Press, 1988.

Murdoch, William W. *The Poverty of Nations*. Baltimore: Johns Hopkins University Press, 1980.

Naisbitt, John. *Megatrends: Ten New Directions Transforming Our Lives*. New York: Warner, 1982.

Naoi, Atsushi and Carmi Schooler. "Occupational Conditions and Psychological Functioning in Japan." *American Journal of Sociology* 90 (1985): 729–752.

Newsweek. "The Japanese Invade Europe." *Newsweek*, 2 October 1989: 28–29.

Nord, Walter R. "Job Satisfaction Reconsidered." *American Psychologist* 32 (1977): 1026–1035.

O'Brien, Gordon E. *Psychology of Work and Unemployment.* New York: John Wiley and Sons, 1986.

O.E.C.D. *Labour Force Statistics, 1965–1985.* Paris: Organization for Economic Cooperation and Development, 1987.

Ogburn, William F. *Social Change with Respect to Culture and Original Nature.* New York: B. W. Huebsch, 1922.

_____. "The Great Man Versus Social Forces." *Social Forces* 5 (1926): 225–231.

_____. "Technology as Environment." Reprinted in Otis D. Duncan (ed.), *William F. Ogburn on Culture and Social Change.* Chicago: University of Chicago Press, 1964 (78–85).

_____. "Cultural Lag as Theory." Reprinted in Otis D. Duncan (ed.), *William F. Ogburn on Culture and Social Change.* Chicago: University of Chicago Press, 1964 (86–95).

Ogburn, William F. and D. Thomas. "Are Inventions Inevitable? A Note on Social Evolution." *Political Science Quarterly* 37 (1922): 83–98.

Olson, Steve. "Year of the Blue-Collar Guy." *Newsweek*, November 6 (1989): 16. (This article was included in the regular feature of *Newsweek* entitled "My Turn.")

Oppenheimer, Valerie Kincaid. *The Female Labor Force in the United States.* Berkeley, Cal.: University of California, 1970.

_____. "Demographic Influence on Female Employment and the Status of Women." *American Journal of Sociology* 78(4) (1973): 184–199.

O'Toole, James et al. *Work in America: Report of a Special Task Force to the Secretary of Health, Education, and Welfare.* Cambridge, Mass.: MIT Press, 1973.

Ouchi, William G. *Theory Z: How American Business Can Meet the Japanese Challenge.* Reading, Mass.: Addison-Wesley, 1981.

Palmore, Erdman. "United States of America," in E. Palmore (ed.), *International Handbook on Aging: Contemporary Developments and Research.* Westport, Conn.: Greenwood, 1980, 434–454.

Parsons, Talcott. *The Social System.* Glencoe, Ill.: Free Press, 1951.

Parsons, Talcott, ed. *Max Weber: The Theory of Social and Economic Organization.* New York: Free Press (originally published posthumously in 1922), 1964.

Parsons, Talcott. "Max Weber's Sociological Analysis of Capitalism and Modern Institutions," in Harry E. Barnes (ed.), *An Introduction to the History of Sociology.* Chicago: University of Chicago Press, 1966, 244–265.

Paukert, Felix. "Income Distribution at Different Levels of Development: A Survey of Evidence." *International Labour Review* 108 (1973): 97–125.

Pearlin, Leonard I., M. A. Lieberman, E. G. Menaghan, and J. T. Mullan. "The Stress Process." *Journal of Health and Social Behavior* 22 (1981): 337–356.

Pearson Report. *Partners in Development: Report of the Commission on International Development.* New York: Praeger, 1969.

Pelling, Henry. *A History of British Trade Unionism.* Harmondsworth, Middlesex: Penguin, 1963.

Petersen, William. *Population* New York: Macmillan, 1975.

Piatier, Andre. "Innovation, Information and Long-term Growth," in Christopher Freeman (ed.), *Long Waves in the World Economy*. London: Butterworths, 1983, 225–236.

Piore, Michael J. and Charles F. Sabel. *The Second Industrial Divide: Possibilities for Prosperity*. New York: Basic Books, 1984.

Plasschaert, Sylvain R. F. *Transfer Pricing and Multinational Corporations: An Overview of Concepts, Mechanisms and Regulations*. Westmead, Farnborough: Saxon House, 1979.

Polunin, Ivan. "Japanese Travel Boom." *Tourism Management* 10(1) (1989): 4–8.

Poole, Michael et al. *Industrial Relations in the Future: Trends and Possibilities in Britain over the Next Decade*. London: Routledge and Kegan Paul, 1984.

Population Crisis Committee. *The International Human Suffering Index*. Washington, D.C., 1987.

Porter, John. *The Vertical Mosaic*. Toronto: University of Toronto Press, 1965.

Portes, Alejandro. "Latin American Class Structures." *Latin American Research Review* 20(3) (1985): 7–39.

Portes, Alejandro and Saskia Sassen-Koob. "Making It Underground: Comparative Material on the Informal Sector in Western Market Economies." *American Journal of Sociology* 93(1) (1987): 30–61.

Power, Margaret. "Woman's Work is Never Done—by Men: A Socio-economic Model of Sex Typing in Occupations." *Journal of Industrial Relations* 17 (1975): 225–239.

Psacharopoulos, George and A. M. Arriagada. "The Educational Composition of the Labour Force: An International Comparison." *International Labour Review* 125(5) (1986): 561–574.

Purcell, John and Keith Sisson. "Strategies and Practice in the Management of Industrial Relations," in George Sayers Bain (ed.), *Industrial Relations in Britain*. Oxford: Basil Blackwell, 1983, 95–120.

Quinn, Robert P. and Graham L. Staines. *The 1977 Quality of Employment Survey: Descriptive Statistics with Comparison Data from the 1969–70 and the 1972–73 Surveys*. Ann Arbor, Michigan: Survey Research Center, University of Michigan, 1979.

Rajan, Amin and Richard Pearson, eds. *UK Occupation and Employment Trends to 1990*. London: Butterworths, 1986.

Randall, Susan C. and H. Strasser. "Theoretical Approaches to the Explanation of Social Change: A Survey," in H. Strasser and S. C. Randall (eds.), *An Introduction to Theories of Social Change*. London: Routledge and Kegan Paul, 1981, 36–87.

Rapaport, Carla. "Japan's Growing Global Reach." *Fortune* 119(11) (1989): 48–56.

Rasmussen, Wayne D. "The Mechanization of Agriculture." *Scientific American* 247(3) (1982): 77–89.

Redfield, Robert. *The Folk Culture of Yucatan*. Chicago: University of Chicago Press, 1941.

Reskin, Barbara F. and Heidi I. Hartmann, eds. *Women's Work, Men's Work: Sex Segregation on the Job*. Washington, D.C.: National Academy Press, 1986.

Reynolds, Lloyd G. *Labor Economics and Labor Relations*. Englewood Cliffs, N.J.: Prentice-Hall, 1959.

Riesman, David. *The Lonely Crowd*. New Haven, Conn.: Yale University Press, 1961.

Robinson, John P., V. G. Andreyenkov, and V. D. Patrushev. *The Rhythm of Everyday Life: How Soviet and American Citizens Use Time*. Boulder, Col.: Westview, 1989.

Robinson, John P., R. Athanasiou, and K. B. Head. *Measures of Occupational Attitudes and Occupational Characteristics*. Ann Arbor, Mich.: Survey Research Center, University of Michigan, 1969.

Robinson, Pauline K., S. Coberly, and C. E. Paul "Work and Retirement," in Robert H. Binstock and Ethel Shanas (eds.), *Handbook of Aging and the Social Sciences*. New York: Van Nostrand Reinhold, 1985, 503–527.

Robinson, W. S. "Ecological Correlations and the Behavior of Individuals." *American Sociological Review* 15 (1950): 351–357.

Rochell, Carlton. "The Role of Computers in the Automated Workplace." *Computers and People* 37(1) (1988): 12–17.

Roethlisberger, F. J. and William J. Dickson. *Management and the Worker*. New York: John Wiley and Sons (originally published in 1939), 1964.

Rojot, Jacques. "The 1984 Revision of the OECD Guidelines for Multinational Enterprises." *British Journal of Industrial Relations* 23(3) (1985): 379–397.

Roos, Patricia A. *Gender and Work: A Comparative Analysis of Industrial Societies*. Albany, N.Y.: State University of New York Press, 1985.

Rosenberg, Nathan. *Inside the Black Box: Technology and Economics*. Cambridge: Cambridge University Press, 1982.

Royal Commission on the Economic Union and Development Prospects for Canada. *Report, Vol. 1–3*. Ottawa: Minister of Supply and Services, 1985.

Rubel, Maximilien. "Marx, Karl." *International Encyclopedia of the Social Sciences*, Vol. 10. New York: Macmillan and The Free Press, 1968, 34–40.

Rytina, Nancy F. and Suzanne M. Bianchi. "Occupational Reclassification and Changes in Distribution by Gender." *Monthly Labor Review* 107(3) (1984): 11–17.

Safarian, A. E. *Governments and Multinationals: Policies in the Developed Countries*. Washington, D.C.: British-North American Committee, 1983.

Sanderson, Stephen K. *Macrosociology*. New York: Harper and Row, 1988.

Sassen-Koob, Saskia. "New York City's Informal Economy," in A. Portes et al. (eds.), *The Informal Economy: Studies in Advanced and Less Developed Countries*. Baltimore: Johns Hopkins University Press, 1989, 60–77.

Schnore, Leo F. "Social Morphology and Human Ecology." *American Journal of Sociology* 63 (1958): 620–634.

Scientific American. "The Mechanization of Work." Vol. 247(3) (1982).

Scott, Peter and Paul Johnson. *The Economic Consequences of Population Ageing in Advanced Societies*. Discussion Paper No. 263. London: Centre for Economic Policy Research, 1988.

Scott, W. Richard. "Professionals in Bureaucracies—Areas of Conflict," in H. M. Vollmer and D. L. Mills (eds.), *Professionalization*. Englewood Cliffs, N.J.: Prentice-Hall, 1966, 265–275.

_____. "Organizational Structure." *Annual Review of Sociology* 1 (1975): 1–20.

_____. *Organizations: Rational, Natural, and Open Systems*. Englewood Cliffs, N.J.: Prentice-Hall, 1987.

Seligson, Mitchell A. "The Dual Gaps: An Overview of Theory and Research," in M. A. Seligson (ed.), *The Gap Between Rich and Poor: Contending Perspectives on the Political Economy of Development*. Boulder, Col.: Westview, 1984, 3–7.

Selznick, Philip. *TVA and The Grass Roots*. Berkeley, Cal.: University of California Press, 1949.

Shaiken, Harley. *Work Transformed: Automation and Labor in the Computer Age*. New York: Holt, Rinehart and Winston, 1984.

Sheppard, Harold L. and Neal Q. Herrick. *Where Have All the Robots Gone? Worker Dissatisfaction in the 70s*. New York: Free Press, 1972.

Shils, Edward and Henry Finch, eds. *Max Weber on the Methodology of the Social Sciences*. New York: The Free Press, 1949.

Simon, Herbert A. "The Steam Engine and The Computer: What Makes Technology Revolutionary." *Computers and People* 36(11–12) (1987): 7–11.

Singer, Charles et al., eds. *A History of Technology, Volume IV: The Industrial Revolution*. New York: Oxford University Press, 1958a.

_____. *A History of Technology, Volume V: The Late Nineteenth Century*. New York: Oxford University Press, 1958b.

Sivard, Ruth L. *World Military and Social Expenditures*. Washington, D.C.: World Priorities, 1985.

Smucker, Joseph. *Industrialization in Canada*. Scarborough, Ont.: Prentice-Hall, 1980.

Spash, Clive L. and Ralph C. d'Arge. "The Greenhouse Effect and Intergenerational Transfers." *Energy Policy* 17(2) (1989): 88–96.

Spenner, Kenneth I. "Deciphering Prometheus: Temporal Change in the Skill Level of Work." *American Sociological Review* 48(6) (1983): 824–837.

_____. "Social Stratification, Work, and Personality." *Annual Review of Sociology* 14 (1988): 69–97.

Staines, Graham L., R. P. Quinn, and L. J. Shepard. "Trends in Occupational Sex Discrimination: 1969–1973." *Industrial Relations* 15(1) (1976): 88–98.

Standing, Guy. "The 'British Experiment': Structural Adjustment or Accelerated Decline?" in A. Portes et al. (eds.), *The Informal Economy: Studies in Advanced and Less Developed Countries*. Baltimore: Johns Hopkins University Press, 1989, 279–297.

Statistical Abstracts of the United States, 1989. Washington, D.C.: U.S. Department of Commerce, 1989.

Statistical Survey of Japan's Economy, 1986. Tokyo: Economic and Foreign Affairs Research Association, 1986.

Stein, Alfred J. and S. Das. "Sustaining and Augmenting Competitive Advantage in Emerging Industries in a Global Environment," in Antonio Furino (ed.), *Cooperation and Competition in a Global Economy*. Cambridge, Mass.: Ballinger, 1988, 157–168.

Stinchcombe, Arthur L. "Bureaucratic and Craft Administration of Production: A Comparative Study." *Administrative Science Quarterly* 4 (1959): 168–187.

Stouffer, Samuel A. et al. *Studies in Social Psychology in World War II, Vols. 1–4*. Princeton, N.J.: Princeton University Press, 1950.

Strasser, Hermann. "The Structural-Functional Theory of Social Change," in H. Strasser and S. C. Randall, *An Introduction to Theories of Social Change*. London: Routledge and Kegan Paul, 1981, 130–191.

Strong, David. "Speech." Reported in *The Ring* (University of Victoria Campus Report). Vol. 16(18): 1, November 13, 1990.

Struik, Dirk J. *Yankee Science in the Making*. New York: Collier, 1962.

Swafford, Michael. "Sex Differences in Soviet Earnings." *American Sociological Review* 43(5) (1978): 657–673.

Syrquin, Moshe and Hollis Chenery. "Three Decades of Industrialization." *World Bank Economic Review* 3(2) (1989): 145–181.

Szalai, Alexander, P. Converse, P. Feldheim, E. Scheuch, and P. Stone. *The Use of Time*. The Hague: Mouton, 1972.

Taveggia, Thomas C. and R. Alan Hedley. "Discretion and Work Satisfaction: A Study of British Factory Workers." *Pacific Sociological Review* 19(3) (1976): 351–366.

Taylor, Frederick W. *Principles of Scientific Management*. New York: Harper and Row, 1911.

Taylor, M. J. and N. J. Thrift. "Models of Corporate Development and the Multinational Corporation," in Michael Taylor and Nigel Thrift (eds.), *The Geography of Multinationals: Studies in the Spatial Development and Economic Consequences of Multinational Corporations*. London: Croom Helm, 1982, 14–32.

Terry, Michael. "Shop Steward Development and Managerial Strategies," in George Sayers Bain (ed.), *Industrial Relations in Britain*. Oxford: Basil Blackwell, 1983, 67–91.

Thompson, E. P. "Time, Work-Discipline, and Industrial Capitalism." *Past and Present* 38 (1967): 56–97.

Thompson, James D. *Organizations in Action*. New York: McGraw-Hill, 1967.

Thompson, Warren S. "Population." *American Journal of Sociology*, 34 (1929): 959–975.

Thurston, Robert H. *A History of the Growth of the Steam-Engine*. London: C. Kegan Paul, 1878.

Tinbergen, Jan. *Reshaping the International Order*. New York: Dutton, 1976.

Toffler, Alvin. *Future Shock*. New York: Bantam Books, 1970.

Tönnies, Ferdinand. "Gemeinschaft und Gesellschaft," in C. P. Loomis (trans. & ed.), *Fundamental Concepts of Sociology*. New York: American Book Company (originally published 1887), 1940.

Towers, Brian. "Running the Gauntlet: British Trade Unions Under Thatcher, 1979–1988." *Industrial and Labor Relations Review* 42(2) (1989): 163–188.

Treiman, Donald J. *Occupational Prestige in Comparative Perspective*. New York: Academic Press, 1977.

Troyer, Steve. "Labour Relations in the Public Service in the United States," in Tiziano Treu et al. (eds.), *Public Service Labour Relations*. Geneva: International Labour Office, 1987, 243–287.

United Nations. *Statistical Yearbook 1948*. New York: United Nations, 1948.

_____. *Statistical Papers, Series M, No. 4*. New York: United Nations, 1968.

_____. *1985/88 Statistical Yearbook*. New York: United Nations, 1988.

Ure, Andrew. *The Philosophy of Manufactures on an Exposition of the Scientific, Moral and Commercial Economy of the Factory System of Great Britain*. London: Frank Cass, 1835.

U.S. Bureau of the Census. *Statistical Abstract of the United States: 1988*. Washington, D.C.: U.S. Department of Commerce, 1987.

Usher, Abbott Payson. *A History of Mechanical Inventions*. London: McGraw-Hill, 1929.

Vaitos, Constantine V. *Intercountry Income Distribution and Transnational Enterprises*. Oxford: Clarendon Press, 1974.

Walker, Charles R. and Robert H. Guest. *Man on the Assembly Line*. Cambridge, Mass.: Harvard University Press, 1952.

Wallace, Walter L. "Overview of Contemporary Sociological Theory," in W. L. Wallace (ed.), *Sociological Theory*. Chicago: Aldine, 1969, 1–59.

Wallerstein, Immanuel. *The Capitalist World Economy*. Cambridge: Cambridge University Press, 1979.

Weber, Max. *The Protestant Ethic and the Spirit of Capitalism*. London: Allen and Unwin (originally published in 1904–05), 1976.

Weiss, Hilde. "Karl Marx's 'ENQUÈTE OUVRIÈRE,'" in Tom Bottomore (ed.), *Karl Marx*. Oxford: Basil Blackwell, 1979, 172–184.

Whyte, William H., Jr. *The Organization Man*. New York: Simon and Schuster, 1956.

Wilensky, Harold L. "Orderly Careers and Social Participation: The Impact of Work History on Social Integration in The Middle Mass." *American Sociological Review* 26 (1961): 521–539.

_____. "Work, Careers, and Social Integration." *International Social Science Journal* 12 (1960): 543–560.

Williams, Mary B., D. Ermann, and G. Gutierrez. "Cautionary Tales and the Impacts of Computers on Society." *Computers and Society* 19(3) (1989): 23–31.

Wilson, Charles Erwin. "Statement to the Senate Armed Forces Committee," in John Bartlett (ed.), *Familiar Quotations*. Boston: Little, Brown (originally published 1952), 1980, 817.

Wilson, John. "Sociology of Leisure." *Annual Review of Sociology* 6 (1980): 21–40.

Wohlers, Eckhardt and Günter Weinhart. *Employment Trends in the United States, Japan, and the European Community: A Comparative Economic Study*. New Brunswick, N.J.: Transaction, 1988.

Wolfe, Alan. *Suicidal Narrative in Modern Japan: The Case of Dazai Osamu*. Princeton, N.J.: Princeton University Press, 1990.

Woodward, Joan. *Industrial Organization: Theory and Practice*. London: Oxford University Press, 1965.

World Bank. *World Tables (3rd Edition). Volume I: Economic Data*. Baltimore: Johns Hopkins University Press, 1983.

_____. *World Development Report 1987*. New York: Oxford University Press, 1987.

_____. *World Development Report 1989*. New York: Oxford University Press, 1989.

_____. *World Development Report 1990*. New York: Oxford University Press, 1990.

World Commission on Environment and Development. *Our Common Future*. Oxford: Oxford University Press, 1987.

Woytinsky, W. S. and E. S. Woytinsky. *World Population and Production: Trends and Outlooks*. New York: Twentieth Century Fund, 1953.

Young, Michael and P. Willmot. *Family and Kinship in East London*. London: Routledge and Kegan Paul, 1957.

1988 World Population Data Sheet. Washington, D.C.: Population Reference Bureau.

Credits

page 5 (Figure 1.1): From "World Development Report 1987." © 1987 by The International Bank for Reconstruction and Development/The World Bank. Reprinted by permission of Oxford University Press, Inc.

page 6 (Table 1.1): From "World Development Report 1989." © 1989 by The International Bank for Reconstruction and Development/The World Bank. Reprinted by permission of Oxford University Press, Inc.

page 6 (Table 1.1): Reprinted by permission from *Fortune* Magazine; © 1991 The Time Inc. Magazine Co.

page 7 (Table 1.2): From *Sociological Review 21*, 1973. Reprinted by permission of Routledge Publishers.

pages 10–11 (Box 1-1): From "Japanese Flexible Manufacturing Systems: Impact on the U.S.," by Ramchandran Jaikumar in *Japan and the World Economy 1* (2), pp. 122–123. Used by permission of Elsevier Science Publishers B.V., Amsterdam.

page 12 (Box 1-2): From "Our Common Future: World Commission on Environment and Development 1987," p. 3. © 1987. Reprinted by permission of Oxford University Press.

page 15: From "Our Common Future: World Commission on Environment and Development 1987," p. 33. © 1987. Reprinted by permission of Oxford University Press.

page 16 (Box 1-3): From *The Victoria-Times Colonist*, 6 September 1989. Reprinted by permission.

page 23 (Table 1.5): *The International Human Suffering Index*, published by the Population Crisis Committee, 1120 19th Street NW, Suite 550, Washington, DC 20036.

pages 24–26 (Box 1-4): From "1988 World Population Data Sheet." Used by permission of The World Bank.

pages 35 - 37: From *American Journal of Sociology 72* (4), pp. 351–362, "Tradition and Modernity: Misplaced Polarities in the Study of Social Change," by Joseph R. Gusfield. © 1967 The University of Chicago Press. Reprinted by permission.

page 51 (Box 2-3): From "Toward a Theory of Social Conflict" by Ralf Dahrendorf from *Journal of Conflict Resolution 2* (2), p. 174. © 1958. Reprinted by permission of Sage Publications.

page 53 (Figure 2.1): Reprinted by permission of Macmillan Publishing Company from "Population," 2/e by William Petersen. Copyright © 1975 by William Petersen.

page 64 (Figure 3.1): From Lenski and Lenski, "Human Societies: An Introduction to Macrosociology." © 1982 McGraw-Hill, Inc. Reprinted by permission of McGraw-Hill, Inc.

pages 68 and 72–73: From "The Industrial Revolution in the 18th Century" by Paul Mantoux. © 1961 Paul Mantoux. Reprinted by permission of Random Century Group, London, and the Estate of Paul Mantoux.

page 72 (illustration): The Granger Collection.

pages 82–84 (Box 3-3): From Henry Ford, "My Life and Word" © 1922. Reprinted by permission of Ayer Company Publishers, P.O. Box 958, Salem, NH 03079.

page 83 (photograph): From the collections of the Ford Archives, Henry Ford Museum, Dearborn, Michigan, and Greenfield Village.

pages 86–87 (Box 3-4) and 90 - 91 (Box 3-5): From Christopher Harvie et al. (eds.), "Industrialization and Culture, 1830 - 1914." © 1970. Reprinted by permission of Macmillan, UK.

page 91 (illustration): The Granger Collection.

page 93 (Table 3.5): From Lenski and Lenski, "Human Societies: An Introduction to Macrosociology." © 1982 McGraw-Hill, Inc. Reprinted by permission of McGraw-Hill, Inc.

page 93 (Table 3.5): From "Modern English Society: History and Structure, 1850–1970" by Judith Ryder and H. Silver. Reprinted by permission of Routledge, Andover, UK.

pages 102–104 (Box 4-1): From "Karl Marx's *Enquete Ouvriere*," by Hilde Weiss, pp. 178 - 184 in Tom Bottomore (ed.), "Karl Marx." © 1979. Reprinted by permission of Blackwell Publishers, Oxford, UK.

page 105 (Figure 4.1): The Granger Collection.

page 109 (Figure 4.2): The Bettmann Archives.

page 113 (Figure 4.3): The Granger Collection.

page 121 (figure): From "Organizations" by James G. March and Herbert A. Simon, p. 41. © 1958 March and Simon. Reprinted by permission of John Wiley and Sons.

page 144 (Box 5-1): From Richard J. Estes, "Trends in World Social Development" (Praeger, an imprint of Greenwood Publishing Group, Inc., Westport, CT, 1988), pp. 2–3. © 1988. All rights reserved.

page 147 (Figure 5.1): From William W. Murdoch, "The Poverty of Nations," p. 238. © 1980 The Johns Hopkins University Press, Baltimore/London.

page 152 (Box 5-2): From "The New Industrial State" by John Kenneth Galbraith. Copyright © 1967, 1971, 1978, 1985 by John Kenneth Galbraith. Reprinted by permission of Houghton Mifflin Company. All rights reserved.

page 173 (Table 6.5): From "Gender and Work: A Comparative Analysis of Industrial Societies," by Patricia A. Roos. © 1985 by State University of New York Press. Reprinted by permission.

page 177: From "The Power of Japanese Women" by Kimind Kusaka, in *Economic Eye*, Spring 1989. Reprinted by permission of Kimind Kusaka and Keizai Koho Center, Japan Institute for Social and Economic Affairs, Tokyo.

pages 193 (Figure 7.1) and 206 (Figure 7.2): R. Alan Hedley, "Formal Organizations," in *Sociology* (K. Ishwaran, ed.), © 1986 by Addison-Wesley. Reprinted with permission of the publisher.

page 208 (Box 7-1): Excerpted from *Newsweek*, 2 November 1987. © 1987, Newsweek, Inc. All rights reserved.

page 208 (Box 7-1): Illustration by David Suter, from *Time*, November 2, 1986, p. 52. © 1987 David Suter. Reprinted by permission.

pages 208–210 (Box 7-1): Condensed from *Newsweek*, 2 November 1987. © 1987, Newsweek, Inc. All rights reserved.

page 226 (Table 8.2): From Ghosh, "Multi-National Corporations and Third World Development" (Greenwood Press, Westport, CT, 1984), p. 52. © 1984 by Pradip Ghosh. Reprinted with permission of Greenwood Publishing Group, Inc.

page 229 (Table 8.3): From M. J. Taylor and N. J. Thrift, "The Geography of Multinationals." © 1982 Croom Helm. Reprinted by permission.

pages 237–238, 239–243, and 244: From Isaiah Frank, "Foreign Enterprise in Developing Countries," pp. 29, 45, 53–54, 60–62, 77, 100, 124. © 1980 The Committee for Economic Development, New York.

page 253: From Steve Olson, "Year of the Blue-Collar Guy," in *Newsweek*, November 6, 1989, p. 16. © 1989 by Steve Olson. Reprinted by permission.

page 262 (table): Source: "Executive Pay," *BusinessWeek*, May 7, 1990, p. 57. Reprinted by special permission of BusinessWeek.

page 270 (Table 9.4): From Robert P. Quinn and Graham L. Staines (1979), *The 1977 Quality of Employment Survey: Descriptive Statistics, with comparison data from the 1969–70 and the 1972–73 Surveys*. Ann Arbor: Institute for Social Research, University of Michigan. Reprinted by permission.

page 275: Reproduced by permission from the *Annual Review of Sociology*, Vol. 13, © 1987 by Annual Reviews Inc.

pages 281–282: From "Making It Underground: Comparative Material on the Informal Sector in Western Market Economies," by Alejandro Portes and Saskia Sassen-Koob, from *American Journal of Sociology* 93 (1), pp. 42–43. © The University of Chicago Press. Reprinted by permission.

page 294: From Roy J. Adams: "North American Industrial Relations: Divergent Trends in Canada and the United States," in *International Labour Review* (Geneva, International Labour Organization), Vol. 128, 1989, No. 1, p. 49.

page 301 (Box 10-2): From R. P. Dore, "British Factory - Japanese Factory: The Origins of National Diversity in Industrial Relations," p. 164. © 1973 by R. P. Dore. Reprinted by permission of The University of California Press.

pages 310–312 (Box 10-3): From "Automating Air-Traffic Control," by Hoo-min D. Toong and Amar Gupta, from *Technology Review*, April 1982. © 1982 Technology Review. Reprinted by permission.

pages 310 - 312 (Box 10-3): From "Work Transformed: Automation and Labor in the Computer Age" by Harley Shaiken. © 1984 by Harley Shaiken. Reprinted by permission of Henry Holt and Company, Inc.

page 320: © Newsweek, Inc. All rights reserved.

page 324: From Kenneth I. Spenner, "Social Stratification, Work and Personality," p. 79. Excerpted, with permission, from the *Annual Review of Sociology*, Vol. 14, © 1988 by Annual Reviews Inc.

page 325 (Figure 11.1): From Gordon O'Brien, "Psychology of Work and Unemployment," p. 89. © 1986 John Wiley and Sons, Ltd. Reprinted by permission of John Wiley and Sons, Ltd., Chichester, England.

pages 332 (Figure 11.2) and 333 (Figure 11.3): Reprinted from "The Rhythm of Everyday Life: How Soviet and American Citizens Use Time," by Robinson et al., 1989, by permission of Westview Press, Boulder, Colorado.

page 343 (Table 11.7): From Donald J. Treiman, "Occupational Prestige in Comparative Perspective," pp. 155–156. © 1977 The Academic Press. Reprinted by permission.

page 346 (Table 11.8): From Binstock and Shannas: "Handbook of Aging and the Social Sciences" (1985). Reprinted with the permission of the publisher (Van Nostrand Reinhold). "All Rights Reserved."

pages 357 (Table 12.3) and 359 (Table 12.4): From "Culture's Consequences: International Differences in Work-Related Values" by Geert Hofstede. © 1980 by Geert Hofstede. Reprinted by permission of Sage Publications.

page 368 (Figure 12.1): Figure from "The Second Industrial Divide: Possibilities for Prosperity" by Michael J. Piore and Charles F. Sabel. Copyright © 1984 by Basic Books, Inc. Reprinted by permission of Basic Books, a division of HarperCollins Publishers Inc.

Name Index

Abbott, D., 74–75
Abegglen, J. C., 202, 211, 239, 299, 300, 304, 305, 313, 355, 373
Adams, R. J., 294
Adams, S. M., 48
Aldrich, H. E., 191, 195, 202, 204, 206, 222
Aldrich, M., 171, 178, 179, 190
Alterman, J., 9
Amaya, N., 276
Anderson, J. C., 295, 319
Andrews, F. M., 326
Andreyenkov, V. G., 332, 333, 334, 335, 336, 349
Arnold, H. L., 84
Argyris, C., 257
Arriagada, A. M., 166
Atchley, R. C., 344, 345, 349, 350
Athanasiou, R., 281

Bain, G. S., 291, 319
Bakker, I., 189
Balassa, B., 155
Banks, A. S., 158
Becker, G. S., 181
Becker, H., 61
Bednarzik, R. W., 3, 166, 183, 255, 277
Befu, H., 362

Bell, D., 81, 161, 169
Bendix, R., 99, 101, 116
Bennis, W., 215
Berberoglu, B., 230, 239, 250
Berg, I., 42
Berk, S. F., 334
Bianchi, S. M., 173, 174, 175
Bidwell, C. E., 93
Biersteker, T. J., 223, 235, 236, 237
Blank, S., 283
Blanpain, R., 247
Blau, P. M., 119, 194
Blauner, R., 270, 276, 283
Bleviss, D. L., 9
Bluestone, B., 278
Bottomore, T., 107
Brandt Report, 132, 133, 134, 155
Braverman, H., 259, 276, 277, 283
Brayfield, A. H., 274
Brown, R. D., 80, 92
Buchele, R., 171, 178, 179, 190
Buckley, P. J., 225, 228, 238, 250
Buckley, W., 201
Bureau of Labor Statistics, 3, 4, 184, 185, 186, 190, 277, 281
Burns, T., 215
Bytheway, W. R., 344

Subject Index